WITH CHARITY
TOWARD NONE

WITH CHARITY TOWARD NONE

A Fond Look at Misanthropy

FLORENCE KING

ST. MARTIN'S PRESS
NEW YORK

Library of Congress Cataloging-in-Publication Data
King, Florence.
    With charity toward none : a fond look at misanthropy / Florence
King
      p. cm.
    ISBN 0-312-07124-8 (hc)
    ISBN 0-312-09414-0 (pbk.)
    1. Misanthrophy—Humor.   2. Charity—Humor.   I. Title.
PN6231.M59K56   1992
814'.54—dc20   91-34803
                                                                     CIP

First Edition: March 1992
First Paperback Edition: May 1993

10 9 8 7 6 5 4 3 2 1

for Tom McCormack, Cal Morgan, and Mel Berger

"I hate and despise the animal called Mankind but I like the occasional Tom, Dick, and Harry."—Jonathan Swift

CONTENTS

ACKNOWLEDGMENTS

He travels fastest who travels alone, and that goes double for she, but sometimes it isn't possible. The following individuals—all of whom, let me emphasize, are entirely normal—traveled a few steps with me and therefore have my gratitude.

Patricia O'Toole, author of the delightful group biography, *The Five of Hearts: An Intimate Portrait of Henry Adams and His Friends, 1880–1918,* for listening to my thoughts on Henry and sharing some of hers with me.

John Siman, professor of classics at Johns Hopkins University, for checking my rusty Latin.

The staff of the Central Rappahannock Regional Library: Fredericksburg Branch, which mouthful is known locally as "the lah-berry," for the reserves, inter-library loans, and copying they did for me. Ginger Burke, Ellen Hagan, Betty Hume, Catherine Luce, Mildred Vittoria, Judith Webster, Mary Storm Westbrook, E. Sue Willis, and Carmela Ballato Witzke all went out

ACKNOWLEDGMENTS

of their way to help me and delivered with efficiency and promptness—and friendliness. You would have to visit this library to believe it: it has the ambience of a neighborhood speakeasy.

My special thanks go to another library staff member, Diane Deuel, who is also my downstairs neighbor. When I had the flu and couldn't go out, Diane very graciously brought inter-library loans home for me and took them back. Moreover—and this is not for publication—she also sneaked back a reference book that I accidentally walked off with. We're still trying to figure out why the alarm didn't go off.

WITH CHARITY
TOWARD NONE

AUTHOR'S NOTE

From *The American Heritage Dictionary:* "*misanthrope* also *misanthropist* n. A person who hates or scorns mankind. [Fr. < Gk. *misanthropos,* hating mankind: *misein,* to hate + *anthropos,* man.]"

Firsthand, behind-the-scenes information is the kind America likes. Not unmindful of other portions of the equine anatomy, we are the land of the horse's mouth. Alcoholics write books about alcoholism, drug addicts write books about drug addiction, brothel keepers write books about brothel keeping, so I have written a book about misanthropy.

As with repressed Victorians and sex, friendly Americans harbor a secret fascination for the forbidden subject of misanthropy. It reared its head when I told certain people that I was writing this book. Their first response was a hungry-sounding "Ohhh," followed by eager suggestions of whom to put in it.

The name proffered most often by intellectual men was Franz Kafka, accompanied by a supporting quotation that they all seem to have underlined: "Nervous states of the worst sort control me without pause. Everything that is not literature bores me and I hate it. I lack all aptitude for family life."

My own favorite Kafkaisms are "A friendship without disruption of one's daily life is unthinkable," and "All that I have accomplished is the result of being alone." As heartwarming as these sentiments are, Kafka's life suggests that his real problem was not so much misanthropy as emotional pulverization by a misanthropic father. According to Franz, the elder Kafka possessed "a knowledge of people and a distrust of most of them," and manifested "aloofness, self-confidence and dissatisfaction with everyone else."

Kafka's free-floating guilt included guilt over his unsociable nature, which he tried to change—something no self-respecting misanthrope would ever do. As a student he took on what we would call extracurricular activities, joining political clubs and even a séance. But despite interesting associates that included Max Brod and Franz Werfel, Kafka never felt comfortable in groups. Writes Louis Untermeyer: "After an hour of talk his nerves would give way, his lips would twitch, his extraordinary black eyes would burn, and he would be racked with headaches."

I know the feeling well, but it is not misanthropy in the strict sense. It is what comes over a touring writer who is too tired to hate. Kafka's whole life was a book tour, which is another way of saying that he was temporarily haunted on a permanent basis. It takes energy to be a misanthrope but Kafka was so overwhelmed by people that he had no strength left to hate them.

My consultants recommended several nihilists and existentialists but I rejected them all. A black turtleneck sweater does not a misanthrope make. Nihilists and existentialists tend to be bohemians, who invariably run in packs; despite their alienated stance they have always struck me as a sociable lot who surround themselves with people because they are forever saying "Nothing matters," and they need someone to say it to.

I have also eliminated pessimists and fatalists such as Oswald Spengler and T.S. Eliot. If we take as one definition of a misanthrope, "Someone who does not suffer fools and likes to see fools suffer," we realize at once that we are dealing with an individual who has something to look forward to. Misanthropes have the "vision thing" down pat. Anticipating the spectacle of seeing fools suffer makes us wake up in the morning with a song in our hearts, even when the suffering fool is an American president with the power to drag us all down with him. A misanthropic Philistine no doubt would have said, "Hey, wouldn't it be a gas if we could get this guy Samson to come over to the temple?" No matter what wastelands we must endure, our motto is: *It was worth it.*

Every woman who volunteered names recommended Dorothy Parker, but she is not to be found herein. A romantic masquerading as a cynic, Parker hated to be alone, and attempted suicide several times after broken romances. Misanthropes love to be alone, and our attitude toward broken romances is the flip side of America's favorite maxim: "A lover is a stranger you haven't met yet."

One woman suggested Jane Austen based on the quotation: "I do not want people to be agreeable, as it saves me the trouble of liking them." This remark bespeaks a standard occupational hazard in an otherwise outgoing lady. Writers are more interested in people than fond of them; life is a laboratory and people are the mice, but it does not follow that all writers are misanthropes. Austen became a writer because people fascinated her,

3

warts and all. I became a writer so I could stay home alone. There's a difference.

Many suggested Greta Garbo but I never seriously considered her despite such promising statements as, "For a Swede it is just as natural to be alone as it is for an American to get together."

Garbo was more "world-weary" than misanthropic and it's just as well; had she been a misanthrope she would have been an exceedingly frustrated one. Her intense desire to be alone paradoxically required her to cultivate legions of people: the rich whose chateaux and hunting lodges she borrowed to find privacy and solitude; and the entourage of sycophantic fixers who made reservations, handled customs, ordered lunch, and shoved her into taxis so she would not have to deal with people.

Two statements by Garbo convince me that she does not belong in this book. Of swashbuckling Douglas Fairbanks she said, "He makes me feel tired," and in *Grand Hotel* she delivered with striking conviction her famous line, "I have never been so tired in my life." Being a misanthrope would have been too much trouble for this listless, phlegmatic woman. The necessary savage indignation would have demanded too much energy and left her even more exhausted than she already was.

I mention W.C. Fields briefly, but I have left out Oscar Levant, Alan King, Andy Rooney, *et al.* They are not misanthropes but pseudocurmudgeons whose function is to give Americans someone we hate to love, but love anyway. These cute grouches also give real misanthropes a bad name, especially when they turn up on Jerry Lewis's telethons. After all, if you can't hate children, whom can you hate?

I am unable to detect anything as simple as misanthropy in the great monsters of history. Some were insane, like Caligula and Ivan the Terrible. Others, like Hitler, Mussolini, and Stalin, exuded a certain heavy-handed bonhomie (Saddam Hussein appears to belong in this category) that suggests normal conviviality, or at least a willingness to give it a try.

As leaders of great masses of people, monsters must be able to use their personalities to mesmerize their followers and forge primal bonds with them by becoming father figures. Whatever this gift is called—heart, the common touch, public relations— no misanthrope could hold such a pose for more than five minutes, and then only on a good day.

Many monsters, like Adolf Eichmann and his French Revolutionary counterpart, the Jacobin prosecutor Fouquier-Tinville, were also solid middle-class citizens given to civic joinerism, good neighborliness, and exemplary behavior toward friends and family. Hannah Arendt attributed this conundrum to "the banality of evil," but Talleyrand came closer to the mark when he said: "A married man will do anything for money."

Finally, I have eliminated "affectless" psychopaths. Misanthropes were sensitive back when sensitive wasn't cool; to us, life is a Chinese water torture and every drop is a tidal wave. This is not to say, of course, that we aren't psychopathic in our own fashion, but we don't commit crimes because we know that prison life is communal. (If ever you meet someone who cannot understand why solitary confinement is considered punishment, you have met a misanthrope.)

All of the misanthropes I discuss in this book portend or illuminate some contemporary American problem. For this reason, Jonathan Swift, perhaps the most famous misanthrope of all time, makes only a passing appearance. If we discount the effect on his temperament of Menière's disease, which is still being debated and can never be known, the chief cause of Swift's misanthropy seems to have been disgust at the many second-rate people he was forced to deal with in his clerical career. Devious peers and their double-crossing sycophants controlled the church livings and deaneries Swift sought to obtain. His story is a miasma of petty intrigues that, while universal in some respects, offers no striking analogy to American life and is, in my opinion, boring: if you have plowed through one Swiftian fight you have plowed through them all.

I have left out H.L. Mencken for similar reasons. So much has been written about him, especially since the publication of his controversial diary last year, that his misanthropy, while indisputable, has become a cliché. I have chosen instead to include a chapter on his forerunner and idol, Ambrose Bierce, about whom not nearly enough has been written.

I had planned to include Mark Twain and Ring Lardner because both have been called misanthropes by many critics. In Twain's case the assessment is based on the emergence, toward the end of his life, of a "dark side" in his writing. I got tired of reading about this late-blooming "dark side" because misanthropes are born, not made. If Twain's outlook grew bleak in his last decade it was because he was hit by family tragedies—and because it was his last decade. "The Man That Corrupted Hadleyburg" (1899) paints human nature as thoroughly rotten, but it is the normal bitter wisdom of old age, not misanthropy, that speaks to us. America expects old people to exit cute, but some old people refuse to exit cute and Mark Twain was one of them.

He has also been taken too literally, as in his essay "The Damned Human Race," about Man's greatest defect, which he says is "permanent, indestructible, and ineradicable":

> I find this Defect to be the *Moral Sense*. He is the only animal that has it. It is the secret of his degradation. It is the quality *which enables him to do wrong*. It has no other office. It is incapable of performing any other function. It could never have been intended to perform any other. Without it, man could do no wrong. He

would rise at once to the level of the Higher Animals. Since the Moral Sense has but one office, the one capacity—to enable man to do wrong—it is plainly without value to him.

I read this not as misanthropy but as an intentionally sophistic jeu d'esprit—the moral sense as the clitoris of the human spirit—that rings with the same love of exaggeration that infused his joyous early works.

In his 1929 critique in *The Nation,* Clifton Fadiman accused Ring Lardner of a "perfectly clear simon-pure, deliberate misanthropy." Why? Because his characters are "mental sadists, four-flushers, intolerable gossipers, meal-ticket females, interfering morons, brainless flirts, liars, brutes, spiteful snobs, vulgar climbers, dishonest jockeys, selfish children, dipsomaniacal chorus girls, senile chatterers, idiotically complacent husbands, mean arrivistes, drunks, snoopers, poseurs, and bridge players."

Anyone who would end a list like that with bridge players betrays a certain desperation, and the use of *dipsomaniacal* for *drunken* is cause for deep suspicion, which I promptly developed. It deepened still more when I came across a 1932 assessment by Ludwig Lewisohn, who found "icy hatred and contempt" in Lardner's "bitter and brutal" stories.

I read some of these bitter and brutal stories but their misanthropy eluded me. What did Lardner do to the Lit Crits to make them so mad? The first hint comes in Lewisohn's remark about the ease with which Lardner continued "to sell his merciless tales to the periodicals that cater to the very fools and rogues whom he castigates." The cat comes completely out of the bag with Harry Salpeter's charge in *The Bookman:* "[Lardner] had too many high-priced magazine fish to fry to worry about his place in the pantheon of American literature."

In other words, Lardner remained popular with readers of *The*

Saturday Evening Post after the literati, closet misanthropes without peer, had deigned to discover him.

The Lit Crits were discovering "tragic visions" right and left during the twenties and thirties—Melville was their chief victim—so I took the misanthropy charges against Lardner with a grain of salt. To me, he was an O. Henry in a bad mood or a Lewis Grizzard liberated from good ole boyitis, but not a "simon-pure" misanthrope. Besides, in the course of my research I came across that Fadiman quotation so many times—writers hand down quotations like family silver—that I decided Lardner deserved a break whether he was a misanthrope or not.

Like any other personality trait, misanthropy is a matter of degree. Taken in the literal sense, the obvious problem is one of logistics: hating the entire human race is hard to do—though a few have done it and I will discuss these heroes in subsequent chapters.

In the figurative sense, however, misanthropy is a realistic attitude toward human nature that falls short of the incontinent emotional dependency expressed by Barbra Streisand's anthem to insecurity, "Peepul who need peepul are the luckiest peepul in the world." Considered in this context, an examination of misanthropy has value for Americans who do not necessarily hate everybody, but are tired of compulsory gregariousness, fevered friendliness, we-never-close compassion, goo-goo humanitarianism, sensitivity that never sleeps, and politicians paralyzed by a hunger to be loved.

With the second sense in mind, I have written this book to try and cut through some of the confusion and win one for the Sonofabitch.

A NATION OF FRIENDLY MISANTHROPES

When millions of people will go anywhere, bear any burden, and pay any cover price to "feel good about myself," you know that the unconquerable worm is doing his thing in the Republic of Nice.

Niceness as practiced by Americans is a festival of misanthropy denied. We are so afraid of the hostility within us that confrontations barely get started before somebody pops up and announces, "The healing has begun." Fear of getting mad is so widespread that nobody says *mad* anymore. The word is *angry*; somehow it sounds less mad than *mad.*

Initially the word of choice among cheese-bound white winos in the informed 'n' concerned class, the A-word has been so thoroughly drummed into our heads by the media that now it has trickled down to looters. During last spring's riots in Washington's Mount Pleasant district, a participant told the *Washington Post:* "We're angry 'cause of being hassled."

To make sure nobody gets *angry* we pre-soften each other constantly in ways that are becoming more and more bizarre. Recently I sent away to a Danish import house for a table that arrived unassembled. I didn't have too much trouble putting it together—it was a five-goddamnit job—but what got me worked up was the packing label: *"Warning! This box contains confusing instructions from Denmark. Please use our friendly instructions packed outside this box."*

Friendly has become a synonym for *clear* and *concise* because clarity and concision are cool qualities. It began with "user-friendly" computers to make cold technology warm, and now nearly every inanimate gismo we use is touted as friendly.

The user-friendly virus has even spread to book reviews, as I discovered recently when I compared the published version of one of mine with the version I wrote.

The fun of writing is in the rewriting. I like to prune every unnecessary word from a piece, to polish and sharpen sentences and arrange them in seamless sequence so that the reader's eye travels effortlessly from left to right in unbroken rhythm as if set on optical cruise control. This is called "tightening"—what Evelyn Waugh was referring to when he wrote in the preface to one of his novels: "If the author had been less industrious, this book would be twice as long."

My review as originally written was as tight as a drum, but when it came out it was loaded up with attributions added by an editorial hand: "according to the author . . . says the author . . . writes the author . . . the author states . . . the author avers . . . in the opinion of the author." All of these grace notes were unnecessary—whom else would I be quoting except the author of the book under review? I had made clear who was speaking with lead-in sentences and colons, but some nervous editor, afraid that *somebody, somewhere,* would misunderstand *something* and get *angry,* had turned my tight copy into an arhythmic sprawl.

The Republic of Nice is embarked on a campaign of no-holds-barred soothing. The entertainment world's time-honored rule, "Always leave 'em laughing," has given way to "Always leave 'em secure." The last segment on news shows now is likely to feature individuals who do strange things for muzzy reasons. A man stands on a street corner every morning and evening during rush hour to wave at passing motorists. A woman in a state that renews driver licenses on the driver's date of birth stands outside the motor vehicles office singing "Happy Birthday" to everyone who goes in. A man cuts the trees on a mountain slope into the shape of a heart that can be seen from miles away so that weary travelers can "take heart": Christ of the Andes meets Burma-Shave.

Asked by the interviewer why he does what he does, the subject shrugs, smiles indulgently at the self-evident question and replies, "I love people." This response has become the designated driver of American attitudes. The psychological test question, *Would you rather work with people or alone?* now ranks with *Own* versus *Rent* on a credit application as an instrument for separating the wheat from the chaff.

The jumpy, black-and-white commercial featuring a tormented soul wringing his hands because his long-distance phone system has ruined his life is usually a prelude to the "Family Of . . ." solution. Americans work for a Family Of, are insured by a Family Of, get their mufflers and brake jobs from a Family Of, buy and sell homes through a Family Of, get moved cross-country by a Family Of. Buy something from a mail-order house and you will become a member of the Damark Family; return it and you will become a member of the UPS Family. What all these firms really are selling is the perfect security of High Middle Ages feudalism, with the CEO as lord of the manor.

Love never shouts, so the new non-jarring commercials feature dulcet voice-overs. Did you know that no dolphins were harmed to bring you Star-Kist Tuna? A hushed female voice-over informs us that except for a tendency to get caught in tuna nets, the creatures are just like thee and me: "Dolphins talk to each other, and as they get more excited they talk faster and at a higher rate. They have friends among dolphins of the same age, they have one baby at a time, mothers babysit for each other, and the bond between a mother and her young lasts for years."

Star-Kist should get an excited dolphin to do this commercial because the woman's voice is so gentle, soft and low that we can hardly understand it. These whispery (raspy when the voice-over is male) tones are all over the tube these days. At first I thought they were intended to simulate the hissing voice of Satan tempting us to buy, but I have changed my mind. I now think they are the latest thing in Make Nice, the aural equivalent of the linked-arms march after race riots, carefully crafted to sound "unthreatening."

In the Republic of Nice, the soft-spoken are King. Television anchors, who must somehow project an air of unthreatening authority, are lately solving this conundrum by swallowing the end of their sentences to avoid a sharp, strident delivery. The worst offender is Peter Jennings. His voice drops and disappears into a prissy smirk and a little nod reminiscent of the unassertive women Colette Dowling describes in *The Cinderella Complex*, whose speech patterns she calls the "Diffident Declarative."

The Republic of Nice has a Rumpelstiltsken Complex. Living in dread of exploding in foot-stamping, purple-faced rage like the foul-tempered gnome in the fairy tale, we have devised comparable precautions.

Plugging up safety valves is our favorite way of keeping everybody calm. In her horrified appraisal of my last book, *Lump It or Leave It,* Martha Peters of the *El Paso Times* insists that "satire is only funny when it is neither embittered nor mean." That would be news to several people in the present book, but Walter B. Schwab of Providence puts Ambrose Bierce and Anatole France in their place in his May 14, 1990, letter to *Time:* "Disparaging humor is verbal abuse and can be as damaging as the physical kind, if not more so. It destroys self-esteem."

A Nashville obstetrics ward became a brooding ground of self-esteem when a couple sued the hospital for $4 million on learning that the nurses had nicknamed their baby daughter "Smurfette" because she was born blue from blue dye injected into her mother's womb during a prenatal test.

"Painful though these events have been, we have all learned a great deal about how sensitive and fragile our society is, how deeply people and groups can be hurt if great care is not taken in conducting public discourse."

No, that has nothing to do with Smurfette. That's CBS president David Burke after suspending Andy Rooney for allegedly making cracks about people of another color, but it fits any self-esteem emergency. It also fits on a Miranda-sized card so that the five remaining spontaneous citizens of the Republic of Nice can carry it around in their wallets in case they slip up and say what they think.

Code words are pretty packages full of friendly instructions in which we wrap our real meanings. Some, like *inner city,* have been around for years, but the one that is all the rage lately is *dialogue.*

I caused a dialogue here in Fredericksburg, Virginia when I wrote an op-ed for our local paper, the *Free Lance-Star.*

Fredericksburg, which lies sixty miles south of the Nation's

Capital, is turning into a suburb of it. Federal government employees who can no longer tolerate or afford the original suburban Virginia counties of Arlington and Fairfax are moving here in droves to find solace in our relaxed "lifestyle," which is being steadily destroyed by their increasing presence.

I got tired of hearing the locals castigate the come-heres in private, so I decided to do what the Republic of Nice calls "explore" the problem and "address" the issue. I called the newcomers Yankee yuppies, said they were either rootless or from Illinois, accused them of eating cheese that looks like a unicorn's miscarriage, and recommended that the counties of Arlington and Fairfax secede from Virginia and form a separate state so the rest of us will not have to pay for their roads.

I gave my op-ed to the editor of the paper, who passed it on to his assistant and then left for a fact-finding mission to China. The night the piece was published, our little corner of the Republic of Nice went up in smoke. I received congratulatory phone calls from people with Southern accents, who identified themselves; and violently abusive anonymous phone calls, including two death threats, from people with Northern accents. The next day I bought my first answering machine and the phone calls changed from spoken words to hard breathing and Bronx cheers.

The paper received more letters than it had ever gotten on any subject. The newcomers called me a fascist, an elitist, a "Fredneck," and that favorite of book reviewers, *mean-spirited.* The Southerners who wrote in support of me called the newcomers "carpetbaggers," blamed them for traffic jams and tax hikes levied "to pay for schools for their doped-up kids," and suggested that the Rappahannock River be turned into a moat to deflect Northern migration.

The uproar attracted the attention of Washington's NBC-TV, who sent a team down to cover it. After a few picturesque shots of Fredericksburg, they interviewed the newspaper editor look-ing pale and drawn behind his letter-piled desk, followed by an interview with me in which I expanded my original secession idea.

"The Northern Virginia counties and the suburban Maryland counties should hook up together and form a separate state with Washington as its capital," I said. "Then they can make one big pothole out of the place."

The television coverage fanned the flames all over again. More letters-to-the-editor poured in, but this time I garnered a fervent supporter from the Yankee-yuppie contingent. A Fredericksburg newcomer originally from Wisconsin, he picked up on my anti-Illinois crack and wrote in to say that he didn't like Illinois people either because they vacationed in Wisconsin and clogged up the roads. This drew a letter from an Illinois native who said that Wisconsin didn't have any roads worth driving on. By the time a Minnesotan got in it, they had forgotten all about me and were fighting with each other.

The paper devoted the lead editorial to my brouhaha, an-nouncing in tones of solemn approbation: "A dialogue has begun."

More recently, the *Free Lance-Star* reported on a speech deliv-ered at Fredericksburg's Mary Washington College by a member of the Nation of Islam. It was the usual Farrakhan farrago: up with Hitler, down with Jews and other whites, plus a locally tailored insult to George Washington's mother, for whom the college is named. As a final fillip, he tossed in a pan review of *Driving Miss Daisy* for its portrayal of affection between the races.

The speech triggered hysteria on campus; so many students were weeping and raging and getting into disputes that profes-sors had to use class time for "tension-defusing" discussions of racial issues. The letters-to-the-editor column divided along black-white lines and a town-gown split emerged, but how did the college administration describe it all?

The banner headline read: MUSLIM SPEECH CREDITED FOR SPURRING DIALOGUE.

Another way the Republic of Nice puts the lid on its Rumpelstiltsken Complex is through "stress management," a phrase so suggestive of gritted teeth that you can almost hear the scrunch.

To keep Americans from dying in the prime of nice, the stress industry has abandoned medicine's earlier claim that letting off steam is good for you. Now we read: TRUST HELPS HEARTS. BLOWING YOUR TOP COULD BE HAZARDOUS TO YOUR HEALTH, TWO STUDIES INDICATE.

One of these "wellness" studies took place at Duke University, the house that tobacco built, and involved 118 male lawyers who scored "hostile" on a personality test. The testees were prone to "antagonistic interaction," and were described as "rude, abrasive, surly, critical, uncooperative, condescending, and disagreeable"—the law firm of choice for litigious Americans.

Among the researchers on this study was Dr. Redford B. Williams, Jr., author of *The Trusting Heart,* who warns: "Having anger is bad for you, whether you express it or not. But we found that people who said they made a point of letting other people know they were angry had higher death rates."

The best way to bottle up anger is to turn men into women. After years of consensus seeking, reaching out, coming together, building bridges, linking arms, and tying yellow ribbons, the feminization of America is now complete. American men have been turned into their own secret police, under orders to kick down their own doors in the middle of the night and arrest themselves for "insensitivity."

A foremost beau ideal of the New Man is columnist Richard

Cohen, the *Washington Post*'s resident oh-dear, who is such a world-class bundle of sensitivity that if he had been on the *Titanic* he would have apologized for damage to the iceberg. Male soul-searching is in and Cohen is its undisputed champ, having searched his own so often that he has become Butterfly Dundee, the man every woman would least like to have with her if she met a mugger.

The feminization of America is so pervasive that it has even changed the way men talk, not just their tones but the whole thrust of their conversations. Persuaded that normal masculine directness and unequivocality might make people *angry,* today's men have adopted the age-old feminine stratagem of hurt feelings and the newer feminist technique of politicized nagging to get their points across. Our national discourse now is conducted in a baritone tsk-tsking tut-tuttery, as when a snippy Dan Rather demanded of his man in Alaska: "Did Hazelwood ever apologize for the Valdez oil spill?"

It has spread beyond the press and academia to such bastions of testosterone as the National Rifle Association, from whom I received an unbelievable computer-written letter signed by Wayne LaPierre.

Since the NRA membership is overwhelmingly male, it would be interesting to know the reaction of the thousands of brawny hunters who must have received one just like it. It is by turns a billet doux, a Jewish mother's kvetch, and a haunting reminder of those sweetly threatening Girls Dorm Council reports about what happens to people who leave starch on the bottom of the iron. It is four pages long thanks to the user-friendly practice of ridiculously short paragraphs; nonetheless, I must quote it in full to render its indescribable flavor, and to prove my contention that Alexander Portnoy never had to put up with anything like it.

Mind you, I have never met or spoken to Wayne LaPierre, but this is what he said:

Dear Florence:

I need to know if we're still friends.

I know you normally receive legislative alerts from me every so often and, after a while, they all start to look alike.

But this is a personal letter from me to you.

You see, I have realized that every person reaches a point where they must take stock of all they have done.

You begin to take inventory of what your life has represented. You reflect on your motives, goals, ambitions and accomplishments.

In the end, you realize that the best gauge of a successful life comes from the friendships you have made.

That's why I am contacting you personally. To see if our friendship, forged in 1989, to fight the anti-gun and anti-hunting crowd is still as strong as ever.

To tell you the truth, this year has been one of the most trying for me and the NRA.

I simply haven't stopped for a minute trying to put out the brushfires Handgun Control, Inc. has started in Congress and in almost all 50 state legislatures.

I'm constantly in and out of state capitals and hearings and continually cross-examined on national and local news programs. Sometimes just for a few minutes, sometimes for hours.

When the big votes come up in Congress, the demands never stop.

But this is the course I have chosen. Because I think it is crucial that we convey our message about our Constitutional right to keep and bear arms.

By taking this path, the times become very trying and exhausting. And time away from work becomes virtually non-existent.

But I'm committed to my job because I know I speak for many Americans who will not allow their gun rights to be abolished. And your voice and mine must be heard!

At this point, I think of you.

Do you approve of what I'm saying and what I'm doing?

Every time someone puts a microphone in my face, I think for a minute how you feel . . . how you might respond. . . .

What worries me the most is that I haven't heard from you in quite a while. I personally checked and found no contribution from you since 1989. Only through your contributions can NRA-ILA continue it's [sic] work. And unless I'm wrong, we haven't even gotten a personal letter of encouragement from you during that time.

Which leads me to ask—do I still speak for you?

I am proud of the fact that when the battle was heating up in 1989, you took the time and stood by me. You added your efforts to mine to help protect our gun rights.

With all that's gone on in the past year, I cannot deny that I miss your ongoing support. I do. Our program desperately needs your continued help. And your NRA dues cannot be used to fight the battles NRA-ILA faces.

But more importantly, I miss hearing from you.

The National Rifle Association is built on our standing together.

That's why it is so important to me that this friendship not just become another fond recollection of the past. Or a friendship that is just forgotten.

I certainly understand that budgets get tight and not everyone can make a gift every year. I know I've called on you to write your

Congressman and Senators and you might have done it and I just don't know about it. And if you have, I want to say thank you. I've asked you to do so much.

But I'd like you to take just a minute to hand write a note or use the enclosed card to check off that I'm on target ... that I'm still on track ... that when I'm interviewed by the press or representing gun owners in the U.S. Congress, I'm still speaking for you.

So, please drop me a line and let me know that we are still fighting for the same goals. And, if you are able to include your special $50 for the cause we have all fought so hard for, that would let me know how much you still care.

This is important. Very important. I'm not just writing to ask you to send a contribution. I'm writing because I want to keep our friendship strong.

We've seen too much as friends to just lose each other in the shuffle of the battles we must fight.

And by hearing from you today, I will be able to continue to produce our hard-hitting ads to fight the anti-gunners and anti-hunters in the media, the Congress, and the 50 state legislatures.

Each time I must walk onto a platform to speak or face a badgering circle of microphones, I will know that the strength of what I say is much more than just words, it's more than my voice, it's yours as well.

Unless you're there, standing with me, the cause we share is greatly diminished.

I will be looking forward to your response.

All my best,
Wayne

How many NRA fund raisers does it take to change a lightbulb? None: "Don't worry about me, go out and enjoy yourself, I'll just sit here alone in the dark."

The feminization of America was supposed to banish Rumpelstiltsken permanently but it is likely to have the opposite effect. Nothing is more infuriating than female stratagems. With her silken weaponry of ambivalence, circularity, and freighted silences, woman burrows into her adversary's very soul—sideways, like a tick crossed with a mole crossed with a crab. This modus operandi has filled everything from the French Foreign Legion to battered-wife shelters, yet America thinks it will keep the peace.

Our feminized niceness has mired us in a soft, sickly, helpless tolerance of everything. America is the girl who can't say no, the town pump who lets anybody have a go at her. We are a single-parent country with no father to cut through the molasses and point out, for example, the inconsistency of embracing warm and compassionate "values" while condemning cold and detached "value judgments."

This popular mental somersault was evident in the case of Jim Dickson, the blind yachtsman who conceived the foolhardy idea of sailing the Atlantic alone. In our motherish rush to give the testy Dickson his way, we forgot all about the sighted sailors whose crafts he could have rammed, and the Coast Guardsmen who might have had to die for the sake of niceness at any price. The only person who dared say *no* to Dickson was William F. Buckley, Jr., whose warnings brought down the wrath of the Republic of Nice on his head, complete with plummy epithets such as "paternalistic sightist."

Our feminized niceness keeps us from solving our most pressing problems, such as crime. In our treatment of criminals we are like the mother-heart in the fable about the boy whose sweetheart commands him to cut out his mother's heart and bring it to her as proof of his devotion. He obediently cuts out the heart, but as he hurries to his sweetheart's house with it, he stumbles and falls, whereupon the heart speaks: "Are you hurt, my son?"

The only way to handle the criminal is to whip his ass till his nose bleeds buttermilk, but the few unequivocal souls who are willing to unleash such curative measures shun politics because they know they would never even get nominated, much less elected. Captive of female priorities, America instinctively shrinks from the only kind of personality capable of solving the problems we constantly deplore. From the White House down, we vote only for candidates whose eyes plead "Like me."

Bruno Bettleheim said, "The deepest of all human anxieties is to be at the mercy of one's own impulses." Instead of "humanizing" men, it would have been far better if women had copied men's stoic *virtus*. A nation of self-controlled people is less likely to blow than one giving off beta-consciousness waves. The hatreds we are trying to tamp down and deny have a much better chance of coming to the surface when people are "in touch with their feelings." And if they do, they will be all the more violent from having been so long subjected to the feminized tactics of the Republic of Nice.

The suspicion that David Souter might be a misanthropic hermit sent the Republic of Nice into a tailspin when the fifty-year-old bachelor was nominated to the Supreme Court.

"Judge Souter is our Rorschach test," wrote *Washington Times* columnist Suzanne Fields, "telling us more about ourselves than about him." He certainly did. The vaunted independence that Americans cherish consists of two things: the single-issue pressure group and the automobile. We boast about our rugged individualism, yet when an avatar of it draws near to a position of power, we go crazy.

Women's groups demanded reassurance that Souter would

"empathize" with women's issues. Presumably they meant "sym-pathize," though with feminists you never know.

Elizabeth Chittick, honorary president of the National Woman's Party, proclaimed: "The fact that he's 50 and not married tells me he's anti-women."

Alan Dershowitz seemed to hint at something really nasty: "I mean, this is a 50-year-old bachelor who lives with sheep in Weare, N.H., out of this world."

Time called him "An 18th-Century Man," forgetting that the Founding Fathers were too, and warned: "The more serious question about Souter's ascetic ways is whether a man who seems to prefer books to people can empathize [there it is again] with and understand the problems of ordinary people."

Kenneth Adelman gave Souter advice on how to handle the hearings: "You have to show yourself in a sincere manner. Don't be afraid to show emotions about the passionate issues of the day. Show concern, show care, show feeling."

Finally, somebody dredged up a Souter date from the early sixties, Ellanor Stengel Fink, who did her best to reassure the citizens of America "Я" Us.

"What doesn't come across in the accounts I've read is what a warm, friendly guy he can be," she rhapsodized. "He comes across as a steely intellectual. All head and no heart. He is a very bright person and very interesting, but he's not all brain. He's a friendly, warm person and extremely considerate." And not only that, his parents were "very warm, friendly lovely people. A traditional, close family."

That does not necessarily guarantee a brilliant Supreme Court career, and it certainly doesn't guarantee a long one. To para-phrase Nietzsche, relatives have probably killed more people than the cholera—a forbidden view in the Republic of Nice but one that rears its subliminal head in the low-fat margarine commercial: *"Love your family twenty-five percent less!"*

Souter is no longer in a position to reveal to the Republic of Nice the title of the steely intellectual's favorite holiday ditty, but there is nothing stopping me. It's called "I'll Be Lone for Christmas, You Can Bet Your Ass."

I have no doubt that many people fully expected Souter's isolated cellar to yield up a dozen or so female corpses murdered by him over the years. And why not? Every newspaper reader in the Republic of Nice knows what murderers are like: SLAYING SUSPECT DESCRIBED AS LONER.

According to the suspect's neighbors, he "kept himself to himself" and "had trouble at work." But the victim? Listen to his neighbors: "Everybody loved him, he got along with everybody. He didn't have an enemy in the world. He was such a happy person, always helping people. I remember he always said a stranger is a friend you haven't met yet. He would give you the shirt off his back. One day a homeless came to the door and asked him for a drink of water, and he invited them in for a meal. He was always smiling, I never saw him frown, no, not once. Our kids were crazy about him."

To suggest that this hot, wet paragon might have had a fatal flaw, and that it might have had something to do with America's blackout of the maxim, "Everybody's friend is everybody's fool," is not permitted. Nonetheless, it is a truth universally unacknowledged that loners go happily through life, keeping themselves to themselves and having trouble at work until they die in their beds at ninety-six. "Hell," said Jean-Paul Sartre, "is other people."

A NATION OF
MISANTHROPIC FRIENDS

Across the border from the Republic of Nice is the Republic of Mean, home of the closet misanthrope, where feeling better about oneself takes the form of a petty, ad hoc, peekaboo loathing of humankind that no real misanthrope would have time for.

How about some proportional misanthropy? It goes well with proportional representation. George Bush in Omaha: "It's good to be away from Washington and out here with the *real* people." Rosalynn Carter's press secretary: "She's in touch with the *real* people." The National Beef Council: "Beef! Real food for *real* people!" Take your pick and hate the rest.

Not since Pompeiians yelled "Run!" have so many people surged in the same direction at once as the great hordes presently going to law school. Asked why they want to be lawyers, these fledgling Perrys and Portias recite various conventional reasons, including, incredibly, "I want to help people." The real reason, never voiced, is: "I want to learn how to be mean."

Egged on by the compassion-impaired, many of the handicapped have turned into ogres who relish every opportunity to hurl epithets at anyone who says "confined" to a wheelchair, or who does *not* say "differently abled" instead of handicapped. Somerset Maugham anticipated these closet misanthropes. "It is not true," he wrote, "that suffering ennobles the character; happiness does that sometimes, but suffering, for the most part, makes men petty and vindictive."

Sick jokes have been officially outlawed by the compassion-impaired but substitutes can be found in perfectly respectable newspapers. Masquerading under the guise of human interest and bearing innocent headings such as "Around the Nation" or "News in Brief" are little squibs about the activities of cretins that get clipped and enclosed in letters exchanged by people who have not yet been rendered brain-dead by the machinations of the sensitivity industry.

I file mine in a folder marked *Idiocy: General* to save for my agent. Among those I have sent him is the one about a man who axed his mother-in-law to death in a dark garage in the belief that she was a giant raccoon. Another, which I reheadlined MURDER AT SECOND BASE, was about two Little League mothers who got into an infield shoot-out that left one dead.

My agent sent me one about a man who sued a saloon after a faulty switch on an adjustable "knock-back" drinking chair catapulted him through a plate-glass window. I responded with BABY FOUND ASLEEP IN GETAWAY CAR (the bankrobber's sitter didn't show up), and UNBURIED CORPSE FOUND ON SOFA (the body of a woman who had been dead for two years was found on a sofa, fully clothed, at the home of her daughter, who told police that she hadn't known what to do with it).

Inevitably, the day came when we sent each other the same clipping: NEWLYWEDS ELECTROCUTED BY TUBSIDE TV.

"Decade-ism" is an ideal sport for the closet misanthrope who wants to remain securely in the closet. Decades are full of people, so if you hurry up and hate the decade just past, you can hate just about everybody now alive, yet be accused of nothing stronger than a sense of history.

Perpetually irritable intellectuals too liberal to admit how irritable they are tend to have a great sense of history. As soon as a zero turned up at the end of their date stamps last year, pundits in the Land of Hopefully and Glory took thoughtful flying leaps into a literal yesterday, turning op-ed pages into festivals of self-flagellation with misanthropic undertones as they condemned the "Reagan Decade" for its buccaneering greed and administered sound thrashings to everyone who did not spend the eighties in a hair shirt.

Decade-ism gives closet misanthropes of the Republic of Mean a perfect out. No matter how much they berate the decade just past, they can still get credit for being good citizens of the Republic of Nice by announcing that they are looking forward to the kinder 'n' gentler decade coming up.

Our eagerness to get away from each other has made the ubiquitous "Ten Most Livable Cities" article beloved by closet misanthropes.

Americans are desperate to escape crime, pollution, noise, rudeness, and traffic jams—*i.e.,* people. Once they move somewhere new to get away from people, they discover they are hated by people who hate people who are trying to get away from people they hate. This is known to Style editors as: "A Town in Transition, Fighting to Preserve Its Historic [rural, traditional, unique, Norman Rockwell] Character."

The new migrations are proving that the Welcome Wagon is dead. I see the handwriting on the mall, and it's a bumper sticker:

27

Seattle: Don't Californicate the State of Washington
Oregon: Come See Us But Go Back Home
Atlanta: General Sherman, Where Are You Now That We Need You?
Fredericksburg: If You Ain't a Rebel, You Ain't Shit

Rainbow misanthropy? It's a mystery to me how anyone can look at the proliferation of support groups and not see them for what they really are: a lunatic quest for birds of a feather by people so sick of our Great Diversity that they unconsciously reject it by joining Tone-Deaf Parents of Left-Handed Anorexic Kleptomaniacs just to be with their own kind.

A leading rainbow misanthrope is Sonny Carson, the black convicted kidnapper who worked in the campaign of New York Mayor David "Gorgeous Mosaic" Dinkins. Accused of being anti-Semitic, Carson replied: "Anti-Semitic? I'm anti-white. Don't limit my anti-ing to just being one little group of people." Spoken like a true misanthrope: Don't think small, I hate everybody.

A movement toward equality of bigotry is leading to misanthropy by accretion. Karen Schwartz of the Gay and Lesbian Alliance Against Defamation (GLAAD) commented on the Andy Rooney flap with the statement: "GLAAD opposes all forms of bigotry and believes that if you scratch a homophobe you'll probably find a racist." By this logic, the scratched racist, if scratched repeatedly, will prove to be anti-Semitic, will prove to be anti-Catholic, will prove to be anti-Slavic, and so on down the list until we achieve raw misanthropy—literally.

A similar accretion is taking shape in the sex war. In the early days of the women's movement, when *misogyny* was on every tongue, some writers, feminists among them, misued *misanthropy* in the belief that it meant hatred of *males*. Misogyny's correct mate is *misandry;* a woman who hates men is a *misandrist.* You can do wonders with a matched set, as Walt Whitman demonstrated when he defined America as the place where "the men hate the women and the women hate the men." If half the population is misogynistic and the other half misandristic, America is thus a misanthropic whole. Misogyny and misandry are simply substitutes for misanthropy among those who are not quite ready to take that giant step for mankind.

The darkling obsessions that feminists develop mark them as closet misanthropes. For the past several years, their leading obsession has been incest. They have gone to the mat with it, but the American media maw demands constant stoking, so they can't get much more mileage out of it. A feminist without an obsession is like Abbott without Costello, so what other age-old perversion is waiting in the wings? Today, incest; tomorrow— what?

We must turn to Mary Daly for a preview of coming attractions. In a May 10, 1989 *New York Times* article about her ongoing struggle to obtain tenure at Boston College, she is quoted as saying that Christianity and all other major faiths, as well as Marxism and Freudianism, are patriarchal forms whose "entire message is necrophilia."

The turning-inward, the retreat into oneself implicit in incest is exceeded only by the ultimate solitude of necrophilia. Feminists who go around looking for either of these perversions have very little love for mankind regardless of how many linked-arms marches and candlelight vigils they participate in.

Involuntary euthanasia is a closet misanthrope's fantasy at the moment but I predict it will catch on. In America no one is evil, things just catch on, helped along by our penchant for inventing words to justify the conclusions we have already reached.

Now that legal abortion has gotten people used to counting in trimesters, the *when* of euthanasia will be easy to manage. We will acquire a new buzzword, "lifeness." Not death but simply less-than-life. If trimesters are valid measurements at the start, why not "lifenesses" at the end? It's bound to appeal to Americans. Awkward words always do.

Old people know perfectly well that a great deal of closet misanthropy is directed at them. Their fear of hatred is pitiful to behold, but worse are their attempts to deflect it. Every once in a while, newspapers and magazines will contain a letter from a senior citizen in defense of young people, particularly teens. "A boy helped me change my tire. . . . it's good to see the young people enjoying themselves. . . . we often sit on our porch and watch the skateboarders. . . . we always schedule our trips to the supermarket on Friday nights so we can enjoy the camaraderie of cruising night as the youngsters drive around and around the shopping center in leisurely fashion, greeting their friends with jaunty halloos [truly!]."

These letters are sometimes triggered by an article critical of kids, but most of the time they are pathetic non sequiturs triggered by nothing—except perhaps the blithe use of the word "geezer" by closet misanthropes in the media.

Lest anyone think that gerontophobia has been driven out by political correctness, think again. Smith College recently made a not-so-subtle change in the definition of *ageism* in its PC handbook. It now means "oppression of the young and old by young adults and the middle-aged." In America, anyone who shares billing with children ends up leaving the stage, often with the help of a vaudeville hook.

The widespread hatred of television is a form of closet misanthropy of special interest to anyone who grew up in the radio era. We didn't hate radio and blame it for all sorts of ills. We didn't worry about how many hours a day our radios were on, we didn't lie about our radio habits ("I never listen to it"). We didn't claim that radio invaded our privacy, and our newspapers did not contain self-help pieces entitled "Turning Off the Radio Habit."

Today we have Judy Mann in the *Washington Post* on "Turning Off the TV Habit," about her family's cold-turkey withdrawal from the electronic beast.

"I don't miss it at all," she insists in the third paragraph. It's a one-sentence paragraph, set apart and standing alone for greater dramatic emphasis.

She goes on to say, "You realize how stupid the sitcoms are," "It is a terrible time-waster," and "Television is a lot like smoking: You only realize what a rotten habit it is once you've stopped." She also quotes her husband—"He thinks it destroys the mind"—and a Washington-area English teacher: "If TV is like a drug that numbs the mind, excessive viewing amounts to drug abuse."

These vitriolic reactions echo the fashionable complaint that television is "an insult to the intelligence," but intelligence is the handmaiden of cool reason, and something hotter is at work here.

Television rouses our instinctive hatred because it is the only medium of entertainment in which the great do not keep their distance. Theater actors perform on a curtained stage, radio is a disembodied voice, and movies of the thirties and forties presented godlike stars who were figuratively larger than life and made them literally larger than life on giant screens. But the democratic size of the television screen and its permanent presence in our homes have deprived us of personages awesome and mysterious, damaging thereby the psychic dynamo that powers religious faith. In the primitive recesses of our minds, television personalities are to us what antichrists and heretics were to the Middle Ages.

The most revolting form of closet misanthropy in the Republic of Mean is the "Oprah's Guest" syndrome. Masquerading as compassionate broad-mindedness but really driven by the notion that dignity is elitist, it demands that people strip themselves of all that is seemly and wallow in maudlin sludge.

MARYLAND COUPLE SHARES A GIFT OF LOVE: HER KIDNEY

After the area's first spousal transplant, the couple "crept together through the hospital corridors, both slightly bent with pain," while their teenage children "hung out with them, looking after mom and dad and making home videos of them."

When they left the hospital to go home, the husband wore a teeshirt inscribed: "My wife gave me her heart and all her love. Now she gave me a kidney." He explained: "I was so glad. I had my catheter and my bag of what we call liquid gold. I said, 'Timmie, look at this,' " meaning that the new kidney was working.

Added the *Washington Post* reporter: "The Warners are the kind of people who view obstacles as challenges—the glass half full, not half empty, as Kenneth Warner put it. And they are 'goal-oriented' people, he said. Warner decided he wanted a transplant kidney, and he set Christmas as his personal deadline."

But who would donate it? Said Mrs. Warner: "We woke up on a Saturday morning and I said 'Why can't I give you a kidney?' " And so she did. And left the hospital wearing a teeshirt inscribed: "I gave my husband my heart and all my love. Now I gave him a kidney."

My coffee cup is half empty. While I pour myself a refill, look at this:

It's a Christmas postcard from Congressperson Patricia

Schroeder, who evidently culled my name from the *MS.* sub-
scription list. The picture shows the whole family, including the
dog, frolicking in the snow. The message reads: "Santa's back!
So are Jim, Pat, Scott, Jamie & Wolfie Schroeder! Jamie is a
sophomore at Princeton studying Chinese. Scott works at ABC
News in D.C. Jim works at paying bills and Pat works at passing
them! Wolfie sleeps! Best Holiday Wishes for a great 1990. Pat &
the gang."

The home address is up in the corner, designed to look hastily
written by hand instead of photocopied: Schroeder, 1600 Emer-
son, Denver CO 80218. And of course, *Pat* contains a smiley face
in the circle of the *P.*

It is not necessary to like people to respect them. The Warners
and Schroeders among us miss a vital point that we of cooler
temperaments instinctively understand and unfailingly honor:
Familiarity doesn't breed contempt, it *is* contempt.

Hatred of smokers is the leading form of closet misanthropy
in the Republic of Mean. Smokists don't hate the sin, they hate
the sinner.

The anti-tobacco campaign never would have succeeded so
well if the alleged dangers of smoking had remained a problem
for smokers alone. We simply would have been allowed to invoke the Right to Die, always a favorite with democratic lovers
of mankind, and that would have been that. To put a real
damper on smoking and make it stick, the right of others not to
die had to be invoked somehow, so "passive smoking" was invented.

The name was a stroke of genius. Just about everybody in
America is passive. Passive Americans have been taking it on the
chin for years, but the concept of passive smoking offered them

a chance to hate in the land of compulsory love, a chance to dish it out for a change with no fear of being called a bigot.

The big, brave Passive Americans responded with a vengeance. They began shouting at smokers in restaurants. They shuddered and grimaced and said "Ugh!" as they waved away the impure air. They put up little signs in their cars and homes. At first they said Thank You for Not Smoking but now they feature a cigarette in a circle slashed with a red diagonal. They even issue conditional invitations—I got one. The woman said, "I'd love to have you to dinner but I don't allow smoking in my home. Do you think you could refrain for a couple of hours?" I said "Go fuck yourself" and she told everybody I was the rudest person she had ever met.

Insisting that there is no difference between tobacco and hard drugs, they equate cigarette smokers with heroin, cocaine, and crack users and call us "addicts." Curiously, however, we are the only ones they are willing to berate publicly. If they really believe all addicts are equal, why don't they walk up to crackheads and mainliners and scream "Ugh! You're disgusting!"

Because they are afraid of getting killed.

Washington Times columnist and smoker Jeremiah O'Leary was the target of two incredibly baleful letters to the editor after he defended the habit. The first one said, "Smoke yourself to death, but please don't smoke me to death," but it was only a foretaste of the second:

Jeremiah O'Leary's March 1 column, "Perilous persuaders . . . tenacious zealots," is a typical statement of a drug addict trying to defend his vice.

To a cigarette smoker, all the world is an ashtray. A person who would never throw a candy wrapper or soda can will drop a lit cigarette without a thought.

Mr. O'Leary is mistaken that non-smokers are concerned about the damage smokers are inflicting on themselves. What arrogance! We care about living in a pleasant environment without the stench of tobacco smoke or the litter of smoker's trash.

If Mr. O'Leary wants to kill himself, that is his choice. I ask only that he do so without imposing his drug or discarded filth on me. *It would be nice if he would die in such a way that would not increase my health insurance rates.* [my italics]

The expendability of smokers has also aroused the closet misanthropy of the federal government. I was taking my first drag of the morning when I opened the *Washington Post* and found myself staring at this headline: NOT SMOKING COULD BE HAZARDOUS TO PENSION SYSTEM. MEDICARE, SOCIAL SECURITY MAY BE PINCHED IF ANTI-TOBACCO CAMPAIGN SUCCEEDS, REPORT SAYS.

The article explained that since smokers die younger than non-smokers, the Social Security we don't live to collect is put to good use, because we subsidize the pensions of our fellow citizens like a good American should. However, this convenient arrangement could end, for if too many smokers heed the Surgeon General's warnings and stop smoking, they will live too long and break the budget.

That, of course, is not how the government economists phrased it. They said:

The implications of our results are that smokers "save" the Social Security system hundreds of billions of dollars. Certainly this does not mean that decreased smoking would not be socially beneficial. In fact, it is probably one of the most cost-effective ways of increasing average longevity. It does indicate, however, that if people alter their behavior in a manner which extends life expectancy, then this must be recognized by our national retirement program.

At this point the reporter steps in with the soothing reminder that "the war on tobacco is more appropriately cast as a public health crusade than as an attempt to save money." But then we hear from Health Policy Center economist Gio Gori, who said: "Prevention of disease is obviously something we should strive for. But it's not going to be cheap. We will have to pay for those who survive."

Something darkling crawls out of that last sentence. The whole article has a die-damn-you undertow that makes an honest misanthrope wonder if perhaps a cure for cancer was discovered years ago, but due to cost-effective considerations. . . .

But honest misanthropes are at a premium that no amount of Raleigh coupons can buy. Instead we have tin-pot Torquemadas like Ahron Leichtman, president of Citizens Against Tobacco Smoke, who announced after the airline smoking ban: "CATS will next launch its smoke-free airports project, which is the second phase of our smoke-free skies campaign."

Rep. Richard J. Durbin promised the next target will be "other forms of public transportation such as Amtrak, the intercity bus system and commuter lines that receive federal funding." His colleague, Sen. Frank Lautenberg, confessed, "We *are* gloating a little bit," and Fran du Melle of the Coalition on Smoking OR Health, gave an ominous hint of things to come when she heralded the airline ban as "only one encouraging step on the road to a smoke-free society."

These remarks manifest a sly, cowardly form of misanthropy that the Germans call *Schadenfreude:* pleasure in the unhappiness of others. It has always been the chief subconscious motivation of puritans, but the smokists harbor several other sub-conscious motivations that are even more loathsome.

Study their agitprop and you will find the same theme of pitiless revulsion running through nearly all of their public-service ads. One of the earliest showed Brooke Shields toweling her wet hair and saying disgustedly, "I hate it when somebody smokes after I've just washed my hair. Yuk!" Another proclaimed, "Kissing a smoker is like licking an ashtray." The latest, a California radio spot, asks: "Why sell cigarettes? Why not just sell phlegm and cut out the middle man?"

Fear of being physically disgusting and smelling bad is the insecure American's worst nightmare, which is why bath-soap commercials never include the flow-restricting shower nozzles that environmentalists push in *their* public-service ads. The showering American always uses oceans of hot water to get "ZESTfully clean" in a sudsy deluge.

Next comes a deodorant commercial. "Raise your hand, raise your hand, raise your hand if you're SURE!" During this jingle we see an ecstatically happy assortment of people from all walks of life and representing every conceivable national origin, all obediently raising their hands, until the ad climaxes with a shot of the Statue of Liberty raising hers.

The Statue of Liberty is a symbol of immigration, the first aspect of American life that the huddled masses experienced. The second was being called a "dirty little" something-or-other as soon as they got off the boat. Deodorant companies see the wisdom in reminding the immigrants' descendants of the dirty-little period in their family histories. You can sell a lot of deodorant this way. Ethnics get the point directly; Wasps get it by default in the subliminal reminder that, historically speaking, there is no such thing as a dirty little Wasp.

Smokers are the new greenhorns in the land of sweetness and

health, scapegoats for a quintessentially American need, rooted in our fabled Great Diversity, to identify and punish the undesirables among us. Ethnic tobacco haters can get even for past slurs on their fastidiousness by refusing to inhale around dirty little smokers, and Wasp tobacco haters can savor once again the joy of being "real" Americans by hurling with impunity the same dirty little insults that their ancestors hurled with impunity.

The tobacco pogrom serves additionally as the basis for a class war in a nation afraid to mention the word *class* aloud. Hating smokers is an excellent way to hate the white workingclass without going on record as hating the white workingclass.

The anti-smoking campaign has enjoyed thumping success among the "data-receptive," a lovely euphemism describing the privilege of spending four years taking notes on the jawboning of asses. The ubiquitous statistic that college graduates are two-and-a-half times as likely to be non-smokers as those who never went beyond high school is balm to the data-receptive, many of whom are only a generation or two removed from the lunch-bucket that smokers represent. Haunted by a fear of falling back down the ladder, and half-believing that they deserve to, they soothe their anxiety by kicking a smoker as the proverbial hen-pecked husband soothed his by kicking the dog.

The earnest shock that greeted the RJR Reynolds "Uptown" marketing scheme aimed at blacks cramped the vituperative style of the data-receptive. Looking down on blacks as smokers might be interpreted as looking down on blacks as blacks, so they settled for aping the compassionate concern they picked up from the media.

They got their misanthropy-receptive bona fides back when the same company announced plans to target "Dakota" cigarettes at a fearsome group called "virile females."

When I first saw the headline I thought surely they meant me:

what other woman writer is sent off to a book-and-author luncheon with the warning, "Watch your language and don't wear your Baltimore Orioles warm-up jacket"? But no. Virilettes are "Caucasian females, 18–24, with no education beyond high school and entry-level service or factory jobs."

Commentators could barely hide their smirks as they listed the tractor pulls, motorcycle races, and macho-man contests that comprise the leisure activities of the target group. Crocodile tears flowed copiously. "It's blue-collar people without enough education to understand what is happening to them," mourned Virginia Ernster of the University of California School of Medicine. "It's pathetic that these companies would work so hard to get these women who may not feel much control over their lives." George Will, winner of the metaphor-man contest, wrote: "They use sophisticated marketing like a sniper's rifle, drawing beads on the most vulnerable, manipulable Americans." (I would walk a mile to see Virginia Ernster riding on the back of George Will's motorcycle.)

Smoking is the only evil that cannot be blamed on white males. Red men started it, but nobody will say so because that would be racist. Meanwhile, smokers are the only people in America who are subject to de jure segregation.

* * *

Here lie I, Timon, who alive all living men did hate;
Pass by and curse thy fill, but pass,
And stay not here thy gait.

Carving "Go Away" on his tombstone is guaranteed to make a misanthrope feel better about himself. One who actually did it was a citizen of ancient Athens who makes a brief appearance in Plutarch's *Lives,* the source for Shakespeare's *Timon of Athens.*

The play opens with the rich, neurotically nice Timon, "that honourable, complete, free-hearted gentleman," practicing the "untirable and continuate goodness" for which he is famed. In the course of a single morning, he adds to a girl's dowry so her beloved's father will consent to the match, sends his servants hither and yon with cash gifts to all who have touched him for a loan, and pays a friend's debts to get him out of debtor's prison. Believing that "we are born to do benefits," he throws regular banquets for the deadbeats of Athens, who are steadily eating him out of house and home.

His only real friend is a good-natured cynic named Apemantus who lives by the Golden Mean that Timon so ostentatiously ignores. Apemantus's opinion of human nature is contained in the table grace he recites by way of warning at one of the banquets.

> *Immortal gods, I crave no pelf;*
> *I pray for no man but myself;*
> *Grant I may never prove so fond*
> *To trust man on his oath or bond,*
> *Or a harlot for her weeping,*
> *Or a dog that seems a-sleeping,*
> *Or a keeper with my freedom,*
> *Or my friends if I should need 'em.*
> *Amen. So fall to it.*

But Timon pays no attention to this shrewd advice. When the debtor that he sprang from jail tries to pay him back, he refuses to hear of it, saying, "I gave it freely ever." Taking him at his word, his other so-called friends don't bother to pay him back either. Nor do they come to his rescue when he finally goes bankrupt.

Realizing that he has been betrayed, Timon throws one last banquet for the freeloaders. Thinking that he has somehow recouped his fortunes, they all show up in their usual expectant mood, but this night they are greeted by the New Timon.

"You knot of mouth-friends!" he screams, and then uncovers the platters. Dinner is warm water and stones.

"Live loathed and long," he tells them, calling them "smiling, smooth, detested parasites, courteous destroyers, affable wolves, meek bears, trencher-friends and minute-jacks." Then he really lets loose:

> *"Burn house! sink Athens! henceforth hated be*
> *Of Timon man and all humanity!"*

We next meet him outside the walls of Athens, where he enumerates the calamities he hopes will strike the city: adulterous wives, disobedient children, thieving servants, slave uprisings, "itches, blains, and leprosy," and sons who "pluck the lined crutch from thy old limping sire, and with it beat out his brains."

He himself won't be there to see it, however:

> *"Timon will to the woods, where he shall find*
> *The unkindest beast more kinder than mankind. . . .*
> *And grant, as Timon grows, his hate may grow*
> *To the whole race of mankind, high and low."*

He becomes a hermit. When his still-loyal steward comes to visit him, he tells the man:

> *"Hate all, curse all, show charity to none,*
> *But let the famished flesh slide from the bone*

> *Ere thou relieve the beggar. Give to dogs*
> *What thou deniest to men. Let prisons swallow 'em."*

Alcibiades has no better luck. "I am Misanthropos, and hate mankind," Timon tells him. "For thy part, I do wish thou wert a dog."

Apemantus the Cynic makes the trek out to the hermitage to try and talk some sense into him. "The middle of humanity thou never knewest, but the extremity of both ends," the wise old man says, but it does no good.

Next, Timon is visited by a delegation of senators. With seeming hospitality he gives them a tour of his hermitage and asks them to take a message back to the citizens of Athens. The senators perk up, thinking he must be feeling better, but this, according to Plutarch, is what he said:

"I have a little yard where there grows a fig tree on which many citizens have hanged themselves. And, because I mean to make some building on the place, I thought it good to let you all understand that, before the tree be cut down, if any of you be desperate, you may there go hang yourselves."

Shortly afterwards Timon himself dies and is laid to rest under his notorious tombstone. Knowing that the curious will ignore the inscription and come anyway, he spent his last days landscaping the spot in such a way that the weight of the crowd will cause it to sink into the sea.

Timon of Athens is universally acknowledged to be Shakespeare's worst play: "two plays, casually joined at the middle," according to Mark Van Doren. Some scholars suspect that the version we have was actually a rough draft that Shakespeare put aside, intending to polish it later, but never got around to it. Others think Shakespeare wrote half of it and somebody else finished it. Whatever happened, the dramatic fault is lack of foreshadowing. The protagonist swings from one extreme to the other with such speed and clumsy motivation that audiences can't believe in it.

The only way to salvage it is to turn it into a screenplay called *Regarding Timon.* Once it's billed as "an American story for the 90's" it will make perfect sense.

THE GOADING
OF AMERICA

Fisher Ames is the Founding Father who draws a blank. When I first discussed the idea for this book with my agent and various editors, none of them had ever heard of him, and neither had any of the people who volunteered the names of their favorite misanthropes.

I told them not to feel bad. I was a history major through graduate school, with A's in *American Revolution* and *U.S. Constitution,* but until a few years ago when I came across him in my private reading, I had never heard of Fisher Ames either.

Yet it was Ames who wrote the final version of the First Amendment, and his speech on Jay's Treaty, delivered when he was the leader of the Federalists in the First Congress, was called the finest example of American oratory by Daniel Webster and Abraham Lincoln, both of whom memorized large portions of it to train themselves in the art.

Why then the blackout on Fisher Ames?

He was born in Dedham, Massachusetts in 1758, entered Harvard at twelve, and graduated at sixteen. After teaching himself law, he went into practice, farming the family lands on the side, until politics called.

The Ames home seems to have been a cocoon of idyllic happiness. His wife evinced none of the nascent feminism of Abigail Adams. She gave him six sons and a daughter, who received large chunks of paternal quality time thanks to the pleasure Ames took in inventing and playing educational games. He also got along well with his in-laws; his letters to brother-in-law Thomas Dwight are as warm as they are voluminous.

Fisher Ames was called a "sweet" man by his contemporaries. His first biographer, writing shortly after his death, spoke of "the charms of his conversation and manners [that] won affection" and "the delicacy, the ardor, and constancy with which he cherished his friends," and said: "He had a perfect command of his temper; his anger never proceeded to passion, nor his sense of injury to revenge."

No one sounds less like a misanthrope, yet Fisher Ames had a bleak opinion of human nature. "Our mistake is in supposing men better than they are. They are bad, and will act their character out," he wrote. He insured his absence from history textbooks with: "Our disease is democracy. Democracy is a troubled spirit, fated never to rest, and whose dreams, if it sleeps, present only visions of hell."

Ames's fellow Federalist and philosophical soulmate, Alexander Hamilton, held the same views and just as frequently aired them. It being impossible, however, to ignore Hamilton in the textbooks, it has been the custom to soft-pedal his opinions of mankind and democracy—*e.g.,* the typical high school or college text will say, "Hamilton distrusted the people," when in fact he said: "The people! The people, sir, are a great beast!"

45

Both Ames and Hamilton, and in a later era Henry Adams, were sociable men with a wide circle of friends who nonetheless qualify for conditional membership in the ranks of misanthropy. As Federalists, Ames and Hamilton believed in a government controlled by "the wise, the rich, and the good," the same philosophy held by Henry Adams, who was nominally a Democrat. The views of all three men amounted to what we now call elitism. Since the elitist hates the masses, and since the masses make up the vast majority of the human race, the elitist conservative is, numerically speaking, a practicing misanthrope.

In Ames's case, his basic outlook was exacerbated by a political event that goaded him into a bitter hatred of mankind. It is no exaggeration to say that he was frightened into misanthropy by the French Revolution.

As word of the excesses of the Terror filtered in—summary executions, blood-drinking, cannibalism, massacres of nuns, the sexual dismemberment of the Princess de Lamballe, accusations of incest against Marie Antoinette—all done in the name of "the People," Ames coined the word "mobocracy" and likened France to "a Cerberus gaping with ten thousand throats, all parched and thirsting for fresh blood. . . . tyranny more vindictive, unfeeling, and rapacious than that of Tiberius, Nero, or Caligula, or any single despot that ever existed."

Ames was not alone; Burke in England reacted the same way. The French Revolution probably created more misanthropes than any other event in history. In other bloodbaths the evildoers have been exotic foreign marauders or nations within nations—Huns, Bolsheviks, Nazis, Khmer Rouge—but in the France of the Terror they were *the People,* humanity's upper-case whole.

The French Revolution frightened Jefferson and his democratic republicans too, but for a very different reason. The conservative Federalists, fearing the people, wanted a strong central government with a powerful executive branch. But the liberal Jeffersonians, fearing kings, wanted separation of powers and checks and balances to control the executive, whom they saw as a potential Louis XVI ever ready to abridge the people's rights. To Ames, this amounted to a deliberate weakening of executive authority inflicted on the Constitution by those who imagined all government to be a Bourbon king.

Ames loathed Thomas Jefferson, considering him a dupe of the French Enlightenment's naive, optimistic faith in the essential goodness of human nature. Whenever anyone quoted Jefferson's "all men are created equal," Ames shot back: "but differ greatly in the sequel."

The "Jeffs," as Ames called the democratic republicans, moved him to savage eloquence: "They learn to throw their eyes beyond the gulf of revolution, confusion, and civil war, which yawns at their feet, to behold an Eden of primitive innocence equality, and liberty. . . . The rights of man are to be established by being solemnly proclaimed, and printed, so that every citizen shall have a copy. Avarice, ambition, revenge, and rage will be disenchanted from all hearts and die there; man will be regenerated. . . . and the glorious work of that perfectibility of the species, foretold by Condorcet, will begin."

To the democratic-republican claim that anarchy could be avoided by giving the people so much freedom that they would have nothing to rebel against, Ames countered that human nature being what it is, people will always find something to rebel against; if nothing else, envy will make them crave "the power to make others wretched."

He predicted the rise of what he called "factions" and we call pressure groups: "A combination of a very small minority can effectually defeat the authority of the national will. . . . Suppose at first their numbers to be exceedingly few, their efforts will for that reason be so much the greater. They will call themselves the People; they will in their name arraign every act of government as wicked and weak; they will oblige the rulers to stand forever on the defensive. . . . With a venal press at command, concealing their number and their infamy, is it to be doubted that the ignorant will soon or late unite with the vicious?"

But, the democratic republicans argued, the majority rules! No, said Ames, they don't. The price of liberty is eternal vigilance, and most people are unwilling to pay it: "The virtuous, who do not wish to control the society, but quietly to enjoy its protection; the enterprising merchant, the thriving tradesman, the careful farmer, will be engrossed by the toils of their business, and will have little time or inclination for the unprofitable and disquieting pursuit of politics."

The only eternally vigilant citizens in a democracy, Ames warned, will be members of factions whose ceaseless demands will cause "a state of agitation that is justly terrible to all who love their ease. . . . it tries and wears out the strength of the government and the temper of the people. It is a game which the factious will never be weary of playing, for conquering parties never content themselves with half the fruits of victory."

Ames opposed the addition of the Bill of Rights to the Constitution, believing that the Magna Charta guaranteed everything that needed to be guaranteed. A member of Congress when the Bill of Rights was introduced, he wrote scathingly in a letter to Thomas Dwight:

Mr. Madison has introduced his long expected amendments. They are the fruit of much labor and research. He has hunted up all the grievances and complaints of newspapers, all the articles of conventions, and the small talk of their debates. It contains a bill of rights, the right of enjoying property, of changing the government at pleasure, freedom of the press, of conscience, of juries, exemption from general warrants, gradual increase of representatives. . . . This is the substance. There is too much of it. Oh! I had forgot, the right of the people to bear arms. *Risum teneatis amici?* [Can we restrain our laughter?] Upon the whole, it may do some good towards quieting men, who attend to sounds only, and may get the mover some popularity, which he wishes.

Ames wrote the final version of the First Amendment, not because he approved of it, but simply to bring literary order to the unwieldy bundle of rights that Madison amassed.

As time went on and his health failed, Ames's bitterness increased. When Jefferson was elected president he said: "We are in the hands of the philosophers of Lilliput." As for the Louisiana Purchase, it was "a Gallo-Hispano-Indian Omnium Gatherum" destined to produce even more factions and lead us down that fatal Roman road from a republic ruled by laws to an empire ruled by power.

He continued to pound away at democracy. "What other form of civil rule so irresistibly tends to free vice from restraint and to subject virtue to persecution?" "There is universally a presumption in democracy that promises everything, and at the same time an imbecility that can accomplish nothing, not even preserve itself." "We are sliding down into the mire of a democracy, which pollutes the morals of the citizens before it swallows up their liberties."

Five years before his death he wrote Thomas Dwight: "Our country is too big for union, too sordid for patriotism, too democratic for liberty." He was glad to be out of politics: "Nor will I any longer be at the trouble to govern this country. I am no Atlas, and my shoulders ache."

In the end, he seemed to adopt a broader misanthropy extending beyond American politics to the entire race of mankind: "Indeed I consider the whole civilized world as metal thrown back into the furnace, to be melted over again."

Most people know that John Adams and Thomas Jefferson both died at a ripe age on the same day: July 4, 1826. Given the superstitious weight of the number *three,* a study of the life of Fisher Ames concludes with a chill down the spine, for Ames died of tuberculosis at age fifty on July 4, 1808.

The Grim Reaper's unhealthy interest in America's birthday takes on ominous significance when we examine our present national mood in the light of Fisher Ames's warnings about factionalism.

Our underlying fear that there is no national glue holding us together has always been embarrassingly obvious. Whenever calamity strikes—Pearl Harbor, Dallas, the Iranian hostages, the Challenger explosion—we give ourselves away with a verbal pat on the back that we recite with conspicuous relief: "It brought us together."

Collecting Gotterdammerungs in the cause of union will no longer work. There is so much pluribus in the unum that everybody is somebody's "them."

Affirmative action is our French Revolution, goading us into misanthropy as surely as the excesses of the Terror goaded Fisher Ames. It has sent a twist through the national belly, as anyone who knows anything about this country might have predicted, for when you hit Americans in the college education, you hit them where they live.

What's the use? is becoming our national war cry. Copious tears have been shed over despairing rage in the ghetto, but there's more than one kind of despairing rage, and more than one kind of ghetto. The talented student who cracks the books to get into college, only to be passed over for someone less deserving, thinks *what's the use?* and then feels the twist in the belly. His parents, who have worked themselves ragged to give him a college education, think *what's the use?* and then feel the twist in the belly. The professor who demands excellence from his students, only to find himself charged with elitism, thinks *what's the use?* and then feels the twist in the belly.

The present mood of America, especially on college campuses, recalls Robinson Jeffers's phrase, "something in the air that hates humanity." Assessing the Civil Rights Act of 1990, Thomas Sowell lays it on the line:

> I see no reason why it can't happen here. Nothing is easier than to start a spiral of racial confrontations, and nothing is harder than to stop it. . . . we will have quotas set in concrete, no matter how much people deny it. And the hatred that is going to grow out of that is going to be something like we've never seen. . . . There's a consolation in being as old as I am. I don't think that I'm going to live to see the terrible trends that are setting in, particularly in race relations, come to their conclusion. I certainly would not want to be here for that.

Affirmative action was designed originally for "women and other minorities" but the phrase has become just another tortured euphemism. Female conscientiousness and eagerness to please have always made women good students and natural test takers. Jews have gloried in scholarship throughout the ages, and Asians of both sexes score so high on SATs and IQ tests that they regard affirmative action as an impediment. Affirmative action really means favoritism for blacks for the sake of racial peace, but the favor is pure chimera, and so, increasingly, is the peace.

Hatred of truth is misanthropy in the fullest sense because it is a denial of the human spirit. Evidence that many blacks have sunk to this nadir is piling up.

In 1919 there was a popular song called "The Irish Were Egyptians Long Ago." Now a growing band of black scholars is insisting that blacks were. Calling themselves "Afrocentrists," they are demanding that curricula at all levels be rewritten to include the contributions of black Egypt. These assay out to just about everything ever invented, written, and built, for by placing themselves in ancient Egypt, blacks can thus claim that they antedated and influenced ancient Greece, and take credit for all the seminal discoveries in mathematics, architecture, sculpture, astronomy, and philosophy that make up Western civilization.

This is precisely what they are doing. The leading Egyptomaniacs—Martin Bernal of Cornell, Asa G. Hilliard III of Georgia State, Theophile J. Obenga of Gabon—contend that Greek philosophers "sat at the feet" of black Egyptian priests, who taught them all they knew. Hilliard also claims that Rameses, King Tut, Moses, Cleopatra, Jesus, Buddha, and Aesop were black or partly so; and that study at "the great African universities" was "fairly common" among the ancestors of American slaves. He concludes: "Since Africa is widely believed to be the birthplace of the human race, it follows that Africa was the birthplace of mathematics and science." *It follows?* If geometry and structural engineering had been based on that kind of logic, the pyramids would have collapsed on the Jewish slaves that the black Egyptians presumably owned.

The most outlandish claim comes from an Oregon teacher, Carolyn Leonard, who has solved the riddle of the Sphinx: "Napoleon shot off its nose to alter the facial features so people wouldn't know it was African." This happened to a lot of old statues, according to Leonard. "They were not eroded by time, but deliberately altered to rid them of the vestiges of African features."

Afrocentrism is catching on. Sphinxologist Leonard is ensconced in the Portland school system with the glorious title of Coordinator of the Multicultural-Multiethnic Education Office. The New York State Department of Education has created a new "curriculum of inclusion," and in Washington, D.C. a former sixties activist, Albena Walker, is conducting an elementary school "pilot program." According to the *Washington Times,* her curriculum employs yoga. ("In through the noses, out through the mouths. . . . all the spiritual sciences have their roots in Africa. . . . Invoke your ancestors, breathe in, breathe out").

John Leo of *U.S. News & World Report* calls Afrocentrism "a sort of Tawana Brawley theory of history, in which facts do not matter, only resentments and group solidarity." However, Leo adds that when he called seven prominent Egyptologists at random to ask their opinion on the Black Egypt theory, all seven said it was not true—"then asked that their names not be used." One told him it was "politically too hot" to get into.

Egyptologists tend to be dependent on grants from foundations, which are dependent on government tax laws. Most people erudite enough to dispute Afrocentrism are sucking on some public or semi-public tit, which explains why only four scholars so far have come forward to do battle. Two of them are unassailable emeriti of history almost as eternal as the pyramids themselves: Henry Steele Commager and Arthur J. Schlesinger, Jr. The other two are William H. McNeill and Diane Ravitch, who was called "Miss Daisy" by the offended Egyptomaniacs.

The four have formed the Committee of Scholars in Defense of History, but who will be brave enough to lend them public support? Certainly not the enterprising merchant, the thriving tradesman, the careful farmer, or the rest of our virtuous citizenry who do not wish to control society, but quietly to enjoy its protection and send their children to its schools. They, who have little time or inclination for the unprofitable and disquieting task of being called racists, will simply grumble in private until they wake up one morning and find that Afro Ed has become a required course in every school in America, and nobody will know how it happened.

A further indication that blacks as a group are becoming misanthropic is their increasingly testy readiness to regard as white anyone who is not black.

Miami is a flashpoint for black-Hispanic tensions. Black accusations of brutality against Hispanic police pulsate with the same frenzied quality of similar cases against white police in the sixties. They also are showing the same tendency to turn into causes célèbres, such as last year's well-publicized trial of an Hispanic officer who shot a black motorcyclist who tried to run him over. The Miami police force itself has divided along racial lines: black officers have charged that Hispanic officers are slow to respond to back-up calls from them.

In "Hispanics vs. Blacks in Houston," about the ongoing struggle for municipal power, *Newsweek* reporter Ginny Carroll writes: "The reigning assumption seems to be that the nation's two largest minorities will have to duke it out, while white control remains intact. . . . the animus between [Hispanics] and Houston blacks is likely to worsen."

Black hostility toward Asians has mounted steadily in the face of Asian business success, which many inner-city blacks attribute to a government plot, and the superior academic performance of Asian students in tests that are supposedly biased in favor of whites.

A personality conflict freighted with irony has also emerged. Explaining what it is about Asians that blacks don't like, the embattled Korean grocer whose Brooklyn store has been the target of a year-long black boycott told the *Washington Post:* "Because we don't laugh so much and don't smile so much, it doesn't seem like we're very kind people." Blacks are now demanding smiling good cheer of Asians just as white Southerners once demanded it of them.

Black anti-Semitism has been around a long time but it entered new realms when Toni Morrison told *Time:* "What I find is a lot of black people who believe that Jews in this country, by and large, have become white. They behave like white people rather than Jewish people."

Rachel Flick confronted the same attitude at a 1988 black-Jewish conference in Atlanta convened to repair the damage between the two groups. "What emerged in Atlanta, moreover, was that interest in repairing the alliance is one-sided," said Flick. "For Jews of the Reform tradition, as most of the civil-rights activists are, an alliance with the downtrodden is an essential part of feeling Jewish. But for blacks, Jews are white—a point tactfully and truthfully offered by Benjamin Hooks of the National Association for the Advancement of Colored People."

As a final fillip, blacks have thrown down the gauntlet to feminists. To repair the damage done to poor black males by their female-dominated, fatherless environments, the growing movement by black educators to segregate boys into separate classes, or even separate schools staffed exclusively by black male teachers, can only undermine the whole concept of sexual equality and re-invent Freudianism, complete with new-old buzzwords like "emasculation."

Hispanics, Asians, Jews, women—blacks are flailing their way into misanthropy minority by minority, group by group, faction by faction. If it continues, our Omnium Gatherum might well achieve a unity nobody bargained for.

A few years ago, while having coffee in my favorite diner, I eavesdropped on a conversation between two good ole boys who were discussing the race for the 1984 Democratic presidential nomination. This is what I overheard:

"Hey, T. J., you know whut?"

"Whuzzat, Dwayne?"

"If the Jews hate Jesse Jackson, they cain't be too bad."

Political scientists would call this a re-alignment but in fact it is a movement of the earth. When Dwayne and T. J. become good ole goys, anything can happen. If blacks continue on their misanthropic way they will eventually goad the rest of the population into a monolithic "white" race. The concept of ethnicity will vanish altogether as Hispanics join other whites in adopting the Eurocentrism of which we presently stand accused. Asians, having given "Protestant Ethic" new meaning with their thrift and hard work, will increasingly think of themselves, and be thought of, as white—as they already are at the Virginia State Employment Commission, which lumps them with whites in the category called "Other."

There is no telling where it will end, though I am willing to venture a guess: Wasps will finally stop describing as "foreign looking" anyone who does not turn pink and blister after an hour in the sun.

TENDER

MISANTHROPES

The word *misanthrope* ought to be inhospitable to qualification and immune to modifiers, but it isn't. Misanthropes come in two models that were defined by the literary historian Irving Babbitt in his monumental 1919 work, *Rousseau and Romanticism.* "The tender misanthropy of the Rousseauist," Babbitt wrote, "is at the opposite pole from that of a Swift, which is the misanthropy of the naked intellect."

The misanthrope of the naked intellect hates people straight down the line with no exceptions and no regrets. Regarding mankind as hopeless, he tends to be apolitical. Regarding mankind as loathsome, he tends to be an apolitical arch-conservative, a purely temperamental stance whose sole purpose is hands-off, apocalyptic revenge. Presented with Thomas Hobbes's assessment, "The life of man is solitary, poor, nasty, brutish, and short," he replies: "If it ain't broke, don't fix it."

The tender misanthrope, on the other hand, despises humanity in general but is ever ready to make an exception for the *real* people. He feels certain that he could love them if only he could find them—or failing that, transform existing false people into his idealized *real* people through social and political programs of his own making.

The world has endured regular bouts of tender misanthropy. The worst upheaval occurred in the fifth century, when early Christian hermits fled to the deserts of North Africa and became their own *real* people. In the early twentieth century, tender misanthropes decided that the *real* people were "the Workers," while to the tender misanthropes of eighteenth-century France, the *real* people were "noble savages."

Jean-Jacques Rousseau's *Discourse on the Origins of Inequality* praised "natural man" over his civilized counterpart, who, he believed, had been ruined by knowledge, culture, luxury, and "insincere" polished manners. Civilization, said Rousseau, really ought to be torn down and all laws abolished so that everybody could be happy like the simple peasants who placed heart over head, emotion over logic, nature over culture, soul over all.

He sent Voltaire a copy of the *Discourse* but the grand old cynic, who was a bona fide liberal, saw through Rousseau's misanthropic liberalism and took a dig at him in his thank-you note: "I have received, sir, your new book against the human species, and I thank you for it. No one has ever been so witty as you are in trying to turn us into brutes; to read your book makes one long to go on all fours. As, however, it is now some sixty years since I gave up the practice, I feel that it is unfortunately impossible for me to resume it."

Jean-Jacques Rousseau was born in Geneva in 1712 to a forty-year-old mother who died two days later. His father was a watch-maker with aristocratic pretensions that he expressed by wearing a sword and keeping it on the equivalent of hair-trigger, resulting in several incarcerations for public brawling.

Jean-Jacques also had aristocratic pretensions but they went beyond his father's simpleminded pleasure in swashbuckling. "What was hardest to destroy in me," he wrote later, "was a proud misanthropy, a certain acrimony against the rich and happy of the world as though they were so at my expense, as though their alleged happiness had been usurped from mine."

Apprenticed to an engraver, he hated the common atmosphere of the workshop so much that he ran away, becoming a nomadic Jack-of-all-trades and, whenever possible, an older woman's kept boy. His relationship with his first patroness, Mme de Warens, is summed up by his pet name for her: *"Maman."*

The ad hoc quality of Rousseau's mind and the hysteria that lay just under the surface of his personality emerge in the story he told of how he came to be a writer. In 1749 as he was walking along the Vincennes road on his way to visit Diderot in prison, he happened to buy a newspaper in which he happened to see a notice that the Dijon Academy was holding an essay contest on the influence of formal manners on French culture. What happened next sounds very much like a fit:

"All at once I felt myself dazzled by a thousand sparkling lights; crowds of vivid ideas thronged into my head with a force and confusion that threw me into unspeakable agitation; I felt my head whirling in a giddiness like that of intoxication." He sat down under a tree, ideas surging through his fevered brain. At last, when he had pulled himself together, he saw that his shirt-front was wet with tears but could not remember having shed them.

He wrote the essay, won the prize, and wormed his way into the homes of bored French aristocrats, becoming the last word in radical chic. Ensconced as the man of the hour, he turned out a plethora of how-to and self-help treatises on subjects ranging from botany to solitary hikes to breastfeeding. He was notoriously a tit man, but instead of admitting it to himself and accepting it as one of life's more pleasurable hang-ups, he rationalized it in the same way that he rationalized his misanthropy, writing and talking so much about primitive scenes, mother's milk, and peasant warmth that breastfeeding became a national fad, even among women of the nobility who had always used wet nurses.

His concern did not extend to his mistress, the scullery maid Thérèse Vasseur, who had given birth to five children by him. Having gained an entrée into Parisian society, he did not want to advertise his connection with the common Thérèse, so he dumped all five little ads in a foundling home and then wrote a book on how to raise children. *Emile,* as it was called, laid out a program of "natural" behavior over rigid discipline, "natural" environments over artificial ones, and "freedom" from stifling rules.

In quick succession came a romantic novel, *La Nouvelle Héloise,* equating sincerity of feeling with manic depression ("I love you as one must love, with excess, madness, rapture and despair"), and a political treatise, *The Social Contract* ("Man is born free but he is everywhere in chains"). After that the Establishment had had enough; Rousseau's books were condemned by church and state and their author exiled.

He lived for a while in England where he met David Hume, with whom he soon broke over some imagined offense, and young James Boswell, who visited him at his next place of exile in Switzerland. They had dinner in Rousseau's kitchen, served by the long-suffering Thérèse Vasseur, who had stuck with him despite the disappearing act he performed with their children. The visit ended abruptly when Rousseau snapped at Boswell,

"You are irksome to me. I cannot help it, it's my nature. Go away."

Boswell was the last man to see him before he went completely round the bend. Two weeks later, Voltaire published a pamphlet poking fun at *Héloise* and revealing the story of the five abandoned children. Thereafter a broken man, Rousseau suffered regular delusions of persecution until his death in 1778.

He was buried on the estate of one of his hard-core fans, the Marquis de Girardin, a forerunner of today's limousine liberals, who planted him on the "Isle of Poplars" in the middle of a lake, the gravesite surmounted by an imposing tomb and surrounded by benches reserved for nursing mothers. His death triggered a new round of sentimental hysteria as thousands of pilgrims (including Marie Antoinette) flocked to his grave, and Elvis-like sightings of him were reported in the press. Fifteen years later during the Reign of Terror, the Jacobins, who rode to power on the primitivism he unleashed, reburied him in the Pantheon where he still lies.

Rousseau's philosophy can be summed up by the buzzword of his day: *sensibilité*—what our age calls "getting in touch with your feelings." His methodology can be summed up by the title of Johnny Ray's 1952 hit song: "Cry."

Rousseauian tears, says Simon Schama in *Citizens,* were regarded as "the soul directly irrigating the countenance. More important, a good fit of crying indicated that the child had been miraculously preserved within the man or woman. So Rousseau's heroes and heroines, beginning with himself, sob, weep and blubber at the slightest provocation."

The *sensibilité* craze spread to other arts. The philosopher Diderot, one of the Encyclopedists, also endorsed coming apart: "Move me, astonish me, unnerve me, make me tremble, weep, shudder and rage." A favorite painter of the time, Jean-Baptiste

Greuze, the Rousseau of the palette, had all of Paris in a sodden mess with his *Girl Weeping Over Her Dead Canary.* An art critic wrote that he went back again and again to gaze at it and cry some more: "I have passed whole hours in attentive contemplation so that I became drunk with a sweet and tender sadness."

According to Rousseau, the best place to cry was in the woods. Nature was particularly well-suited to his overwrought vocabulary. The woods were *wild, untamed, primitive, lush.* The woods were full of *nooks, copses, verdant canopies, umbrageous illusions.* They were also full of sobbing Rousseau fans but never mind that, you could be *alone with nature* in the woods, *lose yourself* in their beauty, *let it wash over you,* sleep *naked* in a *bower* and *become as one* with nature's *torrents.* Afterwards, you could write about your sylvan crying jag and claim to be *drunk with* emotion, a cliché that is with us still.

To understand why eighteenth-century France succumbed to his glorification of unbuttoned hysteria, it is necessary to know what seventeenth-century France had been like. Called the Age of Reason, it was a neoclassical period that modeled its behavior on the stern virtues of Early Rome: honor, duty, courage, and especially *gravitas,* that dignified stoicism in the face of personal pain that was considered the mark of an aristocrat.

In literature and drama these virtues were transmuted into simple logical plots faithful to the Aristotelian model, pithy epigrams modeled on Martial, a reverence for linguistic precision as dictated by the Académie Française, a lofty formalism requiring actors to declaim rather than emote, and a curtain of charity prohibiting scenes of lust and violence from the stage.

In life as in art, the watchwords were self-control and decorum. Rigid perhaps, but Frenchmen of the seventeenth century had a high opinion of human nature and a limitless faith in

Man's capacity for rational behavior. We get from people what we demand of them and the Age of Reason demanded much.

The neoclassicists did not deny emotions altogether. One of their leading lights, Blaise Pascal, penned the famous line, "The heart has its reasons of which reason knows nothing," but he said it and got out, leaving posterity an exquisitely balanced epigram. Rousseau said it and kept on saying it over and over in purple prose until his followers were as conditioned as Pavlov's dogs. If he did not actually cause the French Revolution, he certainly set it up. His message of *I feel, therefore I am* ushered in a self-indulgent emotionalism that spilled over into political anarchy and became the rationale for the Reign of Terror.

Only a tender misanthrope could screw up the world as Rousseau did. The misanthrope of the naked intellect, disdaining such categories as *real* people on the grounds that if indeed they exist, they must be even worse than the other kind, has no wish to liberate the repressions of a species that he already finds intolerable. If he must share the world with people, he wants them to be as decorous and self-controlled as possible. He is thus an Age of Reason unto himself who, for purely selfish motives, places humanity on a pedestal and holds it to the highest standard of behavior. Ironically or not, the misanthrope of the naked intellect is the true friend of mankind.

By contrast, humanity has never regained the dignity and strength of character that Rousseau's tender misanthropy destroyed. His glorification of "natural" behavior foretold the Freudian theory of repression which encouraged man to regard his conscience as his worst enemy, leading in turn to the hippie credos of "Let it all hang out" and "If it feels good, do it," and the coarse sexual honesty that the seventies called "getting down and dirty."

And now we have "out of control," a trendy euphemism describing the behavior of someone who has sunk below the rational level and entered the realm of dark impulse. Bret Easton Ellis's *American Psycho* would have sounded very familiar to the Paris mob that cut out the vulva of the Princess de Lamballe, stuck it on a pike, and held it up to Marie Antoinette's window amid howling demands that she kiss it. They also did the same things that Jeffrey Dahmer did in his gory Milwaukee apartment—except that he did them in secret and they did them in the middle of the Place de la Concorde in broad daylight because they had been saturated, trickle-down fashion, in a Rousseauian ethos that urged them to abandon their unique human capacities for rationalism and civilized behavior and surrender themselves to primitive instinct.

Seeing how much American madness can be traced back to Jean-Jacques Rousseau is like seeing how many words can be formed from *antidisestablishmentarianism.* In both cases the answer is: a lot.

The phrase "pursuit of happiness" has a suspiciously Rousseauian ring, as well it might. The well-read Thomas Jefferson was his contemporary, and served as Minister to France in the period just after his death. The various self-realization and human-potential movements that have shredded our social fabric in the name of "feeling good about myself" are outgrowths of the oxymoronic mass individualism that Rousseau promoted in his posthumously published *Confessions,* which contains the Western world's first mantra: "I am not made like anyone I have seen; I dare believe that I am not made like anyone in existence. If I am not better, at least I am different."

Real people are everywhere now: beating drums in the woods in New Man weekend pow-wows, mooning coeds on campuses, simulating pelvic thrusts under the goal posts, leaping naked out of the stands to steal home plate, and letting unleashed emotions wash over them in today's version of the verdant canopy, the confessional talk show. The cheapness, tawdriness, and utter lack of class that ooze out of Oprah, Donahue, and Geraldo are the recycled *sensibilité* of Jean-Jacques Rousseau, the tender misanthrope who loved people so much that he dumped human dignity in a foundling home.

"A special type of sincerity," wrote Irving Babbitt, "is itself an outcome of the Rousseauistic movement. It seems to be assumed in certain quarters that almost any opinion is justified provided it be held with sufficient emotional vehemence." Homeless advocate Mitch Snyder, who abandoned his wife and children so he could take care of strangers, was vehemently sincere. The self-analysis he gave to a Washington reporter shortly before committing suicide could be slipped into an edition of Rousseau's *Confessions* with no one the wiser—including Rousseau.

> I don't consider myself a good person. I tend to be very impatient,
> I tend to be very short, I tend to make heavy demands on people.
> I don't have much time or energy to give much one-on-one, and
> so I'm very hard on people around me. I take much more than I
> give. I give to people in the shelter, I give to people on the streets,
> I give to people who are suffering, but that's got little to do with
> people who are around me. They pay the price.

"The misanthropist of the Rousseauistic or Byronic type has a resource that was denied to Swift," Irving Babbitt continues. "Having failed to find companionship among men he can flee to nature."

Green grow the Rousseaus, O! Anyone who has received junk mail from Greenpeace has read Jean-Jacques in full throttle: "Listening to 500 dolphins shrieking in panic as they fight and gasp for air. . . . standing by helplessly as living dolphins were dragged aloft thrashing and flailing in terror. . . ." Suddenly, I awoke in the Fredericksburg post office to find tears on the front of my Baltimore Orioles warm-up jacket, yet I had no memory of having shed them.

The current crop of rat lovers, cockroach cuddlers, and assorted environ-mental cases never come right out and say "I am a misanthrope." They prefer to hate human nature through what Babbitt called "an Arcadian haze."

Typical is a letter in the *Santa Barbara News-Press* from one Charles LeCompte: "Think how nice this planet would be with no humans. The air would be super-clean, the oceans super-clean. But no! Humans came along with their ignorance and greed and have just about destroyed this planet. Depending on personal beliefs, God or nature made one big mistake, and that mistake is humans."

Or try this helpful hint from *Earth First! Journal:* "Are you terminally ill with a wasting disease? Don't go out with a whimper; go out with a bang! Undertake an eco-kamikaze mission. . . . The possibilities are limitless. Dams . . . are crying out to be blown to smithereens, as are industrial polluters, the headquarters of oil-spilling corporations, fur warehouses, paper mills. . . . To those feeling suicidal, this may be the answer to your dreams. . . . Don't jump off a bridge, blow up a bridge. Who says you can't take it with you?"

I frankly admit I like that. As a child I was powerfully influenced by Veronica Lake's heroic deed in the World War II movie about Bataan nurses, *So Proudly We Hail,* when she walked into a Japanese barracks with a grenade tucked in her bra. The lustful grinning soldiers surrounded her, and then. . . .

I saw it when I was in elementary school, when the first of many progressive teachers was riding me about being antisocial.

Thereafter, whenever I was accused of aloofness, a picture of Veronica Lake rose in my mind. *They want me to have more extracurricular activities, huh? They want me to join clubs, huh? They want me to go to group functions, huh? Okey-dokey....*

This is definitely a misanthrope's fantasy. *Earth First!* won't tell you; I just did.

The rise of the animal-rights movement has been attributed to "post-industrial" this-and-that but I detect several quasi-misanthropic causes.

Liberals have developed compassion fatigue for their own species but they are too liberal to say so.

The now-famous war cry, "a rat is a pig is a dog is a boy," is simply another way of saying that we have run out of humans to demand rights for. Equality was bound to come to this.

Animal-rights activism gives disillusioned feminists an excuse to go back to being women protecting wee creatures without compromising their radical credentials.

Animal-rights activists are motivated by an unconscious wish to escape the sexual revolution through the evocation of chaste childhood images of a boy and his dog or a girl and her horse.

Like Rousseau, they are hypocritical snobs. Fisher Ames and Alexander Hamilton were honest about their hatred of the masses, as were Sir Harold Nicholson ("I hate the common people"), and John Randolph of Roanoke ("I am an aristocrat. I hate equality, I love liberty"). But the quadruphiles couch their class hatred in jokes about polyester and testimonials to natural fabrics, which they invariably anthropomorphize: cotton "breathes," madras "bleeds" (leather used to do something or other before they swore off it).

They are the same people who sang "We Are the World" but it ought to be "We Are the Graduate School." According to the frequently published statistic, 99 percent of quadruphiles are white, 51 percent are college graduates, 36 percent have done post-graduate work, and a third earn at least $40,000 a year. This means they are "articulate." Articulate? *Speciesism?* Fittingly, you have to have a harelip to pronounce it.

"I detest my fellow-beings and do not feel that I am their fellow at all," wrote Gustave Flaubert.

Flaubert (1821–1880) is France's misanthrope of the naked intellect who turned the literary tables on the tender misanthropy of Jean-Jacques Rousseau.

He was born in Rouen at the mid-point of the Romantic Movement that Rousseau spawned, an era of palmy neuroticism when the affliction of choice was *Sturm und Drang* and the beau ideal was a dead poet, preferably under thirty.

The Romantics were round-the-clock free spirits. Coleridge turned on to opium and Wordsworth bemoaned the invention of railroads because they discouraged vagabondism. Many Romantics led such hectic personal lives that it is hard to see how they managed to get any work done. George Sand left her husband and put on pants, the better to chase Frédéric Chopin, of whom Mme de Staël said: "The only constant thing about him was his cough." Percy Bysshe Shelley was a monster of irresponsibility whose headlong search for universal love made everyone in his orbit miserably unhappy—even including the donkeys he acquired for a trans-Alpine trip with Mary Godwin, when everything that could go wrong did go wrong due to his contempt for bourgeois habits such as planning ahead and thinking things through.

Next to suicide, the spectacle of insanity exerted the most fervid pull on the romantic imagination. The heroine of Sir Walter Scott's *The Bride of Lammermoor* went mad on her wedding night. The period's best-known literary mistress was mad to begin with, as Lord Byron discovered when he tangled with the congenitally beset, self-dramatizing Lady Caroline Lamb, who slashed her wrists at the dinner table. The fad for delirium and brain fever pervaded the recently invented Gothic novels and upped the ante on Rousseau's woods: now they were full of *stygian mists* and *melancholy penumbra*.

None of this suited Gustave Flaubert's practical, easily irritated Norman soul. He was quintessentially middle class, a doctor's son who set out to be a lawyer. When he gave up the law for writing there was no question of starving in a cold garret *à la bohème*. He lived in his family's spacious country home near Rouen with his doting widowed mother, waited on hand and foot by her and a devoted female servant who arranged the household to accommodate his need for solitude and silence.

Visits to Paris to partake of the literary ambience left him overwrought. "Contact with the world, with which I have been steadily rubbing shoulders now for fourteen months, makes me feel more and more like returning to my shell," he wrote his mother. "I hate the crowd, the herd. It seems to me always atrociously stupid or vile."

Life back home also presented problems: "I took a walk in Rouen this afternoon and met three or four Rouennais," he confided to his journal. "The sight of their vulgarity and of their very hats and overcoats, the things they said and the sound of their voices made me feel like vomiting and weeping all at once. Never since I have been in this world have I felt so suffocated by a disgust for mankind!"

He had a mistress, Louise Colet, but she got on his nerves, so he saw her only when the demands of the flesh gave him no choice. The rest of the time she had to be content with the only kind of affection that misanthropes are good at. "The most successful love affairs are conducted entirely by post," said

George Bernard Shaw. And so Flaubert wrote letter after letter to poor Louise who, because she never understood him, assumed that the voluminous correspondence meant that he could not live without her.

She got a taste of the misanthropic point of view when she wrote him that she thought she was pregnant. He replied: "The idea of giving birth to someone fills me with horror. I'd curse myself if I became a father." He enlarged upon the point after her fears had proved false: "This paternity would have made me fall into the ordinary conditions of life. My virginity, with respect to the world, would have been wiped out, and I would have sunk into the abyss of common misery."

That misanthropes are literary classicists is axiomatic but Flaubert didn't know it yet. Determined to master the romantic style, and able to afford leisurely, material-gathering travel, he took an extended trip to the Near East to soak up some Oriental exoticism. After visiting Early Christian sites in North Africa, he returned to Rouen and wrote *The Temptation of St. Anthony,* a long, lush, lyrical fantasia full of demons, meditations, and visions.

He insisted upon reading the six-hundred-page manuscript aloud to a captive audience of two friends. It took four days, and by the time it was over they were in worse shape than St. Anthony. The book was crammed with vivid descriptions and meticulous detail but it did not "move"; the plotless story was as flat and static as its protagonist, who was a psychotic hermit.

At this Maalox moment in literary history, one of Flaubert's friends suddenly remembered a recent local scandal. "Throw it in the fire," he said of St. Anthony, "and write a novel about that doctor's wife who killed herself."

At first Flaubert didn't want to do it, but he soon realized that this stark domestic tragedy was a perfect vehicle for a misan-

thropic author. The story of a woman enslaved by cheap sentiment and puerile romantic dreams, *Madame Bovary* demanded
a writer able to remain aloof from the emotions he had to describe. To "identify" with Emma Bovary, to weep and wallow
with her in Rousseauian fashion, would have dragged both author and story down to her level and turned the book into the
same sort of trashy melodramatic novel that Emma herself read
and identified with.

Flaubert wrote *Madame Bovary* like a bookkeeper looking for a
penny. His detachment, his objectivity, his emotional restraint, his
pitiless insight and savage realism gave her the sympathy and
understanding she craved and put her in a class with Andromeda.

He was equally kind to his readers. Unlike the Romantics,
who believed that a writer should forget about grammar and
spelling and "just let it come," Flaubert was too rigid to confuse
writing with vomiting. He spent whole days searching for *"le mot
juste,"* the right word, the perfect word, the *only* word that would
express exactly what he wanted to say.

He always cut more than he saved. The misanthrope's abrupt-
ness finds a friend in the classicist's economy of expression. It is
easy to imagine how Rousseau would have written the arsenic
scene; Flaubert's laconic sentences twist like short-bladed knives:
"She opened the jar and began to eat it" and "Still there was the
taste of ink."

There is no such thing as a bad translation of *Madame Bovary*
because it is so clear and concise that no translator could possibly
go off the rails. Yet the language is so simple, the sentences are so
direct, the scenes are so logically arranged around unifying points,
that anyone with a few years of French under his belt can read it
with ease in the original, even when schooldays are long in the past.

Madame Bovary, the work of a misanthrope, is the most user-
friendly novel ever written.

YOUR PRESIDENT IS NOT A MISANTHROPE!

Ask any American his opinion of Richard Nixon and you will get an answer as complex and contorted as Nixon himself. The French, on the other hand, respond with childlike simplicity: they're crazy about him. Small wonder, since they know him so well. The "real Nixon" has been a fixture at the Comédie Française since 1666. His name is Alceste, and he's the protagonist of Molière's play, *Le Misanthrope.*

In the Paris of Louis XIV, where style and form are everything, Alceste is notorious for his charmlessness and gaucherie.

> *The soul God gave me isn't of the sort*
> *That prospers in the weather of a court.*
> *It's all too obvious that I don't possess*
> *The virtues necessary for success.*
> *My one great talent is for speaking plain;*
> *I've never learned to flatter or to feign;*

And anyone so stupidly sincere
Had best not seek a courtier's career.

In 1948, Alceste Nixon came face to face with the kind of man
he hated when Alger Hiss was called to testify before the House
Un-American Activities Committee, of which Alceste was a
member.

"Hiss," Alceste wrote later, "was a striking representative of
the fashionable Eastern establishment—a graduate of Harvard
Law School, clerk to a Supreme Court Justice, an aide to Frank-
lin D. Roosevelt at the Yalta conference and one of the major
organizers of the United Nations conference in San Francisco.
He had impeccable social and intellectual qualifications, and the
list of people who he said would vouch for his character ranged
from Adlai E. Stevenson to John Foster Dulles. He, in effect,
pleaded innocence by association."

And when there's any honor that can be got
By pulling strings, he'll get, like as not.

Hiss had been accused of membership in the Communist Party
by Whittaker Chambers, whom Alceste Nixon trusted instinctively and identified with: "Although he was a senior editor of
Time magazine, Chambers was poorly dressed, pudgy, undistin-
guished in appearance and in background." When Chambers
appeared before the committee, the newspaper reporters crowding the congressional hearing room reacted like twentieth-cen-
tury versions of Versailles courtiers. "Most of the reporters
covering the Hiss case were obsessed with style," Alceste wrote.
"They were so dazzled by Hiss's background and his brilliant
conduct on the witness stand that they failed to see that beneath

73

the unimpressive exterior, Chambers was a stronger, more intelligent man."

The graceful Alger Hiss tripped himself up when Committee Chairman Karl Mundt showed him a photo of Whittaker Chambers and asked him if he had ever known him. At this point, it was simply a matter of one man's word against another's. Hiss could have extricated himself with a charmless *no,* but he made the mistake of showing off.

"If this is a picture of Mr. Chambers," he purred, "he is not particularly unusual looking. He looks like a lot of people. I might even mistake him for the Chairman of this Committee."

Hiss's studied urbanity and supercilious sarcasm got Alceste Nixon's goat: "Hiss's friends from the State Department, other government agencies, and the Washington social community sitting in the front rows of the spectator section broke into a titter of delighted laughter. Hiss acknowledged this reaction to his sally by turning his back on the Committee, tilting his head in a courtly bow, and smiling graciously at his supporters."

> *Notice how tolerant people choose to be*
> *Toward that bold rascal who's at law with me.*
> *His social polish can't conceal his nature;*
> *One sees at once that he's a treacherous creature.*

Still gilding the lily, Hiss asked if Whittaker Chambers were present in the hearing room. "He then looked from side to side, giving the impression that he did not have the slightest idea who this mysterious character might be and that he was anxious to see him in the flesh." Told that Chambers was not present, Hiss assumed a theatrical air of disappointment that roused Alceste Nixon's deepest suspicions.

This artificial style, that's all the fashion,
Has neither taste, nor honesty, nor passion.

"It was a virtuoso performance. . . . But even at that time I was beginning to have some doubts. From considerable experience in observing witnesses on the stand, I had learned that those who are lying or trying to cover up something generally make a common mistake—they tend to overact, to overstate their case. When Hiss had gone through the elaborate show of meticulously examining the photograph of Chambers, and then innocently but also somewhat condescendingly saying that he might even mistake him for the Chairman, he had planted in my mind the first doubt about his credibility."

Alceste Nixon's dogged persistence exposed Hiss. He was jailed for perjury, earning for Alceste the undying hatred of the media courtiers. They hated him relentlessly throughout the eight years he served as vice president, and he hated them in return.

And I despise the frenzied operations
Of all these barterers of protestations,
These lavishers of meaningless embraces,
These utterers of obliging commonplaces. . . .

Alceste Nixon ran for president in 1960 but he lost on looks and style in the first televised debates with John F. Kennedy.

No one could possibly be taken in
By those soft speeches and that sugary grin.
The whole world knows the shady means by which
The low-brow's grown so powerful and rich. . . .
Are you in love with his embroidered hose?
Do you adore his ribbons and his bows?

The answer was yes. Two years later Alceste Nixon ran for governor of California and lost that one too. Calling in the courtiers, he announced that they would no longer have Alceste to kick around.

> *Come then: man's villainy is too much to bear;*
> *Let's leave this jungle and this jackal's lair.*
> *Yes! Treacherous and savage race of men,*
> *You shall not look upon my face again.*

It was his finest hour, but he didn't know it.

Alceste Nixon went into retirement and wrote a political autobiography about the Hiss case and other landmarks of his career called *Six Crises*. As it happened, America had several crises of her own, and so in 1968, Alceste ran for president again.

He was bound to win, considering what had happened to the Democrats. He didn't *have* to try to conceal his real personality but he did it anyway, out of long habit. He came up with the "New Alceste," and devised a campaign slogan promising to "Bring Us Together," making a heroic effort to seem warm and friendly even though it clearly made him uncomfortable. His anomalous cold dark eyes gave off an obsidian flatness that betrayed his scornful opinion of political backslappers.

> *I see you almost hug a man to death,*
> *Exclaim for joy until you're out of breath,*
> *And supplement these loving demonstrations*
> *With endless offers, vows, and protestations. . . .*

His victory sealed his fate. Now that he was president—which is to say, First Nice Guy—he had to go on concealing his real personality. That's when the trouble started. The American electorate, who assuage their own insecurity by demanding Nice Guyism of their leaders, have no idea what years of spurious warmth can do to someone like Alceste Nixon. Nothing is more stressful than a misanthrope trying to be nice with no end in sight. It's hard enough on the people who must witness it, but it just about kills the misanthrope. The strain becomes unbearable; if it goes on too long, paranoia normally kept under control suddenly explodes and the misanthrope starts doing things that he would not ordinarily do.

> *Ah, this is what my sad heart prophesied;*
> *Now all my anxious fears are verified;*
> *My dark suspicion and my gloomy doubt*
> *Divined the truth, and now the truth is out. . . .*
> *Yes, now I have no pity, not a shred;*
> *My temper's out of hand; I've lost my head. . . .*
> *A righteous wrath deprives me of my senses,*
> *And I won't answer for the consequences.*

Alceste Nixon got into some trouble that he could have gotten out of very easily, but he let it go on and build up out of an unconscious need to justify the misanthropy he had denied all his life.

> *I'll discover by this case*
> *Whether or not men are sufficiently base*
> *And impudent and villainous and perverse*
> *To do me wrong before the universe.*

They are.

The "excess of zeal" that set Watergate in motion is the sort of thing that invariably goes on behind a misanthrope's back because a misanthrope's back is usually turned. In a word, we are easy to screw. In *The Palace Guard,* authors Dan Rather and Gary Paul Gates write:

> What gave Haldeman such overwhelming power was that he served as sentinel for a President who chose to sequester himself behind a wall of Do Not Disturb signs. Of all the characteristics that define Richard Nixon, none perhaps is more striking than his celebrated sense of privacy, a trait that he personally attributes to his Quaker heritage.

American loners who would never say "I don't like people" will readily own up to a sense of privacy because it sounds like the Constitution. By attributing his sense of privacy to his Quaker heritage, Nixon got two amendments for the price of one, so to speak. Anyone who objected to it could conceivably be accused of religious bigotry as well as illegal search and seizure.

It might have worked in the nineteenth century, but by the time Nixon appeared on the public scene the Quakers had taken on a quaint, harmless glow like the ruddy, smiling burgher on the oatmeal box. His Quaker-heritage allusion was lost on most Americans, who did not know enough about Quakers to know what they had to do with whatever it was about him that they didn't like. Every time he brought it up, they thought he was just being sanctimonious.

The misanthrope who tries to hide his misanthropy is invariably mistaken for a run-of-the-mill hypocrite and roundly despised. The unabashed misanthrope, on the other hand, evokes a surprising response, as Robert Lewis Taylor notes in his biography of W.C. Fields: "Fields' defiance of civilization, over a period of sixty-seven years, became an institution in which the public took pride. . . . Most persons, as a scholar has noted, harbor a secret affection for anybody with a low opinion of humanity."

This secret affection springs from a universal familiarity with the grind of daily life. For the meek majority who never say what they really think and never get even with the people who do them wrong, the misanthrope is a stand-in whom they can cheer from the safety of the sidelines. He has little to offer victims of crushing evil, but he is the nemesis of humanity's little meannesses, the ones that hurt most of the people most of the time. Engaged in his ceaseless battle against such widespread human failings as officiousness, pomposity, and duplicity, the ostensibly uncharitable misanthrope ironically becomes a warrior for the shat-upon.

A politician could benefit from such a stance, but Nixon would not risk it. A misanthrope is *never* a conformist but Nixon is the exception that proves the rule. His desperate desire to fit in and be accepted is his tragic flaw. Determined to bend himself into the requisite American shape, he spurned the gift of misanthropy bestowed on him by the non-Quaker gods, who punished the indomitable prince of darkness by changing him into a vulnerable Gloomy Gus.

The universal fascination for what-might-have-been is used to clever effect in the vegetable-juice commercial featuring people who gulp down candy bars or ice cream for quick-energy snacks, and then, too late, slap themselves on the forehead and say, "I coulda had a V-8!"

But for our sweet tooth, America coulda had a Richelieu.

Commenting on the only Watergate conspirator who did not break down and confess, Stewart Alsop wrote: "In wartime, G. Gordon Liddy would have been festooned with decorations rather than slapped in jail. As so often in wartime, his stubborn silence did no good."

Liddy disagrees. "I became what I wanted to be," he writes in his autobiography, *Will.* An intimate account of the personal code of honor by which he has chosen to live, the book describes boyhood dreams of Heidelberg dueling scars and German military discipline, grisly tests of courage that included cooking and eating a rat, holding his hand over a flame until his flesh charred, and tying himself to a tree during an electrical storm to "defeat the fear of death and welcome the death of fear."

Statements like this have earned Liddy the tag of psychopath because America has forgotten what "dashing" means. Bursting upon the national scene at the height of the feminist movement, Liddy was dismissed as a comic-machismo anachronism, but in fact he is the spiritual twin of Edmond Rostand's Cyrano de Bergerac: the misanthrope as a stubborn blend of idealist and cynic perfectly balanced in one untroubled soul.

Americans, incapable of understanding that idealism and cynicism always travel in tandem, are forever trying to pry them apart as if they were wheat and chaff. Confronted by a complex personality, we tell ourselves he can't be *this* if he's *that,* but G. Gordon Liddy is most gloriously *this* at the same time he is most gloriously *that,* as he demonstrated when he wrote of Watergate Judge John J. Sirica: "Just as I do, John Sirica believes the end justifies the means. . . . The difference between us is that I admit it openly and don't pretend to be anything other than what I am."

> *I carry my adornments on my soul*
> *I do not dress up like a popinjay;*
> *But inwardly I keep my daintiness. . . .*
> *I go caparisoned in gems unseen,*

Trailing white plumes of freedom, garlanded
With my good name—no figure of a man,
But with a soul clothed in shining armor. . . .

The incredible strength that Liddy showed throughout the seven years of his imprisonment can never be sustained by "love." Only a lordly contempt for the human race and a keen eye for its foibles could have kept him sane, and like Cyrano, he has them in abundance.

Senator Sam Ervin: "Do you swear to tell the truth, the whole truth, and nothing but the truth, so help you God?"

Liddy: "No."

It is my pleasure to displease. I love
Hatred. Imagine how it feels to face
The volley of a thousand angry eyes—
The bile of envy and the froth of fear
Spattering little drops about me. . . .
The Spanish ruff I wear around my throat
Is like a ring of enemies; hard, proud,
Each point another pride, another thorn—
So that I hold myself erect perforce
Wearing the hatred of the common herd
Haughtily, the harsh collar of Old Spain,
At once a fetter and—a halo!

Cyrano was so quick on the uptake that he could write poems while he dueled, *"twirling—thus—a bristling wit,"* his meter keeping time with the cuts of his sword, *"making the sharp truth ring, like golden spurs."*

Liddy on Charles Colson's conversion: "If he'd run over his grandmother for Nixon, imagine what he'll do for Jesus."

Liddy lighting his cigar on a peace marcher's candle: "There, you useless son of a bitch. At least now you've been good for something."

Nowadays, Liddy's brand of antiquated honor exists only in jails. Of his fellow inmates he wrote: "Do them a favor or an injury, honor requires them to repay it, and they were constantly looking for some way to do so." The respectable majority is terrified of cavalier panache, but the inmates of Danbury Prison idolized Liddy when he used Watergate methods to expose corrupt wardens. Black prisoners especially respected him because they instinctively understood and identified with his refusal to give in and cooperate with the government like the other Watergate figures.

> *What would you have me do?*
> *Seek for the patronage of some great man,*
> *And like a creeping vine on a tall tree*
> *Crawl upward, where I cannot stand alone?*
> *No thank you!*
> *Be a buffoon in the vile hope of teasing a smile*
> *On some cold face? No thank you!*
> *Make my knees callous, and cultivate a supple spine,*
> *Wear out my belly groveling in the dust?*
> *No thank you!*

Liddy's idealism and cynicism are still going strong. In an appearance last year on the Howard Stern radio talk show, he described George Bush as "a man who can't keep his word," and punctiliously refused to answer questions that verged even slightly on legal opinions because: "I was disbarred. I want you to understand that."

Yet during a "Crossfire" debate about the Iran-Contra hearings, he pointed out dryly that no one should be surprised that Oliver North shredded documents because the government issued him a shredding machine, and what else did they expect him to do with it?

TOURETTE'S MISANTHROPY

The *New York Times* reviewer of *Lump It or Leave It* said that I reminded her of "someone with Tourette's syndrome at a diplomats' ball."

Tourette's Misanthropy is idealism with a short fuse. Its earliest known sufferer was Coriolanus, the patrician general and failed politician of Republican Rome.

The character of Coriolanus in Shakespeare's play has been called a "splendid oaf." A Patton in spirit but lacking Patton's intellectual streak, the Shakespearean Coriolanus is a consummate aristocrat within the original Old Roman definition: honor incorruptible and consumption so inconspicuous that you can't tell by looking whether he is rich or not. As the puzzled senators say of him, "He covets less than misery itself would give."

It goes without saying that Coriolanus would make a great statesman, but in order to be elected consul on the patrician ticket he must first become a great politician. His friend and campaign manager, Menenius, assesses his candidate's chances.

His nature is too noble for the world:
He would not flatter Neptune for his trident,
Or Jove for his power to thunder.
His heart's his mouth:
What his breast forges, that his tongue must vent.

Menenius tries to impress upon his candidate the importance of wooing the plebeians but Coriolanus recoils. He hates the common people and thinks God made far too many of them. Entering the Forum for his first campaign speech, he greets the assembled plebeians in his own inimitable fashion.

What's the matter, you dissentious rogues,
That, rubbing the poor itch of your opinion,
Make yourselves scabs?
Who deserves greatness
Deserves your hate; and your affections are
A sick man's appetite. . . .
He that depends upon your favours swims
With fins of lead. . . .

Menenius, a born spin doctor, whispers urgently, "This is the way to kindle, not to quench." But Coriolanus, cranked up and really into it by now, ignores him and launches into his plan for solving the famine problem.

Would the nobility lay aside their ruth
And let me use my sword, I'd make a quarry
With thousands of these quartered slaves,
As high as I could pick my lance.

85

When the mob starts howling in protest, Coriolanus calls them a "musty superfluity" and bellows, "Oh, go home, you fragments!"

Menenius calls a damage-control confab and puts out the word that Coriolanus's "noble carelessness" often makes him speak roughly, but in his heart he really loves the common people and has proved it many times by his heroic service in the army. He has twenty-seven war wounds, Menenius points out—"every gash an enemy's grave"—and promises that Coriolanus will go to the Forum in a toga of humility and show his wounds to the people.

Coriolanus balks at the idea but Menenius convinces him that it's an excellent way to show his human side. Coriolanus reluctantly agrees, so off they go to the Forum to put a spin on his first disastrous outing.

It might have worked if Coriolanus had told the plebeians a few war stories first and built up gradually to the subject of his wounds, but instead he immediately rips open his toga of humility and yells:

> *Look, sir, my wounds!*
> *I got them in my country's service, when*
> *Some certain of your brethren roared and ran*
> *From the noise of our own drums.*

"O me, the gods!" Menenius groans. "You must not speak of that: you must desire them to think upon you."

"Hang 'em!" Coriolanus replies, not troubling to lower his voice.

"Pray speak to them in wholesome manner," Menenius begs.

"Bid them wash their faces, and keep their teeth clean."

Next, Coriolanus tells the mob point-blank that he wants their votes.

First Citizen: "The price is, to ask it kindly."

Third Citizen: "You have not loved the common people."

Coriolanus: "You should account me the more virtuous, that I have not been common in my love."

As the heckling mounts, Coriolanus loses what little patience he has and yells, "Why in this wolfish toga should I stand here to beg of Hob and Dick?"

The tribunes denounce him as an enemy of the people and demand his banishment. Menenius and Coriolanus's womenfolk beg him to go to the Forum and answer the charges against him.

"You have been too rough. You must return and mend it."

But he still doesn't get it. "Why did you wish me milder?" he asks. "Would you have me false to my nature? Rather say, I play the man I am."

Surrounded by pragmatists, he finally agrees to try and mend his fences once more. "Well, I must do it: Away, my disposition, and possess me some harlot's spirit! I will answer in mine honour."

"Ay, but mildly," Menenius cautions.

"Well, mildly be it, then,—mildly!"

Smoldering all the way to the Forum, by the time he gets there he is so worked up that he explodes at the mere sight of the expectant plebeians, whose value to the state he analyzes in another extemporaneous speech.

> *Mutable, rank-scented mob!*
> *In soothing them, we nourish against our senate*
> *The cockle of rebellion, insolence, sedition,*
> *Which we ourselves have ploughed for*
> *By mingling them with us.*

He calls the plebeians "measles" and their tribune a "Triton of the minnows." When an old man tries to take hold of his arm, he pushes him off, barking, "Hence, rotten thing! or I shall shake thy bones out of thy garments!"

A riot breaks out. Enter the aediles (cops) but the situation is now beyond control. When the tribunes accuse Coriolanus of seeking tyrannical power and urge the plebeians to kill him, he draws his sword and offers to take on the whole crowd.

> *The fires in the lowest hell fold in the people!*
> *You common cry of curs whose breath I hate!*
> *Whose loves I prize*
> *As the dead carcasses of unburied men*
> *That do corrupt my air,—I banish you!*

Infuriated by the slurs on his honor and the compromises he has been forced to make, Coriolanus suddenly compromises himself. Blind to the irony of his action, he decides to avenge his honor by committing treason. He goes over to the enemy, the Volscians, and offers to help them invade Rome, his "cankered country," promising to fight "with the spleen of all the under fiends" of hell. He would rather ally himself with his old adversary, the Volscian general Aufidius, whom he once called "a lion I am proud to hunt," than let his principles be trampled by the Roman mob.

His wife and mother go to the enemy camp to dissuade him. Their pleas are so heartrending that Coriolanus gives in and agrees to return to Rome. But it's too late: now he is a traitor to the Volscians, and their leader Aufidius is not the honorable man Coriolanus has judged him to be. He is subject to peer pressure— "Our virtues lie in the interpretation of the time"—so when the

Volscians demand the death of Coriolanus, Aufidius orders his execution.

When I first read *Coriolanus* in college we had a vigorous classroom discussion about his decision to commit treason. My classmates were either shocked or puzzled by his act but I was neither. I identified thoroughly with him but I kept quiet because my reason was too complicated to explain, and if I had attempted to do so, everybody would have laughed because it involved walnuts.

It happened on Christmas Day, 1940. I was four. Preparing for a day of company, my grandmother gave me a bowl of walnuts in the shell and told me to put them on the coffee table. I carried them successfully through the kitchen, but when I was halfway across the living room, three or four walnuts spilled out of the bowl onto the floor.

There really is something to the expression, "I was so mad I couldn't see straight." Outlines and edges of things shifted momentarily like pictures coming out of their frames. The next thing I knew, I had turned the bowl upside down and dumped all the walnuts on the floor in a deafening tattoo.

My grandmother had seen it. "What in the world did you do that for?"

"If I spill a few, I'm going to spill them all," I said grimly.

Then, my fury expended, I very calmly picked up the walnuts, taking care to get every one, replaced them in the bowl, and put it on the table as directed.

When I told this story to a psychiatrist twenty-five years later, she immediately jumped to the conclusion that I had panicked over failing to meet my grandmother's perfectionist standards of Southern elegance. That's what you get for talking to psychiatrists: they are the master mold of conventional thinking and the very glass of superficiality. My "perfectionist" grandmother's

FLORENCE KING

housekeeping was predicated on the hearty Anglo-Saxon maxim, "A little dirt never hurt anybody"; she would not have cared if I had picked *shelled* walnuts off the floor and put them back in the bowl. As for elegance, the reason the walnuts made a deafening tattoo was that we had linoleum instead of rugs.

The walnut incident was my first episode of Tourette's Misanthropy: idealism with a short fuse. There have been many others since. The most recent one was as fraught with irony as Coriolanus's decision to compromise himself to keep from being compromised and dishonor himself to keep from being dishonored. As far as anyone in the publishing world knows—and just about everyone in the publishing world has now heard this story—I did what no writer has ever done before: raised hell about a favorable review.

I say *favorable* because the reviewer said nice things about *Reflections in a Jaundiced Eye.* It was not, however, a *good* review because it broke just about every rule of the reviewing art—and reviewing *is* an art, which is why I went ballistic. I cherish the review-as-literature; as lapidary journalism in the eighteenth-century mode, the last hard sparkling diamond in the essayist's tarnished crown. To me, writing a good review is not just a way to make extra money, but a sacred duty.

As soon as I read the review of *Eye* I wanted to shoot the reviewer, but since I couldn't do that, I did the next best thing and wrote him a letter. It said, in part:

> You do not know how to write a review. I do. Here are your faults:
>
> 1. A book review is a news story about a book and should carry a short, tight lead with a reader hook. Your Tarleton twins lead rambles on forever and goes nowhere. I told this story in the book

to make a point—that I hate children and hence was quite pleased when Granny told me I had eaten one—but you simply tell it without ever making the point about children, or any point at all. When you finally stop talking about the Tarleton twins, you leave the reader with the idea that the book is about Southern women, which it is not.

2. You wrote: "As she says of the Wall Street guy who skipped the sex scenes in a novel about money, 'I want to get to the good parts.' " In the first place, this is a sliding attribution resulting from a careless reading of the passage. It was the Wall Street guy, not me, who said "I want to get to the good parts." Then in your next sentence you say: "That's what this new book of essays is about. The good parts." This implies that my book is about money, which is one of the few things it *isn't* about.

3. Your description of men as "once chaotic and Heathcliff-like" bears no resemblance to the old-fashioned manly virtues that I praise in the book. You paraphrased something I never said, and you did it with a particularly unthought-out and meaningless choice of words. When were men as a group ever "chaotic?" Were you trying to say dashing, gallant, courageous, daring, devil-may-care? I've known plenty of chaotic women but no chaotic men until I read your review.

4. You don't have an eye and an ear for the telling quote. If you hadn't quoted the shaft I gave Mary Gordon, no one reading your review would have any idea of the tone of my book. Yet by choosing to quote what I said about Gordon, you made things hard on yourself and took up valuable space because you had to quote her twice before my shaft would make any sense. With all the quotable one-liners in my book that can stand alone, why did you decide to get tangled up in that one?

5. You concentrated on too many minor points and in general farted around without ever stating fully the two things that must

be in every review: what the book is about, and what the reviewer thinks of it.

    6. When reviewing a volume of discrete essays such as this one, the reviewer must identify and state the central theme that links them all together. You go from a hokey "She's not real pleased with things" to a quick reference to Alexander Hamilton which you promptly drop. Of the reviews I've had so far, the best statement of theme comes from the *Washington Times:* "Miss King is a fussy old maid who doesn't suffer fools and likes to see fools suffer."

I sent a copy of this letter to the book section editor, and then wrote her a letter saying that her method of choosing reviewers (I maintain that she tries to match reviewer and author too closely by genre and region, something we had argued about before) had produced one "who used my navel for his navel gazing."

According to a New York acquaintance of mine who heard a discussion of this episode at a literary cocktail party, the considered opinion of all present was that I'm crazy.

If I am, so is Carlton Fisk.

The forty-three-year-old Chicago White Sox catcher is a jovial, well-liked man, but he is an old-fashioned New Englander with rigid standards about how and how not to play baseball. Early in the 1990 season, Fisk did something without precedent in the major leagues: he blew his stack and chewed out a player on the opposing team for making a mistake.

The White Sox were playing the Yankees in New York. During the Yankee half of the inning, twenty-two-year-old "Neon" Deion Sanders, so called because of the flashy gold chains he wears on the field, hit an easy pop-up. Assuming it would be caught, Sanders strolled toward first base, then turned and ambled nonchalantly back to the Yankee dugout before the fielder had the ball in his glove.

Suddenly, looming behind him, was the six-foot-two Fisk, bellowing like a bull.

"Run it out, you piece of crud! Go on, run it out!"

Sanders stared at him in disbelief, obviously thinking that he must have lost his mind. He clearly had no idea why Fisk was incensed but he found out the next time he came to bat.

The huge catcher rose from his squat and gave him a murderous look.

"The days of slavery are over," said Sanders, who is black.

"Let me tell you something, you little [epithet not printed in the newspaper]," said Fisk. "There is a right way and a wrong way to play this game. You're playing it the wrong way. And the rest of us don't like it. Someday you're going to get this game shoved right down your throat."

Naturally both benches cleared—something that never happens, unfortunately, in the publishing world. Afterwards Fisk explained why he had castigated Sanders. He did it, he said, for "truth, justice, and the American way, and to keep Lou Gehrig from spinning in his grave."

Washington Post sportswriter Thomas Boswell understood Fisk's violent reaction and wrote a moving tribute to him.

> Call it the last stand of the dinosaurs. We may never see the like again, in any pro sport. So relish it. . . .
>
> Fisk is profoundly anachronistic and proud of it. He's out of step with the times. . . . Perhaps what sets Fisk apart is his antiquated notion that baseball is a calling, not just a silly game. Like a soldier, a cop, a priest, he reveres his forebears and is delighted to think he's worthy of them. What was good enough for Rogers Hornsby and Willie Mays is good enough for him.

Fisk is an idealist with a short fuse who suffers from Tourette's Misanthropy.

Another sufferer, who may well be the reincarnation of Coriolanus, is John Silber, the Democrat who lost the Massachusetts governor's race because his heart is his mouth. "Silber's shockers," as his brusque remarks were called, turned every liberal in America into a spin doctor and had Ellen Goodman agonizing for weeks: should she, could she, vote for a *Republican* to keep the mean-spirited Coriolanus from solving the social problems without which she would have nothing to write about? Her last column before the election ended on a note that was straight out of "The Lady—or the Tiger?" but her deft touch with suspense is about as deft as all her other touches. It was pretty clear that she voted for the palely loitering Wasp.

The prickly, unashamedly elitist Gore Vidal, if not an actual misanthrope, shows great promise. A gentleman of the old school despite such lapses as *Myra Breckinridge,* Vidal definitely has Tourette's Misanthropy on the subject of America's growing egalitarian inclination to deny the existence of inborn talent.

"This is the American attitude," he told *Publishers Weekly.* "Anybody can bull through it, or fake it. Faking it is our great national pastime. They always think that if you write well you're somehow cheating, you're not being democratic by writing as badly as everybody else does."

America's readiness to hurl a charge of elitism at anyone who insists that things be done well puts victims of Tourette's Misanthropy at daily risk of death from a sudden, massive stroke. I thought I was a goner when I read the following letter to the *Washington Post* from one George Wooley.

The many books on "correct" grammar are merely helpful guides to better communication skills. Who decides what grammar rules or spelling are officially correct? It's not set in stone. New words and phrases and new uses for old words and phrases are part of the art of language and the art must not be stifled by a few scholarly decisions.

The sole purpose of any communication, written or oral, is to convey a message, and it is far more important that the message delivered is correctly interpreted than it is that the message is in a "correct" form.

The eye stumbles over that last clause, which should read: *it is far more important that the message delivered be correctly interpreted than that it be in a "correct" form.* But never mind that. Let's make this egalitarian twit run out his pop fly.

In 1327, King Edward II of England was deposed and imprisoned in Berkeley Castle. Three goons hired by the rebellious Welsh barons were standing by to murder him, but they were afraid to act without the protection of written orders from Queen Isabel's chief henchman, a bishop who was in on the plot.

The bishop was equally afraid to put anything in writing. If something went wrong and the queen needed a fall guy, he did not want an execution order in his handwriting floating around. He needed an escape hatch; he had to figure out some way to make his message equivocal enough so that he could claim it was an order of reprieve *or* an order of execution, whichever the situation called for.

What to do?

Taking a leaf from today's anti-elitists, the bishop decided that it was far more important that his message be correctly interpreted than that it be in correct form, so he composed a sentence in which he intentionally omitted a vital comma. The sentence was: *Kill Edward not to fear is good.*

Depending upon where they chose to "see" the comma, the

goons could read it as: *Kill Edward not, to fear is good.* Or they could read it as: *Kill Edward, not to fear is good.* Knowing what they were supposed to do, they chose the second version. But for a comma, regicide was done and all the conspirators were covered.

If you feel like screaming, tearing your hair, and rending your garments over ignorance, incompetence, semiliteracy, and the curious pride so many Americans take in all three, you have Tourette's Misanthropy.

If you want to take slothful, rude, careless, unpunctual people by the lapels and shake them until their teeth rattle, you have Tourette's Misanthropy.

If you get the urge to kill when you hear plangent elegies about "babies having babies" in the inner cities, and then open a woman's magazine to find an interview with a famous movie star about the joys of her unwed motherhood, you have Tourette's Misanthropy.

If you spend the evening snapping and snarling at your spouse because your newspaper contains an op-ed calling Martin Luther King's plagiarism "textual appropriation" and "voice merging," you have Tourette's Misanthropy.

Don't worry about it, don't feel guilty about it, and for God's sake don't waste your money on a psychiatrist to find out what's wrong with you, because there is nothing wrong with you. Remember, *you* are right, and *they* are wrong. If you start feeling depressed, do what I do and recite Cyrano de Bergerac's farewell.

> *Yes, all my laurels you have riven away*
> *And all my roses; yet in spite of you,*
> *There is one crown I bear away with me,*
> *And tonight, when I enter before God,*

WITH CHARITY TOWARD NONE

My salute shall sweep all the stars away
From the blue threshold. One thing without stain,
Unspotted from the world, in spite of doom
Mine own—my white plume.

MS.-ANTHROPES

"Female misanthrope" is an oxymoron. Women are philanthropists in the original sense of the word, before money got involved in it. Despite a quarter century of feminism, people who deal with female raw emotions, from counselors of battered wives to teachers of karate, report that women still say, "I can't get angry enough."

One would expect more women to become misanthropic now that they are hardly ever alone. At least the traditional housewife of the feminine-mystique era had the house to herself for a few hours each day, but today's beset Having It Alls lack even that. Yet when women talk about "privacy" they mean abortion rights, and the millions of words feminists have written about "a room of one's own" refer to psychological space, rarely to physical solitude. For most women, being alone is tantamount to being deserted.

Women meet hatred with salvos of bigger and better niceness

and warnings of "There's more niceness where that came from." However much you pretty it up, this is masochism, and no misanthrope was ever a masochist. The opposite, it must be confessed, is more likely to be the case. My own sadism is the psychological kind known as "gleeful," rather than the physical kind, but both are distinctly unfeminine.

The ranks of distaff misanthropy are therefore thin, but one shining exception has walked this earth, and she makes me look like Little Bo Peep.

A six-foot-one, gun-toting virago whose sobriquet was "the gorilla lady" was not a woman to cross, but somebody finally did. On December 27, 1985, Dian Fossey was butchered at the Karisoke Centre for Mountain Gorilla Research in Rwanda where she had spent eighteen tumultuous years.

She was found in bed, her head split in two by a machete left nearby. Half-empty bottles of beer and scotch sat on her worktable beside an unloaded pistol. The murderer had entered her cabin through a hole cut out of the tin wall. The most puzzling aspect of the macabre scene was the hair clutched in her stiff hands: it was her own.

Solving Fossey's murder was not the purpose of the late Harold Hayes, who died in 1989 just as he was completing his engrossing biography, *The Dark Romance of Dian Fossey*. Whodunit interests him less than whydunit, and here he hits pay dirt, for there were very few people in Dian Fossey's embattled life who did *not* have a motive for murdering her.

Poachers, cattle herders, park officials, Western conservationists, members of her staff, a couple dozen researchers—the parade of possible suspects extended far back into the past. . . . Fossey had shot at her enemies, kidnapped their children, whipped them about the genitals, smeared them with ape dung, killed their cattle, burned their property, and sent them to jail. Anyone who dared to threaten her gorillas, or even to challenge her methods, set her off, and the force of her malevolence was difficult to imagine.

Born in the Bay Area in 1932, Fossey attended San Jose State College. Drawn to children, especially helpless ones, she became a physical therapist at a Louisville, Kentucky hospital. Refusing to live in nursing quarters, she insisted on renting a remote cabin deep in the woods miles outside of town. The landlord, who had advertised the place for a couple, refused at first to rent it to her, saying it was too isolated for a woman alone and he would not be responsible for her safety. She threatened to return to California if she could not have the cabin, so her supervisor at the hospital called the landlord and explained that Fossey's position had been hard to fill and they could not risk losing her.

The landlord relented and Fossey moved into the cottage, where she lived alone for ten years, collecting stray dogs instead of boyfriends. Eventually she moved to an even more remote house when she returned from a vacation and found that the landlord had put a mobile home for his aunts too near her place.

The consensus among her co-workers was that she liked animals better than people. When they gathered for coffee, she refused to join them and took her breaks alone. In what was probably a subconscious decision to insure that others kept their distance, she was less than fastidious in her grooming and often gave off body odor.

A fervent desire to see exotic animals led her to borrow $8,000 to go to Africa. It was on this trip that her enormous ego first reared its head and gave hints of megalomaniacal excesses to come. Completely flat-chested, wheezing with emphysema from her three-pack-a-day habit, and often smelly from not bathing, she nonetheless thought every man she met was trying to seduce her, and hurled accusations of sexual harassment when they did not respond to her up-front offers.

Hiring the last of the Great White Hunters, John Alexander, to take her on private safari, she laid it on the line: "What makes you think sex has anything to do with love? Here we've been three weeks on safari. We could have shacked up together and had a hell of a good time." When Alexander modestly declined, she spread the story that he was "all over me all the time."

Her articles on the trip (and the accompanying photos that she "borrowed" from a more experienced photographer and neglected to credit) attracted the attention of the famous prehistorian Louis Leakey, who preferred female assistants for his ape studies because "women were more patient, more sensitive to mother-infant relations, and less likely to arouse aggression in males." Little did he know that his latest Galatea would nearly start a civil war.

Arriving in East Africa in the sixties "when just to be white was to risk your life," Fossey's Tugboat-Annie nerve became an advantage in the face of Communist-inspired Simba incursions. Much of what happened in East Africa at this time was not reported by a press eager to put a good face on newly emerging nations, but Hayes fills in the blanks with some riveting passages:

> Led by witch doctors, the Simbas believed themselves impervious to bullets. They stoked their courage on hashish, and dressed themselves in monkey skins and whatever else might be at hand—lamp shades, women's panties, chicken feathers. . . . Many [of their victims] died by being forced to drink gasoline, then their stomachs were cut open and set on fire. One specially prized victim, a moderate politician named Sylvere Bondekwe, saw his liver cut out and eaten while he was still alive. . . . In their

extended siege of Stanleyville years earlier, the Simbas had held 1,100 Belgians and Americans hostage. "We shall cut out the hearts of the Americans and Belgians and wear them as fetishes," the Simbas had announced. "We shall dress ourselves in the skins of the Americans and Belgians."

Joseph Mobutu, financed by the United States for his anti-Communist resistance, swore to put down the Simbas. Knowing the limitations of his own army—"In a crisis, Congolese soldiers tended to drop their guns, take off their shoes, and run"—he hired white soldiers of fortune to protect his own position. When the white mercenaries, many of whom held Nazi-style racial views, turned against Mobutu and began killing their black comrades-in-arms, Mobutu announced that Europeans were trying to take over the country and ordered all whites killed.

It was at this time that Fossey claimed she was held for two days in a cage and "raped and raped and raped" by black African soldiers. No one knows what actually happened. One story has it that she was urinated on and otherwise humiliated, but that she escaped actual rape by defying her tormentors with the force of her rage, screaming, "You don't have the balls to rape me!"

It has the ring of truth, given Fossey's hell-for-leather personality, and it might have worked for a woman over six feet tall. Leakey believed her rape story, but the son of Congo colonialists did not: "If any African raped a European in that part of the world," he told the author, "you might as well forget that European's existence. . . . You don't get out of those kinds of camps."

This same ex-colonialist, on discovering that Fossey intended to stay and study gorillas come hell or high water, gave her some practical advice:

"The only option you've got to stay alive is to make yourself into some sort of spiritual witch. You've got to do this with such effectiveness and create such a sense of terror about you, people will give you a wide berth. All over Africa, there have been European women who lived on farms by themselves while their husbands went to war—my mother was one of them. The only way they survived was to become known as some sort of banshee. All Africans, you know, live in a spook land. They believe almost everything is invested with spiritual meaning. . . . I suggested she should make herself into someone no one would want to go *near*—that she should get wailing systems, smoke bombs, false faces, that sort of thing.

"At the same time, I told her she should beat the bejesus out of anybody she felt like beating the bejesus out of. And then they would get the feeling there was a woman up there who was behaving totally unwomanly."

This is precisely what Fossey did. To stop farmers from grazing their herds on the gorilla preserve, she shot a cow and vowed to shoot one a month: the grazing stopped. When farmers kidnapped her dog, she kidnapped eight of their cattle and spread the word that she would shoot one cow a day until she got her dog back: she got it back by nightfall. Abandoning her gorilla work to track the killers of a water buffalo, she fired a clip at them. Spotting one of their children hiding behind a tree, she kidnapped the child and offered to exchange him for his father's spear: she got the spear. "Naturally I returned the brat," she wrote to Leakey.

Word of her incredible courage began to spread. The Africans had never seen a woman like Fossey:

In a country where women were subservient to men, this giant female *mzungu* [European]—looming over the pint-sized Hutu and Batwa—was subservient to no one. . . . So effective were her techniques of terrorizing the Africans that some members of her staff believed she had supernatural powers. One day, a tracker brought the body of a small child into her camp. He asked her to cure it, to bring the child back to life. He had no doubt that the white witch could do this.

Rwanda became her only home. After her affair with Robert Campbell ended in 1972 she sloughed off the few friendships she had ever made back in America and burned the bridges connecting her to her life in her native land. She endured the occasional company of the embassy people, who had to endure hers for political reasons even though she called the wife of one official a cunt.

The "Malthusian nightmare" of densely populated Rwanda drove her to fury as she watched the native peoples overwhelm the preserve, their only source of food and water, crowding her beloved gorillas out of existence. In an extreme reaction to the encroachment of her own species, Fossey became a surrogate mother to infant gorillas, "tending them night and day as though they were her own babies, feeding them, cuddling them, sleeping with them in her cabin, covered with their diarrhea."

She flew into a rage if people interrupted her work. When a group of Chicago tourists showed up unannounced, she fired bullets over their heads and sent them scrambling back down the mountain in fear of their lives. Her own scientific staff felt her iron hand. "The person who runs a field station sets its style. Fossey's was hermitic. She stayed in her cabin all day and all night, and expected the researchers to stay in theirs when they weren't in the field. They all ate their meals alone. If they wanted to say something to somebody, they sent a note."

A National Geographic producer saw her beat four African

porters with her walking stick. Another saw her threaten a captured poacher with castration. "She would approach the poacher, holding pliers or machete, looking at that part of their anatomy. . . . All during the brutal ritual, Fossey shouted obscenities at the prisoner, a mixture of words that came into her head—English, French, German, Swahili, communicating a feeling of absolute outrage."

State Department cables flew when she asked the Rwandan government for permission to kill poachers on sight. "It is now only a matter for the President to give the order—KILL—[because] the prisons are already over-crowded and this is the only way we are going to be able to protect the remaining gorillas," she announced.

But somebody killed her first. She was buried in the gorilla graveyard she started when her special pet, Digit, was killed by poachers. The Rwandan government tried and convicted her African tracker, who allegedly committed suicide in his cell. Her American assistant Wayne McGuire, whom she had bawled out two days before her death, was also convicted in absentia after he returned to the United States, but Rwanda has never tried to extradite him.

I found it interesting that the other reviewers of this book stopped short of calling Fossey a misanthrope. Most concluded that she had "gone bushy"—the African version of cabin fever—which could be construed as another way of saying "better insane than unfriendly." Others, especially female reviewers, said that her ostensible hatred of people proved that she really "hated herself"—a favorite American rationalization for misanthropy.

They either missed or chose to ignore a passage in the book indicating that gorilla ladies do things differently. Speaking on condition of anonymity, another female primatologist told the author: "I didn't like humans. The monkeys allowed me to opt out, to get my need for social interaction and social closeness, so I didn't have to pay the price of human interaction."

So it was with Dian Fossey, a blip on the radar screen of Smile Button America. I suspect that citizenship in the Republic of Nice had a great deal to do with her behavior. In other countries, congenital introverts simply remain introverts all their lives, neither advancing nor retreating, but America's commitment to extroversion as a national art form can abrade some naturally aloof personalities until they flower into deadly nightshade.

Children are admirably gimlet-eyed before adults put them through the American make-over program. When *Snow White and the Seven Dwarfs* came out in 1940, my favorite dwarf was Grumpy, and for once I conformed: Grumpy was the overwhelming favorite of children, and Grumpy dolls outsold all the others. (As children of the Depression we had to choose *one* doll; today's children would get the whole set and this valuable statistic would be unavailable.)

Unfortunately, something happens to change most children from baleful realists to peepulphiles, and that something is school. "Much may be made of a Scotchman if he be caught young," said Samuel Johnson, and he was right.

As the enforced extroversion and other-directedness of school closed in on me, I felt compelled to remain Scotch, as it were. I invented a game called "making it night": closing the blinds and curtains and turning on all the lights during the day. It was, I know now, my way of banishing the Little Mary Sunshine that school, my first American institution, expected me to be. As I got older, I developed a love of rain and cold weather as other symbols of solitude, and instinctively distrusted anyone whose favorite season was summer.

I can identify with Dian Fossey shrouded in the mists of her mountain aerie, but her fixation on that isolated Kentucky cabin and what she went through to get it tell me more about her than any of her African experiences.

I know the panic she must have felt when the landlord refused to rent it to her. I know the blind rage she must have felt when she threatened to quit her new job if she could not live alone. I know the emotional exhaustion she must have undergone when she had to run around making phone calls and explaining herself to people so they would intercede for her. I know the crumple of relief she must have felt when she got the cabin after all. And I know the shame that surely came over her when involuntary gratitude crept into the relief and she found herself saying "thank you" to the landlord for letting her be a loner.

That cabin—and those coffee breaks—are all I need to know to understand why she ended up in Africa beating the bejesus out of anybody who got in her way.

That Dian Fossey was a Mean Green is indisputable. She was as wacky and brutal as today's battlers against "speciesism" who believe in civil rights for spotted owls, but the resemblance ends there. Ready and willing to go it alone, she committed all her outrages without the help of screaming minions on college break. Unlike the tree spikers of Oregon, there was nothing sneaky about her, and she had guts.

In an America drowning in Happy Talk, a woman who refused a rabies vaccine with "I'm no more rabid than usual" has my undying admiration.

Female misanthropes in literature are even rarer than in life, but I found one.

The Prodigal Women, written by Nancy Hale, edited by Max Perkins, published in 1942, is my "desert island book," the one I would want with me if I were shipwrecked and had to read the same book over and over—and I've already read it twenty times.

Set in Boston in the 1920s, its theme is: "People who need people are the unluckiest people in the world."

Leda March, the protagonist, is the bookish daughter of an unimportant branch of a rich Brahmin family. She's happy moping about the woods, hating girls with school spirit and being hated by them, but suddenly she acquires a best girlfriend.

Betsy Jekyll, a Southern transplant who prides herself on her Jazz Age "pep," overwhelms Leda with puppydog friendliness and drags her home to meet the frantically hospitable Jekyll family who have just moved North.

Mother Jekyll would rather fill her house than clean it. Rolling back the rugs and playing the piano for her dancing daughters, screaming "Stay for supper!" over the din, she exudes gregariousness. The older daughter Maizie, the family beauty, is a Southern belle knee-deep in popularity and hysterical gaiety. Chattering a mile a minute, tossing dresses aside, spilling perfume, she puts on a theater of femininity for the rapt Leda and Betsy who gather in her room to watch her dress.

Leda loves all this—yet she doesn't. She senses that the Jekyll women would die without people to validate their existence, and she doesn't want to be that way. She longs to flee from them and the emotional dependency they represent.

Leda turns into a beauty and comes to the attention of her socially powerful aunt who sponsors her debutante year. Her sudden entrée into the top drawer of society gives her a perfect excuse to drop the emotionally threatening Jekylls, who are déclassé, and so she does.

She becomes the toast of the season—with an ironic twist. Rid of the Jekylls' encroachment on her inner space, she must now cope with all of Boston. Savoring her power over the girls who used to make fun of her, she puts herself on automatic pilot and plunges into the social fray, becoming the debutante who never sleeps.

When her handsome older cousin James begs her to marry him, her triumph is complete. She is now in a position to recoup the place in society her dowdy parents lost. With her looks and James's money she can be Boston's leading hostess and most sought-after young matron. . . . except that she doesn't like people.

What she really wants to be is a Boston bluestocking.

[It] was inconceivable to her that people, human beings, could ever awaken the kind of hesitant tenderness, the warmth, that came to her when she read great words, or when words formed themselves in her imagination. . . . Her life would be pure, and severe; spent in learning, absorbing. Her life would be as white as alabaster, never smeared with the soil that came from living minds. . . . she imagined her room, the room where she would study all the days. . . . the thousands of books, the millions of books. . . .

While Leda dreams of sensible shoes, the Jekyll sisters pursue ultrafeminine destinies. Betsy, a monster of other-directedness, goes to New York and becomes the consummate Flapper. Scatty Maizie falls in love with Boston scion-turned-painter Lambert Rudd, an inner-directed creator who puts his work first and needs nothing from people. Virile but wary, he wants an emotionally self-sufficient woman who will leave him alone to paint.

Threatened by Lambert's detachment, Maizie hurls herself against him like a wave at a rock. "He was a hundred worlds away from her, talking about his work. . . . All of her nature was gathered, drawn up in a knot, wanting him and seeking about for a means of getting him. . . . [She was] goaded to desperation by his remoteness, by her impotence to engage him."

She gets pregnant and refuses to have an abortion, so he reluctantly marries her. On their extended honeymoon in South America, Lambert is so morose and distant that the insecure Maizie, desperate to please him, aborts the baby after all and develops a gynecological infection. The trip, which was supposed to give Lambert a chance to paint, turns into a mobile medical unit and Lambert turns into a nurse. Waiting on her, keeping track of her medicines, he can no longer concentrate on his painting and begins to loathe her for "the base hurly-burly that his mind had become."

The inner-directed Lambert and the inner-directed Leda meet and fall in love, but Maizie goes to pieces when Lambert asks her for a divorce. The ensuing uproar is too much for Leda's pristine temperament; "she did not want to be so near to people as that. . . . she had stuck her head into a nest of passion."

She marries the dull, adoring James and salvages her emotional detachment by transmuting it into the society matron's brittleness. Lambert is not so lucky; his emotional detachment is shattered by Maizie's invalidism. Becoming pregnant again, she takes to her bed and stays there to guard against miscarriage. Knowing that his gruffness makes her hysterical, Lambert learns to hide it. "He said everything very softly, smiled cautiously, hoping that he wouldn't get her all upset." Eventually all spontaneity in him is stifled, and with it his artistic talent.

Maizie is happy and calm during her pregnancy, but once the baby is born her old insecurity returns. Now that she's well, Lambert will stop waiting on her, stop speaking softly, stop smiling warmly. Haunted by the specter of his renewed detachment, she has a Grand Guignol nervous breakdown as only a

Southern belle can, complete with auditory and visual hallucinations.

After Maizie enters an asylum, Lambert has an affair with the now-divorced Leda. Because each grants the other his own space, his artistic talent reawakens and she begins writing poetry. Soon their idyll is interrupted by Maizie's psychiatrist, who pronounces her well enough to live on the outside with her husband and daughter. Lambert's cooperation being vital to her full recovery, he goes to live with her in a house in the hospital town. Reluctantly, because Lambert asks her to, Leda takes a country house nearby so they can continue seeing each other.

But Maizie finds out about it and goes to pieces again. Repelled by this spectacle of intimacy turned to cannibalism, and realizing what Lambert's surrender to the world of people has done to him, Leda spurns him and admits to herself that she is a misanthrope.

"My spiritual home . . . my way of life is alone. It always was. I always knew it." Solitude wins, and with it her old dream of writing. "Creation lives alone in a small temple. Only one may worship at a time. That was my gift at birth, that was all I ever had. I was given the private means of purification." She walks off through the woods she loved as a girl, resolving "to live alone, without desire. . . . All sin lies in the life of people, all virtue for me alone."

I don't know how the women's studies crowd has managed to miss *The Prodigal Women* in their eternal quest for the literature of "autonomy." If Leda's ultimate decision isn't one of those vaunted "choices" feminists are always talking about, I don't know what is. Her unequivocal stance contradicts their sacred tenet of Having It All, but life for a woman is such a minefield of conflicts that misanthropy, at least in the figurative sense of "everybody buzz off," is the only thing that really works.

The Prodigal Women contains 556 pages of very small print to accommodate the wartime paper shortage. I first read it from early morning to past midnight for two days in November 1957. I was twenty-one and living alone in an apartment whose rent of seventy-five dollars a month I could barely afford, but that weekend shines in my memory as the happiest interlude of my life.

The weather was blustery and cold, the trees gaunt and bent as the wind stripped off the last of their wet brown leaves. Each time I got up to fix another cup of coffee, I leaned on the kitchen windowsill while I waited for the water to boil, gazing out at the grim day and wrapped in deep pleasure as my mind echoed John Donne's line, "In Heaven, it's always autumn."

OUR LADY'S JUGGLER
SHRUGGED ON THE
INSTALLMENT PLAN

Most misanthropes are easy to understand because we blurt out the simple truths that most people think but never say. The plainspoken have nothing to lose but their friends, so we weigh the risks and behave accordingly.

The exceptional misanthrope, for one reason or another, is driven to spin tangled webs of denial, contradiction, and displacement. Three such puzzles are Anatole France, Ayn Rand, and Louis-Ferdinand Auguste Destouches, who took for his pseudonym his mother's maiden name: Céline.

Anatole France (1844–1924) is the French writer known to everyone who has ever dipped into the ubiquitous paperback, *Great Short Stories of the World*. It always includes "The Procurator of Judea," about two retired Roman bureaucrats talking shop. At the end, one man tries to prompt the other's memory about an incident in Judea during the reign of Tiberius. You were there then, weren't you? You remember that, don't you? But the old procurator shakes his head. "Jesus? Jesus of Nazareth? No, I don't recall," mumbles Pontius Pilate.

When this story was published in 1892, Anatole France was hailed for his pitiless irony and called the "new Voltaire." This in itself was ironic, for irony was no more consistent a trait in him than any of his other traits.

He had my third-year French class in tears when we read a very different short story by him, *"Le Jongleur de Notre Dame,"* about an ignorant, probably retarded, itinerant juggler who passes through a village during its festival in honor of the Virgin Mary.

As the juggler watches in awe, each villager pays homage to the Virgin in his own way and according to his own talents. The village carpenter makes her a new manger, the seamstress makes her a new robe, and so on, placing their tributes before the fine new statue of the Virgin in the village church.

Deeply touched by their devotion, the juggler wants to pay homage to the Virgin too, but how? Juggling is all he knows. Going into the church at night when no one else is there, he performs in front of the statue as he has never performed before. Leaping, spinning, standing on his head, he gives his all in such a tour de force that at last, covered with sweat, he collapses in exhaustion.

Suddenly the door bursts open and the villagers, who have been spying on him, rush in and attack him for committing a sacrilege. But just as they are about to kill him, the statue comes to life and the Virgin Mary steps down from her pedestal and wipes the sweat from the juggler's face with her veil.

The author of this reverent story was the same Anatole France who supported Dreyfus because the Church was anti-Dreyfus and he hated the Church. His books are full of sentiments such as, "Men are the most pernicious race of little odious vermin that

Nature ever suffered to crawl upon the face of the earth," yet his eulogy at Zola's funeral concluded with a line that has been cherished and quoted by humanitarians ever since: "He was a moment of the conscience of mankind."

Misanthropes are born, not made. A traumatic childhood seems to have no more effect on the formation of the misanthropic temperament than a happy childhood, but Anatole France may have been inconsistent in this as well. An early biographer, Barry Cerf, writing five years after his death, paints a classic Oedipal situation in his 1929 study, *Anatole France: The Degeneration of a Great Writer.* I suspect that Cerf was influenced by the Freudian craze sweeping the twenties, but that's all right. No one caught in the storm that was Anatole France can afford to be fussy about ports.

He was born Jacques-Anatole Thibault. His father, a bookseller on the quais of Paris, was a staunch Catholic, militarist, and royalist, the latter possibly explaining why his son took his country's name for a pseudonym. Papa also seems to have had a great deal to do with the atheism, dilettantism, socialism, communism, reactionism, and patriotism that turned up in Anatole at various times, and occasionally all at once.

His mother was a sentimentalist of the same degree as those overheated women who made pilgrimages to Rousseau's tomb to contemplate the wonders of *sensibilité.* Anatole's assessment of her is not for the fainthearted:

> She literally poisoned my life. She made me inconsistent and timid. . . . Love brought the most honest woman in the world to commit acts of the most revolting indelicacy. . . . Until I was thirty-five, she never went to bed until I came home. . . . To the time of my marriage my mother tucked me into bed every night. When she had kissed me and was carrying away the candle, I

sometimes longed to strangle her. There is no more heavy tyranny than mother-love.

Schopenhauer was also a misanthrope and his mother threw him down a flight of stairs, so what can you do? At least Frau Schopenhauer was of this world, whereas Mme Thibault floated around in one of her own making in which everybody was sweet and nice. Writes Cerf: "France's youthful idealism, founded as it was on an unstable basis, collapsed. . . . Had he not dreamed away his childhood and youth, had he learned earlier that human beings are neither saints nor paladins, he might have been able to reconcile himself to the sad facts of life and the dreary mediocrity of mankind when the truth finally forced itself through his doting mother's guard."

One result of Anatole's years under his doting mother's guard had my fourth-year French class in tears. *Le Livre de Mon Ami* is a collection of vignettes about the happy childhood of what even I called "a darling little boy." It was the only time in my life that I have ever loved children, an inconsistency I owe to Anatole France.

He finally got out from under his mother, or as he put it: "And then I married. After the sacrament I learned what hell is."

Although he was already middle-aged in the 1880s, he was drawn to Oscar Wilde's Aestheticism and Ernest Renan's Dilettantism, both of which provided him with the attitudes he needed to cope with his father-mother split. The watchwords of these literary movements were *light* irony, *tolerant* skepticism, *nonchalant* aloofness—in sum, the Mauve Decade's version of "cool."

He achieved the requisite tone in his first novel, *The Crime of Sylvestre Bonnard,* whose *gently* witty protagonist says things like: "He hated fanaticism, but he was fanatically tolerant." Next came *Thais,* about a fifth-century Christian monk and an Alexandrian courtesan who pull the same kind of switch on each other as the young couple in O. Henry's "Gift of the Magi," except that Anatole adds a cutting edge. The monk keeps trying to convert Thais to Christianity at the same time she keeps trying to convert him to sensuality. It goes on like this until the very end, when the monk finally loses his faith and heads for Thais's bed, only to discover that she has finally seen the light and become a Christian.

Anatole lost his cool a few years later in *The Opinions of Jerome Coignard,* whose protagonist is a dramatized representation of French thought in the Age of Reason. A bleak realist, Coignard charges the leaders of the Revolution with naiveté and counters their optimistic opinions of mankind with his own: "He would not have signed a line of the Declaration of the Rights of Man because of the excessive and iniquitous distinction that is established in it between man and the gorilla."

From now on, Anatole vows to be an Age of Reason man, a skeptic who sees human nature as it is, not as it ought to be. Using Jerome Coignard as a mouthpiece, he condemns Rousseau for promoting the inherent goodness of human nature: "He who undertakes to guide men must never lose sight of the fact that they are malicious monkeys. . . . The folly of the Revolution was in aiming to establish virtue on the earth. When you want to make men good and wise, free, moderate, generous, you are led inevitably to the desire of killing them all." As for making them think, their reaction to intelligence could be observed by "pouring ammonia on an anthill."

Rejecting Rousseau's political ideas, he clung to Rousseau's sexy ideas, such as "confidence in the superiority of instinct, the senses, sentiment, emotion, and the superiority of all these to reason, reflection, and intelligence." This exercise in the impossible made Anatole a romantic realist, a primitive rationalist, and a tender misanthrope of the naked intellect, but he saved his best leap of logic for the Dreyfus case. Insisting that he was still a reactionary, he aligned himself with the Dreyfusards against church, state, and the Army of France.

The revelations of the Dreyfus case increased his misanthropy. "I am persuaded that the sum of stupidity and folly in the world is at all times constant," he wrote. "Far from rejoicing when I see an old error depart, I think of the new error which will come to take its place, and I wonder anxiously if it will not be more inconvenient or more dangerous than the first." On this pessimistic note, he threw in his lot with human progress and became a socialist.

The work he published during his socialist period contains his bitterest condemnations of mankind. *Penguin Island* is an all-out attack on French society; *The Gods Athirst* presents a right-wing view of the Revolution that shocked republicans; and *The Revolt of the Angels,* in which angels and devils change places, expresses a savage and unrelieved loathing for the entire human race.

When France entered World War I on August 1, 1914, the seventy-year-old Anatole, who, being a socialist, was an antimilitarist and a pacifist, presented himself at the army recruitment center and demanded a rifle.

His attempts to explain his contradictions only manufactured more. Drawn to Pascal's distinction between pity that leads to sympathy and pity that leads to contempt, he came up with "tender spite" and "benevolent scorn" to describe his attitudes, using the confusing phrases so often in interviews that the critics eventually picked them up and used them in reviews.

An illogical Frenchman is a frightening spectacle and virtually a contradiction in terms. Logic is sacred in the land of Descartes but Anatole's thought patterns seem custom-tailored for America, land of post hocky ergo propter hocky, where Occam's razor wouldn't cut butter. With his gift for oxymorons, if he were resurrected he could go on Oprah and join the gang discussion of "tough love" without missing a beat.

Anatole won the Nobel Prize for literature in 1921. This honor can ruin a misanthrope because the unspoken ground rule for laureates is: "If you can't say something nice about Man with a capital M, don't say anything at all." The pressure is so grandmotherly that a laureate runs the risk of never being the same sonofabitch again, but Anatole wriggled free. Barely a year after his Stockholm triumph he was saying: "I have rarely opened a door by mistake without discovering a spectacle which made me look upon humanity with pity, disgust, or horror."

Summing him up, Cerf calls him "a sensualist to whom love meant carnal desire," who had "little that was fine or lovable in his character. . . . he was not kindly, generous, or even tolerant. . . . while he was surrounded by scores of ecstatic admirers and numerous acquaintances, he seems to have had no devoted friends."

Yet his ultimate contradiction, Cerf believes, contains the key to his personality: "Despite his contempt for man and man's affairs, he loved life intensely."

This view would seem to be supported by the words of one of Anatole's fictional characters: "This dog's life. . . . I love it, brutal, vile, and gross; I love it sordid, unclean, decayed; I love it stupid, half-witted and cruel; I love it in its obscenity, in its ignominy, in its infamy, with its impurity, its hideousness, and its squalor, its corruption and its stench."

A neat evasion, and one calculated to charm romanticists with its Rousseauistic touches, but I don't believe it. Anatole's political and philosophical inconsistencies had their roots in the ultimate inconsistency of trying all his life to combine misanthropy and sensuality.

The misanthrope must either be cold to begin with, or he must turn cold when he finally acknowledges what he has known all along: Sex requires people. There is no greater contradiction than a misanthrope in bed. If he persists in staying there, the primal contradiction will spread like a cancer to his higher brain cells, until nothing he says or thinks will make any sense.

Consistency, thou art a jewel. As with Catholicism, so with misanthropy, the jewel in the crown is celibacy.

Another life-loving misanthrope fled Soviet Russia for America in 1926. Twenty-one-year-old Alice Rosenbaum arrived in New York lugging a Remington-Rand typewriter and some books by a Finnish writer whose surname was Ayn.

Years later as Ayn Rand she would define her philosophy of Objectivism as "the concept of man as a heroic being, with his own happiness as the moral purpose of his life, with productive achievement as his noblest activity, and reason as his only absolute." She devised an oath to this effect and put it into the mouth of the hero of *Atlas Shrugged:* "I swear by my life, and by my love of it, that I will never live for the sake of another man, nor ask another man to live for mine."

Her father's drugstore chain had been taken over by the Soviets in the name of the People, so Ayn's mother sold her jewelry to send her daughter to America. Taken in by her Chicago cousins, she immediately took possession of their cramped apartment in the name of Ayn Rand. A night owl like most writers, she kept her cousins awake with her midnight-to-dawn typing and used up all their hot water for her frequent baths—which she also took at night, running the water full blast until the tub was nice and full.

If her cousins were disturbed, it did not matter because she rejected familial ties. People just happen to be born into a particular family, she believed, and this element of chance made of consanguinity an "unchosen value." Loving one's family or behaving differently toward them simply because they were family was therefore "irrational."

It was a consummately un-Jewish attitude, but Rand also rejected Jewishness in the same sweeping way. Although she was born in Czarist Russia in 1905 and raised in St. Petersburg, she told her biographer Barbara Branden that she had never met with the slightest manifestation of anti-Semitism, nor heard any discussion of it at home. This conflicts with another story she told Branden: that her father had become a pharmacist because the only available Jewish quota at the university was in chemistry, and eager for an education, he took it even though his real interests were history and literature.

In *The Passion of Ayn Rand,* Branden posits that since anti-Semitism was ubiquitous in Russia during Rand's childhood, she had to have encountered it, but probably blocked it out of her mind "because the memory would have carried with it an unacceptable feeling of humiliation." She never denied that she was a Jew, but "it had no significance to her, she had no emotional tie or sense of identification with Jews or things Jewish." Like family ties, Jewishness conflicted with Rand's belief that "man is a being of self-made soul," so she chose to be unchosen.

Rand's Chicago uncle, who was in the movie-distributing business, gave her a letter of introduction to Cecil B. DeMille and she headed for Hollywood with her silent-movie screenplays. Working as an extra and a properties reader, she met a young bit player named Frank O'Connor and fell in love with him at first sight. He was the physical type she went for: "American-looking," as she often said: tall, blond, blue-eyed, long-legged, slim.

He was also an American citizen, and Rand's visa was running out. They were married in Los Angeles and went to Mexico on

121

their honeymoon so that she could re-enter the United States as his wife. Later on she would joke, "Ours was a shotgun wedding—with Uncle Sam holding the shotgun." Barbara Branden believes that this was pretty much the case. She says the couple's early Hollywood friends felt that Frank was not particularly in love with Ayn, and that "everybody knew" he married her so she would not be sent back to Soviet Russia—a selfless act of the sort that Rand would one day castigate in her novels as "altruism."

Now that she had her man, she had to make sure he fit the heroic mold that was the basis of her developing philosophy. Recalling the first time she saw him, she told Braden: "he was enormously anti-social—and of course I liked that. His manner suggested an aloof, confident self-sufficiency. I never caught him speaking to anyone, he always sat alone. . . ."

Rand's capacity for believing what she wished to believe was boundless. As Branden and everyone else who knew Frank quickly discovered, he was actually passive; a sweet, gentle, thoughtful man who was overwhelmed by his dogmatic, self-absorbed wife. He stopped working as soon as Rand began making enough to support them, and gradually became the "wife" while she became the "husband." However much this role reversal conflicted with Rand's heroic philosophy, it suited her on a personal level because she hated women.

"In childhood, all of her life, it appears that her most intense scorn was reserved for women," Branden writes. "The human qualities she cared about were, she believed, specifically masculine attributes: above all, purposefulness and strength."

Rand's hatred of the female role turns up in cloaked form in all her novels. The oath from *Atlas Shrugged* would make an apt masthead motto for *MS.* Howard Roark's final speech in *The Fountainhead* opens with, "I am a man who does not exist for others." Her most detestable villain, Ellsworth Toohey, preaches "the nobility of self-sacrifice in order to rob men of their self-esteem, their courage, their virtue, and their honor and to turn them into willing sacrificial victims"—a passage that needs only one word changed to fit any feminist tract, or to state the theme of *The Cinderella Complex*. Communism itself, with its demands for selfless dedication, undoubtedly reminded her of the demands made upon her sex, and the many women, contemptible to her, who met them.

After the publication of *The Fountainhead* brought her to the attention of conservative intellectuals, a friend told her that the Austrian economist Ludwig von Mises had called her "the most courageous man in America." "Did he say *man?*" asked Rand. Assured that von Mises had indeed said *man,* she was overjoyed.

In everyday life she was a fearful woman who poured boiling water on the dishes to kill germs, worried whether she had locked the door, hated to fly, and could not learn to drive. Obsessed with the need to have full control of her destiny, she was afraid, says Branden, "that she might inadvertently fail to take precautions against an external danger that could be averted."

Called "Mrs. Logic" by Nathaniel Branden, Rand boasted that her philosophy of Objectivism was so tightly reasoned that a person who accepted even the smallest part of it had to accept all of it. Those who did not she called "hooligans"—a favorite epithet of Communism that she evidently picked up in spite of herself—and accused them of "vicious dishonesty," "moral treason," and "social metaphysics" (going along with the crowd instead of being an individualist).

With the connivance of Nathaniel Branden, head of the New York-based Objectivist Institute and chief gremlin of the happy few allowed to sit at her feet, social metaphysicians were actually put on trial in Rand's living room and sent away to reflect on their "volitionally chosen cancer of the spirit"—her redundant name for any opinion she disagreed with.

Rand cloaked her misanthropy in various lesser guises: aloofness and intimidating formality, the half-loaf of misogyny, and contempt, "a term she used again and again to describe her feelings for most of the people around her," writes Barbara Branden. "It is a term that—accompanied by a dismissive wave of her hand and a grimace of distaste—dotted her conversations." She advised her followers, "Don't withhold your contempt from men's vices," a practice she herself followed so often that she was constantly breaking off relations with friends of many years' standing. Said one: "She seemed almost to invite a break, as though it would confirm her attitude toward the world."

These ruptures were invariably cerebral rather than emotional. Ostracism awaited those who expressed admiration for a writer, painter, or composer that Rand considered "irrational." She decreed that Van Gogh was "wild," Rembrandt was full of "grim, unfocused malevolence," Beethoven had a "tragic sense of doom," Shakespeare was an "abysmal failure" because his characters were swept along by their emotions instead of being ruled by reason and free will, and Somerset Maugham's *Of Human Bondage* expressed "a deeply malevolent view of life."

She hated nature lovers so much that she almost threw Barbara Branden out of the house for saying that she enjoyed scenery. To Rand, nature was not only wild and irrational, just as Rousseau said, but also "malevolent," another of her favorite words for anything that did not lend itself to intellectual order and control.

She carried misanthropy of the naked intellect further than it has ever been carried before or since. Anyone who *dared* say a good word for nature had to listen to Rand sing the praises of skyscrapers, concrete, steel girders, smokestacks, and even industrial smoke, for these were the products of the rational mind of Man, who invented them. The individual unwise enough to suggest that these things are inanimate had to sit up until 4 A.M. listening to Rand explain why a blast furnace symbolized an "exalted sense of life."

Everything good was a product of rationalism; all evil proceeded from irrationalism, including cancer: its cause, she believed, was "bad premises."

Blaise Pascal called Man "a thinking reed," but Ayn Rand had no use for reediness. Her fictional heroes are perfect; morally incorruptible, dedicated geniuses with stratospheric levels of exaltation and such stringent ideals that they are as chaste as Hippolytus until the right woman comes along. Reviled and punished by an envious world, they are so secure in their egoism that they never for a moment consider misanthropy as a response to their very real troubles. In *The Fountainhead,* the man who has ruined Howard Roark's reputation and career asks him, "What do you think of me, Mr. Roark?" "I don't think of you," Roark replies.

Randian heroes are ideal candidates for misanthropy of the naked intellect but they never get elected. No matter what they suffer at the hands of people, Rand cannot permit them to hate people because she has drawn them above the battle. The closest she comes to creating an overtly misanthropic character is *The Fountainhead*'s Dominique Francon, of whom she said, "Dominique is myself in a bad mood." The real misanthropes in Rand's novels are the professional people lovers: altruists, humanitarians, social workers, labor leaders, public relations flacks, one worlders, collectivists, socialists, and conformists—in short, tender misanthropes with bad premises.

Mrs. Logic painted herself into a corner. She couldn't admit that she hated people because that would class her with her fictional bad guys, yet if she identified with her good guys—which of course she did—she still couldn't admit that she hated people because her good guys love Man.

She was also stymied by her inordinate self-love, which made the misanthrope's unavoidable philosophical trap repugnant to her. If the human race is no damn good, the misanthrope, being a member of it, is no damn good either. The way out of this is to have a taste for irony and an appreciation of the ridiculous, but she had neither. Barbara Branden recalls "the chastening experience of telling her a joke . . . then being greeted by a blank look of bewilderment—then having to give a lengthy explanation of what was the presumed humor." Rand was suspicious of humor on principle, says Branden, especially the idea of being able to laugh at oneself, a suggestion that drew from her the stony reply: "That's the man who wants a blank check on flaws."

Unable to admit her misanthropy without destroying her Man-centered philosophy, Rand clung to her philosophy and got meaner and meaner from the frustration growing out of her conflict. "Her vision of the human potential made the rest of reality unendurable," writes Branden. Creating paragons on paper made her expect the impossible from the actual people around her. At the age of sixty-three she expected thirty-seven-year-old Nathaniel Branden to find her sexually desirable because she was his "highest value." When her husband turned into a drunk from living with her, she claimed that "his problems were psycho-epistemological" and made him write papers on his thought processes, refusing to believe that there could be anything wrong with his sense of exalted purpose.

Atlas Shrugged finally forced Ayn Rand to confront her misanthropy. In *We the Living,* her autobiographical first novel set in early Soviet Russia, the villains are Communists, a large group as political movements go but by no means a majority of mankind. In her second novel, *The Fountainhead,* the villains are conformists, a larger group but still manageable, especially in post-World War II America, when many other thinkers were bewailing conformity. But in *Atlas Shrugged* the villains are mediocre people, the world's largest majority. Like the aristocrat who hates the masses, she made it in on numbers.

"Makes well-poisoning seem like one of the kindlier arts," wrote reviewer Gore Vidal.

". . . an outpouring of hate," charged Patricia Donegan in *The Commonweal.*

Granville Hicks in the *New York Times:* "Loudly as Miss Rand proclaims her love of life, it seems clear that the book is written out of hate. . . ."

Barbara Branden finds in *Atlas* "a blistering contempt for the world," and speculates: "On a more subtle level, her hatred seemed to be rooted in a deep, terrible fear—as if the outside world was not merely an arena where wrong ideas were held and wrong actions taken: it was an arena fraught with danger."

What was it? Studying this passage, I detect something that Barbara Branden missed in this otherwise superb biography: Ayn Rand's whole shtik was a gargantuan displacement of her never-admitted fear of anti-Semitism.

Her hatred of the irrational, her construction of a laborious philosophy based on individualism, reason, logic, objective thinking, and rejection of emotionalism would, if universally adopted, bring about an immediate end to anti-Semitism, which is a product of the Gentile id. By constructing fictional plots in which logical behavior and rational characters always triumph over the forces of darkness, she spent her entire career as a novelist crusading against anti-Semitism while taking care not to write a word about Jews.

There is not a single Jewish character in all of her work; not even in *We the Living,* which is set in Russia, or in *The Fountain-head,* which is set entirely in Manhattan. She admitted that she modeled architecture critic and free-lance humanitarian Ellsworth Toohey chiefly on Harold Laski, yet Toohey is a Wasp. With the exception of the heroes, to whom she gave Irish names (Roark, Rearden, Galt) in honor of Frank O'Connor, everybody, good or bad, is a Wasp. Peter Keating and Jim Taggart are rats but they are Wasp rats; Gail Wynand was raised in a Hell's Kitchen tenement but he's Wasp; and Dominique Francon, despite her frenchified name, is the procelain Wasp debutante incarnate.

Moreover, they all look Wasp. Toohey is the drip with the bookbag, but everyone else is long and lanky, blond or carrot-top, blue- or gray-eyed. The partial exception is the handsome villain Peter Keating, who has black hair and gains weight. By the time she wrote *Atlas Shrugged* Rand seemed to have recognized the need for a little ethnic variety, but what did she name the heroic pirate who hijacks ships carrying humanitarian aid? Ragnar Danneskjold—just what the copy editor needed.

Despite their overwhelming Gentileness, Randian heroes come off as metaphors for Jews because they are beset by irrational forces that try to bar them from the professions and use their virtues against them to bring about their destruction—what Rand, in a rare unguarded moment, called "the sanction of the victim," a phrase that reminds us of the language of the Holocaust debate.

The major heroes are never permitted to exhibit or even acknowledge the existence of anything that could be construed as Jewish agony. Instead, they analyze their problems coldly and declaim them in long speeches like characters in the neoclassical dramas of Corneille and Racine. But a minor hero of *The Foun-*

tainhead gives it away. New York Wasp sculptor Stephen Mallory's definition of terror echoes the age-old keening *why?* of the persecuted Jew that pervades Bernard Malamud's *The Fixer,* whose real-life model was in a Czarist prison when Ayn Rand was a child in Russia:

> To me—it's being left, unarmed, in a sealed cell with a drooling beast of prey or a maniac who's had some disease that's eaten his brain out. You'd have nothing then but your voice—your voice and your thought. You'd scream to that creature why it should not touch you, you'd have the most eloquent words, the unanswerable words, you'd become the vessel of the absolute truth. And you'd see the living eyes watching you and you'd know that the thing can't hear you, that it can't be reached, not reached, not in any way, yet it's breathing and moving there before you with a purpose of its own.

Barbara Branden writes that Rand regarded "the outside world" as a place of peril and wanted "to create a safe haven around her, a smaller world within the larger irrational world that would consist of people who were predictable, intelligible, in accord with her thinking, devoted to her. . . ."

She did in *Atlas Shrugged.* The Wyoming mountain sanctuary, Atlantis or "Galt's Gulch," into which the rational creators and captains of industry disappear and start their own community, is Ayn Rand's Israel. The Anglo-Celtic inhabitants are the Chosen—by Ayn Rand—People, exiles who actually do what the Jews have always been accused of doing: running the world.

Louis Ferdinand Auguste Destouches (1894–1961), known to the world as Céline, was born and raised behind his mother's lace shop in a canopied arcade near the Paris Opera, which explains much of what you are about to read: the kid lived in a mall.

The flat was grim and dark—literally from the sunless arcade, figuratively from the parsimonious, repressed petit bourgeois mindset that prevailed within. It is easy to imagine the shabby furniture swathed in doilies made from leftover lace. Worse, the family had to eat bland foods like noodles, rice, and bread soup to guard the lace against rich kitchen smells. Céline described all this in his second novel, *Mort à crédit,* translated into English as *Death on the Installment Plan.*

Céline was wounded at Ypres in 1914 and decorated for valor. After the war he resumed his studies at the Rennes Medical School and in 1919 married the dean's daughter. Any other man would have used his father-in-law's connections to feather his nest, but Céline had an aversion to accepting help from anyone. It almost seemed that he had married into an influential medical family solely for the pleasure of spurning their influence; after a few years he took a traveling job as a League of Nations physician and never lived with his wife or their daughter again.

He worked in Geneva, Germany, Cuba, and Detroit, where he studied the medical and psychological aspects of the Ford assembly line. After his American sojourn he returned to Paris, got a job in a free clinic in a workingclass neighborhood, and wrote a novel on the side.

It is here that his resemblance to Somerset Maugham abruptly ends. Maugham emerged from his slum doctoring with a cynical fondness for humanity, but Céline seems to have found in it a justification for his burgeoning misanthropy.

His first novel, *Voyage au bout de la nuit,* rendered in English as *Voyage to the Middle of the Night,* was published in 1932. It's something of an existentialist *Anthony Adverse,* a story of travel and adventure in exotic places by a slum doctor named Bardamu and his friend and alter ego, Robinson, a classic sonofabitch and Social Darwinist who represents the misanthropy that Bardamu feels but can't quite bring himself to express.

The funniest line comes when Robinson tells Bardamu that he understands perfectly why his friend became a doctor: "When people can stand up, they're thinking of killing you. Whereas when they're ill, there's no doubt about it, they're less dangerous." In Part One of the novel, the tormented, confused Bardamu is committed to an insane asylum; when we meet him again in Part Two, he has risen to chief of staff. In the end he admits that the world is mad, but unable to kill himself, he lives on as head of his own private madhouse.

In *Voyage* Céline launched a fusillade against the bourgeoisie, calling it the class that guillotined Louis XVI and then proceeded to treat the common man worse than kings ever had. This made him the darling of the French Left, but as soon as the intellectuals began praising him, he adopted a philistine stance and confided to interviewers: "the very word 'writing' has always struck me as indecent."

Voyage was published in the Soviet Union and Céline was invited, along with Gide and other Communist pets, to visit the Workers' Paradise. The only way he could get his Soviet royalties was to go to Russia and spend the money there, so he went. The Soviets planned to use the visiting French writers for propaganda purposes, but when they asked Céline what he thought of their noble experiment, he told them they were arrogant for thinking they could perfect anything as rotten as mankind.

The only good thing about Christianity, he went on, is that it *tells* man he is inherently evil, so at least the church is honest—unlike Communism, which has the temerity to think that man can be changed. "You have the nerve to dress up a turd and call it a caramel," he said, and then wrapped up the interview with a call for a Franco-German alliance to save France from the Marxist blight.

Returning home, he enlarged upon his Russian comments in a polemic called *Mea culpa.* Published in 1936, it raised a firestorm, not only among the French Left but in polite society generally, because of his remarks about Jews. The bourgeoisie "smells a little Jewish," he wrote, accusing the middle class of cosying up to Léon Blum's Popular Front government for "life insurance." But it really didn't matter, he concluded, because society was so corrupt that "with Jews or without Jews" it was doomed.

Now he became the darling of the French Right, but when he was invited to attend a fascist meeting and the speaker began denouncing the "Jewish-Marxist tyranny," Céline stood up and yelled, "To hell with that Aryan *merde!"* and called the Germans krauts and blockheads. Despite this, Lucien Rebatet, editor of the French fascist newspaper *Je Suis Partout,* asked Céline to write some articles for him. Céline did, but his vituperative racism was too much even for Rebatet and he refused to print them.

No one could figure out where he was coming from. "I adhere only to myself, as much as I can," was the only explanation Céline offered.

He went on to write three more polemics that, as he was later to say, accomplished the impossible: "Left and Right, Monarchist and Communist, all agreed that I was the greatest scum on earth." The polemics, known by the confusing name, "pamphlets," were actually full-length books. They have never been published in English and probably never will be, because they were so full of hate, for Jews and just about everybody else, that they were banned in Nazi Germany.

Bagatelles pour un massacre (trifles for a massacre) rehashed the discredited "Protocols of the Elders of Zion" and claimed that there was indeed a Jewish conspiracy, not of international bankers as the Protocols claimed, but of two modern centers of Jewish influence: "Hollywood la juive" and "Moscou la youtre."

In *Ecole des cadavres* the corpses are the Gentiles who were slaughtered in World War I and who are destined to be slaughtered again in another war engineered by Jews with the connivance of their special Gentile pets, the English (Céline believed the two had "good chemistry"). He also blamed the coming war on liberals, socialists, idealists, the Frenchman-in-the-street, Masons, the Catholic church, and the Communists. Yet the book was dedicated to a Communist sympathizer, Eugene Dabit, whom Céline happened to like.

The last polemic, published in 1941 after the fall of France, was *Les beaux draps* (a fine mess). Between American Jewish movies and Russian Jewish socialism, Céline wrote, the masses were so brain-dead that they might just as well be exploited because it was all they were good for.

Never one to insult just one side when two were available, he also accused the Vichy government of cowardly opportunism: "I didn't wait for the German High Command to be set up at the Hotel Crillon before becoming pro-German."

After *Bagatelles* Céline was forced out of his job at the government clinic. He lived on his seventy-percent disability pension from his World War I wounds, in a Montmartre apartment overtop the one used by the Resistance. They did not make the connection between Dr. Destouches and the writer named Céline, but Céline knew who they were. His own fascist visitors routinely passed Resistance fighters on the stairs but Céline never reported his downstairs neighbors to the German Occupation; moreover, he treated, free of charge, a Resistance member who fell ill.

As the Allied liberation forces closed in on Paris in 1944 Céline, fearing summary execution, fled to Sigmaringen in the Black Forest where he served as house physician to the Vichy exiles holed up in an ancient Hohenzollern castle. True to form, he refused to make radio broadcasts for the Nazis.

When Paris was liberated he took off again, this time for Denmark where he claimed he had buried some gold in the garden of a former girlfriend. Accompanied by his second wife Lucette, he made his way, sometimes by train, sometimes on foot, across war-torn Germany with his cat Bébert in a woolen bag around his neck.

He never found the gold. After the war ended the French government demanded his extradition. Céline and Lucette were both arrested and jailed in Denmark, she for two months and he for fourteen, while bureaucrats in both countries wrangled over his status. In the end the Danish government refused to extradite him. When he got sick they sent him to a prison hospital for several months, then set him free on condition that he not try to leave Denmark without permission. His Danish lawyer lent Céline and Lucette a cottage on the Baltic where they lived from 1947 until France granted him amnesty in 1951.

He was tried in absentia for collaboration in 1950. It was widely believed by the French public that the "monster of Montmartre" had promoted the Holocaust in his pamphlets, but an American biographer, David O'Connell, who read all four in the original French, states that "nowhere in the text of these works are any such calls for mass murder made."

Morally speaking, this is a minor point. Anyone with Céline's unvarnished opinion of human nature knows that the mass of people can be swung like a lariat and are incapable of making fine distinctions between the theory of anti-Semitism and its ultimate practice: to write the former is to invite the latter. Technically speaking, however, Céline called for the expulsion of Jews to England, the United States, the Soviet Union, and Palestine. He was found guilty by a majority of the jurors but the punishment meted out to him was meaningless. He was sentenced to a year in prison, which he had already served; fined 50,000 francs, which he did not have; consigned to "perpetual disgrace," which he was already in; and subjected to the confiscation of his worldly goods, of which he had exactly none.

He returned to France in 1951 and received permission to practice medicine in Menton. At first the literary world maintained a careful silence; later on, when he resumed writing and it became fashionable to say "Céline is a terrible person but a gifted writer," a few supporters like Roger Nimier beat the drums for a Nobel Prize. In 1957 he published *D'un chateau à l'autre* (from one castle to another), a novel about his wartime flight. Various others followed, one dedicated to "Animals, Sick People and Prisoners," and another to Pliny the Elder, who died in the eruption of Vesuvius.

Eerily, he finished his last book a few hours before he died of a sudden massive stroke. Called *Rigadon,* it is an attack on the Chinese. They were going to take over the West, he predicted; Europe was finished and the barbarians were at the gates. He was sure of this, he said, because: "I am a parasitolgist, doctorated!"

Analyzing Céline has become a popular sport. Sartre wrote *Anti-Semite and Jew* with him in mind, but the best comment on his complex personality comes from the lawyer who defended him at his trial: "He was too much of a loner to collaborate with anybody."

Some students of Céline have tried to absolve him of anti-Semitism by claiming that he used Jews merely as a *symbol* of evil, as if that in itself were not anti-Semitic. Some have said that his hatred of Jews was a temporary aberration caused by some personal crisis that just happened to correspond with World War

II; others that he was temporarily insane at this same convenient time. Those of the Freudian persuasion say that he substituted Jews for the parents he hated; other Freudians believe that the image of Jews as beset outsiders was Céline's own image of himself, and he felt they had stolen his show.

Sartre missed by a mile with his venality theory: "If Céline could support the social theses of the Nazis, it is because he was paid to do so." David O'Connell points out that the Soviets tried and failed to get Céline this way, and quotes a witness who was with him in Moscow: "I was highly amused, knowing that Céline, a delicate and honest man, without needs, without vices, without a car, without a servant, a nonsmoker who drank only water, was one of those very rare beings who couldn't be bought."

O'Connell traces Céline's anti-Semitism in part to his origins in the strongly anti-Dreyfus lower middle class, his resentment of Jewish success in medicine, and his unrequited love for an American woman who married a Jew, but he reminds us that all of Céline's behavior owed much to the fact that he was "an eccentric, albeit a vengeful and racist one," whose every act and thought were a "manifestation of his unusually strong spirit of independence."

Here we have a paradox. Anti-Semitism being history's oldest form of groupthink, rugged individualists and eccentrics tend to be its least likely practitioners. Anyone who hears a different drummer probably will be so repelled by the conformity of anti-Semitism and the company that anti-Semites must keep that he might just become a philo-Semite out of contempt for the mass mind.

Why didn't Céline, the consummate eccentric, take this route? Here I must hazard a guess, because of all the misanthropes I examine in this book, Céline is the one who leaves me stumped.

The only thing about him that I can identify with is the fascist-good-neighbor number he did on the Resistance. Basing my theory on what I would do in the same situation, I suspect that he somehow discovered the location of the Resistance apartment and rented another one in the same building purely out of puckishness, delighting in the spectacle of Resistance members and collaborators passing each other on the stairs and exchanging polite greetings—especially the French equivalent of "Have a nice day."

As for his anti-Semitism, I think it was somehow tied up with his laziness.

That he was lazy is indicated by his so-called medical career. He liked to say that he chose to work in government clinics because he could not bear to grow rich from anything as repulsive as sick people, but if he found sick people repulsive, why did he become a doctor at all?

O'Connell believes Céline's clinic work proves that "despite all the shortcomings he found in mankind, he was still committed to helping people without getting rich in the process." That's a generous interpretation but I can't accept it. My guess is that Céline took salaried jobs and appointments to government clinics because it was easier than opening a private practice.

The same penchant for taking the easy way out shows up in his writing. His first novel, *Voyage au bout de la nuit,* is written in a traditional style, but his subsequent works are marred by what he called his "digest" or "telegraphic" method—fragmentary sentences separated by three dots. He claimed that he was trying to capture the way people really think and talk, but as Samuel Johnson pointed out, what is written with ease is never read with pleasure. Céline succeeded in making things easy only for himself.

In the same way, anti-Semitism was easier than misanthropy.

I see the lazy Céline trying to simplify his many hatreds and turn them into a manageable political and intellectual shorthand by using anti-Semitism as a kind of computer mouse.

Armed with his quick 'n' easy mechanical ethic, he moved all over the screen of human nature, finding materialism, arrogance, hypocrisy, manipulation, and exploitation in Communists, socialists, liberals, monarchists, Masons, the church, the middle class, the lower-middle class, the workingclass, the Frenchman-in-the-street, the English, the Germans, the Resistance, the Vichyites, and finally the Chinese—and then dumped it all in the Jew file.

BY FLYING SPIKES IN
F-SHARP POSSESSED

I wish I could say I never met a misanthrope who bored me, but I can't. Three who leave me cold are Ty Cobb, Irving Berlin, and James Gould Cozzens.

Tyrus Raymond Cobb (1886–1961) was born in Royston, Georgia, and named by his scholarly father after the ancient city of Tyre, renowned for having stood up to Alexander the Great.

The Cobbs were big fish in a little pond. W.H. Cobb was a superintendent of schools, newspaper editor, and state senator. His family was a minor branch on the great tree known as the Cobbs of Georgia, who produced the commander of Cobb's Legion (Ashley Wilkes's regiment) in the Civil War. Ty's mother, *née* Chitwood, was the daughter of a well-off landowner. Married to W.H. Cobb when she was only sixteen, she gave him three children, two boys and a girl, of whom Ty was the oldest.

The family was prosperous and Ty's childhood was a Booth Tarkington idyll, although even as a boy he played rough. His father wanted him to become a doctor and Ty rather liked the idea too, but baseball won out. W. H. Cobb, though somewhat disappointed, raised no strenuous objections.

Everything was fine until the night of August 8, 1905, when Mrs. Cobb emptied a .12-gauge double-barreled shotgun into Mr. Cobb, turning him into a pile of shredded meat on the porch.

Eighteen-year-old Ty was in Augusta playing minor-league ball. The two younger children were spending the night with friends, and Mr. Cobb, according to his wife, had left some hours earlier in the family buggy to spend a couple of days supervising some work on his farm. Later that night, however, several people saw him walking around in town.

Mrs. Cobb said she had gone to bed in the room she shared with her husband when she was awakened by a noise and saw the shadow of a man through the tall French windows that led onto the upstairs porch. Although it was a hot Georgia night, the windows were closed and locked. Thinking that the shadowy male figure was a stranger trying to break in, she grabbed the loaded shotgun that was kept by the bed and fired once. Neighbors testified that they heard the blast, and then, "a considerable time later," heard another.

Mrs. Cobb said she went to the shattered window and saw her husband lying in a pool of blood. The family doctor, who was the first to see the body, found a loaded revolver in the dead man's pocket.

Ty was summoned from Augusta and came home to tragedy and triumph: no sooner had he arrived back in Royston than a telegram arrived saying that he had been picked up by the Detroit Tigers and had to report at the end of August.

He did, playing his first major-league season while his mother, out on bail, awaited trial for manslaughter. He returned for the trial—she was acquitted—and soon thereafter made a home for her and his sister in Detroit, where they lived for many years. Although he must have heard the Royston gossip about his mother's alleged lover, he never spoke of it to anyone and remained a dutiful son.

In the following season of 1906, a never-identified illness took Ty out of the Tigers line-up for a time. Rumors went round that he was in a mental institution, but he was seen sitting in the stands watching games on numerous occasions. This mystery, like the circumstances of his father's death, has never been entirely cleared up.

After the 1906 season, Ty began what was to be the longest mean streak in baseball. Assessments of his disposition ranged from Tristram Coffin's rather elegant "a creature without normal motivation" to the more usual jock inarticulateness of Jimmy Austin, who said Ty was "real nasty" on the field.

Ty himself explained his behavior in typical Southern fashion: "I was just a mild-mannered Sunday School boy, but those old-timers turned me into a snarling wildcat." There is a good deal of truth to this. All rookies are teased and made the butt of practical jokes, but Ty's Southernness drew more than the usual amount of fire. The Civil War was only forty years in the past when he entered major-league baseball, and the great majority of players were Irish- or German-Catholic boys from the North. The Wasp Ty with his thick Georgia drawl was a natural target; his teammates ganged up on him, sawing his bats in half, cutting up his uniforms, and hitting him with wet newspapers.

He did not take teasing well, and this too is understandable to anyone who knows Southern men. The touchy pride, the almost universal self-image of the beau sabreur, and the underlying conviction that aristocrats pop off quicker than ordinary people, had to be major ingredients in Ty's psyche.

Put off by his smoldering, chip-on-the-shoulder moods, his

teammates gave him the cold treatment, refusing to sit next to him in the dugout and ignoring him on road trips. He ate alone in strange cities and took solitary after-dinner walks, armed with the pistol he always carried and even slept with, thinking about baseball and how to improve his game. The only breaks in his isolation were bare-chested fist fights with other players whom he invited to his hotel room for that purpose. One opponent was Buck Herzog, whose head Ty banged against the floor until some Tigers pulled them apart. Afterwards, a chastened Herzog told the St. Louis Browns: "Ty likes a funny story. I want you guys to think of some good yarns to tell him before the game. Keep him in a good humor."

Ty's philosophy was simple: "Baseball is a red-blooded sport for red-blooded men. It's no pink tea, and mollycoddles had better stay out. It's a struggle for supremacy, a survival of the fittest."

His object was "a general demoralization of the opposing team." This he achieved by spiking infielders as he slid into a base and sending them limping off the field with their stockings hanging in bloody shreds. But he had other, more subtle methods, such as head games that he played with the icy expertise of a KGB psychiatrist. Picking out an emotionally vulnerable player on an opposing team, Ty would pretend to make friends with him; then, when the player felt confident enough to step into the Tigers dugout before the game to say hello, Ty would turn on him in fury, screaming, "Get away from me! Don't talk to me or I'll kill you!" The hapless victim was so shaken that he could not keep his mind on the game or his eye on the ball.

Ty had nothing but contempt for kind-hearted Walter Johnson, the Washington Senators pitcher who refused to brush back batters for fear of killing them with his lethal fastball. Other pitchers, victims of the war of nerves Ty brought to base stealing, were not so kind. A group of them entered into a conspiracy to finish him off with a "beanball" but they soon regretted their decision. Whenever a pitcher threw too far inside, the Georgia Peach would lay a bunt down the first-base line to make him field it, and then collide with him as hard as he could in hopes of breaking his pitching arm. "The baserunner has the right of way," Ty explained, "and the man who blocks it does so at his peril."

He was "the dirtiest player in baseball," said Connie Mack of the Philadelphia Athletics, and the City of Brotherly Love responded accordingly. Heckling Ty was a Shibe Park speciality, but one day a fan went too far and called him a "half-nigger." Ty exploded, leaped into the stands, ran twelve rows up to where the vocal fan sat, and pulled the man out of his seat. He was a printer who had lost all of one hand and some fingers from the other in a shop accident. As Ty began beating him, someone yelled, "He doesn't have any hands!" Ty yelled back, "I don't care if he doesn't have any feet!" and went on with the thrashing.

He was suspended for the rest of the season, causing the first players strike in major-league history. The Tigers hired semi-pro players as scabs, but when they lost to the Athletics 24-2, Ty told his teammates to play, saying he did not want to hurt their careers. It was probably the only time in his life that he functioned as a peacemaker; the Tigers management showed their appreciation by getting his suspension reduced to ten days and fining him fifty dollars.

Ty's most recent biographer, Charles C. Alexander, writes: "Behaving as most of us would like to were we not bound by convention and our own timidity, Cobb both fascinated people and made them uneasy." It's hard not to admire Ty's scrappiness on the diamond where his adversaries were his equals, but admiration recedes under the vast catalogue of his off-field fights, which were almost always with the little people.

In Detroit he beat up the black groundskeeper, who he said was drunk; when the man's wife came running to his rescue, Ty grabbed her by the throat and started choking her. He might have killed her had not the Tigers catcher intervened and pulled them apart.

On another occasion he stepped into some wet concrete and took umbrage at the black laborer who yelled a warning at him. Ty knocked the man down and was charged with assault and battery. He was found guilty and given a suspended sentence, and later gave the laborer seventy-five dollars to avoid a civil suit.

In Cleveland he got into a knife fight with a hotel elevator operator and a night watchman, playing a doubleheader the next day with his face swathed in bandages. When the hotel employees swore out a warrant against him for "cutting with intent to kill," the Tigers front office paid the men's medical bills and offered them hush money, which so enraged a Cleveland detective that he vowed to yank Ty off any train the moment it crossed into Ohio. The Peach spent the rest of the season sitting out Indians games and bypassing the Buckeye State by taking trains into Canada to get back and forth from Detroit to major-league cities on the east coast.

Philadelphians made dozens of death threats against him. Each time the Tigers played the A's, Shibe Park stationed cops in the visitors' dugout and in the right-field bleachers to protect Ty when he played his position. One time a crowd gathered in front of his hotel but he walked defiantly into it until, seeing the famous glint in his eye, the would-be lynch mob parted and let him pass.

In Detroit as he was driving to the railroad station, three men jumped on the running board of his car and hit at him through the window. Leaping out, Ty took them all on, pistol-whipped one of them unconscious, and got stabbed in the back. With blood soaking through his jacket, he made the train just in time and got three hits in the game the next day.

Learning that the grocer refused to give his wife a refund for some spoiled fish, he grabbed his gun and ran to the store. The grocer relented and apologized but it wasn't over yet. Hearing the loud argument, a store employee emerged from a back room to see what was going on. The employee happened to be black, and because he was a butcher, he happened to have a meat cleaver in his hand. It was all Ty needed; he pistol-whipped the butcher and spent the night in jail. Plea: guilty. Fine: fifty dollars.

In Atlanta he got into an argument with a waitress over his check and the cashier hit him over the head with a glass dish. When the cops came, Ty wrestled them to the ground and demanded that they take him to the station in a taxi instead of the police wagon. They agreed.

His wife left him, thereby earning a place on his "Sonofabitch List" that he always carried with him. Some of the others on it were baseball commissioner Kenesaw Mountain Landis, Dutch Leonard, and as time went on, Eleanor Roosevelt and the entire Democratic party.

Advancing age did not stale his infinite monotony. He even started a fight at the Cooperstown Hall of Fame when he thought somebody had snubbed him. Brooding on the incident, he got drunk and spilled a platter of roast beef into the lap of a dinner companion.

Not surprisingly, he was a gun nut with a passion for blood sports. Writing in 1956 when Ty was still alive, biographer John McCallum describes the Peach holding court at his Nevada hunting lodge:

Ty would sit in a big easy chair, smoke rings curling around his lean head and bronzed features, and dream of the big game he was going to hunt some day in Africa. He was going to do that for years, but he never got closer to the jungles with a gun than Canada. But he dreamed on. Plans were changed and rechanged. Bears, mountain lions, and moose fell before his crack shooting on preparatory trips. He wanted those elephants, crocodiles and rhinos, but something else always came up to postpone the expedition. Still he didn't do too badly. His Lake Tahoe lodge is covered with animals he has killed, bear skins, tanned deer hides, and mounted wild mountain goat heads. He prided himself on being able to take young fellows out and "walk 'em down." He went after birds on horseback, hunted fox at night, and dropped deer with his rifle from a moving speed boat.

The year before he died, Ty summoned a ghost writer to Lake Tahoe with the intention of dictating his memoirs, but nothing came of it. Instead he turned the writer into a combination nursemaid and hostage, nearly frightening him to death by firing a pistol into a motel parking lot, and dragging him on a gambling foray to Reno, where Ty spent his time fighting with waitresses, cashiers, bartenders, maids, and any other breed of little people he could find.

I know this man. I saw him many times during my roadhouse-crawling days in Mississippi and North Carolina, and he always looked the same: a round-faced, pink-cheeked gnome of a man, a mean good ole boy biding his time until somebody had the misfortune to make eye contact with him. That's *all* it takes.

The Southerner's famous mean streak is usually attributed to a murky sadomasochism involving fears and fantasies of interracial sex, but I suspect it is really a reaction against the demands of Southern hospitality.

South Carolina novelist Blanche McCrary Boyd writes: "Southerners are as polite as cattle, except when they're not. When they're not, they might shoot you or chase you around the yard with a hatchet." Living up to a reputation is an exhausting business. It is humanly impossible to be as gracious as Southerners are supposed to be, but we long ago got in too deep. The rest of the country came to believe our propaganda and, fatally, we came to believe it ourselves.

In consequence, we produced monsters of hospitality who cast a pall of incessant, unbearable niceness over the entire region. All classes participated in the torture. The aristocratic prototype of hospitality is the crystalline great lady of whom it is said, "She's kindness itself." The plain-folks prototype was my grandmother, the *miles gloriosus* of the spare cot, constantly braying "We'll *make* room!" and issuing jocular threats about what she would do to a guest who even thought about leaving too soon ("I'll just tie you right up and keep you here!").

Hospitality carried to such extremes is bound to create its opposite, and so we produced the misanthropic good ole boy who greeted out-of-state travelers with speeding tickets or unmarked graves, depending upon his mood. If Ty Cobb had not been a ballplayer he would have made a great Georgia sheriff.

The man who put a song in our hearts and a lilt in our steps was a cold-blooded, foul-tempered, tight-fisted monster. The kindest assessment of him comes from Sid Caesar, who said, "Irving Berlin has an instinct for self-preservation." More typical is composer Harry Warren's quip at the end of World War II: "They bombed the wrong Berlin."

Moses and Lena Baline and their six children left Russia for America in 1893 when Israel, the youngest, was five. Later, when Izzy Baline had become Irving Berlin, he liked to say, "Everyone

147

should have a Lower East Side in their lives." The remark illustrates his blindsided egoism. Young enough to adapt to a new country, he flourished in an environment that turned his parents and siblings into *farloyrene menshen,* "lost souls who spent the balance of their days in a trance of alienation and drudgery," says biographer Laurence Bergreen in *As Thousands Cheer.*

At thirteen Izzy quit school and left home to sing in saloons and live in Bowery flophouses, but the appalling existence never touched the hard inner core of this determined survivor. "He gave no thought to the damage these living conditions could inflict on him or anyone else. Nor did he betray even the slightest self-pity at the loss of his entire adolescence. . . . For better or worse he was free of his family's constraints and the world they had imported from Russia, free not only of their demands, but also of their language and religious rituals."

He did his duty by his mother, taking excellent care of her after his father's early death, but he remained emotionally detached from her, and even more, from his brothers and sisters. They, along with their hopelessness, were what he had to shed as he invented Irving Berlin.

Where work was concerned, Izzy the loner could be as sociable as the next fellow. His first friend in the music world was Harry Von Tilzer, composer of "A Bird In a Gilded Cage," who was born Harry Gumm, uncle of Frances Gumm, who later became Judy Garland. Izzy liked the formality and punctiliousness of Von Tilzer's Germanic pseudonym and decided to copy it, signing his first composition "I. Berlin"—a deliberate change, not the printer's error of legend.

As a singing waiter in a raucous watering hole called "Nigger Mike's," Berlin plugged blackface vaudeville numbers called "coon songs," many of them featuring a character named Alexander, which was considered a comical name for a black man in those days. Shrewdly observing that "syncopation is the soul of every American," Berlin began writing songs, turning out a ragtime festival of ethnicity that would cause mass cardiac arrest in our sensitive era: "Sweet Marie, Make-a Rag-a-Time Dance with Me," "Yiddle on Your Fiddle Play Some Ragtime," and one about Harlem fancy-dress balls called "Puttin' on the Ritz" that he sanitized twenty years later by changing Lenox Avenue to Park Avenue.

An untrained musician, he used only the black keys—he called them "nigger keys"—which restricted him to F-sharp. "The key of C is for people who study music," he sneered. With the help of a transposing piano equipped with a key-changing lever like a gear stick, he wrote so many songs so fast that once during a rare lull, another composer wrote "Izzy, Get Busy and Write Another Ragtime Song."

He did. "Alexander's Ragtime Band" in 1910 catapulted him to fame and triggered the rumor that he did not write his songs himself but had a "little nigger boy" who wrote the melodies. "Imagine how many little nigger boys I'd have to have," he retorted. The rumor persisted throughout his career but Laurence Bergreen lays it to rest with convincing insight into Berlin's loner personality: "His desire for control over his songwriting was so great that he was emotionally incapable of entrusting his work to others."

Sexually fastidious—"His morality was a function of his fierce desire for autonomy"—he detested the rutting Florenz Ziegfeld and rejected the many chorus girls at his disposal. In 1912 he married singer Dorothy Goetz, who died five months later of the typhoid she caught on their Cuban honeymoon. In the twelve years before he married again, "he became more inward, not in the sense of becoming introspective, a mental habit he despised, but less trusting of the world around him: his friends, his business partners, even himself."

His first openly misanthropic statement—his coming out, as it were—was the 1914 anti-war fantasy song, "Stay Down Here Where You Belong," in which Satan tells his sons to remain in hell rather than go to war with mankind. It was a flop, but it was quickly forgotten in the glow of success that greeted "Oh, How I Hate to Get Up in the Morning." When his fame approached legendary proportions after World War I, bringing kidnapping threats from anarchists, he wrote "Look Out for That Bolsheviki Man" and bought a bullet-proof limousine.

In 1925 he met the love of his life, debutante Ellin Mackay, daughter of the devoutly Catholic and devoutly anti-Semitic tycoon Clarence Mackay, who lived in a Long Island mansion surrounded by his collection of medieval armor. After a series of Romeo-and-Juliet crises, Irving and Ellin were married at city hall. His wedding present to her was the copyright to "Always," but contrary to legend, he did not write it for her. It was composed originally in 1913 when the girlfriend of a business associate jokingly challenged him to write a song for her on the spot. "I'll Be Loving You, Mona" was never published but Berlin put it in his trunk and reworked the lyrics some years later for a Broadway show.

He was such a loner that he did not even entirely like the idea of being married, and he suffered a composing block for several years after he and Ellin tied the knot. The negative emotions that marriage triggered in him were remarked on by a reporter who saw him on his honeymoon: "The man is in a highly nervous condition. He is a very different person from the suave and debonair Berlin who once strolled down Broadway after dark. That genial smile he had when he and his bride sailed . . . has disappeared. He is . . . morose, irritable, and snaps out the word 'no' when approached by those not bosom friends."

Part of the trouble was Clarence Mackay's refusal to give Ellin his blessing, part of it was the intrusiveness of the press, but even bosom friends like Alexander Woollcott noted that from his second marriage on, Berlin became more "beleagured and belligerent. . . . he could shift to fury without warning, and those who witnessed his behavior inevitably came away with one overriding question: how could the composer of those lovely, sentimental, romantic ballads. . . . suddenly act so crude, glowering and swearing and carrying on as though fate had singled him out for the misfortune of great fame?"

Violinist Fritz Kreisler was shaken by the conversation they had when Berlin tried to buy one of his songs for his music publishing company: "The dreadful language he used was so awful. He began to curse and swear at me."

He also became stingy with money, and even more with permissions, restricting performances of his songs and raising the roof if anyone dared quote even a few words of his lyrics. He treated Ellin the same way, says Bergreen, guarding her "as jealously as he did his songs, and for the same reason: she was all he had. . . . His mentality remained permanently that of the survivor, always vigilant, forever wary of anything beyond his control."

Clarence Mackay eventually came round, more or less, and acknowledged the births of his three granddaughters, but the Berlin home was not a happy one. Ellin had to shield the girls from his rages, and eventually took refuge herself in a late-blooming career as a novelist. Berlin was enthusiastic about her writing when it came to supplying her with publicity ideas, a specialty of his, but when she asked him for the money to buy a new car he snapped, "You've got your own goddamn money."

They became further estranged over politics: he was an arch-conservative and she was a flaming liberal.

His sojourn in Hollywood during the filming of *Holiday Inn* turned into a debacle. Says Bergreen: "Irving remained in a foul temper long after he returned to New York. His outbursts became more intense. . . . They were a highly unattractive but persistent symptom of the impossible demands he made on himself and the corrosive effects of fame on his personality."

When an employee of his music company had a heart attack and asked for an advance on his Christmas bonus to pay his medical bills, the composer of "White Christmas" refused, snarling, "We're not running a charity here." His nephew got the same reception when he asked for money to pay his mother's medical bills. "She's my sister," said Berlin, "but she's your mother. When you use up all your money taking care of her and you run out, then I'll help you out."

He got his comeuppance in 1964 when he lost his suit against *Mad* magazine, which had parodied some of his lyrics. He claimed it was plagiarism because they had used the same meter, but Judge Irving R. Kaufman ruled: "Parody and satire are deserving of substantial freedom both as entertainment and as a form of social and literary criticism. We doubt that even so eminent a composer as Irving Berlin should be permitted to claim a property interest in iambic pentameter."

Irving and Ellin lived in a Beekman Place mansion, but as time went on they did not live together. He had his apartment and she had hers, one upstairs and one down. They met at dinner but he rarely spoke to her or anyone else. On his walks he chased children away and refused to return the greetings of neighbors. His own children and grandchildren never visited; his eruptions of fury had driven them away.

He refused to attend either the Statue of Liberty Centennial, which was built around "God Bless America," or his own centennial birthday party. By then he was virtually blind and completely alone: Ellin, sixteen years his junior, had died in 1988. His own death at the age of 101 came quietly on September 22, 1989.

It seems to me that Laurence Bergreen leans too heavily on the price-of-fame angle to explain Berlin's misanthropy. In our era, the shoe is on the other foot: fans, not celebrities, are the misanthropes among us.

In religious centuries, when everyone from the King down to the most brutish peasant held the same unquestioning belief in the soul's immortality, fame was unimportant, and indeed, did not really exist as we know it today. The common people of France were permitted to wander in and out of Versailles at will and watch the King at his banquet table. He ate in public so that the people could see, not the King, but God's representative on earth. These public displays were in no way comparable to our gaping autograph hunts and photo ops; they were quasi-religious rituals.

When people said excitedly, "I saw the King!" it was not the same as "I saw Liz Taylor!" The latter is always followed by the expression *in person,* but the idea of seeing the King in person would have been a contradiction in terms. It was his spiritual, not his corporeal, presence that mattered.

In today's secular world, celebrities are the only people left who can be certain of attaining the immortality that the humblest medieval serf took for granted. It is the supreme irony of our enlightened democratic age that *in person* is another way of saying that only the famous have souls. The obscure majority are well aware of the New Calvinism and more and more of them are coming to resent it. The shrinking of immortality to a select few whose names will "live" has ushered in a murderous hatred of celebrities that increasingly results in actual murder. Thanks to the New Calvinism, the misanthropic fan is now a fixture of American life.

As for Irving Berlin's misanthropy, I think he was mean because he was mean. So *nu?* I said he bored me, didn't I?

James Gould Cozzens (1903–1978) never used a simple word when an arcane one was available, so nowhere in his rambling analyses of his temperament do we find the word *misanthrope.* He called his condition *inappetency,* a lack of appetite for living. His publisher, who was probably damaged by years of coping with Cozzens's vocabulary, came up with *anhedonia,* an inability to experience pleasure in life. It never seems to have occurred to anyone to try *bastard.*

Cozzens was a professional Wasp in the manner of John O'Hara, except that he really was a Wasp. The only child of a doting mother and a businessman, he grew up on Staten Island, soaked up high-church Episcopalianism at the Kent School, and carried a walking stick in Harvard Yard. "I feel I'm better than other people," he told *Time* years later.

He did not graduate from Harvard because he had run up so many bills that he could not afford to join Porcellian, and death being preferable to not joining Porcellian, he quit college after his second year.

His first novel, published in 1924, was the well-titled *Confusion,* obviously inspired by F. Scott Fitzgerald's *This Side of Paradise,* about a young man on the brink of life, or the edge of the abyss, or something: the frat rat as Stella Dallas. Five more novels followed; none of them sold well but Cozzens did not have to worry. He had married Bernice Baumgarten, a crackerjack literary agent who supported him. "It could have been a humiliating situation," he told *Time,* "but I guess I had a certain native conceit and felt that her time was well spent."

Guard of Honor, about racial segregation in the World War II army, won the 1949 Pulitzer Prize, but even it did not sell really well. After that came a silence of eight years: Cozzens was busy writing his masterpiece, *By Love Possessed,* published in 1957.

It covers two days in the life of a repressed, eminently respectable Wasp lawyer whose carefully controlled existence is shattered by a rape case, an embezzling partner, a cuckolded partner, an hysterical woman in the throes of conversion to Catholicism, and painful memories triggered by all of the above.

The critics greeted *By Love Possessed* with orgasmic delight. Never, before or since, have so many people typed c-o-m-p-e-l-l-i-n-g so many times in the course of a single season. All the Lit Crit big guns, from Orville Prescott to Jessamyn West, called the novel spellbinding and enchanting, wise and compassionate, distinguished and truly distinguished, as well as magnificent, utterly magnificent, and simply magnificent. Finally, one critic simply gave up and wrote, "about all I can do is ditto the dithyrambs."

Taking note of this blizzard of superlatives, the major book clubs and *Reader's Digest* joined the parade, until *By Love Possessed,* all 570 pages of it, squatted on maple-veneer Early American coffee tables throughout the land. When it drove *Peyton Place* out of the top slot on the lists, Hollywood perked up and completed the cycle of success.

There was only one thing wrong with *By Love Possessed,* but none of the critics wanted to be the first to say what it was. It's dangerous to go against the grain of opinion, especially when the grain comes from the paneled dens of the country's best ivory towers, wherein dwell the kind of people who can't bear to admit that they don't understand something. And if the exalted Lit Crits would not speak out, the matrons of Dubuque certainly were not about to. Instead, they sat on their Early American sofas with Cozzens in their laps, hating themselves for being too stupid and provincial to appreciate what they were reading:

> The sweeping voiceless compliment, the silent, single-minded expression of so real a respect (surely real, being silent, being supposed private) could not but gratify; yet, to most people, pause must also be brought—pause, both on one's own behalf (to protest self-consciously: not so! would be a gross gawkishness; while the grave acceptance of no comment must amount to, be the next thing to, the nod complacent, to oneself proclaiming: *I am not as other men are, extortioners, unjust adulterers . . .);* and on behalf of the single-minded complimenter (not a high look only, but a high aspiration, is apt to go before a fall).

Out of context, you say? Okey-dokey, let's try another one:

> Ah, how wise, how sure, how right, was that genius of the language whose instinct detected in the manifold manifestings of the amative appetite (however different-seeming; however apparently opposed) the one same urgent unreason, the one same eager let's-pretend, and so, wisely consented, so, for convenience covenanted, to name all with one same name! Explaining, sweet unreason excused; excusing, sweet let's-pretend explained. The young heart, indentured (O wearisome conditions of humanity!) to reason, pined, starved on the bare bitter diet of thinking. One fine day, that heart (most hearts) must bolt. That heart would be off (could you blame it?) to Loveland, to feeling's feasts.

There *must* be something without parentheses, you say? You're right, there is:

> Deaf as yesterday to all representations of right, he purposed further perfidy, once more pawning his honor to obtain his lust.

Deaf as yesterday to all remonstrances of reason, he purposed to
sell himself over again to buy venery's disappearing dross.

You won't believe me until you see the sexy parts, will you?
Jessamyn West said they had "lyric power." Maybe she meant:
"the thoroughgoing, deepening, widening work of their connection; and his then no less than hers, the tempo slowed in concert
to engineer a tremulous joint containment and continuance."

Some of the Lit Crits mentioned in passing that Cozzens's style
was a little hard to follow, but then quickly added that the same
was true of Henry James and William Faulkner, thereby elevat-
ing Cozzens still higher. The fraud was finally exposed by Dwight
MacDonald, who reviewed the reviewers in a devastating *Com-
mentary* piece, "By Cozzens Possessed," in which he said that the
sex scene so admired by Jessamyn West read like "a *Fortune*
description of an industrial process." He also accused Cozzens of
making "a dead style even deader" with negative constructions
like "not-unhelped" and "unhasty," said he had a tin ear for
speech, and wrote prose "as Gothic as Harkness Memorial
Quadrangle. . . . Haven't seen 'dross' in print since *East Lynne.*"

The most puzzling aspect of *By Love Possessed* is that Cozzens
had not written this way before. His earlier novels were couched
in what MacDonald called "a straightforward if commonplace
style." But because he was "slimly endowed as either thinker or
stylist, he has succeeded only in fuzzing it up, inverting the
syntax, dragging in Latin-root polysyllables. . . . Like shot in
game or sand in clams, such gritty nuggets are strewn through
the book *to set on edge the teeth of the reader. . . .*"

My italics. I maintain that Cozzens wrote *By Love Possessed*
in this turgid manner not out of creative experimentation or any
other literary reason, but as a deliberate and conscious attempt
to be user-unfriendly. By this time he was virtually a hermit who

never left his home deep in the New Jersey sticks (Bernice had to endure a complicated train trip to New York each day). Unable to stand eating in restaurants unless the nearby tables were unoccupied, compelled to wear gloves year-round to ward off the taint of his fellow man, he made his torturous literary style the final manifestation of his misanthropy. He wanted to make his readers suffer, and if possible, drive the entire country blind and crazy.

Unlike his fiction, Cozzens's journal entries are coherent and valuable for their unvarnished view of mankind. The millions who are presently fiddling with self-esteem while America burns would do well to examine this one:

> The seamy side of human nature. You must be careful how you treat people as your equals. The average person has much more respect for you if, even though he resents it, you make it plain to him that you consider him of no great importance. The line may be a thin one, but if you're 'nice' to him beyond what he, perhaps subconsciously, feels are his deserts he will much more often than not despise you for it.

I have found this to be true. Insecurity breeds treachery: if you are kind to people who hate themselves, they will hate you as well. It does no good to try to help them because they never really change no matter how long they stay in therapy. Even so progressive a spirit as Isadora Duncan admitted as much when she wrote: "It is only in romances that people undergo a sudden metamorphosis. In real life, the main character remains exactly the same."

Insecure people are dangerous and it is best to stay away from them. Especially now, when there are so many of them, only a misanthrope can avoid being exsanguinated by their emotional demands. The mere sonofabitch, in saner times an automatic survivor, has fallen upon hard times and is currently in grave peril.

Cozzens's boorishness was legendary. Like everyone without a sense of humor, he thought he had one. Attending a dinner for his wife's bestselling client Betty MacDonald, he ridiculed *The Egg and I* until he had the author in tears.

His publicly expressed attitude toward his wife defies belief. Describing his feelings on first meeting her, he told *Time:* "I suppose sex entered into it. After all, what's a woman for?" Of his decision to marry: "Mother almost died when I married a Jew, but later when she saw I was being decently cared for, she realized that it was the best thing that could have happened to me."

Both of these remarks pale beside a story told by Cozzens biographer Matthew J. Bruccoli: "They did not want children. Neither one was philoprogenitive, and Cozzens later remarked that he didn't want a son of his kept out of Porcellian because he was half Jewish. Bernice had an abortion when she became pregnant."

I wish there were some way to keep Cozzens out of Misanthropian. He wasn't really one of us at all, merely a mean drunk at the country club.

THE OLD MISANTHROPE

My favorite misanthrope, Ambrose Bierce (1842–1914?), would spin in his grave, wherever it is, if he knew what Hollywood did to him.

In *The Old Gringo,* Bierce is portrayed as a sentimental idealist by Gregory Peck, America's Nice Guy Next Door: Earnest Division, who gave his humanitarian all in the successful campaign to keep Robert Bork off the Supreme Court.

The real Ambrose Bierce, according to a friendly biographer, believed that the Fifth Amendment should be replaced with the medieval trial by ordeal: "Any pressure short of physical torture or the threat of it, that can be put upon a rogue to make him assist in his own undoing is just and therefore expedient."

The Old Gringo was based on the novel by Mexican socialist Carlos Fuentes. The real old gringo wrote: "No people in the world are fit for Socialism. I don't believe in the greatest good to the greatest number. It seems to me perfect rot. I believe in the greatest good to the best men. And I would sacrifice a hundred incapable men to elevate one really great man."

Jane Fonda, a friend of Carlos Fuentes, stars in the movie as a woman who inspired love and trust in the heart of the fictional old gringo, notwithstanding the sentiments that spewed regularly from the real old gringo's pen: "There is positively no betting on the discreet reticence of any woman whose silence you have not secured with a meat-ax. . . . The mind that cannot discern a score of great and irreparable general evils distinctly traceable to 'emancipation of women' is as impregnable to the light as a toad in a rock."

Ambrose Bierce was born on the Ohio frontier, which he hated, and later moved with his family to the Indiana frontier, which he also hated. The sentimental glorification of frontier boyhood in Hamlin Garland's *Son of the Middle Border* inspired him to write a poem about the sun's refraction off the henhouse slime and the maggoty straw on the warped floorboards of the sheep cote.

There were eight little Bierces, all of them given names beginning with *A* by a father who never explained this idiosyncrasy. Ambrose rather liked his father, with whom he shared a taste for reading, but he disdained his mother and all his siblings except his brother Albert, whom he tolerated to the extent of letting him come along on solitary walks through the woods.

Bierce, who was later to define misanthropy as "a hatred of youth and of being young," felt the same way about childhood as Ayn Rand: he was against it. Barbara Branden's comments on this aspect of Rand—"Childhood was an overture, she concluded, a preparation for the future, with no significance in itself"—match those of Bierce's biographer, Richard O'Connor: "Youth, it seemed to him, was something to be gotten over as quickly as possible, with adulthood the only goal worthwhile."

These attitudes recall Jonathan Swift's maxim: "No wise man ever wished to be younger." It was not simply that Rand and Bierce came as adults to dislike children (they did), but that they disliked children while they were children themselves, and resented *being* children. I know the feeling well; it's hard to be a misanthrope when you're that short.

As far as anyone could see, the man who would one day be called "Bitter Bierce" had nothing to be bitter about. He was an Adonis, with thick, curly golden hair, piercing blue eyes, and a perfect physique that was enhanced by the uniform of the Ninth Indiana when the eighteen-year-old Bierce answered Lincoln's call for volunteers in 1861.

Biographer Richard O'Connor believes "repressed idealism" made him rally so quickly to the colors. It certainly was not patriotism in the standard sense; his taste for irreverent verse inspired him to write:

> My country 'tis of thee, sweet land of felony,
> Of thee I sing.
> Land where my fathers fried young witches
> And applied whips to the Quaker's hide
> And made him spring.

Anyone who replaces belief in God with belief in the human comedy ("Death is not the end, there remains litigation over the estate") tends to develop the kind of panache that leads to great courage. Bierce was wounded twice, decorated for valor twelve times, and received a battlefield commission at Shiloh, eventually rising to the rank of brevet major.

Later on, during the post-war "Gilded Age" of greed and political scandals, he was to write: "It was once my fortune to command a company of soldiers—real soldiers. Not professional life-long fighters, the product of European militarism—just plain, ordinary, American, volunteer soldiers who loved their country and fought for it with never a thought of grabbing it for themselves; that is a trick which the survivors were taught later by gentlemen desiring their votes."

War suited him perfectly. Had he been less intelligent, the carnage he witnessed combined with his bleak opinion of humankind would have pushed him over the edge into sadism. As it was, the horrors of war generated a gallows humor and a macabre joie de vivre that pervade his writing, from the definitions in *The Devil's Dictionary* (*"non-combatant:* A dead Quaker") to his short stories.

An early critic predicted that Bierce's work would "never achieve a wide popularity, at least among the Anglo-Saxon race. His writings have too much the flavour of the hospital and the morgue. There is a stale odour of mouldy cerements about them." In *Patriotic Gore,* a study of Civil War literature, Edmund Wilson compared Bierce's writing to his asthma—"an art that can hardly breathe"—and attributed both to psychological causes. Clifton Fadiman acknowledged the morbidity but deemed it non-neurotic: "It merely expresses his fury at our placid healthfulness."

Bierce's fictional objective follows his own maxim: "A jest in the death chamber startles by surprise." We don't want to laugh when the sentry discovers that he shot his own father, or when the Yankee twin turns over a Confederate corpse and looks down at his own face, yet Bierce deadpans his climaxes in such a way that the reader's mind flashes a picture of Peter Sellers as Inspector Clouseau surveying another inadvertency.

To all who criticized his sepulchral bent Bierce replied: "If it scares you to read about one imaginary person killing another, why not take up knitting?"

After the war he worked briefly as a Treasury agent assigned to confiscate Rebel property in Selma, Alabama. Blood and guts on the battlefield hadn't bothered him at all, but witnessing the wholesale plunder carried out by the Reconstruction government offended his rigid sense of honor so much that he came out against peace: "I favor war, famine, pestilence—anything that will stop the people from cheating and confine the practice to contractors and statesmen."

He went to San Francisco and got a job on Hearst's newspaper, *The Examiner,* where he wrote his famous one-sentence book review: "The covers of this book are too far apart." His idealism was soon placed on the line again when he exposed the financial shenanigans of the Southern Pacific Railroad, and Colis P. Huntington tried to buy him off. "Name your price," said Huntington, "every man has a price." Bierce roared: "The price is about seventy-five million dollars, to be handed to the Treasurer of the United States!"

His daily column, "Prattle," became a catalogue of his likes and dislikes. The former included Jews and Chinese, and also Mormons, whom he embraced out of contrariness from having seen them persecuted during his Indiana boyhood. A critic, journalist, and writer himself, he nonetheless hated critics, journalists, and writers—when Jack London was lost at sea Bierce predicted, "The ocean will refuse to swallow him." He hated all sports and said that athletes moved him to "the lofty compassion of an owl for a blind puppy in a dark cellar." Dwight Moody and other evangelists were a "he-harlotry of horribles" and "phylloxera of the moral vineyard."

His hatreds included all "isms" but he readily admitted that laissez-faire capitalism's emphasis on freedom of action encouraged people to behave in ways that provided grist for his misanthrope's mill. Also: labor organizers, socialists, social workers (a misanthropic favorite), teachers, scientists, doctors, lodge members, dishonest people, religious people, and above all, the unintelligent. "That left him a very narrow segment of the population of whom he could approve, a fact which did not dismay him in the least," writes O'Connor.

Above all, he hated women. The three exceptions were George Eliot, the Empress Eugénie of France, and Lillie Coit, a San Francisco eccentric who rode to fires on the back of fire engines. "Lil is a real woman," he said fondly. He admired novelist Gertrude Atherton for her masculine drive and ambition but condemned her spready, run-on literary style as hopelessly feminine—though neither quality stopped him from making a pass at her as they waited for a train.

The rest of womankind were impeded by "the gray batter of their brainettes." Unlike most misogynists, he did not even credit female intuition for occasionally being right for the wrong reasons. "A woman does not leap to correct conclusions," he wrote. "Her saltatory feats commonly land her in a bog. . . . To put the matter with entire lucidity, woman hasn't any thinker." Opinions like these made radical feminist Charlotte Perkins Gilman call him a "public tormentor."

All women got on his nerves but one in particular drove him up the wall: "A sweetheart is a bottle of wine; a wife is a wine bottle." Mollie Day Bierce was the sort of cheerful soft-hearted woman guaranteed to rouse his contempt, which may have been why he married her. Misanthropes can't resist tormenting such people; I once had an affair with a man because he said, "The best thing about a beautiful spring day is being able to share it with someone else." I had to get at him.

Ambrose and Mollie had a daughter and two sons, both of the latter born in London where the Bierces lived for several years while Ambrose worked on a British journal, *The Lantern*. The children got on his nerves. "It's all a gyp perpetrated by women," he said. "Only a fool feels any lasting pride of fatherhood." Refusing to be domesticated, he came and went as he pleased. Although he said, "May Heaven punish the malefactor who invented that deadly dull thing, a good time," he enjoyed staying out late and drinking with his literary confrères, which meant that the only times he saw his family were when he was nursing a hangover. It was on one of these occasions that he lectured his son on blasphemy when he heard the boy say "Damn God." Bierce snapped: "I have told you repeatedly never to say Damn God when you mean goddamn."

The marriage broke up when Bierce found some innocuous letters addressed to Mollie from a platonic male friend. Refusing to listen to her protests of innocence, which several family friends verified, Bierce walked out then and there and never lived with her again. Several commentators have attributed this precipitous action to touchy pride or common-garden jealousy, but it's clear to me that Bierce simply latched onto the letters as an excuse to leave her. To a misanthrope, a sexual relationship is the granddaddy of Reach Out and Touch Someone, a literal rendition of "Peepul Who Need Peepul," the navel as Smile Button. When the resentment of intimacy mounts and the urge to circle the Welcome Wagons comes over us, we frequently turn against our sexual partners as symbols of an activity that, when you think about it, is life's oldest form of teamwork.

Bierce's older son died in a duel. The younger one married a girl his father disapproved of, giving Bierce a perfect excuse not to see him again. When this son committed suicide, Bierce kept his cremated remains in a cigar box on his desk.

Only his daughter Helen remained, and she knew something was up when Bierce visited her in the summer of 1913 with his literary papers in tow and asked her to store them for him. He was going to Mexico, ostensibly as an observer of the Pancho Villa revolution, but his famous rhetorical question—"Why should I remain in a country that is on the verge of Prohibition and Women's Suffrage?"—hints that he did not plan to return to the United States. More telling are his remarks in a letter to his niece: "If you hear of my being stood up against a Mexican stone wall and shot to rags, please know that I think that a pretty good way to depart this life. It beats old age, disease or falling down the cellar stairs. To be a Gringo in Mexico—ah, that is euthanasia!"

Another letter he wrote that summer was typical of a misanthrope saying goodbye to someone he cares for. It was addressed to his brother Albert, the only sibling he ever liked, and it was so violent and abusive that Albert was never the same after reading it. Five months later, after a debilitating bout with insomnia, Albert died of a stroke. Edmund Wilson, who was no bundle of sweetness 'n' light himself, went unerringly to the heart of the matter when he suggested that the letter "may have been Bierce's strange way of trying to diminish the grief that he knew the affectionate Albert would feel at the news of his death."

Bierce presumably died, though not necessarily by execution, in the Mexican revolution. We don't know; his trail dried up suddenly, and no one could be found who had seen the unmistakable gringo, still handsome and impressive at seventy-one. Richard O'Connor speculates that he might have made his way down through Central America and thence into the wilds of the Andes, there to live out his life as a solitary hermit on a mountaintop, chuckling gleefully at the thought of the many search parties combing Mexico for him or his bones. I would like to think that this is what happened.

Whatever happened, his object was to get away from America, which he had come to loathe for its democracy and equality, believing they foretold "the doom of authority." He advocated strong control over the masses, the churches, public meetings, telegraph, and railroads. As for anarchists who committed acts of violence, the proper punishment was "mutilation followed by death."

Living in a blunter age, he did not have to defend his turf via the genteel circuitous route of mailing a check for thirty dollars to U. S. English. "The American eagle has become a buzzard," he announced. "It is the immigration of 'the oppressed of all nations' that has made this country one of the worst on the face of the earth. . . . as always and everywhere, the oppressed are unworthy of asylum, avenging upon those who gave them sanctuary the wrongs from which they fled. The saddest thing about oppression is that it makes its victims unfit for anything but to be oppressed. . . . In the end they turn out to be fairly energetic oppressors themselves."

He looked favorably on eugenics as a way of improving the citizenry—"I think it's very strange that you people who recognize the differences in horses and dogs don't recognize the differences in the human race"—and although he claimed to hate monarchies, he gave them the nod in the area of cultural excellence: "It is the despotisms of the world that have been the conservators of civilization."

Comparing Bierce's reaction against democracy to that of the later Mark Twain, Edmund Wilson wrote: "The insistence of Ambrose Bierce on discipline, law and order, and on the need for the control of the disorderly mob by an enlightened and well-washed minority has today a familiar fascistic ring."

True enough, but the left-wing Wilson forgot to include his own side. Socialists have their own agenda for discipline and law and order, and they also believe in the control of the disorderly mob by an enlightened, though not necessarily well-washed, minority. Extremists right and left are cut out of the same piece of cloth. Both are idealists with lofty standards for human nature who often become misanthropic once the inevitable disillusionment sets in. Right wingers, concluding that mankind is despicable and hopeless, turn to the savage misanthropy of Jonathan Swift and Ambrose Bierce. Left wingers, concluding that mankind is inherently good and needs only one more chance to prove it, turn to the sentimental misanthropy of Jean-Jacques Rousseau and his naive dream of universal love and cooperation. Both are susceptible to totalitarianism, for when human nature invariably declines to be perfected, the only thing left to perfect is the State.

Writing on Ambrose Bierce in the late 1940s, Clifton Fadiman suggested that "the purity of his misanthropy" might one day "speak to us with added vehemence" in some future era of pessimism when an America hungry for leadership had come to hate those "in the saddle." Richard O'Connor echoes the same thought: "He may still be regarded in the future, if it should develop as he foresaw into an anarchic nightmare, as something more than a minor prophet, a disgruntled voice in the wilderness."

We could do a lot worse than Ambrose Bierce. H.L. Mencken accused him of being "quite unable to imagine the heroic, in any ordinary sense," but that more accurately describes Mencken himself. Bierce's credo, delivered as advice to the readers of his column, is a prescription for ordinary everyday heroism that ought to be adopted as the official oath of office in the Republic of Nice:

Be as decent as you can. Don't believe without evidence. Treat things divine with marked respect—and don't have anything to do with them. Do not trust humanity without collateral security;

it will play you some scurvy trick. Remember that it hurts no one to be treated as an enemy entitled to respect until he shall prove himself a friend worthy of affection. Cultivate a taste for distasteful truths. And, finally, most important of all, endeavor to see things as they are, not as they ought to be.

Always depend upon the kindness of misanthropes.

THE MOTHER OF
ALL ATTITUDES

What is it like being a misanthrope on a daily basis? Much depends upon the kind of people you encounter. Generally speaking, they fall into two categories: those who know what the word means and those who don't.

The former always ask the same question in properly shocked American tones.

"How can you hate *people*?"

"Who else is there to hate?"

The others are like the persistent president of a Southern women's club that wanted to take a literary tour of Europe and offered me a free trip in exchange for being their guide. I put her off politely the first two times she called, but the third time I decided to be blunt.

"I can't, I'm a misanthrope."

"Oh, honey, you don't have to let it cramp your style! My sister-in-law's a diabetic and she can go anywhere she wants as long as she takes her little kit with her."

My debut as a misanthrope occurred shortly after I learned to talk. I was being wheeled through a store in my stroller when a child-loving woman exclaimed, "What a darling little girl!" and squatted down in front of me.

"Hello, you sweet thing," she cooed.

"I doan yike you," I replied.

Thereafter I latched onto the sentence as children will, and said it to every stranger who crossed my path. My extroverted grandmother always hastened to explain, "She's just shy"—America's favorite rationalization for misanthropy and one which I was destined to hear time and time again over the years.

America's second favorite rationalization for misanthropy is, "She's been deeply hurt," often pieced out for greater adverbial effect with "somewhere, sometime, by someone." I often get this from reviewers who, as citizens of the Republic of Nice, feel guilty about liking my books. A male reviewer, after placing me "in the first rank of American wits," added: "But like Dorothy Parker, King's success might well have been purchased with the coin of personal happiness."

Female reviewers are even more determined to find hidden tragedy. Said one: "Despite the wisdom and clear, clever observations King makes, the reader can't help but wonder if this woman's acid wit is the result of a lifelong feeling of rejection cushioned by books, which, if true, is very sad."

America's third rationalization for misanthropy is, "Oh, you're just kidding." It goes like this:

"Why don't you go on the 'Today Show'?"

"I'd rather corner them in a dungeon and pull the caps off their teeth. The only thing I have in common with those people is a sofa."

"Oh, you're just kidding."

Oh, no I'm not. The person I admire above all others is the

man who died on the "Dick Cavett Show." I forget his name but it doesn't matter; to a veteran of book-promotion tours who has walked through the valley of the shadow of Happy Talk, he will go down in history as the Man Who Got Even. Having no wish to emulate him, however, I told my publisher that I am through touring books. I went to college with Willard Scott so I was already half dead in 1955, and I have no intention of letting him and his ilk finish me off now.

The American misanthrope who writes has an especially hard row to hoe. Unflagging optimism has been our chief characteristic as a people from the beginning, and our writers have been throwing up their hands in despair ever since. Herman Melville bewailed "the everlasting Yea"; H.L. Mencken spoke scathingly of "the heaven-kissing heroes of the $1.08 counter"; and James M. Cain deplored "the curse of American literature—the sympathetic character."

My own nemesis is the word *upbeat,* used constantly by an editor I once worked with. The most relentlessly cheerful person I have ever met, he seemed to take my temperament as a personal challenge. During the course of our project he enclosed a "Love Is . . ." cartoon in every letter. He also sent me a Norman Cousins roundup; a profile of Marjorie Holmes; a syndicated filler called "Heartstrings"; and a *National Enquirer* clipping about a poll that found that the most popular television shows were those on which married couples sang love songs to each other.

As things turned out, the novel I wrote for him was never published, possibly because I finally told him that if he had been the editor on *Anna Karenina,* he would have said, "Leo, please, take out the train."

The luck of misanthropy is in the chronological draw. History must contain some dawn when bliss it was to be a misanthrope, but I missed it. Instead, I landed in the Age of the Darling Little Girl.

When I was born in 1936, Shirley Temple was at the height of her fame. When I was seven there was Margaret O'Brien, and just as I entered my teens, along came Debbie Reynolds. Between O'Brien and Reynolds there was someone else as well. "Why can't you be sweet and nice like June Allyson?" Granny whispered beside me in the dark. This went on for several years, until Allyson starred as the castrating wife in *The Shrike*.

In view of the misanthrope's icy contempt for helpers and healers, I doubt if psychiatric literature contains any case histories of misanthropy per se. There exists, however, a small amount of material on an aberration connected to misanthropy. Known colloquially as "itchy feet," its clinical name is *dromomania,* from the Greek *dromos,* "to run," and I've had it for years.

Although I hate to travel, I love to move. As a child I collected road maps and gazed contentedly at them by the hour, sounding out the names of strange new places and wondering what it would be like to live in them. When I grew up I did something about it. Since graduating from college I have had some forty addresses in various parts of the country, most for a few months and none for more than three years, until moving to my present apartment, where I have lived for eight years.

The link between misanthropy and dromomania is pinpointed by Kathleen Winsor in her second novel, *Star Money:*

What a relief it was to have anything done, finished, over with for good. So you could throw it out of your life and forget it and go on to something new. Some of her happiest moments had been spent cleaning out closets or drawers, throwing things away, knowing that whatever the symbolism they had had for her, she was destroying it. Each time she finished with some-

thing or someone and knew that she had finished forever, it
gave her in some sense the illusion of having been granted a
new beginning to life. . . .

For some time now I have been planning to move to the
mountains of western Virginia. My object is to live in a place that
does not call itself "the community with a heart." I want one of
those godforsaken towns where all the young people leave and
the rest sit on the porch with a rifle across their knees.

I would have moved by now but I had to wait for the 1991
Census figures to find out which towns are losing population;
then I got involved in this book and didn't want to move in the
middle of it. Meanwhile, to make myself feel that I was doing
something to hasten the day, I cleaned out my closets and drawers with the same absorbing pleasure described by Kathleen
Winsor. (Clutter symbolizes a life filled with people so misanthropes tend to be excellent housekeepers.)

When I finished, my apartment looked like a Spartan barracks, but the mood was still on me, so I had the back seat taken
out of my car.

Ostensibly, it was to make more packing space, but subcon-
sciously I did it for the sheer thrill of shedding something else.
After the surgery, when I looked back at all that beautiful empti-
ness (I'm an agora*phil*iac), I was overcome by an irresistible
impulse to have the buddy seat taken out as well.

I reasoned that I've had only two passengers in ten years, so
I really don't need it; moreover, I'm so used to driving alone that
it makes me nervous to have someone else with me. Best of all,
a car with nothing but a driver's seat would be a bona fide
misanthrope's car. The only trouble was, other people might not
see it that way. The cops might pull me over and ask me what I
was planning to transport, and if I should move to another state

and have to take another driving test, where would the examiner sit?

I didn't do it.

By all rights, a misanthrope should be a Luddite. Being in favor of advanced technology is a progressive stance, and progressive people are full of genial beans and high hopes for mankind. But technology is also "cold," and therein lies its charm for me.

In one of my battles with local feminists in the letters column of the long-suffering *Free Lance-Star,* the president of Fredericksburg NOW latched onto an article of mine in *MS.* in which I said that I had fallen in love with my computer. Taking it literally as feminists will, she wrote: "Erich Fromm described the most disturbing and extreme form of necrophilia as a fascination for machines rather than people. Can this explain Flo?"

When will feminists learn to think before they write? The most disturbing and extreme form of necrophilia is *necrophilia.* Be that as it may, the NOW cow belled me accurately.

After vowing initially that I would never give up my typewriter; that, indeed, I would use a quill or even a stone tablet and a chisel rather than yield to "word processing," I was forced to buy a computer when a reviewing contract with *Newsday* stipulated that I had to send in my copy via modem. My new "system" was delivered on the day of the 1987 stock market crash. Computers were being blamed for the calamity so I began to think better of them, and by the end of the first week I was hooked. I realize that describing something as being "better than sex" has all the stylistic grace of a Levi's Cotton Dockers commercial, but it's true.

I now feel the same way about my new fax machine. The fax is a boon to civilization and Western culture because it helps misanthropes do what we do best: keep the epistolary art alive.

A letter is affection at a distance and a fax gets it there quicker, combining the joy of letterwriting with the speed of phoning, and leaving a record that would otherwise vanish into the sound waves. Thanks to faxing, I can savor the warmth of communication and human contact without leaving the house or talking to a soul. I can even practice my version of Southern hospitality: standing in front of the machine and watching the paper appear over the edge is like standing at the window watching for company, except I don't say "Oh, God, here they come."

Now that high tech has created the growing trend of working at home, the day of the misanthrope is fast approaching. The usual bevy of psychological counselors has sprung up to advise newly minted homeworkers on how to "answer the needs" of family members who "place demands" upon the worker's time and persist in "invading his space." Suggestions abound, including drawing little pictures of computers on the children's calendar, but the handwriting is already on the wall, right up there with the children's crayon scrawls.

Although the counselors will never admit it, the best way to handle invading family members is not to have any in the first place. In lieu of that, you must feel comfortable practicing the dying art of yelling "goddamnit!" But these solutions are *inappropriate,* so most attempts to work at home will founder on the shoals of the Republic of Nice, leaving the way open for misanthropes to corner the market.

Misanthropes have some admirable if paradoxical virtues. It is no exaggeration to say that we are among the nicest people you are likely to meet. Because good manners build sturdy walls, our distaste for intimacy makes us exceedingly cordial "ships that pass in the night." As long as you remain a stranger we will be your friend forever.

We are law-abiding to the point of punctiliousness, not because we are plaster saints, but because criminals must deal with people constantly. Most crimes require a gift of gab and an ability to inspire trust in the victim, so misanthropes do not become con artists. We do not take hostages because once you have them you can't let them out of your sight. We do not commit serial murder because we recoil in moral revulsion at the very word: *serial.* As for child molestation, in order to molest a child you must first be in the same room with a child, and I don't know how perverts stand it.

We are America's last Spartans, for next to the communality of crime is the freemasonry of illness. We ignore pain because our worst nightmare is being in a hospital and coming to the attention of volunteer strokers who serenade us with "You'll Never Walk Alone."

Misanthropes set a valuable example, or at least offer a change of pace, for youth-obsessed America: we don't like being young.

In *The Palace Guard,* Dan Rather and Gary Paul Gates write that Richard Nixon's "deep-in-the-gut loathing for the sixties" was not only political but "an integral part of his personality." Where other politicians strive for an image of eternal youth, say the authors, Nixon did the opposite:

> As a young Congressman, Nixon gave the impression of being older than he was—a man, say, in his middle to late forties. In an eerie sort of way, he has remained frozen in that bracket into his sixties, as though he had made some kind of Faustian bargain to give up the spark of youth in exchange for becoming forever forty-seven.

I think I must have sensed this about Nixon years ago. During his vice-presidency, when I was in college and everyone was saying "There's something about that man I don't like," there was something about him that I *did* like, though I couldn't put my finger on it. As time went on I realized that it was empathy. Like Nixon, I was born to be middle-aged, and now I am.

Ambrose Bierce's definition of misanthropy, "a hatred of youth and of being young," explains much about my earlier life. I no longer drink the way I used to. There hasn't been a bottle of hard liquor in the house for several years now. I didn't try to stop drinking; the craving just petered out gradually, very much the way my menstruation did, and over the same period of time.

I'll still take a drink if somebody offers me one in a social situation, but if you have read this far you know that such situations don't arise very often. Now I have an occasional beer while watching baseball, and burgundy with Italian food, and that's it. Now that my youth is gone I have no more sorrows to drown and no more conflicts to deaden. My temperament and my age are a matched set at last; I like being over the hill.

I expect old age to suit me even better because there is so much more leeway. The younger a misanthrope is, the less he—and especially she—can get away with. I long ago learned that no young woman can be an eccentric; people simply will not accept it. Oblique behavior and outlandish statements from a woman of twenty or thirty are greeted with speechless fury, but when she does and says the same things fifty years later, everyone smiles indulgently and says, "Oh, well, she's old."

My day is coming, and my model is a character in Henry Cecil's novel, *Daughters in Law*.

Miss Pringle, a misanthropic spinster and gardening author *(Weeds Are My Business)*, decides to make her Will. Knowing that she eats the unwary for breakfast, her long-suffering solicitors send her the tyro they have just hired and sit back to see what happens.

Miss Pringle begins by telling the young lawyer that she has no one to leave her money to; no relatives, and no friends either, because she's a recluse.

"It isn't that I mind people so much—they're all right so long as they don't talk. It's then I can't stand them."

She pauses a moment to let the lawyer digest this, then proceeds to dictate the strategy she has devised.

"Take this down. I leave nothing to no one. I know the grammar's bad, but it has rather a pleasant sound about it."

Explaining that this will only deliver her estate into the hands of the government, which she hates, the lawyer suggests that she leave her money to a charity.

Miss Pringle: "There oughtn't to be any charities."

Lawyer: "Some deserving person—an artist or an actor or an author who needs help to keep going?"

Miss Pringle: "What do you mean by deserving? People deserve what they get and get what they deserve. If you give an artist enough to live on he gets lazy."

The lawyer suggests the church.

Miss Pringle: "The church has gone into business."

Lawyer: Animal welfare?

Miss Pringle: "Then they'd say I was potty. Left all her money to a cats' home. I know how they talk."

The lawyer suggests sports, "such as cricket, tennis, or football."

Miss Pringle: "D'you call that sport? No one kills anything."

Lawyer: Research?

Miss Pringle: "There's too much research. People are too inquisitive."

Desperate now, the lawyer suggests nuclear weapons—meaning a peace movement, but Miss Pringle interprets it in her own way.

"For two thousand years we've been preaching peace through

love and a nice mess we've made of it. But peace through fear is better than no peace at all. And, as long as both sides have enough weapons to blow the other side's blooming heads off, they won't use them."

So Miss Pringle leaves her money in trust for the creation of bigger and better bombs.

To answer the question that I am frequently asked: No, I don't worry about "dying alone." There is, after all, no other way to die. We come into the world alone and we leave it alone, regardless of how many presumptive loved ones are clustered around our bed. Even in a suicide pact, as Crown Prince Rudolph must have realized to his dismay on that iron January dawn at Mayerling, someone must go first.

I do worry about dying alone—without the quotation marks. I live alone and intend to keep on living alone, so chances are I'll die at home and nobody will know until somebody in New York starts wondering why they haven't heard from me.

It's an unfastidious thought but if it must be, then so be it. I'd rather rot on my own floor than be found by a bunch of bingo players in a nursing home.

181

EPILOGUE:
A MISANTHROPE'S
GARDEN OF VERSES

Jonathan Odell may be America's most obscure misanthrope. Born into an old established colonial Puritan family, he began life as an army doctor and served in the King's forces in the West Indies.

And then something came over him. Today we would call it Anglophilia, but in Odell's time there was no Alistair Cooke to give it a good name by sitting down in a leather chair and crossing his legs as legs have never been crossed before. In the 1770s it was called Toryism, and Odell became its most implacable purveyor.

He gave up medicine and went to London to study for the Anglican priesthood. After his ordination he returned to the American colonies and set about the daunting task of persuading New England Congregationalists to take the wine. They didn't, but a group of British officers did. They took quite a bit of it on June 4, 1776, during a rousing celebration of the King's birthday hosted by Odell and highlighted by the singing of a song he wrote in honor of George III.

Wakened by the drunken roars pouring out of the rectory in the middle of the night, the local patriots listened to the lyrics and decided that Odell had to go. Escaping one step ahead of the lynch mob, he took refuge behind British lines, serving as a courier in the Benedict Arnold affair and turning out Tory poetry in his spare time.

Odell's writings consist of four satires in verse written between 1779 and 1780. In the preface to one of them he signals the reader what to expect by decreeing that "Ridicule may lawfully be employed in the Service of Virtue." The time had come to do so, he went on, because he had tried everything else he could think of to convince the erring rebels of their duty to their King. He, along with a few other enlightened thinkers, had *explained* why revolution was wrong, but nobody would *listen,* so what else could he *do* but write nasty poetry? "Reason has done her part, and therefore this is the legitimate moment for Satire."

The satire did not come off because the tightly wound Odell had worked himself into such a snit that by the time he took up his pen, he had lost what little sense of humor he might once have possessed.

Worse, he took himself seriously. "There is a note of finality in his judgments that amazes, an infallibility that amuses," writes Vernon L. Parrington. "The Reverend Jonathan frankly acknowledges himself to be the boon companion of Reason, the favored suitor of Truth—from them only has he taken instruction and in their name he professes to speak."

Odell's preferred method of unifying political opinion was to hang everybody who disagreed with him:

> At length the day of Vengeance is at hand:
> The exterminating Angel takes his stand:
> Hear the last summons, rebels, and relent:
> Yet but a moment is there to repent.

He kept an enemies list that sounds sublimely impartial, but only because he hated Federalists and republicans with equal venom. Washington, Adams, Jefferson, Morris, Paine, and just about everybody else in the American pantheon was plunged into a bath of sulphurous ink:

> Ask I too much? then grant me for a time
> Some deleterious pow'rs of acrid rhyme:
> Some ars'nic verse, to poison with the pen
> These rats, who nestle in the lion's den!

He went on espousing his loyalist views right up to the surrender of Cornwallis. At last, when independence was a fait accompli, he went into voluntary exile in Nova Scotia, where he lived long and sullenly on a pension from the Crown. The slight renown he enjoys today comes mainly from a nickname bestowed on him by a leading authority on the literature of the American Revolution, Moses Coit Tyler, who called him "Toryissimus."

Jonathan Odell is an example of how easily misanthropy can lead to treason. He swam against the tide because he hated the tide, whatever it happened to be. It's a good bet that if he had been a Northerner during the Civil War he would have been a Copperhead, and if he had been a Southerner he would have been a Scallawag, because even his different drummer heard a different drummer.

Mad, bad, and dangerous to know was our Jonathan, yet I can't help feeling that at last I have found Mr. Right. I can see

the two of us tucked up together in Nova Scotia, a bundling
board between us, watching Alistair Cooke cross his legs and
working on our garden of verses.

*   *   *

"Anonymous" was a woman,
The Libbers all insist.
She never had a by-line,
For she didn't dare exist.

She scribbled Christian verses,
Penned domestic lucubrations,
Stuffed maxims in her cookbook
To express her aggravations.

She ended up in *Bartlett's*
A queen without a throne,
Where everything she ever wrote
Was classified "Unknown."

But then there came a forum
Where she could sign her spleen,
In letters to the editor
Of *MS.*-fits magazine.

She wrote about her vulva
And the joys of getting head,
And described the hell of marriage
When a husband farts in bed.

She sang of masturbation,
Told the Pope to take a hike,

Then listed her abortions
And announced she was a dyke.

But when it came to signatures
Her courage was dispelled,
So the *Bartlett's* of the future
Will call her "Name Withheld."

       *   *   *

Watching Richard Simmons
As he flaps his little hands,
And kicks his hairless legs up high
And sings along with bands,
A fervent picture leaps to mind
And wishful thought enfolds me
As I visualize him sweatin' to
A quintessential oldie.
It's awfully hard to rhyme it—
After all, I'm not a Horace—
But I'd love to see him buggered
By a Rex Tyrannosaurus.

       *   *   *

A famous politician
Approached the mike one day
To face up to his demons
And lay frailties away.

"I need help," he stated bravely,
"I'm bottomed out, done in,
And now I've come to tell you
That the healing must begin."

WITH CHARITY TOWARD NONE

"The long denial ends today,
I confess to you I'm sick.
The agony is over
But recovery's never quick."

"Out of control for many years,
I let myself get slack,
But now I need your helping hand
As I start the long road back."

The hall was stunned and silent,
You could hear a fallen pin
As every word he uttered
Seemed to touch our hearts within.

We wept with deep emotion,
For we knew he'd hit a skid,
Yet we couldn't help but wonder
Just what it was he did.

We didn't know his substance,
We didn't know his sin,
We didn't even know for sure
What Center he was in.

He never actually named it,
Of light he shed no beam,
But no one dared to question
A search for self-esteem.

He was working through his problems,
Being counseled for abuse,
And anyone who doubted it
Was hopelessly obtuse.

FLORENCE KING

He was dancing to the 12-step,
That was fundamental,
And anyone who looked askance
Was nothing but judgmental.

We told ourselves with great relief
That nothing mattered but belief.
We offered him our hopes and tears
And prayed that he was with his peers:

"Ask Betty Ford to kiss him, Lord,
Ask Liz to make him well,
Let Skitty Kitty Detoxis
Share with him her hell."

At some point in his absence
Came a startling discovery:
We had scrapped the national anthem
To sing "We're In Recovery."

He came back home to cheering throngs
Whose deepest needs he met
When he said, "I offer nothing
But blood tests, spoils, and sweat."

He wept on Sally Jessy,
And Oprah hugged his pain
When he said he had a habit
Of snorting up cocaine.

He slapped a high five with Sonya Live,
And confessed he had really botched it,
He said a prayer on MacNeil and Lehrer
And for once somebody watched it.

"Larry, I'm no human being,"
"Phil, I'm beyond the pale,
"I've nowhere to go and I've sunk so low
That I might as well be a white male."

The U.S. Constitution
Has no anchor, just a sail,
So it wasn't any wonder
That he hit the campaign trail.

He got elected as expected
And what do you suppose?
Everyone knew but none would say
"The President has no nose."

* * *

A Nineties man sat drinking
And tried to do some thinking
But the woman on the barstool hurled her flak.
She talked of her agenda
And the needs of her pudenda
And why she wouldn't ride the Mommy Track.
She said, "Now, you see here, if I gave up my career
I would be a little nothing on the shelf.
I would suffocate and smother being just a wife and
    mother,
I need options and a lifestyle for myself."
Her husband turned around
To escape the steady sound
But her manifesto carried to great lengths.
She talked of her profession
And the value of aggression

And why she wouldn't give up female strengths.
He said, "This chick is sick," then he heard a little *click!*
Now he knew exactly what was wrong.
He kicked her in the tushie and she fell into the sushi,
Then he stood up on the bar and sang a song:

"I want a girl just like the girl
That majored in Home Ec.
She loved to cook, never read a book
Nor even wrote a check.
With her I wouldn't need paternal leave,
She had no career ambitions up her sleeve,
That's why I want a girl just like the girl
That majored in Home Ec."

* * *

One night while watching "Crossfire"
In the privacy of home,
I fell asleep and woke up in
A show called "Twilight Zone."

The Lib Flit started leaking
From a ceiling vent o'erspread,
And in a flash it melted down
That tiny little head.

Next the scrawny chicken neck,
And then the bony chest
Had vanished in an acid bath
As quickly as the rest.

The end was not long coming,
Though it was a little crass.

WITH CHARITY TOWARD NONE

A fer-de-lance slid through the stage
And bit him in the ass.

The long snide night was over,
He would pass this way no more.
Obnoxious Michael Kinsley
Was a grease spot on the floor.

BIBLIOGRAPHY

When I got the first tenuous idea for this book more than a decade ago, I began to gear my private reading along lines likely to result in a steadily increasing knowledge of misanthropy without actually Doing Research, which I hate: going to college once is one time too many, in my opinion.

I also tried to influence my reviewing assignments in the same way, which produced a memorable office exchange that I overheard while waiting on the phone.

"Florence is interested in misanthropes."

"So what else is new?"

Several of my book editors came through, bless them. In fact, I had them so well-trained that one called up and simply said, "I've got one here about a real shit so I thought of you." (Never let the intellectuals bamboozle you into thinking that the field of literary criticism is any more of an Arcadian glade than life's other fields.)

I proceeded in my own fashion, writing down everything that appealed to me in my quotations notebook, which is always at my side whenever I read; scribbling my original ideas on pieces of scratch paper and tossing them in a file marked *Misan;* and reading and clipping both Washington papers and my own local paper every day.

The following list is not complete by any means. I have read hundreds of books over the last ten years, and bits and pieces of hundreds more, but these are the ones I read or reread in the last year or so while outlining and writing *With Charity Toward None.* I have starred those I particularly enjoyed and recommend for general reading.

Adams, Henry *The Letters of Henry Adams, 1858–1891*
Adams, Henry *The Education of Henry Adams*
Alexander, Charles C. *Ty Cobb*
Ames, Fisher *Works of Fisher Ames.* W. B. Allen, ed.
*Babbitt, Irving *Democracy and Leadership*
*Babbitt, Irving *Rousseau and Romanticism*
*Bergreen, Laurence *As Thousands Cheer: The Life of Irving Berlin*
Boswell, James *Boswell on the Grand Tour: Germany and Switzerland, 1764.* Frederick A. Pottle, ed.
*Branden, Barbara *The Passion of Ayn Rand*
*Cecil, Henry. *Daughters in Law*
Cerf, Barry *Anatole France: The Degeneration of a Great Writer*
Cooper, James Fenimore *The American Democrat*
Drabble, Margaret, ed. *Oxford Companion to English Literature*
Durant, Will *Rousseau and Revolution*
Durant, Will *The Age of Voltaire*
Elder, Donald *Ring Lardner*
Fecher, Charles A., ed. *The Diary of H.L. Mencken*
Geismar, Maxwell *Writers in Crisis*
Gerber, John C. *Mark Twain*
*Kirk Russell, ed. *The Portable Conservative Reader*
Lardner, Ring *Gullible's Travels, Etc.*
*Leider, Emily Wortis *California's Daughter: Gertrude Atherton and Her Times*
*Liddy, G. Gordon *Will*
*Loomis, Stanley *Paris in the Terror*
*Loomis, Stanley *Du Barry*
McCallum, John *The Tiger Wore Spikes*

McCarthy, Patrick *Céline*
Molière *Le Misanthrope.* Richard Wilbur translation.
Nixon, Richard M. *Six Crises*
O'Connell, David *Louis-Ferdinand Céline*
*O'Connor, Richard *Ambrose Bierce: A Biography*
*O'Toole, Patricia *The Five of Hearts: An Intimate Portrait of Henry Adams and His Friends, 1880–1918*
Parrington, Vernon L. *Main Currents in American Thought*
Patrick, Walton R. *Ring Lardner*
Pobedonostsev, Konstantin *Reflections of a Russian Statesman.* Foreword by Murray Polner
Rostand, Edmond *Cyrano de Bergerac.* Brian Hooker translation
*Schama, Simon *Citizens*
Starkie, Enid. *Flaubert: The Making of the Master*
Steegmuller, Francis. *Flaubert and Madame Bovary*
Twain, Mark *Letters From the Earth.* Bernard DeVoto, ed.
Twain, Mark "The Man Who Corrupted Hadleysburg"
Untermeyer, Louis *Makers of the Modern World*
Vicinus, Martha and Nergaard, Bea, eds. *Ever Yours, Florence Nightingale: Selected Letters.*

KERRELYN SPARKS

THE
UNDEAD
NEXT DOOR

AVON
An Imprint of HarperCollinsPublishers

This is a work of fiction. Names, characters, places, and incidents are products of the author's imagination or are used fictitiously and are not to be construed as real. Any resemblance to actual events, locales, organizations, or persons, living or dead, is entirely coincidental.

AVON BOOKS
An Imprint of HarperCollins*Publishers*
10 East 53rd Street
New York, New York 10022-5299

Copyright © 2008 by Kerrelyn Sparks
ISBN: 978-0-06-111845-6
www.avonromance.com

First Avon Books paperback printing: February 2008

Avon Trademark Reg. U.S. Pat. Off. and in Other Countries, Marca Registrada, Hecho en U.S.A.
HarperCollins® is a registered trademark of HarperCollins Publishers.

Printed in the U.S.A.

10 9 8 7 6 5 4 3 2 1

With gratitude to my editor,
Erika Tsang,
for her patience and expert guidance.
The Undead have been very kind to us.

Acknowledgments

Another book completed, and I remain reasonably sane! My thanks to all those who have stood by me with love and support: my husband and children, my parents, and my writing buddies—Vicky, MJ, Sandy, and Vicky. My thanks also to fellow writers of PASIC and the Houston chapters of RWA. And finally, my gratitude to those of you who read my books. Your letters and e-mails are treasures that I hoard for the rainy days. Bless you! May you become heroes and heroines in real life!

THE
UNDEAD
NEXT DOOR

Chapter 1

Heather Lynn Westfield was in hog heaven. Who would have believed that a famous fashion designer from Paris would open a fancy store smack dab in the middle of Texas Hill Country? Whatever Jean-Luc Echarpe had been drinking when he'd made that decision, it had to be strong enough to knock your socks off. In his case, two-hundred-dollar silk socks embroidered with his famous fleur-de-lis logo.

Heather wanted to buy some kind of souvenir to commemorate the grand opening of Le Chique Echarpe, but the socks were the cheapest thing she could find. Hmm, should she buy a pair of socks she didn't need or make next month's payment on her Chevy four by four? With a snort, she tossed the socks back onto the glass shelf.

A brilliant alternative popped into her head. She'd grab one of the free hors d'oeuvres, stuff it in a plastic bag, label it *Echarpe's Grand Opening*, and hoard it in the freezer for all eternity.

"Heather, why are you looking at men's socks?" Sasha's baffled look shifted into a sly grin. "Oh, I know. You're buying something for a new lover."

Heather laughed as she nabbed a crab cake from a passing waiter. "I wish." She'd never had a lover. Even her ex-husband didn't qualify for that. She wrapped the crab cake in a paper napkin, then slipped it into her small black purse.

Female customers strutted about, wearing gowns that cost enough to rebuild New Orleans, their stilettos clicking on the gray marble floor. Heather hoped they couldn't tell that her black cocktail dress was homemade.

Glass counters displayed purses and scarves, designed by Echarpe. An elegant staircase curved up to the second floor. A portion of the second floor was lined with reflective glass. One-way mirrors, Heather figured. As much as this merchandise cost, there was probably an army of security guards up there watching the customers like hawks.

The walls on the ground floor were painted a soft gray and boasted a series of black-and-white photos. She wandered over for a closer look. Wow, Princess Di wearing an Echarpe gown. Marilyn Monroe in an Echarpe dress. Cary Grant in an Echarpe tuxedo. This guy knew everybody.

"How old is Echarpe?" she asked Sasha. "In his seventies?"

"I don't know. I've never met him." Sasha pivoted like she was working the runway while she looked around to see who was watching her.

"You never met him? But you were in his show in Paris just a few weeks ago." Heather and her longtime friend Sasha had both dreamed of glorious careers in the world of high fashion from the moment they'd discovered their Barbie dolls had cooler clothes than anyone else in the small town of Schnitzelberg, Texas.

Heather was now a schoolteacher, while Sasha had become a successful fashion model. Heather waffled between being enormously proud of her friend and being reluctantly envious.

Sasha snorted through her surgically shortened nose. "No one sees Echarpe anymore. It's like he disappeared off the planet. Some say he's suffered the cost of his own genius and lost his mind."

Heather winced. "How sad."

"He stopped coordinating his own shows. And he certainly wouldn't be bothered with a shop like this in the middle of nowhere. He has little people for that." Sasha pointed at a slim man across the room and whispered, "That's Alberto Alberghini, Echarpe's personal assistant, though I have to wonder just how *personal* he is."

Heather eyed the man's frilly lavender shirt. The lapels on his black tuxedo were encrusted with lavender beads and sequins. "I see what you mean."

Sasha leaned closer. "Do you see the two women by the old man with a cane?"

"Yes." Heather noted the two emaciated women with pale flawless skin and long hair.

"They're Simone and Inga, famous models from Paris. Some say Echarpe's involved with them. *Both* of them."

"I see." Maybe Echarpe was more like Hugh Hefner than Liberace. Heather eyed the two models. She probably weighed as much as their combined weight. *Nonsense.* Size twelve was normal. She turned to admire a daring red gown on a white mannequin.

"The media can't decide whether Echarpe is gay or into multiple partners," Sasha whispered.

The gown had to be size two. "I could never get into that."

"Threesomes? I didn't care for it much, either."

Heather blinked. "Excuse me?"

"Though I'd probably like it better if it was me and two guys. Better to be the central focus, don't you think?"

"Excuse me?"

"But with my luck, the guys would be more interested in each other." Sasha lifted her hand and studied it. "I'm thinking about adding some collagen to my hand. My knuckles are so bony."

Heather took a moment to assimilate. Sheesh, she and Sasha didn't have a lot in common anymore. Their lives had certainly gone in different directions since high school. "Maybe instead of cosmetic surgery, you could try something really radical. Like eating food."

Sasha tittered with laughter. Men in the room turned to stare at her, and she rewarded them by flipping her long blond hair over her shoulders. "You're such a hoot, Heather. But I do eat food. I swear I have no control whatsoever. I've eaten two mushrooms tonight."

"You should be flogged."

"I know. Let me show you the new gown I'll be wearing soon." Sasha led her over to a gray mannequin posed on top of a glossy black cube. The mannequin wore a stunning white gown with no back and a front neckline that plummeted to the navel.

Heather's eyes widened. Never in a hundred years would she have the nerve to wear such a dress. Never in a hundred years would anyone want to see her in it, either. "Wow."

"It's very clingy fabric," Sasha explained, "so I can't wear a stitch underneath. I'll be incredibly sexy."

"Right."

"I might wear it at the charity show in two weeks."

"I heard about that." The proceeds were going to the local school district, Heather's employer. "It was very nice of Echarpe to do that."

Sasha waved her bony hand in the air. "Oh, he

doesn't have anything to do with it. Alberto's arranging it. Anyway, I'm thrilled to be in the show."

"Congratulations. I hope I get to see it."

"I'm only on the runway once." Sasha stuck out her collagen-enhanced lower lip. "It's not fair. Simone and Inga get two walks down the runway."

"Oh, I'm sorry."

"I've been trying not to worry about it 'cause it would just give me lines. But I swear, who do you have to sleep with around here to get some respect?"

Heather winced. "Why don't you just talk to Alberto?"

"Oh. That's a good idea." She waved at the young man.

"Sasha, darling, you look fabulous." Alberto rushed over and kissed her on both cheeks.

"This is my dear friend from high school, Heather Lynn Westfield." Sasha motioned to her.

"How do you do?" Heather smiled and extended a hand.

Alberto leaned over to kiss her hand. "Charmed." His eyes widened when he noticed her dress.

Shoot, she felt like a hillbilly. Heather opened her mouth to speak, but Sasha beat her to it.

"Alberto, darling, could we go somewhere private?" Sasha curled her hands around his arm and gave him a smoky look from under her false eyelashes. "I'd like to . . . talk."

Alberto's gaze was riveted on Sasha's low neckline. "I have an office nearby. We could . . . talk there."

"That would be lovely." Sasha leaned closer so her breasts were pressed against his arm. "I'm feeling very . . . talkative."

Heather watched, fascinated. It was like being in a live soap opera. Was Sasha offended that Alberto was conversing with her breasts? Were her breasts real?

Would she slap him into next week or go to his office with him? And what about Alberto? Was he gay or metrosexual? Would they actually *talk*?

Alberto escorted Sasha across the store. Heather sighed. The show was over. She was always the observer, never the action figure.

Sasha glanced back and mouthed the word *bingo*.

Heather nodded with a sudden feeling of déjà vu. It was high school all over again. Sexy Sasha was making out in the classroom while Helpful Heather waited by the lockers and served as lookout. Would it always be this way? Why couldn't she be the daring one for once? Why couldn't she wear one of these sexy, revealing gowns?

Well, she couldn't afford it, for one thing. And she was too overweight. She circled the gown Sasha had talked about. So what if she couldn't wear it or buy it? She could make something similar to it. And she could probably do it for about fifty bucks.

White had never been a good color for her. She was too fair and freckly. No, she would do it in midnight-blue. Instead of cutting the neckline to the navel, she'd back it up to the top of her breasts. And she'd put a back on the dress. And sleeves. The ideas were coming faster than she could think them through. She opened her purse and found a pencil and pad of paper that the folks at Schnitzelberg Hardware had given her at their last gardening sale.

Jean-Luc Echarpe could take his multithousand-dollar price tags and toss them off the Eiffel Tower. She might be one of *Les Miserables*, but she didn't have to look like it.

"To Jean-Luc and the opening of his fifth store in America." Roman Draganesti lifted a champagne flute filled with Bubbly Blood.

"To Jean-Luc," the others toasted, and clinked their glasses together.

Jean-Luc took a sip, then set his glass aside. The mixture of synthetic blood and champagne did little to boost his spirits. "Thank you for coming, *mes amis*. It makes this exile easier to bear."

"Don't think of it that way, bro." Gregori patted him on the back. "This is a great business opportunity."

Jean-Luc gave Roman's vice president of marketing an annoyed look. "This is an exile."

"No, no, it's called expanding your market. There are a lot of people here in Texas, and we can safely assume they all wear clothes. Or most of them. I heard about this lake near Austin where—"

"Why Texas?" Roman interrupted. "Shanna and I were hoping you would stay in New York, close to us."

Jean-Luc sighed. Paris was the center of the universe, as far as he was concerned, and any place would be dreary in comparison. But New York City would have been his second choice. "I wish I could, *mon ami*, but the media in New York knows me too well. The same in Los Angeles."

"Aye," Angus MacKay agreed. "Neither of those places would work. Jean-Luc has to—"

"I swear, Angus," Jean-Luc interrupted him. "If you say I told you so, I'll ram one of your claymores down your throat."

Angus simply arched an eyebrow that dared him to try it. "I did warn ye to leave ten years ago. And again five years ago."

"I was busy building my business," Jean-Luc protested. He'd started off in 1922, designing evening wear just for vampires, but in 1933, he'd expanded his business to include the Hollywood elite. After realizing how much mortals liked his designs, he made his big move in 1975. He started creating all sorts of clothes and marketing them to the general public. Soon, he had become a celebrity in the mortal world. The last thirty years had sped by in a whirlwind of success. When you were a vampire more than five hundred years old, the years passed by in the blink of an eye.

Angus MacKay had warned him. Angus had started his investigation and security business in 1927 and was now posing as the grandson of the original founder.

Jean-Luc picked up a copy of *Le Monde* from his desk. "Have you seen the latest?"

"Let me see." Robby MacKay grabbed the Parisian newspaper and scanned the article. A descendant of Angus, Robby worked for Angus's security company. For the last ten years, Robby had been in charge of security for Jean-Luc.

"What does it say?" Gregori peeked over Robby's shoulder.

Robby frowned as he translated. "Everyone in Paris is wondering why Jean-Luc hasna aged in over thirty years. Some say he's had cosmetic surgery half a dozen times, and others say he's found the fountain of youth. He's run away, but no one knows where. Some believe he's hiding in a mental institution, recovering from a nervous breakdown, while others say he's undergoing yet another facelift."

Jean-Luc groaned as he collapsed in the chair behind his desk.

"I warned ye this would happen." Angus dodged to the right when Jean-Luc threw a ruler at him.

Roman chuckled. "Don't worry about it, Jean-Luc. Mortals have very short attention spans. If you stay hidden for a while, they'll forget about you."

"And forget to buy my merchandise," Jean-Luc grumbled. "I am ruined."

"Ye're no' ruined," Angus argued. "Ye now have five stores in America."

"Stores selling clothes from a designer who has disappeared," Jean-Luc growled. "It's easy for you, Angus. Your company exists in secrecy. But when I vanish, all interest in my clothing line may vanish along with me."

"We could make a statement to the press that ye did have cosmetic surgery," Robby offered. "It might put an end to the speculation."

"*Non*." Jean-Luc glared at him.

Gregori grinned. "Or we could tell them you're locked up in a psycho ward, completely loony. Everyone would believe that."

Jean-Luc arched a brow at him. "Or I could tell them I'm in prison for murdering an obnoxious marketing vice president."

"I vote for that one," Angus said.

"Hey." Gregori adjusted his tie. "I was just joking."

"I wasn't," Jean-Luc muttered.

Angus laughed. "Whatever ye do, Jean-Luc, doona let anyone take a photo of you. Ye must remain hidden for at least twenty-five years. Then ye can return to Paris, posing as yer son."

Jean-Luc lounged back in his chair, staring mournfully at the ceiling. "Exiled to a land of barbarians for twenty-five years. Just kill me now."

Roman chuckled. "Texas is not a land of barbarians."

Jean-Luc shook his head. "I've seen the movies. Gunfights, Indians, someplace they keep fighting for called the Alamo."

Gregori snorted. "Dude, you are so behind the times."

"You think so? Have you seen the people down there?" Jean-Luc rose to his feet and strode to his office window that overlooked the store on the ground floor. "The men are wearing strings around their necks."

"Those are ties." Gregori gazed through the one-way window. "Sheesh, you're definitely in Texas. There's a guy wearing a tuxedo jacket with blue jeans. And boots."

"They must be barbarians. They're wearing their hats indoors." Jean-Luc frowned. "They remind me of the bicorne Napoleon used to wear, but they're wearing them sideways."

"Those are cowboy hats, bro. But what do you care? Look, they're spending money. Lots of money."

Jean-Luc leaned his forehead against the cool glass. After the charity show in two weeks, Simone, Inga, and Alberto would return to Paris. Then Jean-Luc would close the store under the pretense that it had failed miserably. His other Le Chique Echarpe stores in Paris, New York, South Beach, Chicago, and Hollywood would hopefully flourish, but this building in Texas would be empty and forgotten. From here, he would continue to design clothes and oversee the business, but he could never show his face in public for twenty-five long years. "Just kill me now."

"Nay," Angus said. "Ye're the best swordsman we have, and Casimir is still in hiding while he grows his evil army."

"Right." Jean-Luc gave his old friend a wry look. "Such a waste for me to die here when I could do it so well in battle."

Angus' mouth twitched. "Aye, exactly."

The buzzer on the office door sounded.

"'Tis yer wife, Angus," Robby announced as he opened the door.

Angus turned to greet his wife with a smile.

Zut. Jean-Luc looked away. First Roman, and now Angus. Both married and madly in love. It was embarrassing. Two of the most powerful coven masters in the vampire world reduced to doting husbands. Jean-Luc wanted to pity them, but the sad truth was, he was jealous. Damned jealous. That sort of happiness could never happen to him.

"Hi, guys!" Emma MacKay strode into the room and straight into her husband's arms. "Guess what? I bought the cutest little handbag. Alberto's wrapping it up for me."

"Another handbag?" Angus asked. "Ye doona have a dozen already?"

Jean-Luc peered through the window and noted which purse Alberto was wrapping. "Good news, Angus. It's one of my lower-priced handbags."

"Och, good." Angus hugged his wife.

Jean-Luc smiled. "*Oui*, it's only eight hundred dollars."

Angus stepped back, his eyes wide with shock. "Forget the bloody army. I'll skewer ye now."

Roman laughed. "You can afford it, Angus."

"So can you." Jean-Luc smirked at his old friend. "Have you seen what your wife is buying?"

Roman hurried to the window and looked for his wife in the store below. "God's blood," he whispered.

Shanna Draganesti was carrying their seventeen-month-old boy on her hip while she filled his stroller with clothes, shoes, and purses.

"She has good taste," Jean-Luc observed. "You should be proud."

"I'll be broke." Roman watched forlornly as the pile in the stroller grew steadily higher.

Jean-Luc surveyed the showroom. As much as he grumbled about his self-imposed exile, he was pleased with the prison he'd designed for himself. It was nestled among the hills of central Texas. The nearest town was Schnitzelberg, founded by German immigrants a hundred and fifty years earlier. It was a sleepy, forgotten place with Spanish oaks dripping moss and white Queen Anne homes with lace curtains.

All his stores in America boasted a similar design, but this one in Texas was different, for it included a large underground lair where Jean-Luc would hide during his exile. It was imperative to keep this lair a secret, so Jean-Luc's mortal assistant, Alberto, had reached an agreement with the contractor who'd built it. The contractor was on the local school board, so Jean-Luc agreed to make a hefty contribution to the school district through the upcoming charity fashion show. As long as Jean-Luc was generous with the town of Schnitzelberg, they would keep quiet about the bankrupt store that a foreigner owned on the outskirts of town.

And just to be safe, Robby had teleported into the contractor's office and removed all the blueprints and work orders related to this site. After the charity show, Robby and Jean-Luc would erase a few memories, and no one would remember there was a huge cellar beneath the abandoned store. Pierre, a mortal who worked for MacKay Security and Investigation, would guard the building during the day while Jean-Luc lay in his death-sleep.

He watched the party below. Simone and Inga were flirting with a white-haired old man, hunched over a cane. He had to be rich, or they wouldn't waste their time.

Jean-Luc's gaze wandered about the store. He'd always enjoyed people watching. The thought of this building being empty for the next twenty-five years was damned depressing. Ah well, he was accustomed to loneliness.

He spotted the new model Alberto had hired for his last show in Paris. Sasha Saladine. She was talking to someone standing behind a mannequin. Alberto approached, and Sasha introduced her companion. Alberto accepted a gracefully extended hand and kissed it. A female. And possessing an arm that wasn't pencil thin. She wasn't a model. A customer, then. Most likely mortal.

Alberto and Sasha wandered off together, leaving the showroom. What was that about? Jean-Luc forgot to speculate when his gaze drifted back to the customer and stuck. She was moving into view, and what a view. She had curves. And breasts. A derriere a man could grab on to. And mounds of curly auburn hair that fluffed around her shoulders. She reminded him of lusty tavern wenches from medieval pubs who laughed heartily and made love with wild abandon. *Mon Dieu*, how he had adored those women.

She was like the old movie stars he had loved to design clothes for. Marilyn Monroe, Ava Gardner. His intellect might design clothes for a size zero, but the rest of him yearned for a lusty, full-figured woman. And here was a beautiful one right in front of him. Her black dress clung to a luscious hourglass figure. And yet the most important feature, her face, remained hidden. He moved to the left and peered closely through the glass.

He caught a glimpse of a pert nose, slightly tilted up at the tip. Not a classical nose like all his models possessed, but he liked it. It was natural and . . . cute. *Cute?* Not a word that could ever apply to his models. They all aspired to perfection, even by artificial means, but the end result was they all looked alike. And in their quest for perfection, they lost something. They lost a sense of personality and unique sparkle.

The woman in question pushed her thick, curly hair behind her ear. She had high, wide cheekbones and a sweet curve to her jaw. Her eyes were wide and intent as she focused on the white gown. What color were her eyes? he wondered. With her rich auburn hair, he hoped they were green. Her lips were wide, yet delicately shaped. No collagen there. She was a natural beauty. An angel.

She retrieved some items from her purse—a small writing pad and a pen. No, a pencil. She was writing something. No, sketching. His mouth dropped open. *Zut!* She was drawing his new gown, stealing his design.

His eyes narrowed. What nerve she had to blatantly copy his gown right in front of everyone. Who the hell was she? Had she come from New York with Sasha Saladine? She probably worked for one of the other major fashion houses. They would love to have copies of his latest designs.

"*Merde.*" He grabbed his tuxedo jacket off the back of his desk chair.

"Where are ye going?" Robby asked, ever vigilant.

"Downstairs." Jean-Luc shrugged on his jacket.

"To the showroom?" Angus frowned. "Nay. Someone might recognize you. Ye shouldna risk it."

"They're local people," Jean-Luc explained. "They won't know who I am."

"Ye canna be certain of that." Robby moved toward the door. "If ye want something from the store, I'll bring it to you."

"It's not a thing. It's a person." Jean-Luc motioned to the window. "There's a spy down there, stealing my designs."

"You're kidding." Emma ran to the window to look. "Where is he?"

"She." Jean-Luc glanced out the window. "By the white—no. *Zut*, she's moved to the red gown."

"Let us deal with her." Angus joined Robby at the door.

"No." Jean-Luc strode toward the exit and stopped in front of the two Scotsmen blocking his way. "Move. I need to find out who's paying her to spy on me."

With a stubborn lift to his chin, Angus folded his arms and refused to budge.

Jean-Luc arched a brow at his old friend. "Your company works for me, Angus."

"Aye, we're paid to protect you, but we canna do it if ye behave foolishly."

"And I'm telling you these local people don't know who I am. Alberto always acted as my go-between. Let me pass before that damned spy leaves with my designs."

Angus sighed. "Verra well, but Robby will go with you." He whispered instructions to his great-great-grandson, "Doona let anyone take his photo. And watch his back. He has enemies."

Jean-Luc snorted as he left his office. With a few strides, he reached the back staircase. Did Angus think he was a weakling? He knew how to protect himself. Sure, he was on Casimir's hit list, but they all were. And Jean-Luc had other enemies as well. A man couldn't live more than five hundred years without making a few vampires angry. But now he'd acquired a new foe. A thief with the face of an angel.

He reached the bottom of the stairs and headed down the side hallway for the showroom. Robby's steps thundered down the stairs behind him.

As Jean-Luc entered the store, heads turned in his direction, then turned away. Good. No one recognized him. The scent of different blood types wafted past him, a sweetly appetizing human buffet. Socializing with mortals had presented a problem for his self-control until Roman had invented synthetic blood back in 1987. Now Jean-Luc and all his Vamp friends made sure they were full before venturing among mortals.

He noticed Robby edging around the perimeter of the room, looking for photographers. Or assassins. Jean-Luc stepped around the old man with a cane and proceeded to the female thief. He stopped a few inches behind her. She was tall, the top of her head reaching his chin. The scent of her blood was fresh and sweet. She was mortal.

"Begging your pardon, mademoiselle."

She turned. Her eyes *were* green. *Zut.* Her beautiful eyes widened as she looked at him.

There was nothing sadder than a fallen angel.

He frowned at her. "Give me one good reason why I should not have you arrested."

Chapter 2

Heather blinked. "Excuse me?" The gorgeous man's French accent took some time to adjust to, but she could have sworn he'd threatened to arrest her. She smiled brightly and extended a hand. "How do you do? I'm Heather Lynn Westfield."

"Heather?" His odd pronunciation sent a tingle down her spine. It sounded like *Eh-zair*, soft and sweet like an endearment. He took her hand and encased it in both of his.

"Yes?" She continued to smile and prayed that none of the feta cheese spinach puff was lodged in her teeth. He studied her with his beautiful blue eyes. And his face—that chiseled jaw and mouth belonged on a Greek statue.

His grip tightened around her hand. "Tell me the truth. Who sent you here?"

"Excuse me?" She tried to retrieve her hand, but he held on tight. Too tight. A shiver of alarm crept up her neck.

His blue eyes narrowed. "I saw what you did."

Oh God, he knew about the crab cake. He must be some kind of security guard. "I—I'll pay for it."

"It is twenty thousand dollars."

"For a *crab cake*?" She ripped her hand from his grasp. "This place is outrageous." With a huff, she pulled the napkin from her purse. "Here. Take your silly crab cake. I don't want it anymore."

He stared at the napkin-wrapped crab cake in his hand. "You are a spy *and* a thief?"

"I'm not a spy." She winced. Had she just admitted to being a thief?

He frowned at her. "There is no need to steal food. It is free. If you are hungry, you should eat."

"It was a souvenir, okay? I'm not really hungry. Do I look like I've missed any meals?"

His gaze wandered over her slowly with an intensity that made her heart race. Well, what was good for the goose . . . She checked him out, too. Were the black curls on his head as soft as they looked? Did he have trouble with his hair tangling? Shoot, as long as his eyelashes were, they probably tangled, too.

She cleared her throat. "I doubt you arrest people for taking crab cakes. So I'll just be going now."

His eyes met hers. "I'm not done with you."

"Oh." Maybe he'd drag her away and ravish her. No, that only happened in books. "What did you have in mind?"

"You will answer my questions." He motioned to a waiter and dropped her balled-up napkin on the tray. "Now, tell me the truth. Who is your employer?"

"SISD."

"Is that a government agency?"

"It's the Schnitzelberg Independent School District."

He tilted his head with a confused look. "You are not a designer?"

"I wish. Now if you'll excuse me—" She pivoted to leave.

"*Non.*" He took hold of her arm. "I saw you copying the white gown. It is twenty thousand dollars. Since you are so interested in it, you should buy it."

She snorted. "I wouldn't be caught dead in that gown."

"*What?*" His eyebrows shot up. "There's nothing wrong with that design."

"Are you kidding?" She pulled away from his grasp. "What was Echarpe thinking? The neckline plunges past the navel. The skirt slits up to North Dakota. No woman in her right mind would wear that thing in public."

His jaw shifted as he ground his teeth. "The models are happy to wear it."

"My point, exactly. Those poor women are so malnourished, they can't think straight. Take my friend Sasha. Her idea of a three-course meal is a celery stick, a cherry tomato, and a laxative. She's killing herself to fit into these clothes. Women like me can't dress like that."

His gaze drifted over her again. "I think you could. You would look . . . *superbe.*"

"My breasts would fall out."

"Exactly." The corner of his mouth tilted up.

She huffed. "I'm not showing my breasts in public."

His eyes twinkled. "Would you do it in private?"

Damn him and his pretty blue eyes. She had to think a moment to remember the gist of the conversation. "Are you going to arrest me or drool on me?"

He smiled. "Can I do both?"

What a confusing man. "I haven't done anything wrong. I mean, other than the crab cake. But I wouldn't have taken it if I could actually afford anything in this place."

His smile faded. "You are in need of money? You plan to sell the designs you copied to another house?"

"No. I just wanted to make one for myself."

"You are lying. You said you would not be caught dead in one of these gowns."

Lying? This guy was full of rotten accusations. "Look, I would never wear one of these gowns the way Echarpe designed them. I tell you, the guy is completely detached from reality. Does he even know any real people?"

"Not like you," he muttered, then held out his hand. "Let me see your sketchings."

"All right. If it'll help clear things up." She showed him her notepad. "The first one is the white gown, but I fixed it."

"*Fixed* it? I can hardly recognize it."

"I know. It looks so much better now. I could actually wear it without getting arrested for indecent exposure."

He gritted his teeth. "It's not that bad."

"If a young boy saw me in it, I'd be listed on a website as a sex offender. But the point is moot, since I could never afford the dress in the first place. I can't even buy a pair of socks here without getting my truck repossessed."

"This merchandise is designed for an elite few."

"Oh, pardon me. I'll just have Cheeves bring around the Rolls-Royce, so I can putter over to the airport and take my private jet back to my villa in Tuscany."

His mouth twitched as he turned to the next page. "And this is the red gown?"

"Yes, but much better after I fixed it. There are four more designs there. I was coming up with so many ideas all at once, I just had to get them down before they were lost. If you know what I mean."

"Actually, I do." He gave her an odd look.

It *was* odd. He didn't look like the type to understand the whimsical creative process. He looked more like an athlete, but with the build of a swimmer, not a weightlifter.

Could he actually have her arrested? His strange accusations combined with his handsome looks had confounded her to the point that she'd babbled like a nervous idiot. She needed to relax and be nicer. "I'm really sorry. I didn't mean to steal anything. Am I in trouble?"

He glanced at her with a hint of a smile. "Do you want to be?"

She stopped herself from saying yes. Good Lord, this guy was sexy. And much too gorgeous for his own good. No doubt he had trouble finding clothes that fit those broad shoulders and long legs. He probably had problems with women, too. They took one look at him and their clothes accidentally fell off.

Aha! That's what she'd do if he arrested her. She'd offer herself to him as a sacrifice. How noble. How ridiculous. She would never have the nerve.

He finished studying her drawings. "These are actually quite good. I can see how they would be more flattering for a woman with a . . . more luscious figure."

He really liked her designs? Heather's heart swelled with pride and joy. She liked being called luscious, too. "Thank you. And thanks for not calling women like me fat."

He stiffened. "Why would I say that when it's not true?"

Whoa. This man was serious trouble. Not only was he gorgeous, but he knew the right things to say to women. Double the danger. And double the fun? No, she slapped herself mentally. She'd just rid herself of one male disaster. No way was she hanging around for the sequel. "I'd better be going." She turned to leave.

"You forgot your sketchings."

She pivoted to face him. "You'll let me keep them?"

"On one condition." He glanced behind her. "*Zut.* We must go."

She looked over her shoulder. A big guy in a kilt was confiscating a young woman's camera phone.

"But I wanted a picture for my blog," the young woman objected.

"Come." The gorgeous security guard grabbed Heather's arm and led her toward a set of double doors with the word *Private* printed above them.

"Wait a minute." Heather slowed down. "Where are you taking me?"

"A place where we can talk."

Talk? Wasn't that code for something else? Good Lord, he *was* dragging her off to ravish her. "Uh, I don't *talk* with strangers."

"You've been talking to me." He gave her a wry look as he pulled her through the double doors and into a hallway. "You've given me quite an earful."

"Well, yes." She glanced back at the showroom. "I just hope you're not expecting something more."

He halted by another set of double doors and returned her notepad. While she stuffed it in her purse, he punched in a number on a keypad. "What I am about to show you is very private."

Oh God, she was afraid of that. "Only seen by an elite few?"

"Exactly. I know you're a tough critic, but I think you will be impressed."

Her gaze wandered south. "I'm sure I will."

"Heather."

His soft way of saying her name made her feel all melted and gooey inside. She lifted her eyes to meet his.

His mouth curled up. "Are we talking about the same thing?"

"I don't know." Her heart pounded. It was hard to think when he looked at her like that.

"I'm going to show you the rest of the fall collection."

"Oh." She blinked. "Right. That's what I thought."

"But of course." The twinkle in his eye was suspicious. He opened the door and escorted her inside.

"It's dark—" She hushed when some lights came on.

A quick glance at the high ceiling let her know he'd turned on only half the lights. Her gaze moved downward. The room was huge, much bigger than the showroom. Shelves lined the walls, filled with bolts of beautiful fabric. Her fingers itched to touch it all. In the back, she spotted two sewing machines. They were reflecting off the glass of French doors along the back wall. To the left of the room sat two large cutting tables. To the right, rack after rack of fabulous clothes. In the center, a host of male and female mannequins stood in a circle like the Stonehenge of high fashion.

Good Lord, what she would give to have a workroom like this. It was heaven. "This is where the magic happens."

"Magic?" He shut the door. "I would call it hard work."

"But it *is* magical." She wandered toward the first rack of clothes, her heels clunking on the wooden floor. "This is where ideas give birth to beautiful things."

He followed her. "Then you like the design studio?"

"Oh yes." She eyed the cleverly cut jackets and skirts on the first rack. "Adorable." She rubbed the fabric between her fingers and frowned.

"What's wrong?"

"It's wool."

"It's a winter jacket."

"And this is Texas. You might sell it in the Panhandle, but down here, you'd have to turn on the air conditioning to wear it, even in the winter."

"I didn't realize that." He crossed his arms, frowning.

"The cut is remarkable, though." She admired one of the jackets. "The guy's a genius."

"I thought he was completely detached from reality."

Heather laughed. "That, too." She proceeded to the second rack.

"Did you make your dress?"

She winced. "Is it that obvious?"

He shrugged. "It is well made, actually. The fabric is crap, but so much of it is these days."

"Oh, I know. I've bought things that literally fall apart after two washings." She halted in front of a beaded bolero jacket as a thought suddenly occurred to her. Since when did security guards know anything about fabric?

"Is it your own design?" he asked.

"Sorta. I like to combine different features from different patterns to make something . . . unique."

He nodded. "It *is* unique."

"Thank you." Who was this guy? "Do . . . do you work for Echarpe as a designer?"

"Would *you* like to?"

Her mouth fell open. "Huh?"

"You've convinced me that I'm neglecting part of the market, and women such as yourself deserve to look your best."

"Oh."

"I believe more of these designs could be adapted for fuller figures, and you might be just the person to do it."

"Oh."

"Come back Monday evening if you wish to start."

"Oh." Good Lord, she was sounding like a moron. "I could work here? In this magical place?"

"Yes."

"Oh my gosh!" Obviously this guy wasn't security. "Are you the manager? I—I hope you weren't offended by some of the things I said. I did say Echarpe was a genius."

"And that he was completely detached from reality. And that you had to *fix* his designs."

Heather winced. "I got a little carried away. But it's only because I feel so passionately that women like me deserve to look as good as our skinnier sisters."

"You have passion." He motioned to her dress. "And talent. Otherwise, I would not hire you."

She grinned. "Oh, thank you! This is a dream come true." She pressed a hand to her chest. "I'm so excited, Mr.—uh, what shall I call you?"

He bowed slightly. "Allow me to introduce myself." His eyes gleamed as he slowly smiled. "I am Jean-Luc Echarpe."

Chapter 3

Jean-Luc expected her reaction to be entertaining, and it was. Heather's mouth fell open. Her lovely green eyes widened in horror. Blood rushed from her face, leaving her so pale, even her freckles faded away.

He grinned. He hadn't had this much fun in years. She opened and shut her pretty mouth, but no words came out, so she looked rather like a fish. An adorable fish.

He tilted his head. "You were saying?"

She managed to choke out a few strangled squeaks. "How can you be—I—I thought you were really *old*."

He arched a brow.

"I mean . . . oh God, I'm sorry." She pushed back her thick curls. Her purse tumbled to the floor. "Aw, shoot."

He leaned over to retrieve it.

"No, I'll get it." She grabbed her purse so fast, she stumbled as she was straightening.

He reached out to steady her.

"I'm okay." She stretched an arm toward some clothing to catch herself. Unfortunately, the clothes parted like the Red Sea, leaving her to plummet to the floor. "Aagh!"

"I've got you!" He grabbed hold of her sleeve. *Rip*.

She crashed onto the floor with him holding her sleeve in his hand. *Merde*.

He leaned over her. "Are you all right?" Her skirt had ridden up, revealing her shapely legs. He couldn't help but imagine those thighs wrapped around his waist. Or his neck.

"Are you really Jean-Luc Echarpe?" she asked.

"*Oui.*"

She moaned and covered her face. "Do you have a cellar I can crawl into for about fifty years?"

Actually he did, and he was tempted to invite her there. She would certainly brighten up his long exile. But he had no right to imprison a mortal just to entertain himself.

He sat on the floor beside her. "There's no need to be embarrassed."

"I'm mortified. Just kill me now."

He chuckled. "I was saying the same thing earlier this evening. We are too melodramatic, *non*?"

"I said some awful things about you." She lowered her hands. "I'm really sorry."

"Don't apologize for being honest. I like it. In this business, very few people are honest."

She sat up and winced when she noticed her skirt. She hurriedly adjusted it. "I don't understand how you can be so hand— young. You've designed clothes for people like Marilyn Monroe."

Had she almost called him handsome? His smile faded when he realized it was time to start lying. *Zut*. She'd been so honest with him. "I'm the . . . son of the original Jean-Luc Echarpe. You may call me Jean, so you won't confuse me with my father."

"Oh. That's great that you inherited his talent."

Jean-Luc shrugged. He hated deception. That was why he normally preferred the company of Vamps. Any relationship with a mortal required a number of lies, especially now that he had to go into hiding. He handed Heather the ripped sleeve. "I'm sorry it tore."

"That's okay." She stuffed it into her purse. "Like you said, the fabric is crap." She looked around the room and grinned. "I can't believe I'm sitting in a real design studio with a famous fashion designer."

He smiled as he rose to his feet. "Are you coming Monday to work?" He extended a hand to help her up.

"Oh, you bet. This is a dream come true for me." She placed her hand in his.

He pulled her up so quickly, she bumped against his chest. His arms instantly surrounded her. She glanced up with her lovely eyes. Such a dark, vivid green. He could hear her heartbeat speeding up now that she was in his arms. He liked that. "Do you know how beautiful you are?"

She shook her head.

Apparently he could also make her lose the ability to speak. Desire sizzled through his veins. She felt so warm and sweet, but he had to stop before his eyes glowed red. She was too great a temptation, and he was always careful to avoid real relationships.

He released her. "I'm afraid I can only hire you for two weeks." Once the store closed, the only mortal allowed inside would be his security guard, Pierre.

"I understand." She stepped back, her face sad. "I realize I have no experience. And I have to go back to teaching in September."

"Are you assuming I'll find fault with you?" Her responding blush indicated he'd touched a nerve. He suspected her feisty attitude was hiding a pit of self-doubt. It was a trick he recognized, having used it himself.

But why would Heather Westfield doubt herself? Had someone tried to strangle her spirit? If so, he felt a sudden compulsion to ram his fist into that person's face. "My concern is not that I'll be unhappy with you. Quite the opposite. I could be *too* happy with you." Too tempted to keep her here to ease the loneliness of his exile.

She gulped audibly.

"And I have a rule I always follow. I never involve myself with employees. No matter how attracted I am." He allowed his gaze to wander over her luscious body.

"Oh my gosh," she whispered. She took another step back. "I—I'm not looking for—I'm not ready—I mean I—"

"The idea of a relationship leaves you speechless?"

"More like horrified!" She winced. "Oh, I didn't mean with you. I just meant with anybody. I went through a nasty divorce a year ago and—"

He held up a hand to hush her. "I will behave myself." He smiled slowly. "Can you?"

"Of course. I'm always . . . good." She looked a bit forlorn about that.

Did she have a secret wish to be naughty? Desire flooded back, and he clenched his fists to keep from grabbing her. It had been so long since he'd . . . He shoved the thought aside. He had to leave mortal women alone. He'd learned that in the most painful way possible.

She strolled down the aisle, touching the clothes as she passed by. "These are cool." She stopped in front of an assortment of belts made of leather, brass, and silver.

"This is my first season to design belts." He moved

closer. Only mortal models could wear the belts made of silver. Simone and Inga stayed far away from anything that would burn their delicate skin. "What do you think?"

"They're lovely. I especially like the big, chunky ones that rest on the hips."

Click. Jean-Luc's superior hearing picked up a sound. He held up a hand, and Heather hushed with a questioning look. A footstep, another click.

He'd never heard the door open or close. Only someone knowing the combination could open the door. A vampire teleporting in from outside the building would set off an alarm. So this person must have teleported from somewhere inside the building. His Vamp friends would have called out, so chances were the visitor was not a friend.

Jean-Luc raised a finger to his lips to warn Heather to remain quiet. He eased toward the end of the aisle and the center of the room. He peeked through the space between the clothes and long rod they were hanging from.

There he was. The old man with a cane. *Click.* He planted the cane on the hardwood floor, then shuffled his feet forward. He remained hunched over, his face hidden.

Jean-Luc sniffed. Heather's aroma was behind him, definitely mortal, but he sensed nothing from this man.

The old man halted with a final click of his cane. "I know you are here, Echarpe."

Jean-Luc stiffened. *Mon Dieu*, it was Lui. He hadn't seen his most dreaded enemy in more than a hundred years.

"I am a patient man. I knew in time you would grow careless. And here you are, unarmed, without your precious bodyguards." The old man straightened slowly, unfurling his spine. "You were impossible to reach in Paris. Surrounded night and day by half a dozen guards." He lifted his chin.

Jean-Luc dragged in a deep breath when he saw the man's eyes. Lui had assumed many identities over the centuries, always managing to look different. Except for the eyes. They were always dark, cold, and filled with hate.

Jean-Luc eased back to Heather as Lui continued to boast.

"You have made your last mistake, Echarpe. I went to the openings of all your stores, but you remained hidden like the coward you are. Now, at last, you have made an appearance. Your final appearance."

Jean-Luc reached Heather and lifted a finger to his lips. She nodded with an anxious look.

He whispered in her ear, "Do not let him see you. Escape out the doors in the back. Run."

She opened her mouth to protest, but he stopped her with a finger pressed against her lips.

Go, he mouthed the word. He pushed her gently toward the opposite end of the aisle.

"Come out of hiding, you coward," Lui shouted. "I have decided to kill you once and for all. I will miss having you around to torture, but Casimir has offered me an enormous sum. I could not refuse."

Jean-Luc marched down the aisle toward the center of the room. "*Zut alors*, I thought you were dead. But no matter, you will be soon enough." He was a better swordsman than Lui, but unfortunately, he was unarmed at the moment. He sent out a psychic message.

"I can hear you," Lui sneered. "Whining to your friends to come and save you."

Jean-Luc stepped into the clearing. "I fight my own battles. Tell me, how long did it take for you to recover from our last encounter? If memory serves, your guts were hanging out."

With a growl, Lui twisted the knob on his cane and ripped the wooden sheath away from a slim, lethal foil. He tossed the wooden sheath aside, and it clattered on the floor. "Your friends will be too late." He charged.

Jean-Luc leaped to the side, grabbed a nearby mannequin, and swung it hard to deflect the first attack.

Lui's sword sliced through, decapitating the male mannequin. "Ah, that brings back sweet memories of the Reign of Terror." He swung again and shattered the mannequin's torso.

Jean-Luc was left defending himself with a mannequin leg. At least it had a metal bar through it. And Robby would be here any second with a real sword.

Jean-Luc ducked, feeling the whir above him as Lui's foil sliced the air. He ran to the right, planted the mannequin leg on the floor, and used it to pole vault onto a cutting table.

Lui swung at his legs, but Jean-Luc jumped and landed on the floor on the far side of the table. When Lui circled to the right to catch him, he moved to the right, too. He could keep Lui dancing around the table until Robby arrived with a sword.

Jean-Luc had completed one circle when he spotted movement behind Lui. He froze. Heather was sneaking up behind Lui with nothing but a handful of belts. What was she thinking? He didn't dare yell at her to stop. That would alert Lui to her presence, and he'd stab her with his sword. *Merde!* He made a face at her and motioned with his head for her to get the hell out of there.

She ignored him, her eyes focused on Lui.

The only thing Jean-Luc could do was draw Lui away from her. He ran to the center of the room and engaged in battle with the mannequin leg. Bits of plaster flew through the air as Lui hacked at Jean-Luc's inferior weapon.

"Stop it!" Heather swung her belts at Lui.

Lui stiffened as silver metal struck the back of his head. A coil of smoke curled up. He turned toward her, his face contorted with pain. "You vicious bitch." He raised his sword.

"Heather, run!" Jean-Luc leaped forward and clobbered Lui on the head with the mannequin leg.

The metal rod sent Lui stumbling to the side. His foil clattered to the floor. Jean-Luc ducked to retrieve the sword, then jumped out of the way when Heather took another swing at Lui.

"Take that, you creep!" Her eyes glittered with excitement.

Lui raised his hands to protect his head, and the silver hissed across his palms, sizzling the exposed flesh.

The front door burst open, and Angus and Robby ran inside, their claymores drawn. Robby tossed a foil across the room to Jean-Luc.

He caught the foil, then turned to face Lui. The bastard had retreated, hiding among the racks of clothing. From the corner of his eye, Jean-Luc spotted Angus slipping between two racks. No doubt the Scotsman intended to catch the bastard from behind.

Jean-Luc handed Lui's foil to Heather. "If he comes after you, do not hesitate to use it."

She nodded, her eyes meeting his. His heart stuttered. *Mon Dieu*, what had he gotten her into?

"I will return for you, Echarpe," Lui announced. "But first I will kill your woman. Just like old times, *non*?"

"She is not my woman! Leave her out of this."

"Ah, but I can see that you care for her. I wonder if she will be as accommodating as your last mistress?"

"Damn you." Jean-Luc strode toward the racks. "Watch her," he yelled at Robby; then he ran down an aisle. He spotted Angus coming from the opposite direction.

Jean-Luc shoved clothes aside, hunting for Lui.

"Bugger," Angus muttered. "He must have teleported away. I'll keep searching." He dashed away at vampire speed.

"Did you get him?" Heather called.

"No. He . . . escaped." Jean-Luc stalked back to the center of the workroom. Seething with frustration, he whipped his foil through the air. Heather's eyes widened.

Robby paced around her, his claymore clenched in a tight fist. "I need to search the grounds. *Now.*"

Jean-Luc nodded. "Go."

Robby sprinted toward the French doors along the back wall and let himself out.

Jean-Luc took a deep breath. "Are you all right?"

"I guess." Heather dropped the belts and Lui's foil onto a cutting table. "But I don't understand what's going on. What's the deal with all these swords? And why would anyone want to kill a fashion designer?"

"It's a long story." And a painful one. "I wish you had run like I told you to do."

"I meant to, but when I saw him attacking you with that sword, and all you had was a mannequin—I don't know. I should have been afraid, but I've been afraid all my life, and I'm sick and tired of it. Then all this anger came pouring out. Anger at myself for being a wimp. Anger at my ex for being an asshole. I just had to take action. And—and I was good!"

Jean-Luc took her hand in his. He suspected it was her ex-husband who had left her immersed in self-doubt. But she was fighting back, and his heart swelled with pride for her. "You were very brave. You may have saved my life."

Her cheeks turned pink. "I don't know if I helped that much. You were doing really well. Who was that guy?"

"I have never known his real name. I call him Lui."

"Louie?"

"*Non*, Lui."

She frowned. "That's what I said."

Jean-Luc sighed. "*Lui* means 'him' *en français*. He is an assassin of many names. Jacques Clément, Damiens, Ravaillac. He incites murder and delights in death."

Her hand trembled. "Why does he want to kill you?"

"Because I have tried to stop him over the cen—years. I succeeded once, and he has wanted me to suffer ever since." Jean-Luc squeezed her hand. "Heather, I regret to tell you this, but you are in terrible danger."

Her face paled. "I was afraid of that. He thinks I'm . . ."

"He believes you are my lover."

She pulled her hand from his grasp. "I'd better stay away then. I guess I can't work here after all."

"*Au contraire*, you should work here. I have security guards who can protect you. In fact, you should live here until we can . . . take care of Lui."

She scoffed. "I can't *live* here. I have a house in Schnitzelberg."

"You must live here. Lui has killed two women in my past."

Heather gulped. "He kills your girlfriends?"

"Yes. I am sorry this happened to you. I did warn you not to let him see you."

She winced. "I should have done what you said."

"If you had, I might be dead. Let me protect you, Heather. I owe you that much."

"I can't stay here. My daughter—"

"*Non.*" Jean-Luc felt as if he'd been pummeled in the stomach. "You have a daughter?"

"Yes. Oh my God. Are you saying she's in danger, too?"

Jean-Luc swallowed hard. A vision of mutilated bodies flashed through his mind. Yvonne in 1757. Claudine in 1832. He couldn't bear this pain and guilt again. "Do not be afraid. I will protect you both."

Chapter 4

She should have known he wasn't perfect. Anyone as gorgeous as Jean-Luc Echarpe had to possess a few serious flaws. Flaw number one: stubborn as a mule. After Heather had recovered from the initial shock, she had refused Echarpe's offer of protection. He'd looked stunned, but then he'd announced his intent again as if he'd automatically passed a law.

After she'd lived for six years with a control-freak husband who legislated everything, even down to what kind of underwear she could buy, Heather's dictator-approved, white cotton panties were in a twist. God help her, she needed to escape domineering men. And she also needed to buy new underwear—something wild that symbolized her newfound courage. Thank goodness there was a giant discount store on the way home. Where else could an independent gal like her purchase lacy underwear and shotgun shells in one convenient stop?

"Mr. Echarpe, I appreciate your kind offer, but I really don't need a protector." She motioned toward the locked door. "If you'll just let me out—"

"In a moment." He frowned at the door. "I don't think you realize how dangerous Lui is."

Grrrr. The man never gave up. "Louie didn't seem that dangerous to me. He was downright wimpy when I hit him with those belts. And you fought him with a broken mannequin. For a villain, he was rather easy to beat."

"It was *not* easy! It only appeared that way because I am the best swordsman in all of Europe."

Flaw number two: overinflated ego. Though she had to cut him some slack. She'd never met a man yet who didn't suffer from that problem. "Maybe y'all still do swordfights in Europe, but here in Texas, we use guns. If I'd been packing, Louie would be on his way to the morgue."

Jean-Luc's brows drew together in a fierce scowl. "Are you saying you can fight him better than I?"

"I've got more faith in my shotgun than any man, that's for sure."

"But I'm trying to save you!"

"I'm already saved. Hallelujah, praise the Lord. Now unlock that door and set me free, brother."

His eyes widened with a look of exasperation. "I cannot let you go until you agree to let me protect you."

"You'll be waiting a long time 'cause I don't need you."

"Ungrateful woman."

"Arrogant man." Her heart raced. Good Lord, this was just as exciting as the time she'd slammed a pie into her ex-husband's face. Even better, actually. The pie had been an act of desperation, tainted with the sad knowledge that her marriage was a failure. This—this was a glorious declaration of independence. She'd never felt stronger or more fearless. Whipping Louie with those belts had made her feel like Wonder Woman, and she liked it.

"It was nice to meet you, Mr. Echarpe. And I appreciate your offer of employment, but under the circumstances, I feel it's best for us not to see each other again." Heather turned, quite proud of her little speech, and marched toward the door. The muttered curses behind her made her smile. "If you'll just unlock the—"

The door suddenly burst open, and a crowd of people swarmed into the room.

"About time," Jean-Luc grumbled.

A kilted Scotsman shut the door and leaned against it. The stern look on his face and the long sword in his hand meant business. Heather's dignified exit was ruined. More than ruined. She was trapped. Somehow, Jean-Luc Echarpe had managed to call in backup.

Flaw number three: he was more than stubborn. The man was relentless.

He introduced her to his friends, but she barely paid attention. This was too damned frustrating. She'd fought too hard to learn how to take care of herself and her daughter, Bethany. Letting a man protect her felt like a giant step backward.

Yet she had to admit he'd seemed very charming at first. She'd been so flattered that he found her attractive. She'd certainly found him attractive before his Napoleon complex had kicked in. He'd offered her the job of her dreams. Chances like that didn't come along often, so she'd be crazy to pass it up. Was she overreacting because he pushed the wrong buttons? He *was* overbearing, but he'd lost two girlfriends. His desperation was understandable.

The guy wanted to be a hero. Was that so bad?

But what did she know about him? If you judged a man by his friends, Jean-Luc would be caring and loyal. That was how his friends appeared. There was a tall, serious man named Roman Dragon-something with his blond wife and baby boy. There was another guy named

Gregori who grinned a lot. The two Scotsmen were both named MacKay. Brothers, maybe. The one named Robby was still guarding the door. The other one, Angus, was married to a beautiful brunette named Emma. Come to think of it, they were all exceptionally good-looking.

"Are you models?" Heather asked as the men hustled Jean-Luc across the room, leaving her with the women and baby.

Shanna laughed as she jiggled the baby in her arms. "No way. I'm a dentist. My husband's the owner of Romatech Industries, and Gregori's one of his VPs. Angus is CEO of MacKay Security and Investigation."

"Oh." Heather glanced at the door. Robby was still guarding it. She wasn't going anywhere for a while.

Emma smiled at her. "You fought very well."

"Thanks." Since she was trapped, Heather figured she might as well fish for more information. "What do y'all know about Louie?"

Shanna shifted the plump toddler to her hip. "It's a sad story. Jean-Luc has been plagued with him for a long time."

"Angus explained a bit while we were coming downstairs," Emma continued with a slight British accent. "Lui has murdered two of Jean-Luc's girlfriends from the past."

"I'm not a girlfriend," Heather muttered. "I only met Mr. Echarpe tonight."

"It doesn't matter," Emma said. "As long as Lui thinks you two are involved, you will be a target."

"I can understand your reluctance to accept Jean-Luc's protection," Shanna admitted. "I was once in a similar situation where Roman had to protect me. That was before we were married."

Heather glanced at the men, huddled across the room and whispering urgently to one another. They were a handsome bunch, but still, there was something different about them, something she couldn't quite put a finger on.

"It took me a while to get to know Roman and trust him," Shanna continued. "I understand your reluctance to trust a stranger, but I've known Jean-Luc for two years now, and he's a totally trustworthy guy. Sweet as can be. He's always watched out for Roman and me."

"He came to my rescue, too," Emma added. "He's the best swordsman in all of Europe."

"So I heard." Heather sighed. His friends were laying it on thick. She glanced at Jean-Luc. She had no doubt he was a capable guy. He had the body of an athlete, and she'd seen how quick and resourceful he was in action. His elegant tuxedo didn't conceal his aura of strength and danger. It just made him look more like James Bond. And James Bond always got the pretty girl in the end.

Her heart constricted in her chest. God help her, she wanted to be that pretty girl.

Flaw number four: too gorgeous for his own good.

"He's a handsome man, don't you think?" Shanna whispered.

Heather jumped. Shoot, she'd been caught ogling him.

Emma gave her a knowing smile. Even the baby on Shanna's hip snickered along with his mom.

"Okay, so he's good-looking. That doesn't mean I need his help," Heather protested. "I can take care of myself."

Emma's smile faded. "You don't understand how terrible Lui is."

"The guy ran away as soon as he was outnumbered. He's not so tough."

Emma lowered her voice. "Locked doors cannot stop him. He has the ability to enter your house whenever he chooses. You would never hear him. He could appear behind you at any moment. Before you knew what was happening, your throat would be sliced in two."

Heather gulped and fought an urge to look over her shoulder. Dammit, they were starting to scare her. Her voice began to rise. "He can't be that bad. It's not like the guy can actually vanish or appear at will. You make him sound like some kind of *supernatural creature of the night!*" Her loud words echoed in a suddenly quiet room.

The circle of men all turned to stare at her. Heather's face heated with a blush. Even in the classroom at Guadalupe High, she didn't get this kind of undivided attention.

The silence stretched while the men exchanged glances. Emma and Shanna looked at each other, then laughed. The toddler squealed and waved his arms toward Heather.

"He wants you to hold him." Shanna thrust him into Heather's arms.

The baby grabbed a handful of Heather's hair, and it brought back pleasant memories of Bethany's infancy. Heather smiled at the little boy's chubby red cheeks and bright blue eyes. "He's adorable. What's his name?"

"Constantine," Shanna answered. "I heard you have a daughter?"

Heather could see where this was going. They'd use her daughter to ratchet up the guilt and make her accept Jean-Luc's offer. "She's four years old. And I can protect us both. I inherited a shotgun from my father."

Shanna winced. "You keep a weapon in the house with a child?"

Heather gritted her teeth. There was nothing she took more seriously than being a good mom. "I don't keep it loaded. Of course, now I need to get some shells for it."

Emma's eyes gleamed with approval. "You know how to shoot?"

"Yes. My dad taught me everything about gun safety. He was an expert."

"What happened to him?" Shanna asked.

"He was . . . shot."

Shanna grimaced.

"In the line of duty," Heather added. "He was the town sheriff."

"Unfortunately, that just goes to show you that even the best of professionals can be killed," Emma said. "You need help to protect your daughter. You cannot stay awake and alert 24/7."

"Fidelia is packing, too."

Shanna gasped. "Your four-year-old has a gun?"

"No, of course not!" Heather huffed. "I would never allow my daughter around guns." She winced. That wasn't quite true. Fidelia had made it clear that she never went anywhere without her pistols. "Fidelia is my live-in babysitter and an old friend of the family. She would do anything to protect Bethany and me."

"So there are two women in your household who know how to shoot?" Emma asked, smiling. "Would you like to make it three?"

Shanna grinned. "That's a great idea!"

"What?" Heather settled the baby Constantine on her hip.

"But do you think Angus will mind?" Shanna leaned toward Heather and whispered, "They're newlyweds."

"We've been married a year now, so I don't think a few nights apart will kill Angus," Emma protested. "What do you think, Heather?"

"It's very kind of you to want to help, but—" Heather winced when the baby tugged on her hair.

"I'm vice president of MacKay Security and Inves- tigation," Emma explained. "And I'm a former employee of MI6 and the CIA, so I'll make a very good bodyguard."

Heather was impressed. "I really appreciate your offer, but my funds are very limited—"

"No charge," Emma interrupted. "Jean-Luc helped Angus and me when we were in trouble. I owe him one."

"It's the perfect solution," Shanna concluded.

Constantine tugged once again on Heather's hair, and she glanced at his face. His eyes captured her attention.

"My days are . . . tied up, so I can only guard you at night," Emma continued. "But that'll give you and your babysitter a chance to sleep, so you'll be better able to protect yourselves during the day."

"I understand." A calm acceptance seeped into Heather as the baby smiled at her. "Thank you, Emma. I'm delighted to have your help."

"Great! I'll let the men know what we decided, then we can go." Emma strode toward the group of men.

Constantine released his grip on Heather's hair. "You can put me down now."

She blinked. The toddler's voice was remarkably clear. And there was something oddly intelligent about his eyes. She set him on his feet. "How old is he?"

"Seventeen months," Shanna replied.

Heather watched him stroll calmly back to his mother. "He's a special little boy."

Shanna beamed with pride. "Yes, he is."

Thirty minutes later, Heather pulled her Chevy truck into the driveway of her home in Schnitzelberg.

"What a lovely house." Emma opened the passenger door to get out.

"I inherited it from my parents." Heather loved the old Queen Anne with the wide porch and hanging swing. She loved the gingerbread woodwork around the porch and second-floor balcony. But most of all, she loved the fact that she could raise her daughter in the same house where she'd grown up.

She grabbed her purse and the shopping bag containing her newly purchased lacy underwear and shotgun shells. Emma hadn't batted an eyelash at the discount store, so Heather liked her already. "This way." She headed up the stairs to the front door.

Emma hitched a tote bag over her shoulder and scanned the front yard. "Your house is off the ground?" She leaned over for a closer look. "No cellar?"

"I wish. I could use the extra storage." Heather unlocked the front door. She could hear the television inside. Fidelia might still be awake.

Emma frowned as she ascended the porch. "It's a lovely home, but very vulnerable. Whose room is off the balcony?"

"Mine, but I keep all the windows and doors locked."

Emma didn't look impressed. "Let me go in first."

Heather's heart lurched. "You think Louie is here?" With her baby inside?

"I'm not taking any chances." Emma retrieved a stick from her tote bag and eased into the foyer.

A stick? It would be quieter than a shotgun, but Heather doubted it was more efficient. She followed Emma in and locked the door.

Emma peered into the living room, then whispered, "Is that Fidelia?"

Heather looked inside. Fidelia was snoozing on the couch with the TV blaring in Spanish. "Yes." The living room opened into the dining room, which appeared empty.

Emma slipped past the staircase toward the back of the foyer and the swinging door that led to the kitchen.

Heather had no patience for this. She had to know if Bethany was all right. She charged up the stairs to her daughter's room.

The nightlight barely illuminated the pink roses Heather had stenciled across the walls and around the windows. White lace curtains let the sun shine in during the day, but for now, the blinds were shut.

Heather tiptoed past the giant dollhouse and wicker doll carriage to the bed topped with a Sunbonnet Sue quilt her mother had made. She dropped her purse and shopping bag on the foot of the bed. Her daughter's feet reached only halfway down the length of the bed. At the head, strawberry-blond curls lay strewn across the pillow. The sight always squeezed Heather's heart. She brushed the curls away to reveal a soft cheek. If she never accomplished any of her dreams, if she never designed clothes or saw Paris, it would be no great loss, for she'd already created the most perfect little masterpiece.

I will protect you, sweetheart. Heather went to the windows to make sure they were locked.

"Don't run away from me again," Emma whispered from the doorway.

Heather turned. "I had to make sure my daughter was okay."

Emma nodded as she entered the room. "The first floor is clear, and all the rooms upstairs."

Wow, she was fast. And thorough. "There's a guest bedroom across the hall that you're welcome to use."

"Thank you, but no." Emma hitched her tote bag higher on her shoulder. "I'll be up all night."

"Then please help yourself to anything you want in the kitchen." Heather had to admit she would sleep a lot easier with Emma standing guard. Thank God she'd managed to avoid having Jean-Luc Echarpe over. The last thing she needed was another domineering man in her life. And a famous fashion designer? He'd probably go through her closet and throw everything out. Or worse, he would stand there and laugh.

Emma eased closer to Bethany's bed and whispered, "She's beautiful."

Heather nodded. "She's everything to me."

"I understand." Emma's smile held a hint of sadness. "I'd like to see the attic now."

"This way." Heather went to the hall and pulled the rope that lowered the folding ladder. "Do you need a flashlight?"

"I see quite well in the dark." Emma ascended the ladder. She stayed in the attic for a moment, then came down. "It's clear. I'd like to check outside again."

"Okay." Heather folded the ladder and let it swing back into the attic. Emma had already moved down the stairs and out the door, so Heather decided to get ready for bed.

She retrieved her purse and shopping bag from Bethany's room and proceeded to her own bedroom. She closed the blinds over the French doors to the balcony. What a night. A job offer from a famous designer and a death threat all in one evening. She replayed the night's events in her mind as she dragged her desk chair over to her closet. Why would a deadly assassin pick on a fashion designer? Unless . . . he was more than a fashion designer? Jean-Luc did have a James Bond aura of mystery about him.

With a snort, she rejected that theory. International espionage was not interested in Schnitzelberg, Texas. She climbed onto the chair, located the shotgun on the top shelf of her closet, then took it to her bed. Didn't Jean-Luc say something about Louie's other names? Cadillac? No, something else. She inserted two shells.

Maybe if she relaxed a bit, she could remember. She'd always had a great memory. She'd given her ex-husband, Cody, the shock of his life when she'd recalled his every insult and threatening remark in court.

She undressed and put on her favorite green silk pajamas. She adored the feel of silk against bare skin, and the sensation always calmed her. She sat on her fuzzy chenille bedspread, snuggled against the pillows, and closed her eyes. An assassin who had taken many names. Not Cadillac, but Ravaillac. Jean-Luc had admitted to stopping Louie, and that was why the assassin wanted revenge.

What kind of fashion designer stopped an assassin from carrying out his evil plan?

James Bond music started playing in her head. No, it couldn't be. She was letting her imagination go crazy.

She turned on her computer, then dragged her chair back to the desk while it booted up. She Googled "Ravaillac" and sat there, stunned. This was even crazier than her James Bond theory.

François Ravaillac had been executed in 1610 after assassinating King Henri IV. Four horses had ripped him into four parts. Sheesh, did they do his death certificate in quadruplicate? One thing was for sure, the man was definitely dead. Even if Louie managed to live four hundred years, he couldn't be Ravaillac. And the French government had ordered the infamous name never be used again.

At the bottom of the web page, there was a link to another assassin named Damiens. That was another name Jean-Luc had mentioned. She clicked on the link.

Robert-François Damiens had tried to kill King Louis XV in 1757. He'd failed, but had still won the grand prize—death by drawing and quartering. Once again, the French had ordered the name never to be used again.

A search for Jacques Clément yielded similar results.

He'd killed King Henri III in 1589. He'd been quartered and burned. As a history teacher, Heather found it all fascinating, but confusing. It just didn't make sense. Either Jean-Luc was mistaken or purposely lying or . . . something very strange was going on.

That brought Jean-Luc's list of flaws up to number five: ambiguity. How could she trust him if his story didn't make sense?

There was a soft knock on her door, and Heather quickly minimized her screen. "Yes?"

The door cracked, and Emma peered inside. "I just wanted you to know everything is safe. You can relax for the night. I'll be leaving shortly before dawn."

"Thank you."

"Fidelia woke up, so I told her what was going on. She insists on reading my future."

"Oh, right." Heather nodded. "She does her tarot cards for anyone who comes to the house. It's her way of protecting us."

"Along with her guns? This should be interesting." Emma glanced at Heather's computer. "Catching up on e-mail?"

"Yes. I'll be down in just a minute."

"All right. Please keep the door open a bit, so I can check on you during the night."

"Okay." Heather waited for Emma to leave, then turned back to her computer. She Googled "Jean-Luc Echarpe" and found a few sites that sold his clothing. She ignored those and looked for personal information. She found a picture taken a year ago at his annual show in Paris. Dark curls, blue eyes, a hint of a dimple with his debonair smile. Sheesh, could the guy get any more gorgeous? Back to flaw number four: too handsome for his own good.

She found a recent article, translated from the Parisian newspaper *Le Monde*. Everyone was wondering why Jean-Luc Echarpe hadn't aged in thirty years. Hmm, they had to be referring to Jean-Luc's father. The Jean-Luc she had met looked only about thirty years old. Apparently the elder Jean-Luc had not been seen for several months. The media suspected he was undergoing another facelift.

Heather found another article dating back thirteen years. This one had a photo. Sheesh, he looked exactly the same as he had tonight. This wasn't making any sense. She searched for Jean-Luc's date of birth, but found no personal information at all.

Back to flaw number five: ambiguity. Some women might call an aura of mystery a plus, but Heather didn't like surprises when it came to men. Though it was intriguing . . .

Why would he call Louie a bunch of names that had disappeared centuries ago? And why did he look exactly the same after thirteen years? Cosmetic surgery or . . . A thought flashed through her mind. A totally bizarre thought, no doubt triggered by the late hour and her overactive imagination.

It had always been one of her favorite TV shows—the immortal Highlanders who lived for centuries, fighting their old enemies with swords. It would explain why Jean-Luc and his friends fought with swords. And why he talked of assassins who lived centuries ago. He even had the kilted Highlander friends. The way they had huddled across the room, whispering to one another, had definitely looked like a bunch of guys with a secret.

Could Jean-Luc be immortal?

With a snort, Heather turned off her computer. Her theories were becoming more and more ridiculous. Immortal men? She might as well believe in elves and fairies, too. Unfortunately, she'd learned the hard way that trolls existed. She'd lived with one of those for six years.

As she descended the stairs to fetch a glass of water, she noticed the television was off. She could hear Fidelia's slightly accented voice. "The reversed Hermit card could mean you are suffering from a deep loneliness."

That didn't sound like Emma. Heather stopped at the entrance of the living room. Her mouth fell open. It wasn't Emma.

Jean-Luc stood. His slender foil was propped against the wingback chair. His blue eyes glimmered as he checked out her pajamas. "I stopped by to see you. Emma let me in."

She'd been tricked. Heather gritted her teeth. She should have known Emma was in league with this guy. "Where is Emma?"

"She's upstairs, guarding Bethany." Fidelia winked at Heather. "This young man says it is his sworn duty to guard you. He's *muy macho*, no?"

Jean-Luc bowed. "I am at your service."

Heather bit back an angry retort. The man refused to take no for an answer. Back to flaw number one: stubborn as a mule. And the way Jean-Luc Echarpe bowed—it seemed old-fashioned. Extremely old-fashioned.

She had to wonder just how old a mule could get.

Chapter 5

She was beautiful even when she was angry. Jean-Luc admired the glittering green fire in Heather's eyes. And the way that silk top clung to her breasts wasn't bad, either. She glared at him as she planted her hands on her hips. The movement caused her breasts to jiggle ever so slightly. No bra. He'd always had a good eye for detail.

"Jean-Luc," she muttered. "I wasn't expecting you."

"Please call me Jean." It would be so easy to slip his hands underneath her top and fill his palms with the sweet, soft heaviness of her breasts. He lifted his gaze to her face and noticed her reddening cheeks. He caught the scent of her blood as it rushed to her face, engorging the delicate veins beneath her skin. Type AB.

Hunger coiled in his belly and sent flickers of desire throughout his body. Luckily he had some bottles of synthetic blood stashed in a cooler outside in his car. That would take care of his physical need, but he was slowly becoming aware of a different hunger, a hunger brought on by years of abstinence. He missed making love, but it went deeper than that. He missed the satisfaction, the peaceful contentment of feeling emotionally connected to a loving woman. Because of Lui, that joy had long been impossible.

Heather folded her arms across her chest, which only pulled the sleek material tighter against her breasts. "Don't tell me you're planning to spend the night here."

"I must. It is my duty and honor to protect you."

"That is so romantic," Fidelia said from her seat on the couch. She shifted her square body sideways so she could see Heather at the doorway. "Don't you think so?"

"No." Heather frowned at her. "It's not romantic if he's forcing himself on me."

"*Chica*, it's not like he's trying to seduce you. He just wants to protect you." Fidelia's eyes twinkled as she glanced at Jean-Luc. "At least that's what he says."

Seduce her? Jean-Luc had avoided mortal women since Claudine's murder in 1832. His sense of honor had demanded that he not expose another innocent female to Lui's twisted vengeance. But Lui already believed he was involved with Heather. The most pressing reason to resist her was gone. That realization sent a jolt of desire straight from his heart to his groin. *Seduce her. You know you want her.*

But why would she welcome any advances from him? Her life and her daughter's life were in jeopardy because of him. She was more likely to slap him than succumb to passionate kisses.

He took a deep breath. "I assure you, *mes dames*, that my intentions are honorable."

Heather snorted and gave him a dubious look.

Did she question his honor? *Merde.* But she was correct, given the direction his thoughts were going.

"From what Emma told me, I could be in danger, too." Fidelia's brown eyes glimmered with mischief. "Where's *my* bodyguard? Do you have like a . . . catalog?"

Jean-Luc blinked. "I can protect you both, but if you prefer a guard of your own, I could call Robby—"

"Roberto?" Fidelia fluffed up her long, straggly black hair. Unfortunately, two inches of gray showed at the roots. "Is he *muy macho* like you?"

"I . . . wouldn't know." Jean-Luc retrieved his cell phone from the inside pocket of his tuxedo jacket.

"He's a Scotsman in a kilt," Heather muttered. "He's got a bigger sword than Jean."

What the hell did that mean? Jean-Luc paused in the middle of dialing to meet her challenging glare. "A claymore is naturally larger than a foil, mademoiselle, but its very weight causes the swordsman to be more slow."

She gave him a bland look. "Slow's good. I like slow."

He stepped toward her. "Finesse is better. And do not forget experience and perfect timing. I am a champion, you know."

"Right." She yawned. "But you know how it is. Only those who are lacking claim that size is not important."

He gritted his teeth. "I lack nothing, mademoiselle. I will gladly prove myself. As *slowly* as you like."

Fidelia burst into laughter. "Ooh wee, if only I was twenty years younger. Well, make that thirty, but anyway, I'm not into swords or men in skirts. I've got all the men I can handle."

Jean-Luc dragged his eyes off Heather to focus on the babysitter. "You do not want Robby?"

"Hell, no, I was just foolin' with you." Fidelia hefted her large purse into her lap and fumbled inside. "What would I do with a Scotsman when I have this nice German *muchacho*, Mr. Glock." She removed a revolver, patted it fondly, and set it on the cushion beside her.

She pulled out another one. "Then there's Mr. Makarov from Russia with love." She set the pistol next to the first one. "And my Italian honey, Mr. Beretta."

While Jean-Luc slipped his cell phone back into his pocket, he noticed there were trigger locks on all her pistols. "How many guns do you have?"

"One for every husband I went through. At least these honeys don't shoot blanks." Laughing, Fidelia stuffed the pistols back into her purse. "My favorite, Mr. Magnum, is upstairs in my bedroom. Too heavy for my purse." She winked. "But talk about size—"

"Fidelia, I need something from the kitchen." Heather motioned with her head toward the back of the house.

"Then go get it." Fidelia's eyes widened when Heather angled her head once more to the kitchen. "Oh, right. Let me help you." She stood, cradling her purse against her large bosom. "We'll be right back, Juan. Don't go."

"Of course." He bowed slightly as Heather strode down the hallway.

Fidelia waddled after her, her long skirt swishing. She glanced back with an amused smirk. "I'm sure she's just lost something. Like her senses."

Jean-Luc eased toward the foyer to watch them, and once the kitchen door stopped swinging in their wake, he zoomed at vampire speed out the front door to his BMW.

He removed a bottle of synthetic blood from the cooler and chugged it down. He hated cold meals, but in his case, it was the best thing. Filling himself with cold blood was the vampire equivalent of taking a cold shower. Just what he needed, for he was hungry for more than food.

He surveyed Heather's two-story, wood-framed

house. Blue with white trim. So warm and appealing. So different from his stone chateau north of Paris. It was flawless and formal, chilly like a mausoleum. This house was full of vibrant people, and looked so . . . lived in. His eye for detail had noted all the signs. A pair of small, wet sneakers left on the porch. A half-crocheted afghan spilling from a basket next to the fireplace. Seat cushions on the couch that remained permanently indented. A cross-stitched sampler on the wall, beseeching God to bless their house. Exuberant artwork, obviously drawn by Heather's daughter, displayed on the mantelpiece with pride.

It was a real home. A real family. Like he had never had. *Merde.* You would think in five hundred years, he would have gotten over it. One thing was for sure, he couldn't let Lui destroy this family. The battle would be difficult, though, because he didn't know when or where Lui would strike next.

Jean-Luc's most dreaded fear, the feeling of powerlessness, lurked in the shadows, waiting for a moment of weakness. He would not succumb. For Heather's sake, he had to protect her and vanquish Lui.

He scanned the yard and street before zipping back into the house. He quietly shut the front door. With his superior vamp senses, he heard Fidelia's whispered voice.

"Why not let him protect you? What do you have against him?"

There was a pause. He silently locked the door.

"There's something odd about him," Heather finally said. "You can see the obvious flaws, but there's something else I can't quite figure out."

"What obvious flaws?" Fidelia asked.

Exactly. What obvious flaws? Jean-Luc eased down the foyer, frowning.

"He's too good-looking," Heather announced.

Jean-Luc grinned.

"And arrogant," she continued, and his smile faded. "I swear, if I have to hear about his championship one more time, I'll take that sword of his and make him a champion blue ribbon steer."

He winced.

"Don't be silly," Fidelia hissed. "If you mess with a man's equipment, then what good is he for?"

"I've been wondering that for about four years now," Heather muttered.

Jean-Luc restrained himself from marching into the kitchen and tossing Miss Heather Westfield onto the table for some much-needed illumination.

Fidelia chuckled. "Well, if he stays here for very long, you might find out."

Damned right. Jean-Luc nodded.

"He's not staying here," Heather insisted.

Damned wrong. He scowled at the door.

Heather lowered her voice. "I want to know if you're getting any sort of strange vibes off him."

"Nothing yet. You know most of my visions come in my dreams at night."

"Then go to bed."

Fidelia laughed. "I can't guarantee I'll dream of him . . . but you might. I can tell you like him."

Jean-Luc tiptoed closer to the kitchen door. He needed to hear Heather's response, but instead, there was a fumbling sound.

"Are we out of triple chocolate ice cream?" Heather made a sound of exasperation as the freezer door slammed shut.

"You're in denial," Fidelia announced.

"No, I'm fully aware that I'm overweight."

"No," Fidelia countered. "You will not admit that you are attracted to Juan."

"His name is John."

He grimaced. Neither one of them pronounced it right.

"He's very handsome," Heather whispered. "But he's too domineering."

"No, no. *Chica*, he's nothing like your ex. You just think all men are bad right now."

"There's something weird about him I don't trust."

Fidelia made a clucking sound. "Then let's finish his reading and see what the cards reveal."

Jean-Luc dashed back into the living room and eyed the cards on the coffee table. After Fidelia had shuffled them, she'd invited him to select seven cards. Only one had been turned face up so far, that damned Hermit card. He didn't normally believe in such nonsense. He'd seen too many charlatans over the centuries. Still, hearing someone announce his loneliness had pricked his pride.

Of course he was lonely. How could he court a woman knowing that Lui would try to kill her?

"I'm not sure he's what he says he is," Heather's soft words drifted from the kitchen. "He has . . . secrets."

She was a perceptive woman. Jean-Luc leaned over the coffee table and flipped the next card. His heart froze.

The Lovers. It was so tempting to hope for a happy future and a glorious union with a loving woman. But how could it possibly happen with Heather? Even if she survived Lui and forgave him for endangering her, how could she accept a lover who was undead?

He heard them enter the foyer. Quickly, he grabbed the Lovers card and stuffed it back into the deck. He picked another card at random and set it facedown where the Lovers card had been. Then he sat in the wingback chair and assumed a bored expression.

"We're back!" Fidelia marched into the room, her

long skirt swishing. She flopped down onto the middle dip in the couch and set her purse beside her.

"Can I get you something to drink?" Heather motioned to the kitchen with a hand that held a glass of ice water. The cubes clinked together like musical chimes.

"No thank you." Jean-Luc clenched the arms of his chair to keep from standing. He'd lived through several centuries when good manners dictated a male should stand whenever a female was standing. Such habits were hard to break, but it would be even harder to explain why he had such a habit. Heather already suspected too much.

"How about we finish your reading?" Fidelia leaned forward, propping her elbows on her knees.

Heather set her glass on a coaster close to the cards. "Do you mind if I watch?"

"No. I have nothing to hide." He was such a liar.

She gave him a suspicious look as she perched on the sofa arm. She dragged a powder-blue chenille pillow into her lap and twisted the fringe around her fingers.

"All right, the second card." Fidelia flipped it over.

Thank God he'd gotten rid of the Lovers. Whatever he'd substituted had to be an improvement.

"The Fool," Fidelia announced.

He winced.

Heather chuckled, then pursed her lips when he glared at her.

"It doesn't mean you are foolish," Fidelia assured him with a smile. "It means you have a secret desire to leap into the unknown and start a new life."

"Oh." That might be true. He glanced at Heather. She hugged the pillow to her chest, her fingers lightly stroking the soft chenille.

She likes texture. She liked to touch and feel things.

His groin reacted. Hopefully she enjoyed hard things as well as soft.

Fidelia turned over another card and frowned. "Oh dear. Ten of Swords."

"Is that bad?" A dumb question since Jean-Luc could see the card's depiction of a dead man on the ground with ten swords in his back.

"Desolation," Fidelia answered. "Your fate is tracking you down, and there is nothing you can do to avoid it."

"Louie," Heather whispered, and squeezed the pillow tighter.

"I won't let him harm you," Jean-Luc assured her.

Fidelia turned the fourth card. "Eight of Swords, reversed. Your past has come back to haunt you."

He shifted in his chair. This was too close for comfort.

Fidelia flipped over the fifth card. "Knight of Swords." She shook her head with a confused look.

"That's bad, too?"

"No, good. You are brave like Sir Lancelot and a defender of women." Fidelia sighed. "I just find it odd that you would select so many Sword cards. There are three other suits. The chance of picking cards from only one suit is rare."

Jean-Luc shrugged. "I *am* a swordsman."

"The swords stand for reason." Fidelia narrowed her eyes. "It must mean you have been concentrating on your intellect and ignoring the needs of your heart."

"I had no choice. I couldn't risk a relationship with anyone because of Lui."

"How old is Louie?" Heather whispered.

Jean-Luc stiffened, then forced himself to lounge back in the chair nonchalantly. "He is . . . older than I."

Heather watched him closely, her fingers digging into the soft chenille pillow. "How old would that be?"

Merde. She was on to him. How could he gain her

trust if he had to keep lying? "I don't know his exact age." At least that much was true.

Fidelia revealed the sixth card. "The Moon." She gave him an odd look.

Jean-Luc swallowed. "Something to do with hunting?"

"No. It means deception." Fidelia glanced at Heather. "It could also mean something supernatural."

Heather's eyes widened.

He sat forward. "Do not be swayed by superstition. I have sworn to protect you, and I will."

"I want to believe you. I'm just not sure I can." Her eyes searched his, and he tried to pour all his concern and admiration for her into his gaze. She didn't look away. A spark of hope ignited inside him. He wanted her trust, her friendship, her respect. He wanted everything she could give him.

"Time for the last card," Fidelia announced. "This one is very important, for it signifies the outcome of our current dilemma." She reached for the card.

The doorbell rang.

Heather jumped to her feet.

Fidelia reached for her purse. "Who would come at this time of night?"

Jean-Luc strode into the foyer with the women following close behind. He heard Angus on the front porch, sending a psychic message to his wife. "It's not Lui. He would never bother to ring the bell."

Heather flipped on the porch light and peered through a pane of leaded glass in the door.

"It's all right," Jean-Luc assured her. "I think it's Angus. Allow me." He opened the door.

Angus slipped inside and nodded at her. "Good evening, lass. How is everything here?"

Heather shrugged. "Okay, I guess. I didn't expect Jean-Luc to show up."

Angus frowned. "He had no choice. 'Tis a matter of

honor." His face brightened when his wife skipped merrily down the stairs. "There ye are."

Emma grinned and walked straight into his arms. "Miss me already?"

"Aye." Angus hugged her tight.

Jean-Luc groaned inwardly. Angus was so easily distracted these days. "Is there any news to report?"

"Nay." Angus rested his chin against Emma's brow. "Robby and I looked all over town. There's no sign of Lui."

Frustration gnawed at Jean-Luc. He desperately wanted to hunt for Lui, but he couldn't ignore his duty to guard Heather. "We need more men."

"I'm going to New York to arrange for more guards," Angus assured him.

Jean-Luc nodded. Roman and Gregori had already teleported back to New York, taking Shanna and the baby with them.

Angus turned to Heather. "We'll bring someone here to help you during the day, too."

Her eyes widened. "Is all this really necessary?"

"Yes," Jean-Luc answered at the same time Angus said, "Aye."

Angus opened the door. "I'd like a moment alone with my wife before I go. Good night." He led Emma onto the front porch.

She glanced back at Heather, smiling. "I'll be back in just a moment." The front door shut.

There was an awkward pause while the others waited in the foyer, then some sounds drifted through the closed door—a squeal from Emma, followed by masculine chuckling and feminine giggling.

Jean-Luc sighed. "Newlyweds."

Heather nodded. "That much cheerfulness can really get annoying."

"*Oui.*" Jean-Luc crossed his arms. "Especially when it is not possible for the rest of us."

Fidelia snorted. "You two are so depressing, you're driving me to drink." She headed for the kitchen. "Anyone else want a beer?"

"No thanks." Heather watched the kitchen door swing, then slanted a curious glance toward Jean-Luc. "You sound almost . . . envious of Angus and Emma."

"What man would not wish to be loved with a passion as great as theirs?"

"Some might find that kind of passion too confining."

"Only if love was used to imprison them." Jean-Luc watched her closely. "Is that what happened to you?"

She shrugged and looked away, but he could sense that was a yes.

He stepped toward her. "I think love should make you feel more powerful and strong, more free and capable of achieving whatever you desire."

Her gaze met his. "A love like that is very rare."

"Do you have that kind of love with your daughter?"

Her eyes widened, then glimmered with moisture. "Yes. I do."

"Then it is possible for you."

She bit her bottom lip. "Why do you think it's not possible for you?"

"I never wanted to expose a woman to Lui's deadly vengeance." Even with Lui gone, there would still be the problem of his being undead. But Roman and Angus had worked around that problem. Maybe he could, too. "It would be difficult to find a woman who could love me as I am."

Heather's mouth quirked. "Are you that hard to get along with? Let me guess. You snore like a buffalo stampede."

"No. I'm actually rather quiet in my sleep."

"You don't stay up all night polishing your fencing trophies?"

He grinned. "No."

She spread her hands in exasperation. "I give up. I can't tell what's wrong with you."

He stepped closer. "Then you are ready to admit that you like me."

Her cheeks blossomed a pretty pink, and the sweet scent of Type AB blood wafted toward him. She lifted her chin. "You're awfully sure of yourself."

He smiled slowly. "An unfortunate by-product of my arrogance."

Her mouth curled with a reluctant smile. "I'm having trouble disliking you."

"Give it time. You'll come around."

She laughed, and the happy sound filled his heart with warm joy. He hadn't enjoyed a woman's company this much in years. Hundreds of years. He realized with a jolt that Heather was a rare woman. Her quick mind was a delightful challenge. Not only was she beautiful and intelligent, but she possessed a courageous and caring heart. She'd come to his rescue tonight when she hardly knew him. And even though he owed her, she refused to take advantage. There was an old-fashioned nobility about her that touched his soul.

The phone rang, and she jumped.

"Good Lord, who would call this late? It's just after midnight." She dashed into the living room and grabbed the phone from the small table next to the wingback chair. "Hello?"

With his superior senses, Jean-Luc could hear an angry masculine voice on the phone. He hovered by the room's entrance, close enough that he could eavesdrop, but far enough away to look like he wasn't.

Heather's shoulders tensed. "Do you know what time it is?"

"Yeah, it's real late for you to have a boyfriend over," the masculine voice sneered. "Why don't you wait till the weekend when I have Bethany? I don't want her exposed to the lowlifes you sleep with."

Jean-Luc sucked in a deep breath. This had to be Heather's ex-husband.

"I have several out-of-town guests spending the night," Heather gritted out. "And it's none of your damned business." She slammed the phone down. "God, I hate Thelma."

"Who is she?" Jean-Luc asked.

"My next-door neighbor. She's best friends with Cody's mother, and she spies on me. She calls Cody's mother, who calls Cody—"

"And he calls you," Jean-Luc finished the sentence. He wished this Cody would show up in person. The bastard needed to learn how to respect women.

"I'd better check on Bethany." Heather rushed from the room. "The phone might have woken her up." She jogged up the stairs.

Jean-Luc moved to the base of the stairs so he could admire her swaying hips.

Fidelia swooshed through the kitchen door with a beer bottle in her hand. "Enjoying the view?" She chuckled as she headed for the stairs. "*Ay, caramba*, but you are *muy macho*. I am glad you are here, Juan."

"It is my pleasure." He wondered if the older woman had been eavesdropping. Probably.

"Good night." Fidelia started up the stairs.

She must have forgotten about the tarot card left from her reading. "Good night." Jean-Luc wandered back into the living room.

The last card remained facedown on the coffee table. Supposedly this was the card that foretold the outcome of their dilemma. He reached down and flipped it over.

He jerked his hand away as if it'd been burned with silver. A skeleton rode a horse.

Death.

Chapter 6

"Come on, sweetie. There are some people I want you to meet." Heather led her daughter down the staircase.

Bethany had been half awake when Heather had checked on her, and she'd thought it best to introduce the four-year-old to their new bodyguards. The last thing she wanted was for her daughter to be frightened if she woke up and found a stranger in her room.

Bethany held tight to her mother's hand, taking each step one at a time.

Heather reached the foot of the stairs and turned to face her daughter. "Sweetie, we have two people visiting us. I want you to meet Emma 'cause she'll be staying in your bedroom tonight."

"Why?" Bethany scratched at her pink pajamas.

"Just to make sure you're safe. Sorta like your own personal guardian angel."

"Oh." Bethany blinked. "Does she have wings?"

"No, but she's as pretty as an angel." Heather led her daughter to the living room and spotted Jean-Luc at the coffee table. He stepped back and stood stiffly by the wingback chair.

Heather narrowed her eyes. She'd detected a hint of guilt in his expression before it had gone blank. What had he been up to? She glanced at the coffee table. The tarot cards had been gathered together into a neat stack.

She wondered what the seventh card had been. Had Jean-Luc seen it? She dragged her gaze from the stack of cards back to him and realized he was staring curiously at her and her daughter. "I brought Bethany to meet you."

"She looks so much like you."

"Yeah. It's called genetics." Heather got the impression he wasn't around children very much. "Sweetie, this is Mr. Echarpe."

Bethany raised a hand. "Hi."

Jean-Luc bowed. "I am honored to meet you, *Bezanie*."

She tugged on her mother's pajamas and whispered, "He talks funny."

"He's from France. Like Belle," Heather whispered back, aware of the wry look he was giving her.

"And the Beast?" Bethany asked.

Heather returned his wry look. "Exactly."

"Is he my guardian angel, too?" Bethany asked.

"No. Emma is yours." Heather glanced around, but Emma was apparently still on the front porch.

"I will be guarding your mother," Jean-Luc explained.

"Oh." Bethany nodded. "Then you get to sleep in my mama's room."

Heather coughed. "That's not going to happen."

"I will abide by your mother's wishes." Jean-Luc's eyes gleamed as his gaze raked over her. "It is my most fervent desire to see her well . . . pleased."

Heather's skin prickled with goose bumps. Good Lord, he was visually undressing her right in front of her daughter. He *was* a beast. Her cheeks grew hot.

He merely smiled.

A sound at the front door distracted her, and she saw Emma slipping inside.

"I checked the grounds after Angus left." Emma locked the front door. "It's clear."

Bethany wrapped an arm around Heather's leg. "Is that my angel?"

"Yes. Emma, this is Bethany. I wanted her to meet you since you'll be in her room tonight."

"Of course." Emma approached them, smiling at Bethany. "Good heavens, you're as pretty as a princess."

Bethany giggled and let go of her mother's leg. "I was a princess for Halloween. Mama made my costume."

"I'm sure it was lovely."

Bethany looked up at her mom. "She talks funny, too. Is she from France?"

Emma chuckled, casting an amused glance at Jean-Luc. "I'm from Scotland. I live in a castle."

Bethany wandered toward her. "I have a castle in my room. It's pink."

Emma leaned over. "Super. I'd love to see it."

Bethany glanced back at her mom. "Can I show it to her?"

"Of course." Heather held out her arms for a hug. "Let me kiss you good night."

As Bethany lunged into her arms, Heather continued, "Don't stay up too late."

"Okay." Bethany turned back to her new friend. "I have a dollhouse, too."

"I saw that." Emma took Bethany's hand to lead her upstairs. "It's so big."

"There's a family living inside," Bethany announced

as she took the stairs one at a time. "There's a mommy and a little girl."

"I see," Emma murmured.

"There was a daddy," Bethany added, "but the mommy made him leave."

Heather winced.

"He's okay," Bethany continued as they reached the top of the stairs. "He lives in the closet now."

Heather covered her mouth to stifle a groan.

"The closet is too good for him," Jean-Luc whispered.

She spun about to find him standing right behind her. Heat burned her cheeks. She'd finally resigned herself to accepting his protection, but she wasn't comfortable with him learning so much about her personal life. "Maybe now you understand why I refused to stay at your place. Bethany's been through too much lately."

"How long ago were you divorced?"

"It's been over a year since it was legal, but we moved here almost two years ago." Heather sighed as she wandered toward the couch. "My mother had just died and left me the house. Thank God we had a place to go." She sat on the couch. "Not all women are so lucky."

"You were not so lucky with your marriage." He crossed the room, then took a seat in the wingback chair.

"Cody's a jerk, all right, but I can't regret it." She dragged the chenille pillow into her lap. "I have Bethany."

Tears crowded her eyes, and she blinked them away to keep from getting too emotional in front of this guy she hardly knew. But never a day had passed that she didn't thank God over and over for her daughter.

Because of her daughter, she'd kept fighting when the situation seemed impossible. She'd refrained from wallowing in despair or self-pity, even when she wanted to, because she refused to look weak or insecure in front of Bethany.

Jean-Luc leaned forward, propping his elbows on his knees. "You're a good mother. She's fortunate to have you."

What a wonderful thing to say. It would be so easy to fall for a guy like this, but she still knew very little about him. That was why she was here on the couch after midnight even though she was exhausted. She needed to find out more about this sword-wielding, mystery man in a tuxedo who insisted on protecting her.

She took a deep breath. "How long has Louie been killing your girlfriends?"

"A long time." Frowning, he tugged at his black tie till it unraveled. "But I assure you, I will not let him harm you or your daughter. His reign of terror has ended."

His frown suddenly transformed into a look of relief and hope. "The Death card. Of course. It meant *his* death."

"Excuse me?"

He motioned to the stack of tarot cards. "I looked at the last card. It was Death. I didn't say anything because I didn't want to alarm you."

Heather laughed. "The Death card wouldn't scare me. I've drawn it myself many times over the last two years. It doesn't actually refer to death, but rebirth. Like the death of my marriage allowing me a new beginning."

"Ah." He nodded. "That sounds much better. I hope to have a new beginning, too."

"Really?" That seemed odd. Wasn't he already rich and successful? But then wealth and success didn't always equal happiness. What had the cards said about him? The poor man was lonely. That made sense if he avoided relationships because of Louie. "If you can . . .

get rid of Louie, then you could have your life back. You could have your new beginning."

He sat forward. "I haven't planned that far ahead. I regret that you're now in danger, and my main concern is keeping you safe."

"But it could be a good thing that he's come back. You can resolve this mess once and for all and be free to enjoy your life." *And stop being lonely.*

"You describe an enticing future for me, but still, I would give it up gladly if I could remove Lui's threats against you."

Heather swallowed hard. What an unselfish, honorable man. He seemed too good to be true. What had the Moon card indicated—deception? She'd been fooled before by men, so she needed to be careful. But the card could also mean something supernatural. The immortal theory simmered in the back of her mind. Gorgeous immortal men trying to chop each other's heads off. Then would Louie be immortal, too? It would certainly explain those old names that Jean-Luc had called him.

"You are an unusual woman," he said quietly.

She sure had an unusual imagination. "I'm fairly normal, I think."

"No. I sense that you're . . . irritated with me for invading your home, but you don't seem angry that I've put you in danger. Most women would be furious about that."

"But you're not doing it. Louie is."

"Most women would still blame me." Jean-Luc rubbed his brow. "And they would make me feel even more guilty than I already do. But you, you take it in stride, and you remain so positive. And courageous."

His lovely compliments warmed her heart, although it was hard to completely accept them. Cody had done a good job of making her feel inferior. "Actually, I've been a coward most of my life."

"I saw you tonight, attacking Lui. You were very brave."

"I've been trying to improve. After my mother's death, I realized how much I had let fear control my life. It stole my dream. It killed my parents. So I've declared war on fear."

His eyes gleamed with what she could only interpret as admiration. "You're a fighter. I like that."

She grinned. She could really get accustomed to this. Cody had always put her down to make himself feel better. But Jean-Luc was different. There was a quiet, self-assured strength that emanated from him, and it was so attractive. Of course he was attractive, she realized wryly. He made her feel good about herself.

"You said fear killed your parents. How can that be?"

Her grin faded. "It's a long story." And a painful one. But if she confided in Jean-Luc, maybe he would tell her about himself. Or maybe it would put him to sleep.

"I would like to hear it." He lounged back and waited.

She had to admit she was curious how he would react. So she took a deep breath and dove in. "My father was the town sheriff. He was very good at his job, but my mother lived in terror that he'd be killed. She nagged him for years to quit."

"Did he?" Jean-Luc asked, apparently interested.

"No. He wanted to make a difference. And he did." Heather smiled, remembering. "When I was about six, there was a boy who went missing. Everyone was trying to find him. There was no ransom note, so my dad believed the boy had wandered into the woods and was lost."

"Did they find him?"

"My dad organized people into search parties, but no luck. Then he sought the help of a psychic in a nearby town. He took some flak over that. There were a few old ladies in town who thought Fidelia was some kind of Satan worshipper, but she did help my dad find the boy."

"Fidelia was the psychic?"

"Yep. My dad never needed Fidelia's help again, but my mother was thrilled to find someone who could give her the reassurance she needed." Heather leaned back to regard the ceiling as she recalled all the times her mother had dragged her to Fidelia's old, crumbling house. "Every week we went to see her, and Fidelia would announce that my dad was going to be safe for another week."

"For a price," Jean-Luc added.

Heather laughed. "Yep. I didn't realize till my mom passed away that we were Fidelia's main source of income. She was broke, and I needed a babysitter, so we teamed up."

Jean-Luc nodded. "I can tell she cares for you and your daughter."

"Well, yeah, if I can just keep her from shooting someone to prove it."

Jean-Luc smiled. "It is a good sign of your character that you inspire such loyalty."

Heather sucked in a deep breath. That had to be the most awesome compliment she'd ever received. She could really get addicted to Jean-Luc. "Thank you."

He shrugged as if it wasn't a miracle for a man to say wonderful things. "You were telling me about your father?"

"Oh, right. When I was sixteen, I went with my mom to Fidelia's. I was studying for a test in the kitchen. Then I heard all this shouting from the living room."

"An argument?" Jean-Luc asked.

"A bad reading. Fidelia tried to calm my mother down, but after ten years of readings, my mom knew what all the cards meant. She was totally freaked out. By the time we got home, my mom was hysterical. She called Dad and insisted he come home right away. He knew she was upset, so he stopped by a grocery store to buy her some flowers."

Heather rubbed her forehead, suddenly reluctant to go on with the story. "Two guys in ski masks barged in, waving pistols. My dad tried to stop them, and he was . . . shot."

"I'm so sorry."

Heather's eyes filled with tears. "If Mother hadn't called him so upset, he wouldn't have been in that store. It was her fear that grew and grew until it came true."

Jean-Luc stood and paced across the room. He seemed deep in thought.

Heather took a big breath to regain control. She'd come too far in life to turn into a blubbering weakling.

"Did your mother blame herself?" he asked quietly.

"No, that never occurred to her. In fact, she felt justified, for her fear had been proven right."

Jean-Luc shook his head as he continued to pace.

Heather wished she knew what he was thinking. "My mother's obsession with fear increased, but with a new focus. Me."

He halted and stared at her.

Heather lowered her gaze to the pillow in her lap and tugged at the fringe. "My dream of leaving Schnitzelberg and becoming a fashion designer was deemed too dangerous. I needed to stay home and have a safe career. The boy I was dating in high school was too dangerous, too, 'cause he wanted to go into law enforcement."

She dug her fingers into the pillow as a surge of anger rushed through her. "I let Mom order me around. She was so miserable after Dad died, and I wanted her to be happy. But she was never happy. The more I gave, the more she demanded. She even picked out my husband for me."

"Cody?"

"Yes. He was so dependable. So predictable. And even more controlling than my mother. I felt so smothered, like every creative need inside me was slowly being strangled to death."

Jean-Luc sat beside her on the couch. "At least you have a beautiful child."

Heather smiled. Boy, this man knew how to say the right thing. "Bethany makes everything good. She's the most perfect creation."

"What happened to your mother?"

"Fidelia called her one morning. She'd had a bad dream about a car accident. My mom was supposed to go see her that day for a reading, but Fidelia begged her to stay home. Well, my mom refused to drive anywhere then. She was calling me every day to run errands for her, and I had my own house and a two-year-old to keep up with. It was so annoying, but I did what I could."

"You have the patience of a saint."

"You mean doormat. My mom went outside one day to get the mail." Heather motioned toward the front yard. "The mailbox is out by the curb. A neighbor's cat ran into the street just as a car was coming by. The car swerved to miss the cat—"

"And hit your mother?"

"No, they managed to brake in time." Heather turned on the couch to face Jean-Luc. "My mother was so afraid, so certain of her own death that she had a heart attack. It was fear that killed her."

"How terrible."

"It was. I was devastated. But at the same time, I had this sudden revelation." She leaned toward him. "I had let fear control my life. Fear triggered my parents' deaths. Fear caused me to make all the wrong decisions. I wasn't living. I was cowering in a self-made prison!"

His eyes narrowed. "I understand. Too well."

"And that's when I declared war on fear. I filed for divorce the next day. Everyone thought I was behaving strangely out of grief, but it took something as bad as grief to make me open my eyes and reclaim my life."

Jean-Luc rested his hand on top of hers. "You realize what you must do?"

"Hmm?" It was hard to think with his slender fingers wrapping around hers.

"You must pursue your dream. Take the job I offered you."

"I don't want you to feel beholden to me because of this Louie thing."

He clasped her hand in both of his. "I offered you the job before Lui came. You have talent, Heather. It is not too late for your dreams to come true."

"How do you always know the perfect thing to say? I'm not used to men being that . . . smart."

His mouth quirked. "I suppose that's a compliment. Whatever wisdom I have, it's from watching people over the years. They live and die, their lives so short and precarious. I know your life is too short to be wasted."

Once again she wondered how old he was. "You're . . . very kind." She retrieved her hand from his grasp. "Not at all like my ex. I swear that man is like a . . . vampire."

Jean-Luc stiffened. "*Non*. He is not."

"I mean he's like an emotional vampire. He completely drained me. All my dreams, my self-esteem, my beliefs, my energy—it was all sucked out till all that was left of me was a lifeless doormat."

Jean-Luc regarded her, a look of dismay on his face. "That is how you envision a vampire?"

"An emotional one, yes. Thank God the real, creepy, monster ones don't exist."

"Right." Jean-Luc loosened his collar.

"But you, you're completely the opposite."

He eyed her warily. "How's that?"

"You listened to me. You accepted my story and my conclusions. You recognized my dream as something precious and worthwhile, and you're willing to help. You don't tear down others in order to build yourself up." She touched his arm. "You're a sweet man, Jean-Luc. Thank you."

He placed his hand on top of hers. "You believe I am good?"

"Yes." She smiled. "And I'm not just saying that because you're my new boss."

He smiled back. "Then you're coming to work Monday?"

"Yep." Her grin widened. She was going after her dream.

"I am glad." He squeezed her hand.

Her heart felt light enough to float to the ceiling. The friendly gleam in his eyes looked so genuine. Good Lord, had she finally found the perfect man? A man who understood her dreams and wanted her to succeed.

His gaze lowered to her mouth and became more heated. Her throat went dry. The light, airy feeling grew more dense, more electric. More heavy with desire.

With a jolt, she realized he meant to kiss her. A flood of emotions swept through her as her heart raced. She was flattered. Excited. Tempted. Terrified.

She jumped to her feet. "Time for bed. I mean—" Her cheeks blazed with heat. "Time for me to say good night." She eased past him and the coffee table.

He stood. "As you wish."

"Good night, Jean-Luc."

"Jean."

Whatever. She hurried into the foyer. She much preferred the name Jean-Luc. It made him sound like a starship captain, but young. And with hair. "If you need anything from the kitchen, just help yourself."

"I'll be fine." He followed her. "Emma and I will be leaving shortly before dawn. I'm afraid you'll be on your own during the day until Angus can send a bodyguard."

"We'll be fine." She headed up the stairs.

"I'll return tomorrow evening right after sunset."

Her heart skipped. Saturday night with a gorgeous man. "Okay."

"Heather, a moment please."

She paused with her hand on the banister. "Yes?"

"You mentioned how Fidelia found that missing boy. If she could help us locate Lui, that would be a tremendous help."

"Oh. That's a good idea. It would be easier if she could handle something that belongs to Louie."

Jean-Luc's eyes lit up. "We have his sword and the cane he used as a sheath. I'll bring them tomorrow night."

"Okay." She paused, not knowing what to say. "Good night." She ran up the stairs.

"Sleep well, Heather." His whispered words followed her up, reaching her like a soft caress.

She slipped into her room, her heart still pounding. Emma had asked her to leave the door ajar, but she closed it firmly. She needed a barrier between her and Jean-Luc. He was too attractive, too appealing, and too damned mysterious. She knew next to nothing about him, except that he seemed too good to be true. He'd learned a whole lot about her tonight. And still, he had wanted to kiss her.

She should have let him, an inner voice scolded. She shouldn't have chickened out. Wasn't she at war with fear? But she had to be careful. Where men were concerned, she'd made some bad mistakes. But hadn't she learned from them?

Tomorrow night he'd come again. She'd have another chance to get to know him. And maybe, just maybe, tomorrow night she'd let him kiss her.

Chapter 7

The next night, Jean-Luc sped toward the town of Schnitzelberg with an ice chest filled with bottled synthetic blood strapped into the passenger seat of his black BMW. The sun had set ten minutes ago. He gulped blood from a bottle of Type AB positive, still cold since he'd been in too big of a hurry to warm it up.

The problem was, if he was awake, so was Lui. And if Lui had discovered who Heather was and where she lived, he could already be there. Jean-Luc had wanted to teleport to her house immediately after awakening, but Emma had convinced him he needed to arrive like a normal mortal.

Heather should be all right, he reassured himself as he turned off the highway and entered the town. Emma had teleported to her backyard five minutes ago. She would have alerted him telepathically if something was wrong.

Still, he hated not being there. He hated that Heather and her daughter had been dragged into his feud with Lui. If anything happened to them . . . how could he endure the guilt of more innocent mortals dying?

Heather's story last night had made him take a hard look at himself. He now realized what lay hidden beneath his guilt and anger. Fear.

He'd risen far from his humble beginnings as an orphaned stable boy. He was a knight by the time Roman transformed him in 1513. He'd become a musketeer, owner of the most prestigious fencing academy in Paris, a lieutenant-colonel in the Vamp army, and now he was coven master of Western Europe, in addition to being a designer and successful businessman. He'd poured all his energy into outward success in an effort to be the master of his own destiny. But beneath it all, the same old torment continued to plague him. The fear of being powerless.

As a lowly stable boy, he'd been powerless to the whims and political machinations of the masters over him. He'd sworn never to be a pawn again. And he'd succeeded until Lui came into his life in 1757.

He should have let Louis XV die that year. But no, Jean-Luc had done his duty as a royal bodyguard, and he'd stopped the mortal assassin Damiens.

The mortal had only been a pawn. Lui enjoyed using mind control to make mortals do his dirty work. He'd succeeded twice before, using mortal scapegoats to kill two kings—Henri III in 1589 and Henri IV in 1610.

Jean-Luc had foiled Lui's third royal assassination. The next night, he'd received a note. *Because of you, the king lives. Because of me, your queen dies.* There'd been no signature on the note, but the paper had been folded and sealed with a dollop of wax, imprinted with the letter *L*.

Two nights later, he'd found the mutilated body of his mistress, Yvonne. In addition to knife wounds and fang marks, he'd found the letter *L* burned into her flesh.

He had declared war against the enemy he dubbed

Lui. After twenty years of evading capture, Lui had disappeared. Jean-Luc had hoped the bastard was dead. Then in 1832, he'd discovered his mistress, Claudine, murdered, with the letter *L* burned into the flesh over her heart.

Jean-Luc had decided the only honorable course of action was to avoid another relationship. But Heather's talk had made him realize the truth. His honor had masked the fear that if he entered into another relationship, he would be powerless to save the woman's life. He wasn't living an honorable life. He was living with fear.

That revelation caused him shame. And anger. Dammit to hell, if he wanted a relationship with Heather, he would take it. He would put an end to Lui's torture and kill the bastard once and for all.

Jean-Luc pulled into her driveway. As he exited the car, Emma emerged from the shadow of a large oak tree. She was sipping from a bottle of cold blood, her bag of stakes slung over her shoulder. She'd kept her presence a secret, so it would appear that they had arrived together.

"They're fine," she reported quietly. "I heard their voices inside. Calm and happy. And the perimeter's clear."

"Good." He exhaled with relief, then took Emma's empty bottle and set it inside his car. From the backseat, he retrieved Lui's sword and cane, along with his own sword. He locked the car and headed for the front porch.

"You're hoping Fidelia can locate Lui?" Emma asked.

"Yes." He noted the small pair of roller skates next to the front door and the paperback book resting on the seat cushion of the porch swing. Life had continued here during the day, and he'd missed it.

"I'm psychic, too," Emma whispered. "More so than

the usual Vamp. I've been listening for any sign of vampire telepathy in the area, but so far, it's been quiet."

Jean-Luc sighed as he rang the doorbell. "Lui is very good at staying hidden. God knows I have tried for centuries to find him." And always failed.

His depressing thoughts vanished when the door swung open and Heather stood there, smiling. She was wearing a turquoise sundress and matching sandals. The twinkle in her eyes and her glowing complexion ignited a spark of desire in Jean-Luc. She seemed genuinely happy to see him.

"Come on in." She stepped back. "We have some lasagna left over from supper, if you're interested."

"That's very kind, but we've already eaten." He hoped he didn't have blood breath. He shut and locked the door.

The little girl, Bethany, sidled up close to her new friend. "Hi, Emma." She glanced shyly at Jean-Luc. "Hi."

He bowed slightly. "Good evening, Bethany."

"Hello, love." Emma knelt to give the little girl a hug. "Did you have a good day?"

"Yes." Bethany leaned close and whispered loudly, "My mommy wanted to look pretty for Mr. Sharp."

"Bethany!" Heather's face turned pink. "Why don't you take Emma upstairs and show her . . . something."

"Like my new book?" Bethany asked brightly.

"Yes. Please." Heather glared at Fidelia, who was standing by the staircase chuckling.

Jean-Luc felt like laughing, too, but he managed to stay quiet.

"Let's go." Emma led the little girl toward the stairs. She glanced back at him, her eyes sparkling with mirth.

"I see you've brought Louie's sword and cane," Heather hurriedly changed the subject. "Fidelia's ready to help us locate him." She motioned toward the living room.

Jean-Luc followed her. "You succeeded wonderfully."

"On what?" She glanced back. "Staying alive? It was very peaceful today."

"That's good. But I was referring to what your daughter said. You look very pretty."

Heather waved a hand in dismissal. "Bethany turns everything into a romance. Even her stuffed animals are married to each other. She has me perform the ceremony. Today I married a male Chihuahua to a lady gorilla."

Fidelia chuckled as she settled on the couch with her purse. "That dog is barking up the wrong tree."

Jean-Luc rested his sword next to the wingback chair. "My friend Roman always says that with love, anything is possible."

"*Sí*, like double homicide." Fidelia patted her purse.

Heather snorted. "Or child custody battles."

Jean-Luc gave her a wry look. "Have you lost all faith in love?"

She looked away, her cheeks pink. "No. There's always hope. Shall we get started?"

"Very well." He placed Lui's sword and cane on the coffee table in front of Fidelia.

She took the cane into her lap. Closing her eyes, she ran her fingers up and down the polished wood. Heather sat quietly beside her. Jean-Luc settled in the wingback chair and waited.

"It is a dark place," Fidelia whispered.

That was hardly surprising. All vampires needed a dark place for their daily death-sleep.

"A cellar," Fidelia continued. "Made of stone. No windows." She shook her head. "It's too dark. I can't see anything."

"Can you tell how far away it is?" Jean-Luc asked.

"Not far, but not too close. Not in town, I think."
Fidelia inhaled sharply. "He senses me." Her eyes
opened wide, and she shoved the cane onto the table.
"This was a mistake. I—I think he may be psychic."

Lui would have a vampire's psychic abilities, but
that wasn't something Jean-Luc could admit to.

Fidelia gave him a worried look. "He sensed me. I
could feel it. He was cold, so cold." She shuddered.

"It's all right." Heather rubbed the older woman's
back. "It's over now."

Fidelia shook her head. "I was trying to trace his location. I think he was doing the same to me."

Jean-Luc winced. *Zut*, he should have taken Fidelia
somewhere else to do this.

Heather's face paled. "He's hunting us."

"Heather, I must ask you again to move to my place,"
Jean-Luc said. "It is only a matter of time before Lui
figures out who you are and where you live."

"We'll just have to find him before he finds us. If we
knew more about him, it might help." Her eyes narrowed. "Who is he exactly?"

Jean-Luc sat back. "I wish I knew. If I knew his real
name, I would have hunted him down and killed him
many years ago."

"You would . . . commit murder?"

"I would do anything to protect those I love."

Fidelia nodded approvingly. "You are good man,
Juan."

He glanced at Heather, wondering if she agreed. She
looked puzzled.

"You said *many* years ago," she murmured. "How
old are you?"

Merde. There was no way to answer this.

"I'm twenty-six," she announced. "And you?"

He shifted in his chair. "I am older than you."

"How much?"

"I was twenty-eight when . . ." He rubbed his forehead. "I was three when my mother died . . ."

"I'm sorry. I didn't realize . . ." Her eyes warmed with sympathy. "Emotional wounds take the longest to heal."

"Yes." He heard a car pulling up in the driveway. He stood, grabbing his sword. "We have company."

Heather jumped to her feet. "It couldn't be Louie, could it? Not this fast."

"I'll be ready for him." Fidelia dug in her purse.

"I don't think it's Lui." Jean-Luc doubted his arch nemesis used cars very often. Even so, he strode into the foyer with his sword. He heard a car door slam outside, then heavy footsteps pound up the steps to the front porch.

Heather arrived at the front door just as a fist knocked hard enough to shake the door's panes of leaded glass. Jean-Luc stayed close by her side.

"I can see him!" a male voice shouted. "You've got that boyfriend spending the night again, don't you?"

"Oh no, it's Cody," Heather groaned. "Thelma must have seen you arrive, and she called his mother."

Jean-Luc peered through the door window. The man on the porch was large and flushed with alcohol-rich blood.

"I can see you, you asshole!" Cody yelled. "You want to screw my ex, go ahead, but lay one finger on my daughter and I'll—"

"Stop it!" Heather hissed as she unlocked the door.

"You shouldn't let him in," Jean-Luc whispered.

"Oh please, let him in," Fidelia drawled. She stood by the stairs, waving her Glock in the air. "Make my day."

"Fidelia, put the gun away," Heather ordered. She opened the door. "How dare you—"

Cody barged into the foyer and glowered at Jean-Luc. "Who the hell are you?"

Jean-Luc glared back. "I do not answer to you."

"Jean—" Heather started, but her ex interrupted.

"*John?* So you're bringing your johns home?" Cody turned to Jean-Luc. "You keep leaving your car parked out front. Now everyone in town knows you're screwing my wife!"

"Ex-wife." Jean-Luc narrowed his eyes. "You are the fool who let her go."

"Enough." Heather stepped between them. "Cody, lower your voice before Bethany hears you. You're drunk, and you have no right to spy on me or pass judgment."

He sneered at her. "I do, too. My daughter's living here, and I can sue for full custody now that everyone knows you're a slut."

"I am not. And I will never let you take her from me."

Cody snorted. "Watch me."

Two hundred years ago, Jean-Luc would have simply skewered the bastard and tossed his body into a river, but the modern world tended to frown upon that solution. He assaulted the man with a psychic wave. *You are a cockroach.*

In his inebriated state, Cody had no resistance at all to vampire mind control. He fell to the floor and scurried around the foyer on all fours.

With a squeal, Heather jumped back. "Cody, what is your problem?"

"I am a cockroach," he muttered in a squeaky voice.

"Hmm, about time you figured that one out," Fidelia stepped back as he brushed against her long skirt.

Cody attempted to go up the stairs, but tipped over and landed on his back. He squirmed, arms and legs flailing.

"Cut it out, Cody," Heather demanded. "Get out of here before you scare Bethany."

"What's going on?" Emma descended the stairs, looking askance at Cody's wriggling body.

Fidelia chuckled. "Let's get a can of bug spray."

"*Raid!*" Cody flipped onto all fours and scuttled out the front door.

You will return to normal at sunrise, Jean-Luc ordered.

"Yes, Master." Cody tumbled down the porch stairs.

"Good Lord, the man's gone crazy." Heather shut the door and locked it.

"That was interesting." Emma gave Jean-Luc a pointed look. She'd probably heard his psychic commands.

He wondered briefly if Lui had heard him, but he doubted he'd said enough for Lui to trace.

"Is Bethany all right?" Heather rushed up the stairs.

"Ooh wee, I need a drink." Fidelia waddled toward the kitchen, still holding her Glock. "I need a beer, that's what I need. You want a beer, Juan, Emma?"

"No thank you." He wandered back into the living room and rested his sword against the wingback chair.

Emma leaned against the entrance, smiling. "A cockroach?"

He smiled back. "The man deserved it."

She nodded. "I'll go back upstairs." She paused, then added, "I think you've made quite an impression on Bethany. The toy mum who lives in the dollhouse has a new boyfriend named John. He's a G.I. Joe doll who looks like he could beat the crap out of the Ken living in the closet."

"Really?" Jean-Luc's heart squeezed in his chest. Could he actually be welcomed into this family? He'd always wanted to be part of a family. His father had died when he was six, three years after his mother had passed away in childbirth. Roman and Angus were the closest he'd ever come to having real brothers.

He gazed about the living room and realized how truly lonely he'd been over the centuries. Heather appealed to him in many ways, but her family, Bethany and Fidelia, were touching his heart, too. How different his life could be if he had true companionship and love filling each night. Such a life made all his previous centuries seem empty and meaningless.

But could they accept him as he was? Could Heather love him?

"I'm so sorry you had to witness that scene with my ex," Heather said as she entered the room.

He turned to face her. *Zut*, he'd been so deep in thought, he hadn't realized that Emma had left and Heather had returned. He needed to stay more vigilant than that. "I didn't mind."

Heather sighed. "I don't know what got into Cody."

"Is Bethany all right?"

"Yes. Thank goodness." Heather flopped down on the couch. "She was watching a DVD with the volume turned up, so she didn't hear anything."

"That's good." Jean-Luc sat beside her. Instantly, he heard her heartbeat speed up. A good sign.

She glanced shyly at him. "Where did Fidelia go?"

"To the kitchen for a beer."

"I wish she wouldn't drink and handle those guns at the same time."

He extended an arm along the back of the couch. "The guns have trigger locks."

"You bet. It was the one requirement I made before she could move in here."

"You've lived in this area all your life, correct?"

She sighed. "Yes. I always wanted to travel, but it never happened."

He made a mental note that he needed to take her to all the places she wanted to see. "Can you think of anyplace that matches Fidelia's description? A place on the outskirts of town. Most probably abandoned."

"With a stone cellar?" She tilted her head, considering. "The state park has an old stone building built during the Depression."

"I'll check it out." He could leave Emma here with the women and take Robby with him.

"I'll come with you."

He blinked. "No. Absolutely not. It's too dangerous."

"I'm already in danger. I fought Louie before and I did well. And I know where the park is."

"I can look up the park's location on the Internet."

Her chin lifted. "I'm going. I'm not cowering here in fear. I'm at war with fear, remember?"

"There's a difference between courage and bad judg—" He paused when his superior hearing detected a sound outside. "Someone is approaching your front porch."

He jumped silently to his feet and grabbed his sword.

Heather stood and whispered, "Should I get my shotgun?"

"No." He hoped Lui was outside. He would destroy the bastard and . . . But what if he made a fatal error and lost? Lui would simply walk into the house and slaughter Heather. "Yes, get your gun. Tell Emma, and wait inside. If he comes in, aim for his chest."

"If he comes in, then you would be . . ." She squeezed his arm. "Be careful."

The concern in her eyes was genuine. *Mon Dieu*, she did care for him.

He touched her cheek. "Go."

Her eyes glazed over with a dreamy look, then she blinked. "Right." She ran to the stairs. The carpet muffled the sounds of her sandals as she dashed up the steps.

"What's up?" Fidelia sauntered from the kitchen,

holding a half-empty beer bottle. She glanced at Heather's disappearing form. "You chased her off again?"

Jean-Luc lifted a finger to his lips, then pointed outside.

Fidelia's brown eyes widened. "I left my German *muchacho* in the kitchen. I'll be right back."

"I don't want you outside. It could be dangerous." Jean-Luc groaned when Fidelia scurried into the kitchen. He'd better act fast before the women in the house charged to the rescue. He smiled to himself. No wonder he liked them so much.

Silently he unlocked the door, then yanked it open.

Chapter 8

Jean-Luc leaped onto the front porch, aiming his foil at the trespasser.

A blond woman yelped and stumbled back. Her stiletto heel caught between two wooden planks, and she crashed onto the porch. "Shit!"

She looked familiar. "Who are you?" he demanded. She was mortal, but that didn't mean she was safe. Lui enjoyed using vampire mind control to coerce mortals into performing his assassinations.

"Damn." The woman rubbed her bony ankle. "I'd better be able to walk a runway." She glared at him. "You crazy imbecile! You scared me to death with that sword!"

He recognized her now. Sasha Saladine, the model Alberto had hired. Obviously she had no idea who he was.

Still sprawled on the porch, she pulled off her shoes and examined the rhinestone-studded heels. "I swear, if my shoes are damaged, I'm suing your ass. These were four hundred bucks, you know. I only buy the best."

Already he missed Heather. When she challenged

him, he liked it. She was witty and fun. This woman was simply annoying. While she continued to berate him with her shrill voice, he scanned the yard for any sign of movement.

"You gonna stand there all night like an idiot or help me up?" She looked around the porch. "This is Heather's house, isn't it? This is where she lived in high school."

She glanced over her shoulder at his car. "Shit. She told me she didn't have a boyfriend." She gave him a wary look. "What are you doing with a freakin' sword?"

"You prefer a gun?" Fidelia shoved past Jean-Luc, holding a beer in one hand and her Glock in the other.

"Oh my God!" Sasha jumped to her feet and raised her hands. "Don't shoot. I thought this was Heather's house."

"Fidelia, be careful!" Heather rushed out onto the porch, her shotgun in her hands.

Sasha gasped. "And I thought New York was dangerous."

Jean-Luc groaned inwardly. "Heather, didn't I tell you to stay inside?"

Heather ignored him and turned to the blond model. "Sasha? What are you doing here?"

"I'm about to get shot or skewered, I don't know which."

"Well, make up your mind. I don't have all night." Fidelia set her beer on the porch and removed a set of keys from her skirt pocket. She fumbled with the key, trying to release the trigger lock on her pistol.

"Don't do that," Heather warned her. "You've had too much to drink."

Fidelia snorted. "I'm not drunk. I'm in complete control." She tore off the trigger lock.

Bang! The gun fired, ripping into a nearby oak tree.

The women screamed. Jean-Luc winced.

A squirrel plummeted from the tree and landed in the yard with a thud.

Fidelia shrugged. "I meant to do that. Damned rodent's been gnawing on the house. And stealing all the nuts from our pecan tree."

Heather planted her hands on her hips. "Haven't I told you a million times to keep the locks on?"

Fidelia hung her head, looking properly remorseful. "I'll be more careful." She switched on the safety, then shot Jean-Luc a pointed look. "I know how to deal with a scumbag with nuts."

His mouth twitched. "I'll take that under advisement."

At that moment, Emma burst onto the porch, a stake in her hand. "Is he here?"

"No," Jean-Luc answered. "False alarm."

Emma looked around. "But I heard a gunshot."

"Yes." Jean-Luc motioned toward the front yard. "We suffered a casualty."

Emma's eyes widened. "We were attacked by a squirrel?"

"Damned right," Fidelia said. "And I took care of it."

"Oh my God, Heather," Sasha whispered. "You're dealing drugs?"

"What?" Heather turned to her. "No!"

"Oh." Sasha looked disappointed. "Then what's the deal with all the weapons?"

Heather sighed. "I can explain. Later."

"Since everything's fine, I'll go back to my post." Emma slanted Jean-Luc an amused glance as she headed back into the foyer. "And you thought you'd be bored in Texas."

He nodded. Life had become much more interesting lately.

"I've had enough excitement for one day," Fidelia

announced and waddled after Emma. "I'm taking a long hot bath and going to bed."

"Good night." Heather set her shotgun down on the porch. "Great. Now I get to deal with the squirrel."

"There is nothing to deal with," Jean-Luc assured her. "The squirrel is dead."

"I can't leave it lying there. Bethany will see it, and she thinks it's SpongeBob's friend Sandy."

Jean-Luc had no idea what she was talking about. "I could bury it. Even say the Last Rites." He knew them by heart after hearing Roman perform them more than a hundred times for their fallen comrades during the Great Vampire War.

Heather's pretty mouth tilted up at the corners. "I didn't realize our squirrel was Catholic."

Was she laughing at him? "If you rather I didn't—"

"No, please. I want you to." She gifted him with a brilliant smile. "I think you're very sweet."

His heart expanded. *Mon Dieu*, a man could grow addicted to this feeling. "You have a shovel?"

"Yes, in the garage." She motioned to her left.

He hurried down the porch steps and took a left turn toward the driveway. He kept his sword with him, just in case Lui was hiding in the shadows. Or the garage.

Sasha Saladine watched him as he passed by, then hissed at Heather. "You big liar! You told me you didn't have a boyfriend."

"He's not my boyfriend," Heather whispered.

Jean-Luc continued to pick up their conversation as he strode toward the detached garage.

"Where on earth did you find him?" Sasha whispered.

"I met him last night at the grand opening."

"You're kidding! That handsome hunk was there? Damn, I screwed the wrong guy."

"Sasha!"

"Have you slept with him yet?"

"Of course not," Heather huffed. "I just met him yesterday."

Her indignation made Jean-Luc smile. He paused at the garage's side door to hear more.

"If you don't want him, I'll take him," Sasha continued. "Alberto was kinda disappointing. But he did promise me more turns on the runway. So, what do you say?"

"Uh, congratulations?"

"No, I'm talking about the hunky guy with the sword. Can I make a move on him or not? Do you want him?"

He strained to hear a response.

"Jean!" Heather called. "Is the door locked?"

He twisted the doorknob, and the door creaked open. "It's fine!" He slipped inside, but left the door ajar so he could hear. He glanced around. The garage was empty.

"John?" Sasha asked. "John who?"

"Jean Echarpe," Heather replied. "He's Jean-Luc Echarpe's son."

Sasha gasped. "You're kidding! Oh, crap! I really did screw the wrong guy."

Jean-Luc shook his head. As if he could possibly desire that vain shrew. Now Heather was another story. He'd love to see her green eyes grow dazed with pleasure when he palmed her breast or stroked her between her sweet thighs. He'd like to see her cheeks flush with heat, her mouth open with a throaty groan. He'd. . .

He'd better stop before his eyes started glowing. He grabbed the shovel and left the garage. The women were still talking, but he was no longer the subject.

"Where's your rental car?" Heather asked. "How did you get here?"

Sasha was lounging on the porch swing, pushing it

with a bare foot on the porch. "Alberto dropped me off. We just had dinner, and he thought I'd drunk too much to drive. But I swear I only had two margaritas."

"Did you eat anything?"

"Sure. But I didn't keep it, if you know what I mean." Sasha pointed an index finger into her mouth.

Jean-Luc grimaced. She was bulimic. This was precisely why he used Simone and Inga as his main models. They were Vamps, so they never had to damage themselves to stay thin. Unfortunately, the media was beginning to question why they never aged, either.

"You shouldn't joke about bulimia," Heather grumbled. "It's a disease."

"It's desperation. I'm twenty-six years old, trying to compete with babies." Sasha noticed Jean-Luc passing by and scrambled to her feet. "Oh, Mr. Echarpe, it's such a pleasure to meet you. I hope you weren't offended by anything I said." Her gaze wandered to the sword, still in his right hand. "Heather said you were here to protect her. I think that's so noble of you."

She was buttering him up. Jean-Luc was used to that. It had nothing to do with him. He'd realized many years ago some models would jump the Hunchback of Notre Dame if it could further their careers.

"I am honored to meet you." He shifted his gaze to Heather. "Where would you like the burial site?"

She looked around the front yard. "How about under the oak tree? That was his home, so I think he'd like that."

"As you wish." Jean-Luc sauntered toward the tree. He spotted a blank space between two patches of flowers and started to dig. If only the women would go inside, he could use vampire speed and finish the task in a few seconds.

The porch swing creaked when Sasha sat once again. "People talk about how friendly small towns are, but it's so not true. Old Mrs. Herman threw me out of her bed-and-breakfast. Can you believe it?"

"That's odd," Heather answered. "She's a widow. I would have thought she'd need the money."

"She's an old prude. I invited Alberto over last night, and when she saw him leave this morning, she got all huffy and told me she wasn't running a bordello. Then Alberto and I tried to go back there after dinner, and she wouldn't let us in. I swear, she's just a frigid old bat!"

"She was our Sunday school teacher," Heather murmured. "Do you have a place to stay?"

"Well, I really don't want to stay with my psycho mom in her dinky trailer, so I thought I'd crash here," Sasha mumbled. "What do you think?"

"Where's your luggage?"

"Don't need it. I sleep in the nude."

"Great," Heather muttered.

"I'll get my stuff and my rental car in the morning. I can't wait to get out of this town. I'm going to the Spa d'Elegance in San Antonio tomorrow. You want to come?"

"I need to stay here."

"How can you?" Sasha's voice turned shrill. "I can't stand it anymore. There are no shopping malls, no nightclubs. I ordered an orange frappaccino at the diner, and they looked at me like I was some kind of alien."

Heather sighed. "You lived here for eighteen years. You know how it is."

"Believe me, I made sure I forgot everything about this godforsaken cesspool."

Heather's voice was low and tense. "I still live here."

Jean-Luc paused in his shoveling to look at the women on the porch. He could see the pink tint of Heather's cheeks, and the green flash of anger in her eyes.

Sasha shrugged. "Well, that's your loss."

He considered digging a bigger grave.

"Since you have no car and nowhere else to go," Heather continued, "I'm going to ignore your insulting comments and show you to the guest room."

Jean-Luc's mouth tilted with a slight smile. In spite of her recent divorce, Heather still had a forgiving and compassionate nature. But would she be so understanding if she knew the truth about him? His smile faded as he recalled her description last night of a vampire. *Creepy monster.* How could she ever accept him?

"Geez, Heather." Sasha's thin shoulders drooped. "I didn't mean to hurt your feelings. You're the only real friend I have. Everyone else just wants to use me. Well, I use them, too. But you're the only one I can really talk to."

Heather's face softened, and she gave the model a hug. "Okay." She opened the front door. "Let's get you to bed."

As the door shut, Jean-Luc surveyed the house once more. It was more than a home; it was a shelter for those in need. Heather had opened it to Fidelia, and now Sasha. With her generous, loving heart, Heather would always have friends and family.

A picture flashed through his head. A family picture—Roman and Shanna Draganesti and their little son, Constantine. Jean-Luc fisted his hands around the wooden shovel handle. He'd never had a family. He never would.

He rammed the shovel into the ground. With his vampire strength, the blade sliced into the ground all the way past the hilt, neatly chopping through a tree root. The grave was big enough now for the squirrel, so he walked toward the dead animal. After two steps, he halted.

A white police car rolled to a stop in front of Heather's house. Along the side of the car, fluorescent letters spelled the words *County Sheriff. Merde.* Like most Vamps, Jean-Luc was wary of law enforcement. A Vamp could never allow himself to be interrogated in one of those rooms with one-way reflective glass, not when their bodies didn't reflect.

He glanced at his sword where it rested, propped against the tree. He strode back and slid the sword under some thick bushes at the base of the tree.

Meanwhile, the officer had exited the squad car. He marched toward the house, looking very official in his neatly pressed khaki uniform complete with belt and gun holster. He watched Jean-Luc with narrowed eyes and rolled a toothpick from one side of his mouth to the other.

"Step away from the tree. Raise your hands where I can see them," he ordered.

Jean-Luc took one step to the side and opened his hands, palms forward. "Is there a problem, Sheriff?"

The young officer halted and chewed on his toothpick. "Who the hell are you?"

"I am Jean Echarpe."

"Johnny Sharp, huh? Where you from, Mr. Sharp?"

Jean-Luc figured it was best to leave the misunderstanding alone. "I'm from Paris."

The sheriff nodded knowingly. "Up north of Dallas. I've been there."

Jean-Luc was taken aback for a few seconds. "There is a Paris in Texas?"

"Yep. But you talk too weird, even for someone from up north. Guess you're one of those Frogs."

Jean-Luc gritted his teeth. "I am from France."

"That's too bad." The sheriff's gaze focused on the recently dug grave. He plucked the toothpick from his mouth and tossed it on the ground. "I got a report from one of the neighbors that a gun was fired here. And now I catch you in the act of digging a grave."

Jean-Luc motioned to the hole. "As you can see, it is a very small grave."

"Well, maybe you like cutting up your victims and burying them in parts." The sheriff rested a hand on his gun holster.

Jean-Luc glared at him. "I have not murdered any-one." *Yet.* He pointed to the side. "The victim is lying there."

"Shit." The sheriff strode toward the dead squirrel, then glowered at Jean-Luc. "Look, Mr. Sharp, I don't appreciate foreigners coming here and shootin' our squirrels."

"I didn't shoot it."

The sheriff snorted. "Right, it was a suicide." He held up a hand as Jean-Luc approached. "Stay back. This is a crime scene, and I don't want you mucking it up."

Jean-Luc sighed. Obviously, not much happened in this town. "I told Heather I would bury the squirrel for her."

The sheriff's eyes narrowed. "You know Heather?"

"Of course." Jean-Luc lifted his chin. "This is her house, in case you didn't know."

"I knew that." The sheriff widened his stance and crossed his arms. "I dated her for two years in high school. How long have you known her?"

So this was the guy Heather's mother had decided was too dangerous. If she hadn't interfered, would Heather have married this big lummox instead? An angry, snakelike sensation coiled in Jean-Luc's belly. With a jolt he recognized it. Jealousy. *Merde.* He hadn't felt that in more than two hundred years.

"Billy!" Heather yelled from the porch. "What are you doing here?" She shut the door and descended the steps.

"Hey, Heather." The sheriff raised a hand in greeting.

"Thelma called about a gun going off." He gave Jean-Luc a suspicious look. "And I found this Frog digging up your yard. Probably looking for snails to eat." He snickered at his own joke.

Heather frowned at him. "Jean is my guest. And he's kind enough to help me with this poor dead squirrel."

She was defending him. Again. Jean-Luc loved it. But he could tell Billy was not impressed. Billy looked downright pissed.

"You gonna ask some foreigner to bury your squirrel? That's a job for a *real* man." Billy grabbed the dead squirrel and strode toward the grave.

Jean-Luc glanced at Heather to see if she was swayed by Neanderthal tactics. Thankfully, she was not regarding Billy with hero worship in her eyes. She looked really annoyed.

"That's not necessary, Billy. Jean has everything under control."

Billy dumped the squirrel in the grave. "You should have called me, Heather. I told you before if you needed anything to call me." He grabbed the shovel, but it was stuck fast. He yanked it hard, but it didn't budge.

"Shall I?" Jean-Luc strode toward the grave.

"Stay back." Billy widened his stance and grasped the shovel with both hands. He strained. A low growl reverberated in his throat. Sweat popped out on his brow.

The shovel didn't move.

He glared at Jean-Luc. "What did you do to this damned thing?"

"Let me see." Jean-Luc curled one hand around the handle and jerked the shovel out of the ground. "Ah, you were correct. The job required a *real* man."

Heather covered her mouth to hide her grin.

Billy glowered uncertainly as if he wasn't sure if

he'd been insulted. Before he had time to figure it out, his walkie-talkie crackled and a voice came on. He punched a button. "Sheriff here. What's up?"

"Someone called about a public disturbance behind Schmitty's Bar," a woman's voice reported.

"Cathy, use the proper code number," Billy growled.

"There ain't no number for a guy acting like a cockroach!" the woman yelled. "He climbed into their Dumpster and he's wallowing in the trash."

Cockroach? Jean-Luc glanced at Heather. It had to be her ex-husband. She frowned, but remained silent.

"Damned drunkard," Billy muttered into his mike. "I'll be right there." He scowled at Jean-Luc. "I'll be watching you, Mr. Sharp." He strode toward his squad car.

Jean-Luc used the shovel to scoop dirt onto the squirrel.

"I think my ex has gone crazy," Heather whispered.

"He was crazy to let you go." Jean-Luc used the flat end of the blade to tamp down the mound of dirt.

"That's kind of you, but I'm worried about leaving my daughter with him."

"It is hard to find people you can trust."

"You can say that again." She frowned at the squad car as it drove away.

Jean-Luc retrieved his sword from under the bushes and used the tip to etch a cross in the loose dirt on top of the grave. "You don't trust the sheriff?" When she shook her head, he continued, "I thought not. You didn't tell him about Lui."

She gave him a quizzical look. "You didn't, either."

He started toward the garage to put up the shovel. "I am accustomed to taking care of my own problems."

She walked beside him. "And I'm one of your problems."

He stopped. "No, not at all. I am enjoying my time with you. It is my greatest regret that you and your daughter are in danger."

She gave him a calculated look. "Then you admit I'm in danger because of you."

Where was this going? "Yes." He resumed his walk to the garage.

"Then you will agree to let me come with you to look for Louie."

He stopped again. "I did not agree."

"But you will. You understand I'm at war with fear."

"Yes, I do, but I don't want to endanger you more than—" He stopped when she moved close and rested a hand on his chest. The way she was looking at him, with such beseeching eyes, he was hard-pressed not to drop his shovel and sword and pull her into his arms. "Ms. Westfield, are you trying to sway me with your feminine wiles?"

She jerked her hand off his chest. Then she smiled and placed her hand back on him. "Do you think I could?"

"Perhaps. How . . . persuasive can you be?"

She curled her hand around the lapel of his black coat. "I've been bossed around so much of my life. I need to take charge."

"Then you plan to seduce me?"

"No. I just want to go with you. I need to take an active role in this."

"How disappointing."

She huffed. "That I want to determine my own destiny?"

"No, that I'm not being seduced. I think I'd like a strong, self-determining woman to seduce me."

She laughed, then gave him a flirtatious look. "The night is still young."

He smiled. "Yes, it is."

"Then we have an agreement," she announced. "I'm coming with you."

Merde. His smile faded. When had he lost all control in this relationship? Heather Westfield was wrapping him around her little finger. And God help him, he liked it.

Chapter 9

"The entrance is a few miles down this road," Heather said, glancing at Jean-Luc as he drove.

"All right." His hands rested lightly on the BMW's steering wheel as if he was accustomed to doing ninety-five mph.

It was a clear night with the stars and a half-full moon shining overhead. Heather's purse rested on the floorboard with Fidelia's Glock inside. She felt the comforting weight of the pistol against her leg. Robby MacKay was in the backseat with his claymore and Jean-Luc's lighter weight foil. Jean-Luc had insisted on picking up the Scotsman on the way.

Robby had objected to her accompanying them, but Jean-Luc had defended her decision. That was a good sign. He wasn't such a control freak after all. He could honor her decisions even when he disagreed with her.

There was still a lot she didn't know about Jean-Luc, but she really liked everything she'd learned so far. She slanted a look at him as he drove. He had a lean face, beautifully accented with a strong jaw and high cheekbones. Last night he'd been clean shaven and all neat and tidy in his elegant tuxedo like a sexy James Bond. Tonight he looked even sexier. Black stubble shaded his jaw, and black curls tumbled carelessly over his head as if he'd been in too much of a hurry to shave or comb his hair. His black slacks and T-shirt looked worn and comfortable, and his long black coat lent him an air of danger.

No wonder Billy had regarded him with suspicion. Jean-Luc looked mysterious. And wild. He was strong enough to pull the shovel from the ground with one hand. He was imaginative and creative with the clothes he designed for women, and yet he hunted down assassins like Louie. She'd never met such an intriguing, complex man. He definitely harbored secrets. But good Lord, what a sexy man he was.

Did he really hope she'd seduce him? From the way he talked and looked at her, Heather suspected he was the one doing the seducing. Her mind raced, imagining all sorts of possible scenarios. If she jumped him, he wouldn't stop her. She was certain of that from the way he looked at her.

His gaze would focus on her face with a hot intensity that curled her toes, then it roamed down her body, lingering here and there. Just thinking about it made her tingle all over. She was so aware of him. The air between them seemed to hum with some kind of magnetic current that sought to pull them together.

"Are you all right?" He glanced at her.

"Yes." She looked away. He must have felt her gaze. He was aware of her, too. "There's the entrance." She pointed at a dimly lit sign on the right.

Jean-Luc slowed and turned onto the narrow road.

"'Tis verra isolated here," Robby observed. "A good hiding place."

"The campers are down there." Heather gestured at a dirt road that veered off to the left.

"Campers?" Jean-Luc glanced back at Robby with a worried look.

"Bugger," Robby muttered.

A chill crept over Heather's bare arms. "You think the campers could be in danger?"

"If Lui has been here, yes." Jean-Luc eased down the road, glancing right and left. "He might need money and . . . food. Is that the place?" He pointed ahead.

Heather squinted and could barely make out the stone structure ahead. "Yes. You can park over there by the playground."

The slides and swing sets gleamed stark and gray under the overhead lamp. A corona of light circled the lamp, filled with buzzing insects. The swings dangled perfectly still in the warm, humid air.

Heather exited the parked car, then removed the flashlight from her purse and clicked it on. In just a few seconds, she was flanked by Jean-Luc and Robby. Both carried their swords.

She slung her purse over her shoulder. "Ready?"

Jean-Luc rested his fingertips lightly on her elbow. "Stay close to me."

Robby moved ahead to enter the stone shelter first. She climbed the steps with Jean-Luc at her side.

Large, open windows lined all four sides of the shelter to let breezes drift through on hot summer days. Leaves lay scattered across the cool cement floor, and the fluttering of bird wings echoed high in the rafters. A series of wooden picnic tables cut across the middle of the room.

Robby marched around the perimeter, apparently able to see without a flashlight. "There's no cellar door here."

"It's outside." Heather lit the way down the steps. "To the right."

Robby strode ahead while Jean-Luc remained glued to her side.

The warm air felt thick and moist against her bare skin. A mosquito buzzed by her ear, and she brushed it away. "Damned bloodsucker."

"Where?" Jean-Luc raised his sword, pivoting to look around.

Heather laughed. "You're going after a mosquito with a sword? Good luck with that."

He gave her a sheepish look. "I thought you meant something a little bigger."

"Like what? A bat? I don't think we have any vampire bats in Texas."

"You never know," he muttered, then motioned toward Robby. "He's found the cellar."

Heather heard the rattle of chains. She pointed her flashlight toward the noise and spotted Robby leaning over the cellar door. "Don't tell me they locked it. The cellar's supposed to be a tornado shelter for the campers."

Robby pulled the chains away from the looped door handles. "The lock was broken." He exchanged a look with Jean-Luc.

Heather wondered if the Scotsman was being entirely honest. He must be. He couldn't be strong enough to rip open a padlock.

"Let me help." Jean-Luc heaved open one of the doors while Robby opened the other.

Heather pointed her flashlight into the gaping dark hole. Sheesh, what had possessed her to come here? "So, who wants to go into the black pit of doom first?"

"I will." Robby started down the steps, holding his claymore ready.

"Don't you need the flashlight?" Heather asked.

"I can see," Robby muttered.

She kept the light aimed into the hole. "You were right," she whispered to Jean-Luc. "I shouldn't have come."

"What about being master of your own destiny?"

"I still believe that, and I believe I can protect myself. I'm just afraid you'll be more concerned with protecting me than catching Louie."

"You are correct. That's why I brought Robby."

"I don't want to hold you back. Or endanger you."

"I'll be fine." He moved to her right with his foil in his right hand. "Stay close behind me." He started down the stairs.

She took a deep breath. *You're at war with fear*. She followed him down, resting a hand on his shoulder.

When he reached the bottom, he took her hand to escort her toward the center of the room. She pivoted, shooting a beam of light in a circle around the dark cellar. It fit Fidelia's description. Dark. No windows. Stone walls. A thick layer of dust on the stone floor made her nose itch. Dirt and debris were swept into small mounds along the walls.

"Check the ceiling," Jean-Luc said quietly.

The ceiling? She aimed her flashlight up. Did they really expect Louie to hang around the ceiling? That was weird.

"It's clear," Jean-Luc announced.

She breathed a sigh of relief. "Great. No homicidal maniacs here."

"Nay. 'Tis safe enough." Robby circled the room. As he approached a dark corner, little scurrying feet pattered away from him.

"A rat!" Heather grabbed Jean-Luc's arm and pressed close. Her flashlight waved about wildly.

He took the flashlight and located the creature. "Don't worry. It's just a mouse."

"Are you kidding? That thing is huge!"

"It's a harmless little field mouse."

"Haven't you heard? Everything is big in Texas."

"Our rats in France would laugh at your mouse." Jean-Luc looped an arm around her shoulders. "You haven't lived until you've seen the rats of Paris."

"Oh, that's so romantic . . . *not.*"

"Ah, now there's a big one with giant claws and sharp teeth." He laughed when she flung her arms around his neck. "*Not.*"

"What?" She realized her face was pressed close to his.

"I was kidding." His arms wrapped around her. "But I can't apologize. I'm quite happy with the results."

"You rascal. You scared me." She should have swatted him, or at least pulled away from him, but it felt so good to have his strong arms around her and the solid warmth of his chest pressed against her.

He rubbed his chin against her brow. The soft scrape of whiskers was both masculine and comforting.

"I doona believe Lui was ever here," Robby announced. "As dusty as the floor is, there would be footprints."

"I agree." Jean-Luc kept his arms around Heather.

Robby muttered something under his breath. "Shall I leave ye two alone?"

Jean-Luc chuckled. "We're coming." He released Heather and handed her the flashlight. "We've done enough for tonight."

Enough searching for Louie or enough hugging? She would have enjoyed a few more minutes of hugging. Or an hour or two. She followed them to the staircase and took Jean-Luc's hand to ascend the steps. The night air smelled fresh compared to the musty, dank air of the cellar.

"We'll try again tomorrow," Jean-Luc announced as he and Robby shut the cellar doors.

Tomorrow? That was Sunday. "I have other plans, but we can go somewhere afterward."

"What plans?" Jean-Luc escorted her back to his car. "I cannot leave you unprotected."

"I already volunteered to help out at the fair. The church is trying to raise money for some playground equipment. I have to be there early to set up chairs and stuff. Fidelia and Bethany will be there, too."

Jean-Luc frowned. "A public place could be dangerous. Robby and I will have to come."

Robby groaned.

Heather grinned. "Great! It starts at seven. At Riverside Park."

"Fine." Jean-Luc pressed his keypad to unlock his car, then opened the door for her. "And afterward, we will continue our hunt for Lui. If you can, think of more places that fit Fidelia's description."

"Okay." She climbed into the car, and he shut the door.

She could hear Jean-Luc and Robby discussing something quietly. Probably the best strategy for keeping her and Bethany alive. She slipped her flashlight into her purse, next to the Glock. With the arrival of Jean-Luc Echarpe, her life had become much more exciting. She was not going to let Louie take her life away.

But she might just lose her heart to Jean-Luc.

The next evening, Heather was setting up chairs at Riverside Park. It had been another uneventful day with no sign of Louie. They'd gone to church in the morning, then they'd goofed off the rest of the day. Jean-Luc had promised to come soon after sunset. She'd found herself eagerly wishing for the day to pass by so she could see him again.

"Need some help with that?"

She cringed at the sound of the booming voice and prayed it was not directed at her. She glanced up. Nope, Coach Gunter was swaggering toward her. The football coach at Guadalupe High had been trying to score for more than six months. The fact that Heather hadn't let him get a first down did not deter him.

"No thank you." She turned her back to him as she unfolded a metal chair. She still had the last row to set up in front of the gazebo where the children would sing.

Coach Gunter circled in front of her so she couldn't help but see him and assumed his usual Superman pose—feet spread, hands on hips, chest thrust out. He also wore his usual attire—a sleeveless T-shirt to show off his bulging biceps, and shorts to show off his muscular calves.

Heather considered him a miniature caveman—short in stature and shorter on brains. There were eligible women in town who collected miniatures. He really should try his luck with them. Some women did ogle his manly physique, and Coach knew it. Heather could tell he expected her to stop her work and admire him, but she continued to unfold chairs and line them up. Bethany was her assistant, sitting in each chair to make sure it worked properly.

"How do you like my swim trunks?" Coach swiveled, no doubt to showcase his buns of steel.

"They're okay." Heather dragged another folding chair off the nearby stack.

"I'm doing the dunking booth," Coach continued. "You should come by later and see me all wet." He winked.

Heather made a noncommittal, grunting sound as she snapped another chair open and placed it in line. She smiled at her daughter. "How does this one work?"

Bethany wiggled onto the chair. "It's fine, Mama." She glanced up at the coach. "I'm gonna sing tonight."

"Yeah, whatever." Coach gave her a dubious look, then his face brightened. "Hey, how'd you like to go out with your mom and me for some ice cream later tonight?"

Bethany squirmed on her chair, grinning. "I love ice cream!" She looked at her mom expectantly.

Oh, foul play. Heather had just picked up another metal chair, and she contemplated whacking the coach on the head with it. But would he feel it? With her luck, he'd consider it some kind of Neanderthal foreplay.

She jerked the chair open and gave her daughter a sympathetic look. "I'm sorry, sweetie, but Coach should have asked me first." She straightened, glaring at the coach. "We already have plans for tonight."

He jutted out his chin. "So the rumors are true? You have a new boyfriend?"

Sometimes this town was a little too small. Heather glanced at the sun skimming along the tops of the trees. In less than an hour, Jean-Luc would arrive. "I have some friends coming later."

"Yeah, right," Coach muttered. "You don't know what you're missing." He stalked away.

With a sigh, Heather grabbed another chair. Only three more to set up. The fair started in five minutes. There was already a line of people at the ticket booth.

"Don't you like him, Mama?" Bethany asked quietly.

"Coach?" Heather positioned the chair next to her daughter. "He never did help me with the chairs, did he?"

"I'm helping you." Bethany climbed onto the one she'd just set up.

"Yep, you're doing quality control. And doing a great job." Heather retrieved another chair from the stack.

Bethany scrunched up her little nose as if in deep thought. "He thinks he's pretty."

The coach? Heather laughed as she opened the chair. "I think you're right. You're a smart cookie."

Bethany shrugged like it was a given. "I like Emma."

"So do I." Heather picked up the last chair.

"Will she see me sing?"

"I believe so." Heather opened the last chair and sat next to her daughter.

"I like the man who talks funny, too."

Heather's heart did a little flip. "Mr. Echarpe?" She'd tried hard not to think about him all day, but he'd still crept into her thoughts a dozen times. Per hour.

Bethany crossed her little legs, mimicking an adult, then folded her arms and rested her chin on one palm. She tapped her chin with a finger. It was her serious thinking pose. Heather considered it adorable, and it always made her want to drag her daughter into her arms for a big hug. She refrained, however, since she knew she should encourage her daughter to think for herself. She glanced at the sun once more, trying to estimate how long it would take to set. And how long before she'd see Jean-Luc.

"Mr. Sharp doesn't know he's pretty," Bethany announced. "But he is."

Heather's mouth dropped open. Good Lord, she'd given birth to a genius. "I think you're brilliant."

"I'm hungry. Can I have some cotton candy? I want the pink one."

"We can do that. After supper." Heather glanced at the gazebo. "Look. Miss Cindy wants you up there."

Bethany squirmed off her chair and ran toward the

gazebo where all the preschoolers were gathering. One of the teachers, Miss Cindy, proceeded to arrange them into two rows, the taller children in the back.

Heather rubbed her neck. The physical labor, Texas heat, and lack of sleep were catching up with her. At least once the sun set, the temperature would fall a few degrees. Jean-Luc was smart to wait.

There he was again, in her thoughts. She'd tossed and turned for an hour last night before sleep had finally overtaken her. She'd been tempted to go downstairs and keep him company all night. God knew there was still a lot she needed to learn about him. She'd shared her life story with him, but he'd shared very little with her.

What was he doing in Schnitzelberg, Texas, when the fashion world was centered in Paris? What was the real story behind Louie? Was she really in as much danger as Jean-Luc claimed? In spite of all her questions, she was drawn to him. Her heart raced whenever she looked into his sky-blue eyes. And she wanted his arms around her again.

But she'd known him only two nights. It was dangerous to fall for a man so fast. It should be dangerous, but it felt wonderful and exciting. Even more reason for her to keep her guard up. She'd survived too much upheaval in her life to screw it up now. Her first priority should be to maintain a calm, loving environment for her daughter.

Fidelia plopped down beside her and set her purse in her lap. In honor of the festive occasion, she'd worn her bright red skirt with gold spangles. "Those silly old church ladies. I offered to do a fortune-telling booth, but they turned up their snooty noses and said it was too pagan for a church function."

Heather winced. "I'm sorry." No doubt one of those church ladies was Cody's mother. Mother Westfield had already informed Heather that she was abusing Bethany by allowing a gypsy woman to live in her house.

When it came to her daughter's safety, Heather was more concerned with Fidelia's gun-toting habits than her card reading. She glanced at the infamous purse. "Are you packing?"

"Only the Glock. I cut back." Fidelia hung her head. "I felt kinda bad about the squirrel."

Heather patted her arm. "I was relieved to have your gun with me last night."

Fidelia nodded. "If that Louie shows up, I'll blow his head off. Don't care if I go to prison for it, either. You were kind enough to give me a home, even after I failed your mama." Her eyes glimmered with tears.

Heather turned to face her old friend. "You didn't fail my mother. You tried your best to warn her."

"If I'd kept my mouth shut, both your parents might still be alive. Maybe those church ladies are right. Maybe I'm no good."

"I won't let you say that! My mother paid for your services, and she would have pestered you to kingdom come for your advice. You know that. It was impossible to tell my mother no."

Fidelia sniffled and wiped her eyes. "I'll do anything to protect you and the baby girl. I owe you that much."

"You don't owe me anything. You were always there for me. Like a second mother." Heather laughed to keep her own tears at bay. "But a lot more fun than my real mother."

Fidelia nodded. "She was a strong-willed woman."

"Stubborn and fearful," Heather corrected her. "I'm not living with fear anymore. I don't want you to, either."

Fidelia patted her purse. "I've got my courage right here."

"You've got courage inside you. And you're a good person. If I wasn't a hundred percent sure of that, I wouldn't trust you to take care of my daughter."

Fidelia blinked away her tears, then assumed her tough face. "I checked out the crowd and the surroundings like you asked. No strangers with white hair and a cane."

"Good. Thank you." Heather glanced at the sun. About thirty minutes to go before Jean-Luc arrived. "Did you have any dreams last night?"

"I did have a strange one. I think it was Juan, but it was hard to tell. He looked like a guy from that movie you watch so much. Pride and something."

"*Pride and Prejudice*? He looked like a Regency guy?"

Fidelia narrowed her eyes, trying to remember. "I think so, but only for a second. Then he looked like . . . George Washington, but fancier."

"That's weird."

"*Sí*. And then he looked like—I don't know. He had on tights and funny shorts that filled out like balloons."

"Like a Renaissance man?"

Fidelia shrugged. "I don't know what it means."

Heather took a deep breath. She'd dismissed her immortal theory as too bizarre, but now she wondered.

Fidelia watched her closely. "You have an idea?"

"It's too strange."

"You're talking to me, honey. Nothing's too strange."

"I think Jean might be . . . different somehow."

Fidelia laughed. "He's a hell of a lot different from any men in this town. But he might be just right for you."

"I mean really *different*."

"You mean in a supernatural way?" Fidelia tilted her head, considering it. "That could be."

"You could believe that?"

"I've told you a million times. There are many things

we do not know. That doesn't make them not true."

An immortal man? If Jean-Luc was one, then Louie was one, too, and they were locked in a struggle that had gone on for centuries. In spite of the heat, Heather shivered.

"Mama! Aunt Fee!" Bethany ran up to them. "Did you see me on the stage?"

"We sure did." Heather pulled her onto her lap. "You looked fabulous."

"Will you sit on the front row to watch me sing?"

"Of course." Heather adjusted the barrette in her daughter's hair. It was topped with a blue grosgrain ribbon bow to match Bethany's blue sundress.

"I'm hungry."

Heather smiled. "You're always hungry."

"I checked out the booths," Fidelia said. "We have our choice of German sausage on a stick or a hot dog."

Great. Heather grimaced. Pork or pork.

"I want a hot dog!" Bethany jumped off her mother's lap. "With lots of ketchup."

A mental picture flashed through Heather's mind as they strolled toward the hot dog booth—Bethany on stage with her blue sundress and a giant ketchup stain down the front. "Let's go easy on the ketchup."

"You should try a foot-long," Fidelia told her.

"I'm not that hungry."

"Honey, who's talking about food?" Fidelia winked.

With a snort, Heather shook her head.

"You should try one with some nice French buns."

Heather laughed. "Yeah, I've been carb-free for too long."

"Look! A Care Bear!" Bethany pointed at a huge yellow bear on display at a game booth. "Can I have that one?"

"I can try." Heather pulled a wad of dollar bills from her jeans pocket. She purchased five balls for five dollars. Four times she managed to hit the stack of milk bottles, but they never fell.

"It's rigged," Fidelia muttered.

"I realize that." Heather sighed. "At least it's for a good cause." Another five dollars later, the milk bottles were still standing. The man handed her a tiny, green bear.

"I'm afraid that's all we get." Heather gave the bear to her daughter.

"That's okay. He's a baby." Bethany cradled it in her arms as they walked away. She looked wistfully back at the huge yellow mama bear.

They ordered their hot dogs and sat on a bench under a giant oak tree. Fidelia teased Heather about settling for a six-incher, while Heather kept an eye on the crowd. There were a few white-haired men with canes, but she recognized them from church.

The sun disappeared over the horizon. The street lamps surrounding the park on three sides came on. Each booth was lit, and the gazebo sparkled with white twinkle lights. The only dark area was down by the river. It was deserted except for a few teenagers stealing kisses. Most of the townspeople were crowded around the booths, laughing and spending money.

The high school students were gathered around the dunking booth, trying in vain to get Coach Gunter wet. He goaded them, his booming voice carrying across the park.

Fidelia was still working on her foot-long hot dog, so Heather left Bethany with her to purchase some cotton candy. Unfortunately, the cotton candy vendor was right across from the dunking booth.

"Come on, you wimps!" Coach shouted at the kids. "Who's gonna dunk me?"

"We're out of money, Coach," one answered.

"You lazy bums! Get a job!" Coach yelled at them.

"Hey, Mrs. Westfield!" several students called out. She greeted them by name.

"Mrs. W.," Coach shouted. "Come and play with me!"

Students snickered. Heather groaned inwardly and turned her back to wait in line for cotton candy. Sometimes this town was really too small.

"I found you." The deep, softly accented voice made her heart leap.

She whirled and found Jean-Luc standing behind her.

Chapter 10

"Oh. You made it." Heather scolded herself silently for sounding too breathless. "I . . . are you hungry?"

"I already ate." He turned to Robby, who had opted for black jeans instead of a kilt. "We'll be fine."

"I'll check the perimeter then. Good evening, Mrs. Westfield." He inclined his head, then marched off.

Heather noted how Robby's T-shirt was stretched across his broad back. Definitely no weapon hidden there. "No swords?" she whispered.

"He has a dagger strapped to his calf," Jean-Luc whispered back. "And I have this." He tapped the ground with a mahogany cane. "There's a sword inside."

Heather eyed the ornate brass handle. "It looks like an antique." Was the owner one, too?

Jean-Luc surveyed the crowd. "I'm overdressed."

Heather smiled. His gray slacks were classy, and his blue dress shirt matched his eyes. "You look good to me."

"Miss?" The vendor interrupted. "It's your turn."

"Oh." She'd been too distracted to notice she was next in line. "One pink cotton candy." She glanced at

Jean-Luc as she dug money out of her pocket. "Unless you want one?"

"No. Allow me." He whipped a five-dollar bill from his wallet and handed it to the vendor.

"Thank you." Heather frowned as she took the stick of spun sugar. She wasn't sure she wanted him paying.

Jean-Luc waved away the change the vendor attempted to give him and smiled at her. "It's for playground equipment, *non*?"

"Right." She smiled back. He was being generous for the preschool. She shouldn't read more into it than that.

"Is that your *friend*, Heather?" Coach's voice roared.

Heather winced. "Ignore him."

Jean-Luc glanced at the coach. "Who is that man? What is that machine?"

"It's a dunking booth."

"Ah, I understand." Jean-Luc nodded. "If he does not drown, then he is a witch."

"No, he's just a creep. It's a game." *A witch?* That sounded medieval. Score another point for the immortal theory. Heather motioned toward the bench where her daughter and Fidelia were sitting. "They're waiting."

"Hey, Mrs. W.," the senior quarterback greeted her.

"Hi, Tyler." She grabbed Jean-Luc's arm, but he didn't budge.

"Wow." Tyler's girlfriend looked at Jean-Luc and gave Heather a thumbs-up. "Way to go, Mrs. Westfield."

"Thank you," Heather muttered, tugging on Jean-Luc's arm. This town was way too small.

Jean-Luc leaned close. "You know all these people?"

"They're students. I'm their history teacher. And everybody knows everyone in this town."

"Heather!" Coach roared. "Where'd you find that sissified city boy?"

Jean-Luc stiffened. "Is he referring to me?"

"Ignore him," Heather begged. "I do. Constantly."

Jean-Luc studied the coach, then turned to Heather with a wary look. "Every man in this town wants you."

She laughed. "Yeah, right. The old guys from the nursing home go into cardiac arrest whenever I walk by."

His gaze drifted over her. "I can believe that."

Was he crazy? She was wearing worn-out blue jean shorts, and the afternoon heat had left her skin almost as pink as her tank top. Her hair was escaping its pony-tail to curl around her forehead and neck. She was a mess, and Jean-Luc was looking at her like she was as sweet as the pink cotton candy she was holding.

"Hey, you! City boy!" Coach shouted. "I bet you can't dunk me."

Jean-Luc turned toward the booth, his eyes narrowing.

"Why don't you get some balls, huh?" Coach yelled.

The kids snickered.

"Dude, you got burned," Tyler muttered.

Jean-Luc's jaw shifted.

Heather yanked on his arm. "Let's go."

"He has insulted my honor," Jean-Luc announced. "I should challenge him to a duel."

"What?" Heather wondered if he was serious. Did they still duel in France? "You mean pistols at dawn?"

"I always preferred swords." Jean-Luc marched toward the dunking booth.

"Wait!" Heather followed him. "You can't be serious."

He stopped, and a corner of his mouth tilted up. "Don't worry, *chérie*. I no longer duel."

"Oh. Well, that's good." No longer?

"But the man has clearly challenged me, and I must defend my honor in some way."

"That's easy." Heather motioned to the stack of balls on the counter. "You just buy some balls and dunk him."

Jean-Luc glanced at the counter. "That would be simpler than killing him."

"Yes, it would." She couldn't believe she was having this conversation.

Jean-Luc smiled slowly, his eyes twinkling. Good Lord, was he just teasing her? Her cheeks grew warm.

"I shall dunk him forthwith." Jean-Luc slapped a ten-dollar bill on the counter and was given two balls.

"Oh, so you finally got some balls, huh?" Coach goaded him. He pulled off his tank top and tossed it aside. "Look, Heather. I'm still dry." He flexed his arms to show off his bulging biceps.

Thwack. Jean-Luc's first ball slammed into the target, knocking it back a foot. Coach's perch gave way, dumping him into the vat of water.

The students cheered. Coach splashed and sputtered in the water. The water was only five feet deep, but for Coach's height, it was practically the deep end.

"Righteous." Tyler patted Jean-Luc on the back.

"I know, right?" another jock agreed.

"Dude, it's like . . . karma, you know," Tyler said. "Coach is always making me run till I puke."

Coach scrambled up the ladder. His burr haircut was flattened on his square head, and his swimsuit was dripping. "Big deal, candy ass! So you had one lucky shot." He pushed on the stool to make sure it had locked back into place, then settled onto it. "You'll never do it ag—"

Thwack. Coach plummeted back into the water.

The students went wild, bouncing up and down. Two cheerleaders performed some leaps.

"Dude, you are awesome!" Tyler held up his hand for a high five.

Jean-Luc raised a hand and looked a little surprised when it was slapped.

"We've been trying to dunk Coach forever," Tyler's

girlfriend shouted over the noise. "But it's so expensive, we ran out of money."

"I understand." Jean-Luc handed Tyler a wad of twenty-dollar bills. "You should all continue to play."

"Dude, you are totally righteous!" Tyler turned toward the other jocks, waving the money. "Balls for everyone! Thanks to Mrs. W.'s new boyfriend!"

Heather winced. Now the whole town would think that was true.

The students cheered, calling Jean-Luc the coolest dude in town. They all lined up to buy balls.

Coach glared at Jean-Luc as he settled back onto his perch. "You bastard!"

Jean-Luc smiled. "I believe my work here is done." He took Heather's arm in his.

She led him toward her daughter and Fidelia. "You realize you're a hero now?"

He nodded, still smiling. "Is that the maypole?"

Heather followed his gaze. "No, it's a flagpole."

"Ah. That's right. This is August. Is it always this hot in Texas?"

"In the summer, yes. And the summer goes on about eight months." Heather groaned inwardly when she spotted Billy headed their way. He was in full uniform, with the usual toothpick in his mouth.

He stopped in front of her and gave Jean-Luc a dismissive glance. "Heather, I want to talk to you alone."

"Why? I haven't done anything wrong."

Billy frowned. "You want to talk about your ex-husband in front of this foreigner?"

Heather winced, remembering her ex's strange behavior the night before. "What did Cody do?"

"I had to lock him up last night. He was babbling like an idiot, claiming to be a cockroach. This morning he was fine, so we let him go. He says he doesn't remember anything."

Heather nodded, her heart sinking. How could she leave Bethany alone with him? "Thanks for letting me know."

Billy tossed his toothpick to the ground. "I guess being married to you drove him crazy."

Ouch. Heather barely had time to register the hurt before she realized there could be a more serious problem. Jean-Luc had stepped in front of her, his hands fisted around his cane.

His voice was soft, but deadly. "Do not insult this woman's honor."

Billy hooked his thumbs in his belt, close to his gun holster. "Are you threatening an officer of the law?"

"That's enough." Heather eased around Jean-Luc and glared at Billy. "Did you know Sasha was in town? She was at my house last night. What a shame you missed her."

Billy's face went pale. "She's here? Sasha came back?"

Heather wanted to kick his teeth in. "She went to San Antonio this afternoon. But she'll be back. She's starring in the charity show at Jean's store in two weeks."

Billy nodded. "Great. I'll be there."

"Excuse us." Heather tugged on Jean-Luc's arm to get away. She headed for the bench where Fidelia and Bethany were waiting. Emma had joined them, and Bethany was talking to her nonstop.

"You're upset with the sheriff, and not just because of his insult," Jean-Luc whispered.

"It's a long story," Heather grumbled.

Jean-Luc stopped. "I like your stories."

She gazed at his sky-blue eyes, and her anger dwindled away. "It's an old wound. I shouldn't let it bother me."

"You said it yourself. Emotional wounds take the longest to heal."

He actually remembered things she said. Amazing.

"My mother wanted me to break up with Billy since he was going into law enforcement. When I did, he said he'd only been hanging around me so he could be close to Sasha."

"The bastard." Jean-Luc turned to glare at Billy's retreating figure. "Still, I suspect he cares for you more than you think. He's clearly angry when he sees you in my company."

"Maybe, but I'm just second choice. If he thinks Sasha is available, he forgets all about me." Heather led Jean-Luc toward her daughter.

Bethany was in the middle of explaining how she'd acquired her new bear. "This is a baby bear, but I really wanted the great big yellow bear. Aunt Fee said it was fixed so that no one can get the big yellow bear."

"That's right, honey." Fidelia nodded. "Your mother tried her best."

With a sigh, Heather handed the cotton candy to her daughter. "Here, sweetie."

"Yummy!" Bethany grinned as she started stuffing pink fluff in her mouth.

Heather figured she was forgiven for her giant bear failure. "Thank you for coming, Emma."

"I'm happy to help." She glanced at Jean-Luc. "Was there a problem with the sheriff?"

Jean-Luc shifted his weight. "There's a . . . bug problem."

Emma's brows lifted. "The cockroach?"

"I'm so worried about it." Heather motioned with her head toward Bethany. "I don't know if it's safe for her to be with him now."

"I'm sure it'll be fine." Emma gave Jean-Luc a pointed look. "Perhaps you could give some reassurance?"

Did he know something? Heather looked back and forth from Emma to Jean-Luc. There was something unsaid going on between the two of them.

Jean-Luc rubbed his brow. "Heather, if I could speak to you alone—"

"Great idea!" Fidelia pointed toward the river. "Why don't you two take a walk? We'll be fine here." She winked at Heather.

Heather glowered back. Could Fidelia be any more obvious? "I have to get Bethany back to the gazebo in ten minutes for the show."

"We have it covered," Emma declared. "You two go on."

It was a conspiracy. Jean-Luc took her by the elbow and led her toward the dark end of the park. Without the crowd of people and park lights, the air felt a bit cooler. The noise of the crowd gave way to the drone of locusts.

She tucked some wayward curls behind her ear. "There's a bench at the end of this path, overlooking the river."

"I can see it. It's occupied."

"It is?" Heather squinted, but couldn't make out the bench yet. Maybe she needed to get her eyes checked. "You have really good eyesight."

"Yes." He escorted her off the path to stroll between two rows of pecan trees. "I understand you are concerned about your daughter's safety with her father."

"I am. It's so unlike Cody. He's always been so . . . normal, I mean in the totally predictable, boring sense. The guy has a ten-step plan for everything and never veers off the set routine."

"*Ten* steps?" Jean-Luc sounded amused. "What if something can be done in nine steps?"

"Then the world will come to an end." Heather laughed. "Seriously, he has ten steps to polish his shoes, ten steps to gut a fish, ten steps to do the yard. The only exception is making love." Oops. She winced.

That shouldn't have slipped out. Jean-Luc was way too easy to talk to.

"But of course. That would require much more than ten steps."

She winced again. Better to keep her mouth shut.

"How many steps did it take?"

She looked around, even though she couldn't see much of anything. "Looks like we're going to have a good crop of pecans this year."

He stopped. His hand tightened around her elbow, making her stop, too. "How many steps to make love?"

She exhaled. "Three. And I'd rather not discuss it."

"*Three?* How can that be possible?"

She gritted her teeth. "I did divorce him, you know."

"That is not making love." Jean-Luc's voice deepened with anger. "That is . . . an abomination."

She stepped back. "It's over. Don't let it bother you."

"But he clearly had no desire to give you pleasure, and that is the main purpose for making love. A man cannot be satisfied if his woman is not."

Heather fluffed her hair off the back of her neck. The temperature must have risen about ten degrees.

"Making love should take hundreds of steps," Jean-Luc announced. "Even a kiss would take at least ten steps."

Heather snorted. "I don't think so. Lips meet, lips part. That's only two steps."

"No tongue?"

"Oh, right. You're *French*. Okay, lips meet, insert tongue, lips part. Three steps."

He sighed. "You have not been properly kissed."

"Excuse me. I've been kissing for twelve years."

"I have been kissing much longer."

She crossed her arms. "Yeah, I kinda figured that."

He stepped toward her. "Ten steps for a proper kiss."

"And an improper one?" She groaned inwardly. Smart aleck. Now she was asking for trouble.

His teeth flashed white when he grinned. "There's only one way to find out." He dropped his cane on the ground and moved closer. "We shall have to put it to the test."

Chapter 11

Jean-Luc was delighted with the turn of the conversation. The minute he'd spotted Heather this evening, he'd wanted to touch her. Her long bare legs tormented him. Her pink skin, flushed with blood, made his vampire nerve cells hum with energy.

Mon Dieu, but it seemed that every man in town wanted her. How could they not? Her shorts hugged the sweetest derriere. Her T-shirt clung to full breasts, then dipped at her waist. He wanted to rip her clothes off with his teeth.

But for now, he'd settle for a kiss.

Emma had scolded him telepathically for making Heather worry, and she'd insisted he explain about Cody. He'd intended to, but he had no idea how to explain the hypnotic trance he'd cast on her ex-husband without opening himself to a lot of unwanted questions. But kissing—this kind of reassurance he could handle. And ten steps would be easy.

He touched one of her curls and rubbed the silken strands between his thumb and forefinger. "Step one is the birth of the idea."

She shrugged. "That's obvious."

"But essential. I find this first step very exciting." He touched her neck, resting his fingertips against her carotid artery. It pulsed strong and quick. In spite of her nonchalant demeanor, she was as excited as he.

"Our lips would not meet purely by accident." He studied her mouth. "I would wonder how your lips feel, how they taste. And my desire would increase until it overwhelmed me. My every thought, my every breath would be focused on my need to kiss you."

Her mouth was slightly open, her breath coming faster. "That's . . . a good start."

He smiled. "Step two is awareness. You are now aware of my desire."

"Okay." She licked her lips.

"Ah, you have moved to step three."

Her eyes widened. "I did?"

"Yes. Step three is your response. You have acknowledged my desire and issued an invitation."

She tilted her head, frowning. "I don't think so."

"You said yes when you licked your lips."

"I did not. You shouldn't make such broad assumptions." She licked her lips again, then grimaced. "Ignore that. It was an involuntary lick."

"I think not. Your body is reacting to me." He stepped closer. "Your body is screaming, *Yes, take me.*"

"In your dreams." She stepped back, folding her arms across her chest. "I'm in complete control of myself."

"For the time being."

She eyed him warily. "Which step are we on?"

"Three. Your body issued an invitation. Step four, my body responds."

"So we're entirely brainless at this point?"

He laughed. "Normally, this would all happen in a matter of seconds, and I wouldn't give you time to challenge everything I say. But for some strange reason, I actually enjoy your challenges."

"Oh." Her mouth twitched. "That's very kind of you."

"You're welcome. Step four, I respond to your invitation. I move in for the kiss." He stepped close and slipped his hand around the back of her neck.

"I still haven't said yes."

"That's why I'm waiting. Step five is your agreement. Even your clever brain must agree now. If a man skips this step, he risks offending his lady and losing her forever."

"'Cause I could walk away," she whispered.

"Yes, you could." He leaned closer, just a few inches from her mouth. "But I know you want it. And you wouldn't want to break my heart."

"No fair using guilt."

He stroked the side of her neck. "I can be ruthless when it comes to getting what I want."

"And I can play hard to get." In spite of her tough words, she tilted her head to make it easier for him to caress her neck.

"Go ahead, *chérie*. Make it hard for me." He smiled because he was definitely hard. He skimmed his fingers along the line of her jaw. "The harder I work, the sweeter will be your surrender. And you will surrender. You want this kiss."

She shivered. "What about you? Do you want this, or do you just want to prove you're right about the ten steps?"

He took her gently by the shoulders. "I don't give a damn how many steps it takes. Your happiness is the only thing that matters."

She sighed. "How do you always know the perfect thing to say?"

"I feel like I know you. I know your heart. It is . . . so much like mine."

"Jean-Luc," she whispered. She touched the hair at his temple.

He moved closer till his forehead rested on hers. "Step six is acceptance. We know the kiss will happen."

"Speak for yourself."

"Woman," he growled. "You continue to challenge me."

She laughed. "I know. It's so much fun. I feel so . . . tough. Completely opposite from the old doormat. It's the new me."

Smiling, he touched her cheek. "I like the new you. You're beautiful, strong, and . . . exciting."

She slid her arms up his chest and around his neck. "You're in big trouble now, buddy. If we kiss, that will only be seven steps."

"But there are many steps attached to the kiss, and I will insist on doing them all. Tasting, touching, nibbling, sucking, the tongue, the scraping of teeth—"

"Okay!" Her hands tightened on the back of his neck. "Bring it on."

His heart lurched. She was surrendering. His blood raced to his groin. No doubt his eyes were glowing red by now. He kept his eyelids partially closed, hoping she wouldn't notice. "Step seven. The test kiss." He pressed his lips gently against hers.

Her eyes flickered shut. "Did we pass?"

"Oh yes." He brushed his lips across her cheek, then planted small kisses back toward her mouth. She opened for him, her lips soft and moist. Her body leaned into him.

He took her this time, kissing her thoroughly, making her lips move with his. She was soft, pliant, delicious. He wrapped one arm around her waist and pulled her hard against him. She gasped, her breath mingling with his own. No doubt she could feel the full length of his erection now, pressed against her belly.

He deepened the kiss, exploring her mouth with his tongue. She tasted of mustard and relish, modern and American, but foreign and exotic to him. She stroked his tongue with the tip of her own, drawing a gruff moan from deep in his throat.

Her fingers delved into his curls, pulling him closer. "What step is this?" She breathed against his mouth.

He rested his forehead against hers. "I can't remember." He needed to back off. His erection was nearing maximum level of torture endurance. He would explode soon.

He took a deep breath. The scent of her blood ensnared him, refusing to let him go. Her pounding heart thrummed into his pores, into his bones. God help him, he couldn't stop.

With a growl of surrender, he drew her earlobe into his mouth and suckled. Her moan reverberated through him. He thought he moaned back, but he was no longer sure. He could no longer distinguish between her thumping heart and his own, her sighs of pleasure and his own. They were becoming one. He wanted inside her. He belonged inside her.

He splayed his hands over her rump and pulled her harder against him. She gasped and tightened her grip on his shoulders. He rubbed his nose against her carotid artery, letting his head fill with the scent of her rushing blood. His gums tingled. He gripped her rear, grinding her against his erection.

"*Mon Dieu*, I want you." He tilted his head back, trying to regain a modicum of control. He couldn't allow his fangs to shoot out. Or his dick to shoot off. He attempted to think through the haze of lust. He couldn't bed her here. If he teleported, he could have her in his bedroom within seconds, but no doubt she'd notice the sudden change of scenery.

The stars overhead winked at him, mocking him for being without a woman for so long. But this wasn't just any woman. This was Heather. She was standing on tiptoe to feather kisses across his neck. She was sweet and generous. He squeezed her rump. Maybe she'd invite him back to her house and her bedroom. Yes, that was the plan. After Bethany was sound asleep, he would sneak into Heather's bedroom and make love to her all night.

In the distance, he heard angels singing, sweet with innocence. His heart soared. Maybe this time, it would work. Maybe this time, he would find a true and lasting love. He would kill Lui and win Heather's heart. For the first time ever, he would have a family.

With a jolt he realized his mistake. The singing was real. With her inferior abilities, Heather probably couldn't hear it.

He grabbed her by the shoulders. "Heather, the children have started singing."

The dazed look in her eyes cleared in a flash. "Oh my God!" She pushed him away. "This is terrible!"

Heather sprinted back to the gazebo as fast as she could. Good Lord, she was too late. Already, the three-year-olds were leaving the stage and the four-year-olds were lining up to sing. She spotted two empty seats on the front row next to Fidelia and Emma. Thank God they had saved some seats for her and Jean-Luc.

It would be all right. She slowed down, struggling to breathe. Jean-Luc stopped beside her, not even winded. Just then, Cody's mother and another woman plopped down into the two empty seats, ignoring Fidelia's protest.

"Oh no!" Heather gulped down some oxygen as she scanned the rows of chairs she'd set up earlier. All the seats in the first eight rows were taken. "This is terrible! I told her I'd be in the front row. She'll look for me, and I won't be there!" Her voice rose in panic.

"Shh!" An elderly woman in the last row turned to hush them.

Heather fought for another breath. Good Lord, she was panicking. How could she have done this? How could she get so wrapped up kissing a guy she'd known only a few days? What kind of mother was she?

"I'll find an empty chair and move it to the front row," Jean-Luc offered.

"Too late," Heather's heart sank. Bethany was on stage, her eyes wide as she examined the front row. She grinned and waved at Fidelia and Emma, then a confused look of dismay came over her face.

Heather waved a hand high in the air, but Bethany didn't see her. She was surveying the first several rows of chairs, and her wounded expression pierced Heather's heart. Miss Cindy started them on their first song, but Bethany didn't join in. With her search for her mom, she didn't even notice Miss Cindy.

Heather jumped up and down, waving both arms in the air. Bethany caught sight of her and instantly brightened. Heather blew her a kiss, and Bethany grinned, then joined in with the singing.

Heather took a deep breath and blinked back tears of relief. "She's okay." She turned to Jean-Luc.

He was gone.

Damn. How could he disappear like that? Was he embarrassed that he'd made her late to Bethany's performance? A surge of guilt flooded Heather. It wasn't entirely his fault. She'd been a very willing participant, totally distracted by that kiss.

And good Lord, what a kiss. Her cheeks blazed with

heat. That rascal—he'd hinted that he could make her lose control, and he had. She didn't want to think about how far she might have gone if he hadn't stopped.

And where was he now? Did he seduce women, then leave them? And wasn't he supposed to be protecting her?

The first song ended, and Heather clapped as she peered around her. Robby was standing off to one side, partially hidden by a copse of pine trees. He nodded at her as her gaze swept past. She raised a hand in greeting, then turned back to watch her daughter. The children started "God Bless America," always a crowd favorite.

"Maybe this will help," Jean-Luc whispered.

She jumped. Good Lord, the man could move quietly. She glared at him, suddenly resenting him for barging into her life and upsetting the delicate balance she'd worked so hard to achieve.

Then her gaze fell to what he was carrying in his arms, and all her resentment melted away. Tears threatened, for it felt like a piece of her heart had melted, too.

Without a word, he handed her the huge yellow Care Bear. She wrapped her arms around its softness, hugging it to her chest. She didn't know if he'd won it or bought it, but she did know he was the sweetest man she'd ever met.

She spotted Bethany on stage, grinning and bouncing up and down. Heather's sight blurred with tears. Jean-Luc understood how much her daughter meant to her. He understood love. He had to be one in a million, and she was seriously attracted to him.

But with her history of failed relationships, she had to be careful. And realistic. There was probably no future with Jean-Luc. As wonderful as he was, he had secrets he didn't seem willing to share. To safeguard her heart, she wouldn't allow the relationship to go any further. She'd keep her feelings to herself, enveloped like a seed package so it couldn't take root and grow.

Still, it felt good. It felt good to know there were still good men in the world. And it felt good to know her relationship with her daughter was as sweet as ever. After all the upheaval she'd endured the last few years, she'd learned the surest way to remain solid and strong was to count her blessings. So she did that now. Life was good.

She closed her eyes, rested her chin on the bear's big head, and let the sweet voices of children wash over her. For this small moment in time, all was right in the world. She would enjoy the moment while it lasted.

The song ended, and the crowd cheered.

She opened her eyes. "Thank you." She turned to Jean-Luc, but he was gone once again. Ah, well. She sighed. She'd known it couldn't last. The guy was different somehow. Immortal, maybe. Or worse.

She spotted him next to Robby, deep in conversation with his bodyguard and the other Scotsman, Angus MacKay, who had apparently returned from New York. There were three more guys, standing in the shadow of the pine trees. A teenager in a plaid kilt and two tall young men wearing khaki pants and navy polo shirts. One guy was white and the other one black. They all looked upset.

Heather frowned. These guys were definitely keeping secrets. They remained in the shadows, but still, heads in the audience were starting to turn. Strangers in town always got noticed.

With the show over, Bethany had skipped down the gazebo steps to join Fidelia and Emma. Heather headed their way slowly. Since most of the crowd was leaving, she was going against traffic.

Everyone gasped when the alarm went off across the town square at the volunteer fire station. A handful of men dashed from the park. People gathered in small groups to gossip and speculate. Heather weaved around them to get to her daughter. In less than a minute, the siren blared from the town's only fire truck. With the whole town watching, the firemen had made record time.

Heather reached her daughter and gave her a big hug.

With a squeal, Bethany grabbed the bear. "Mama, you did it! You got the bear!" She hugged it tight. "Did you see me sing?"

"I sure did. You were wonderful." Heather smiled at Fidelia and Emma. "Thank you for taking care of her."

They followed the crowd away from the gazebo.

Emma eased close to Heather. "Where is Jean-Luc? He should be guarding you."

"He's over there." Heather motioned to the copse of pine trees where the men were huddled. "He's talking to a bunch of guys. Your husband's there."

"Angus is back? Come on." Emma strode toward the huddle of men as Jean-Luc approached Heather, Bethany, and Fidelia.

Emma embraced her husband, and he began to whisper to her urgently.

Heather noted how worried Jean-Luc looked. "What's wrong?"

"There's been some trouble." He dragged a hand through his black curls. "You remember my friend Roman Draganesti from New York?"

Heather swallowed hard, recalling the handsome man, his wife, Shanna, and their adorable baby. "What happened?"

"They go to Mass every Sunday night at Romatech. Roman had a chapel built there, and Mass always starts at eleven. We think the bomb must have gone off early, thank God."

"The *bomb*?"

"*Oui*. Fortunately, no one was seriously injured. But if the bomb had gone off when the chapel was full . . ." Jean-Luc grimaced, and his voice choked. "We could have lost them all."

Heather cringed at the thought of that lovely family getting killed. "Who would do such a thing?" She jolted with a sudden thought. "Was it Louie? Is he targeting all your friends?"

"We know who did it, and it wasn't Lui," Emma explained as she joined them. "It's been a terrible night."

"Aye." Angus MacKay strode toward them. "In one night, there have been four bombings. The first one hit Zoltan Czakvar's home in Budapest. He lost two cov—friends."

"That's terrible!" Heather wondered who this Zoltan guy was. And Budapest? Were these guys a secret clique of immortals?

"Jean-Luc's chateau in France was also hit," Angus continued. "No one was injured, but I hear the damage was extensive."

"You have a chateau?" Heather asked Jean-Luc.

He shrugged. "Only half of one now."

Scowling, Angus wrapped an arm around Emma's shoulders. "Then our castle in Scotland was hit."

"At least no one was killed." Emma gave him an encouraging look. "And we can always rebuild."

"Aye." Angus continued to scowl. "From what I can tell, Casimir has targeted everyone who came to rescue Emma and me in the Ukraine."

"Who's Casimir?" Heather asked. She wasn't sure,

but she thought Louie had mentioned that name the night he'd attacked Jean-Luc.

"He's the one paying Lui to kill me." Jean-Luc confirmed her suspicions. "Though I wager Lui wouldn't mind doing it for free."

Heather shook her head. "I don't understand. Y'all seem like really nice guys. Why do these creeps want to kill you?"

Jean-Luc, Angus, and Emma exchanged looks.

"Are you sure Roman and his family are all right?" Jean-Luc changed the subject.

"They're fine," Angus answered. "Connor wants to take them into hiding. Roman balked at first, claiming it was cowardly, but he finally listened to reason. We canna let anything happen to Shanna or Constantine."

Jean-Luc nodded. "Where will they go?"

"Connor refuses to tell anyone. I agreed. Emma and I will be going to Eastern Europe to hunt for Casimir. If we're captured . . . well, we doona want to know more than necessary."

Heather grimaced. This sounded like war.

A fierce look came over Emma's face. "We need to take care of Casimir once and for all."

"I'll go with you." Jean-Luc grasped his cane with both hands.

"Nay. Ye belong here." Angus glanced at Heather.

She stiffened. "We can take care of ourselves."

Jean-Luc's gaze wandered over her, Bethany, and Fidelia. "*Non*, Angus is right. I must stay here."

"Casimir and Lui already know ye're in Texas," Angus warned him. "So ye're verra vulnerable. Since Connor is leaving with Roman tonight, I had a few men I could spare." He motioned to the group next to Robby. "Ian, Phineas, and Phil—they're here to help ye out."

"*Merci*." Jean-Luc touched Heather's shoulder. "We

have plenty of guards now. You and your family will be safe."

"Thank you." With a shudder, Heather wondered what would happen next.

"Heather!" The yell from the distance caught her attention. Billy was striding toward her, his face grim.

Something unintelligible crackled on his walkie-talkie, and he turned down the volume. "Heather, I have some bad news. Someone set your house on fire."

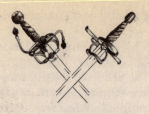

Chapter 12

Damn that Lui! Jean-Luc had no doubt the bastard was behind this. The horrified look on Heather's face tormented him as he rode to her burning house. He'd wanted to drive Heather there, but the sheriff had insisted she go with him. So Jean-Luc sat in the front passenger seat of his BMW while Robby drove. He'd been to her house only twice, yet he was feeling a loss. Heather had to be feeling it a thousand times more.

Her suffering hurt him much more than his own half-destroyed chateau in France. He'd bought it thirty years ago, so he could pretend he had roots going back to an old noble family. But the truth was, he'd never had a family, and a cold pile of stone had not produced the feelings of warmth and comfort he'd craved.

As they drove through the small business section of Schnitzelberg, Jean-Luc noticed a few old buildings were boarded up. "These places could have stone cellars."

"Aye," Robby answered. "We should check them later."

"Ye think Lui could be hiding in one of them?" Ian asked from the backseat of the BMW. "Angus told us a wee bit about Lui."

"Yeah, what a bad dude," Phineas MacKinney added. "Been killin' all your old ladies, huh?"

Jean-Luc shifted in his seat to look behind him. He'd known Ian for centuries. The Vamp might look fifteen, but he was much older. Angus had transformed him at the Battle of Solway Moss in 1542. Seated next to Ian was a tall black man with the unlikely surname of MacKinney.

"I don't believe we've met. I'm Jean-Luc Echarpe."

"The name is Phineas, but you can call me Dr. Phang."

"Thank you for coming." He turned to the third man in the backseat. "You're one of Roman's daytime guards."

Phil nodded. "With Roman and Connor gone, there's no one left for me to guard during the day." The mortal smiled. "But someone's got to watch over you guys."

"You're cool, brother," Phineas announced.

Jean-Luc agreed. A trustworthy mortal was hard to find. The Malcontents viewed mortals as inferior cattle and enjoyed feeding off them and killing them. The Vamps had fed off mortals, too, before Roman's invention of synthetic blood, but they had never been killers. In fact, they tried to protect mortals from the Malcontents. They'd killed hundreds of Malcontents in the Great Vampire War of 1710.

But now, the Malcontent leader, Casimir, was transforming thieves and murderers to swell the ranks of his foul army. Their mission—wipe the good Vamps off the planet and terrorize the mortal world.

Angus had been the Vamp general in 1710, with Jean-Luc as second in command. Angus was always looking for good Vamps to recruit. Finding trustworthy mortals was even trickier. Only a few mortals were willing to risk their lives to protect Vamps. Phil was one of those few.

"Thank you for coming," Jean-Luc told him.

"Not a problem. But I'm going back on a plane." He cast Ian a wary look. "I really don't like hitching a ride when you're teleporting. I just know I'm going to re-materialize someday with my head on backwards."

Ian chuckled. "Angus always checks under his kilt to make sure he dinna lose anything important."

Robby cleared his throat as he turned onto Heather's street. "Do ye think Lui set this fire?"

"Yes." Jean-Luc gripped the brass handle of his cane. "When he attacked two nights ago, he heard me call Heather by name. She was relatively safe until he figured out her last name and where she lives. This fire is his way of announcing that he now knows everything."

"Why didn't he attack her at the fair?" Phil asked.

"He enjoys playing cat and mouse. He'll stretch this out to torture me." Guilt flooded Jean-Luc when he spotted the fire truck in front of Heather's house.

A crowd of people had gathered in the street. The sheriff's car, parked across the street, illuminated the scene with flashing lights. Heather had been so stricken by the news, she hadn't protested at all when Billy dragged her off to his car.

Angus had asked for the keys to her truck, so he could bring her daughter and babysitter to the house. Dazed, Heather had handed over the keys without question. Angus had carefully checked her truck for any explosive device before allowing Emma, Bethany, and Fidelia to climb in.

Robby slowed the BMW to a crawl as they approached the crowd. "Mrs. Westfield canna remain in her house."

"I know." Jean-Luc nodded. "I have to convince her to

move in with me. It's the only safe place for her now."

Robby parked behind the sheriff's car. As Jean-Luc climbed out, he surveyed the scene. The air was thick with the smell of charred wood, but there were no flames to be seen. The firemen had already put the fire out.

He tapped his cane on the street as he examined the crowd. Lui might still be lurking about.

"The house looks fine from the front," Robby commented. "It must have been a small fire."

Jean-Luc nodded. "His intent wasn't to destroy, just to send a message."

Angus parked Heather's small pickup behind the BMW. Emma, Fidelia, and Bethany had all crammed inside, and now they climbed out. The frightened look on the four-year-old's face struck Jean-Luc like a punch in the gut.

Angus strode toward his employees—Robby, Ian, Phineas, and Phil. "Search the area. If Lui engages ye in battle, call for backup."

The guards separated quietly.

Angus stepped close to Jean-Luc and handed him Heather's keys. "Emma and I will be leaving now. 'Tis too late to teleport to Budapest, but we'll go to New York tonight and travel east tomorrow."

"I understand." Jean-Luc pocketed Heather's keys. He knew the hazards of traveling east. A vampire would fry if he teleported into sunlight. "I hope you find Casimir."

"We need to kill him before another war breaks out."

Jean-Luc's chest squeezed with trepidation. He'd known Angus since 1513, the year Roman had transformed them both. They'd become the brothers he'd never had. If he lost them, he would truly be alone. "Be careful, *mon ami*."

"You, too." Angus rested a hand on Jean-Luc's shoulder. "I've always admired ye in battle. Ye charge in, strong and fearless." He glanced toward Heather's house. "Ye should live the same way. Ye deserve to be happy."

Jean-Luc nodded, comprehending the unsaid message. Angus approved of Heather. The bigger question would be if Heather could approve of him. "God go with you."

"And you, too." Angus turned quickly away. No doubt the big Scotsman didn't want to be seen all teary-eyed. He took Emma by the hand, and the two strode down the street.

Jean-Luc knew they would teleport away as soon as they found a secluded place. A little hand curled around his fingers, and he looked down to see Bethany holding his hand. In her other arm, she held the yellow bear he'd won. After he'd smashed three pyramids of milk bottles in rapid succession, the vendor had gladly handed over the bear in order to keep his entire inventory of milk bottles from being destroyed.

"There's too many people. I can't see," the little girl whispered. "Is my house still there?"

"Yes, and it looks all right from the front. The fire is already gone."

Her bottom lip trembled. "I want my mama."

I want her, too. "We'll find her." He led Bethany through the crowd.

"Who do you think started the fire?" Fidelia asked as she walked alongside them. "Was it that bad guy, Louie?"

"I believe so."

"I should have stayed home. He'd be full of lead if I'd caught him." She patted her purse.

Bethany halted and tugged on Jean-Luc's hand. "I don't want my dollies to get hurt."

His throat constricted at the sight of a tear rolling

down her cheek. He squatted in front of her. "If you lose anything, I will replace it."

Her green eyes were the same shade as her mother's. Whereas Heather's eyes could flash with anger, twinkle with mirth, or harden with suspicion, Bethany's eyes were simply wide with worry and need. Deep inside, he felt his heart responding. Was this how a father felt? *Mon Dieu*, it was something he had never expected to feel. It was . . . odd.

He'd always thought parenthood was all about protection and duty. He hadn't expected such a strong surge of . . . tenderness. He wasn't sure he liked it. It felt so damned vulnerable. If anything happened to this little girl, how could he live with himself?

"It will be all right." He wiped her tear away with his thumb and hoped he'd sounded convincing.

He straightened and escorted her through the crowd.

"Mama!" Bethany broke loose and ran to the left. The little green bear fell from her pocket onto the street.

Heather was standing about fifteen yards away, talking to the sheriff. She turned at the sound of her daughter's voice, leaned over, and opened her arms.

"Mama, are my toys all right?" Bethany leaped into her mother's arms.

Heather straightened, still holding her daughter. "It's okay, sweetie. The fire didn't reach your room." Her gaze met Jean-Luc's, then she looked away.

He winced at the pain he'd seen there. He picked up the little bear and walked toward them. "I'm so sorry."

"Why?" Billy eyed him suspiciously. "Did you have something to do with this?"

"Of course he didn't," Heather jumped in. "He was with us at the fair."

"He could have paid someone to do it," Billy muttered. "He's got a hidden agenda, I can tell."

"I got my hidden agenda right here," Fidelia growled, clutching her purse to her chest.

"How much damage to your house?" Jean-Luc handed the little green bear to Fidelia for safekeeping.

"We were lucky." Heather set her daughter down on the street. "We only lost the kitchen in the back. My dad enlarged it when I was little, so there was an extension jutting off the back of the house. It's mostly gone, but the main part of the house is okay."

"You're lucky to have such a nosy neighbor." Billy pointed to the house on the right. "Thelma saw a strange man lurking around the back of Heather's house. She was already calling 911 when the fire started."

Jean-Luc had no doubt the strange man was Lui. "Did she describe the man?"

"Why do you care, Mr. Sharp?" Billy glowered at him. "Is he someone you know?"

Jean-Luc gritted his teeth. "I would never cause harm to Heather or her family."

"Well, someone has," Billy snarled. "You got any enemies, Heather? Any other boyfriends?"

"No."

"Piss off any students?"

"No."

Billy rocked back on his heels. "I guess it could be your ex. Cody's been acting real weird lately."

Heather pulled her daughter close and glared at Billy. "This is not the time to discuss that."

"For now, the house is off limits. No one goes in."

Heather looked stunned. "But our clothes—"

"Not going in," Billy repeated. "Can't have you mucking up the crime scene."

"That's ridiculous," Heather countered. "The crime happened in the kitchen. We could go through the front door and straight up to our bedrooms."

"I want my toys," Bethany whimpered, hugging her giant yellow bear.

Billy pointed a finger at Heather. "You're not going in. That's final."

Heather's cheeks flushed with anger.

"Don't worry," Jean-Luc assured her. "I'll make sure you have everything you need."

She gave him an exasperated look. "I can't let you bear that expense." She turned to glare at Billy. "How soon can we get back in?"

He shrugged. "Could be a few weeks. Or months. I'll post a deputy on the street to make sure no one goes inside to take your stuff. Do you have a place to stay?"

She sighed. "I'll figure out something."

"They will stay with me," Jean-Luc announced. "I have a guest room they can use."

Billy's eyes narrowed. "Don't you own that fancy new store on the edge of town?"

"Yes. Le Chique Echarpe."

"Whatever," Billy muttered. "So the store is your residence, too?"

"For the time being, yes."

"Excuse us one minute." Billy grabbed Heather's arm and pulled her a few yards away.

Jean-Luc rested a hand on Bethany's shoulder to keep her from running after her mom. He turned to look at the house, but he could still hear Billy's whispered words.

"I don't know why, but the guy's after you, Heather. He could have set the fire to force you to live with him."

"He wouldn't do that," Heather muttered.

"How do you know? How long have you known this guy?"

Heather sighed. "Since Friday."

"And you're going to live with him? I didn't think you were that stupid."

Jean-Luc clenched the brass handle on his cane. He'd had enough. He marched toward them.

"Do you actually trust him?" Billy asked.

Jean-Luc halted, holding his breath while he waited for Heather's answer.

"Yes," she whispered. "I do."

It was exactly what he'd hoped to hear, but it still sizzled through him like a small shockwave. She turned and met his gaze. A hesitant smile tugged at the corners of her mouth, but her eyes retained some wariness. She might say she trusted him, but he had the distinct impression she was not entirely comfortable with it. He would have to proceed carefully. If she found out the truth about him too soon, he might lose her completely.

There was something unique about Heather. He wasn't sure what it was exactly, perhaps a combination of things. She had a beautiful face and hair, but in his line of work, he saw that often. She had a body that made his mouth water. He wanted to nibble every inch of her.

Even so, his feelings went beyond simple lust. He liked the way she talked, the way her mind worked, her sense of humor and compassion. He simply liked her. It was so simple, yet felt so profound.

"Will you come home with me?" he asked.

She studied his eyes, and her expression softened. "Yes. Just give me a minute."

Billy made a grab for Heather's arm and scowled when she pulled away. "I'll stop by tomorrow to make sure you're all right." He shot Jean-Luc a warning look.

"She'll be safe with me." He touched her shoulder. Thankfully, she didn't step away.

Billy turned and strode across Heather's front yard. He yelled at a deputy to bring the crime scene tape.

"I can't believe this is happening," Heather whispered as they began running the yellow tape across her front porch. "We have no clothes."

"You're in luck. I make clothes."

She gave him a dubious look. "Do you have designer wear that'll fit me or Bethany? Or Fidelia?"

He glanced at the older woman. She was almost as wide as she was tall. "I have some designer sheets."

Heather rolled her eyes. "The toga look could get old in a few days. I'll just drop by the discount store and pick up a few things. Luckily it's open 24/7."

He winced. "I would prefer you have something nice."

"It's all I can afford right now."

"You will not pay for it." He motioned toward her house. "I am responsible for this."

"You didn't start the fire."

"I know who did."

Her eyes widened. "Are you sure it was him?"

"Yes. This is Lui's sick way of announcing he knows your identity."

A fleeting look of panic crossed her face before she regained control. "I was afraid of that."

"Then you fully realize the danger you are in. Lui will try something worse next time."

"That's why I'm desperate enough to move in with you."

"I thought you trusted me."

She gave him an exasperated look. "Do I have any choice now?"

That hurt. "You can trust me, Heather. I promise I will keep you and your daughter safe."

She searched his eyes. "I do want to trust you. I think I do trust you, but everything is happening so fast. The bear you won for my daughter—that was really very sweet, about the sweetest thing I've ever seen from a man."

"Thank you." He moved closer. "The kiss wasn't bad, either."

Her cheeks blossomed a rosy pink, and she looked away. "I don't usually . . . I don't know what—"

He hooked a finger under her chin to force her eyes to meet his. Her gaze rose to his chin, then stopped. "I need you to promise me something."

Her gaze lifted and locked with his. "What?"

"You must never leave the studio without a guard. That goes for Fidelia and Bethany, too. You must be protected at all times."

"We can do that."

"And you must follow my orders without hesitation."

She pulled back. "I won't let anyone control me."

"I have no wish to control you. I want to keep you alive."

She bit her bottom lip. "Well, I wouldn't argue with that."

"Good. When Lui attacks, there won't be any time for arguments. You must do as I say."

Her mouth thinned. "You plan to kill him, don't you?"

"I have no choice. It's either him or us."

She shuddered. "For once I'm glad Fidelia has all those guns."

"I'll take you shopping now. My car's over there." He motioned to his BMW.

She frowned. "We'll just get a few things. Some clothes and a few coloring books to keep Bethany occupied. She may go crazy without her toys."

"Really?"

"Have you ever seen a four-year-old with nothing to do? It's not a pretty sight."

"Oh." He glanced at the house, now completely cordoned off with yellow tape. A deputy stood guard at the front steps. "Don't worry. I'll take care of it."

"How?"

"Trust me." He pointed to his BMW. "Wait in the car. It's not locked. I'll be there shortly."

"What about my truck? My purse was inside."

"I have the keys. Robby will bring it to the studio later."

"Okay." She walked over to Bethany and gave her a hug. While she talked to Fidelia, Jean-Luc sent out a psychic message to Robby, Ian, Phineas, and Phil.

Meet me by Heather's truck. If you see Phil, bring him, too. He wasn't sure how adept the mortal guard was at picking up psychic messages.

Robby was the first to show up. Jean-Luc handed him the keys to Heather's truck with instructions to drive it to the studio. Ian, Phineas, and Phil joined them.

"No sign of Lui?" Jean-Luc asked.

"Nay," Ian answered. "It would help if we knew what he looks like."

"I've never seen him look the same way twice. I recognize his voice, though. And his eyes. They're black with an odd gleam. You can feel the hatred, but there's something more, something . . . unhinged."

"So the dude's a psycho," Phineas observed.

"And verra dangerous," Robby added. He gestured toward the crowd. "These people are mortal. Ye can smell the difference."

Phil chuckled. "Are you saying we stink?"

Robby grinned. "Some might say so, but no' me. I think mortals smell . . . sweet."

Phil shook his head. "I'm so not flattered."

Phineas sniffed and gave the mortal a curious look. "You smell kinda different, bro."

Phil's smile faded, and he exchanged a wary look

with Robby. Jean-Luc frowned, sensing an undercurrent he wasn't privy to, but this wasn't the time to discuss it. He asked Phil to join him on the shopping trip, then explained the undercover mission to the three Vamps. "Can you do it?"

"Aye, 'tis a piece of cake," Robby answered. "We'll see ye later."

Jean-Luc was relieved to see Heather and her family sitting in the backseat of the BMW. He climbed into the driver's seat.

Phil settled in the passenger seat, then turned to face the females. "I'm Phil Jones. I'll be guarding you in the daytime."

"Nice to meet you," Heather murmured.

"*Hola*, Felipe," Fidelia said in a husky voice.

Phil quickly faced front.

At the discount store, Phil was told to accompany Fidelia, while Jean-Luc watched Heather and Bethany.

In the young girls' department, Heather selected a few little T-shirts and shorts from the fifty-percent-off rack. The more she tried to save him money, the more irritated Jean-Luc became. He spotted the best dress the store had to offer and tossed it into the cart.

"She has nice dresses at home," Heather protested.

"You said you wouldn't argue."

She snorted. "That was for times of extreme danger."

"Which could be now. Lui could be lurking in the toy aisle as we speak."

"We'll see about that." She pushed the cart to the toys. One of the wheels made an annoying squeak with every rotation.

Jean-Luc walked behind her, his cane clicking on the linoleum floor, his eyes ever watchful. The store seemed mostly deserted.

Bethany skipped alongside her mother, hugging her yellow bear. She stopped suddenly, her eyes wide.

"Look, Mama. That Barbie comes with a crocodile."

Heather turned away and selected a few coloring books. "You have plenty of Barbies at home."

"But not a crocodile-hunting one." Jean-Luc tossed it into the cart.

"Yeah!" Bethany jumped up and down.

Heather whirled around to glare at him. "That was *my* decision to make."

She was right, but it surprised Jean-Luc how much he enjoyed making the little girl dance with joy. He shifted his weight, frowning. "I will try to restrain myself."

Heather's mouth twitched. "Is it that hard? I swear, if you have any children, they'll be spoiled rotten."

His heart froze for a second, then plummeted to his stomach. He couldn't have children. In that moment between death and transformation, a vampire's sperm died. At sunset each night, his heart jolted back to life, his blood resumed its race through his veins, and his mind snapped back to consciousness. But the sperm remained dead.

Roman, being a brilliant scientist, had found a way around it. He'd taken live human sperm, then erased the donor's DNA and inserted his own. Shanna was already pregnant when Roman had discovered a problem. A Vamp's DNA was not quite the same as a mortal's. Roman had lived in fear with what he'd done to Shanna, but after nine months she'd delivered a healthy baby boy with no fangs and an appetite for his mother's milk.

Jean-Luc realized with a jolt that he could have children. With Roman's procedure, he could actually be a father. His gaze settled on Heather, and he imagined her swelling with his child.

"Is something wrong?" she asked.

"No. Everything's fine." But it wasn't. Now that the seed was planted in his mind, he couldn't ignore it.

He'd envied Roman for his loving wife and adorable son. It had never occurred to Jean-Luc that he could have a family, too. Lui had always been in the way, lurking in the shadows as a hidden threat. But the assassin's recent emergence could be a blessing in disguise. Finally Jean-Luc would have the chance to be rid of him. And that opened all sorts of new possibilities.

"You had a strange look on your face." Heather dropped a box of crayons into the cart. "I thought you might be angry."

"I am angry at Lui and determined to be rid of him."

Heather rolled the cart toward the women's department. "I'll be so glad when things are back to normal."

Normal? Was that what she wanted? His vision of the future wavered. How could he convince Heather to marry a vampire and give birth to a child with mutated DNA? It wasn't exactly the American dream.

And was it truly what he wanted? He was very attracted to Heather, but were his feelings true or merely a reaction to the danger they were in? Could he have the kind of love for her that would last through the years? Could he handle marriage to her? Could he handle marriage to any mortal?

Was it fair for Heather to be stuck with a man who was dead during the day? It gave new meaning to the term *deadbeat dad*. He could be very supportive financially, but he would be inaccessible every day of his family's life.

Still, Roman and Shanna seemed very happy. Jean-Luc wanted that for himself. Was Heather the one?

He frowned while he watched her select the cheapest items from the women's department. Well, he certainly didn't have to worry about her putting him in debt. But she deserved so much more. He would make his own selections for her when they returned to the studio.

"Do I need to dress up for work?" she asked.

"No. You'll be alone during the day, except for Alberto and the guards."

She gave him a curious look. "When do you work?"

"At night. Jet lag. I haven't adjusted yet." He cringed inwardly at his lies. "I feel more creative at night." That much was true. He couldn't even create a heartbeat during the day.

She frowned, apparently confused by the work schedule or lack thereof. "How many hours do you want me to work each week?"

He shrugged. "Let's not worry about it. In fact, if you don't want to work at all, I completely understand. You can take off a week to rest if you like."

"That's very kind, but I think I'd rather stay busy."

He nodded. "Our first priority is your safety. The second one is to stop Lui. The fashion world can survive without us for a little while."

"I understand." When she turned to examine a rack of jeans, he picked up the cheap bra she'd dropped in the cart and quickly checked the size. C cup. That brought a smile to his face.

Bethany's giggle gave him away, and Heather turned to see him holding her bra.

Her eyebrows raised. "Is there a problem?"

He dropped the bra. "*Non.* It is a lovely size."

A blush invaded her cheeks. "I need to lose ten pounds. Well, twenty actually."

"Heather—"

"I couldn't lose the last ten pounds of baby fat—"

"Heather, I think—"

"And then I gained ten more with too much chocolate therapy during my divorce."

"Heather, I think you are perfect the way you are."

Her blush deepened. "You're just saying that."

"Because I believe it, yes."

"But you design for skinny models."

He shrugged. "People expect to see them on the runway. It doesn't mean I prefer them that way. I like you, Heather. I thought I made that clear earlier tonight."

She tossed a pair of jeans into the cart and turned away. He realized it was hard for her to accept a compliment. "You don't say my name right. Or Bethany's."

He smiled. Was this a challenge? "You don't say my name right, either."

"I do, too." She dropped a plain green T-shirt into the cart. "But I like Jean-Luc better than Jean. Jean is so plain, but Jean-Luc is powerful and sexy and . . . captainish."

He liked the powerful and sexy part. "What is captainish?"

"Like a starship captain. You're Captain Jean-Luc." She gave him a wry smile. "You're used to giving orders."

"You say it like John-Luke."

"Well, duh. That's your name."

"Not in French. You should say it as the French do."

"Oh, really?" She planted a hand on one hip and shifted her weight to one foot. "Enlighten me."

"As you wish." He stepped closer. "First, we do not pronounce the *n* in *Jean*."

"How lazy of you."

He lifted a brow. "The *n* signifies a nasal *a*. *Jean*. Try it."

She wrinkled up her nose and produced the most nasal-sounding *a* he'd ever heard. "Was that French enough for you?" She smiled sweetly.

He stifled a grin. "Not yet. There's the matter of *Luc*."

"Luke."

"*Non. Luc* with the French *u*."

"Was that a vowel, or did you just suck a lemon?"

He laughed. "Come now, give it a try."

"I wouldn't know how to produce such a strange sound."

He stepped closer. "It is easy, *chérie*." He raised her chin with one bent finger. "Pucker your lips."

Her cheeks flushed pink. "I'm not puckering up in the middle of a store. Or in front of my daughter."

"What are you afraid of?" He grazed her lips with his thumb. "I thought you trusted me."

Bethany giggled. "Go ahead, Mama!"

With a huff, she stepped back. "It's a conspiracy."

Jean-Luc winked at her daughter. "Bethany is a very clever girl."

"I am!" She bounced around, grinning.

Heather glared at him. "You're still not saying *our* names correctly."

He knew his *th* sounds came out wrong. It was a typical problem since the sound didn't exist in French. Still, he couldn't resist goading her, so he repeated her earlier words. "Enlighten me."

"It's quite simple really. Watch how I do it. See how the tongue goes against the top teeth?" She demonstrated.

He moved close and leaned over to study her mouth. "I see."

"Now you try. Tongue against the top teeth."

He stuck out his tongue and with a quick movement, he pulled her against him and touched his tongue to her teeth.

"Aagh!" She pulled back. "Your teeth, not mine!"

Bethany erupted in giggles.

Jean-Luc stepped back with an innocent look. "I must have misunderstood."

"Yeah, right." She glowered at him, but then her mouth twitched. She looked away, grinning. "You are impossible."

He smiled. "But you still like me?"

She slanted him an annoyed look. "Yes. I must be out of my mind."

Bethany hugged her yellow bear. "I like you, too."

A soothing warmth settled in Jean-Luc's chest. Here, in this godforsaken discount store far away from the glamorous world of high fashion, he was experiencing one of the most beautiful nights of his long existence.

Chapter 13

It looked more like a museum than a store, Heather thought as she stood outside her new temporary home. Greek columns, made of stone, stretched to the high gabled roof. Close to the front porch was a sign with *Le Chique Echarpe* painted in a pretty cursive script.

"It's big," Bethany whispered.

"And expensive," Fidelia added. "Juan must be very rich."

"It's Jean—" Heather winced as she recalled the way Jean-Luc had practiced his pronunciation.

He was at the front door of his store, his cane gripped in his right hand as he talked to Phil and another man dressed just like Phil. Apparently khaki pants and a navy polo shirt were the official guard uniform. The two guards disappeared into the building with the bags of newly purchased stuff from the discount store.

Jean-Luc descended the steps to where Heather waited on the circular driveway. "Phil and Pierre are taking the bags to your room." He glanced around the grounds. "You'll be safer inside with the alarm system on."

"I'll show you safe." Fidelia plopped her purse on the hood of the BMW and pulled out her Glock. "If Louie shows up, I'll be ready for him. Now where's the key to this damned trigger lock?" She rummaged through the purse.

"Pierre is the other guard?" Heather had never been good at remembering names, and she'd a met a lot of new people in the last two days.

"*Oui*. A daytime guard." Jean-Luc tapped his cane impatiently on the brick driveway. "We should go in now."

"I heard we have company," a voice said from the front door.

Heather turned and recognized the speaker. He was the one Sasha had "talked" to on Friday night. Alberto Alberghini. He was sandwiched between the two beautiful models Sasha had gossiped about. Heather couldn't recall their names, but she remembered there were rumors about them and Jean-Luc. At least they were clinging to Alberto and not Jean-Luc. Still, when the young Italian man escorted them down the steps, she wished they would trip over their long evening gowns.

Jealousy, she chided herself. What an ugly emotion. It would be easier to bear if the two women weren't so damned flawless. Perfectly pale complexions, perfectly applied makeup, perfectly proportioned bodies. Together they were even more striking because they were opposites.

One had long black hair and dark, almond-shaped eyes. She wore an elegant black gown of satin that gleamed in the moonlight just like her perfect curtain of black, silky hair. The other model's hair cascaded down her back with curls of the palest blond. Her eyes were a translucent, icy blue. Her skin was as pale as her white, shimmering gown.

"Is she a princess?" Bethany whispered.

The two models glanced at the little girl, but no expression registered on their perfect faces. Their gazes passed over her and Fidelia, then rested on Jean-Luc.

Heather knew she'd been dismissed.

Jean-Luc motioned toward the one in black. "This is Simone." His hand moved to the one in white. "And Inga."

"Pleased to meet you. I'm Heather Westfield, and this is my daughter, Bethany."

"Aha!" Fidelia extracted a key ring from her purse. She did a double-take at Inga. "*Santa Maria*, girl, eat some tacos. And get some sun. You look like a skinny ghost."

The blonde gave her a bland look, then turned away.

Simone glared at Jean-Luc, her dark eyes simmering with anger. "They are beneath you."

Jean-Luc said nothing but stared back, his eyes intense.

Heather wondered how long the staring contest would continue. Bethany yawned. Fidelia cursed softly in Spanish as she worked on the trigger lock.

Finally Simone lowered her gaze. She bowed slightly as if acknowledging surrender. When she straightened, she directed a look at Heather, a look so full of hatred, it made Heather flinch.

Inga's cold eyes drifted past Heather like a chill wind, then focused on Jean-Luc. "It is not like you to have such poor taste." She pivoted and went up the stairs alongside Simone, Alberto scrambling after them.

Heather hunched her shoulders as she slid her hands

into the pockets of her jean cutoffs. "That was one hell of a welcome wagon."

Jean-Luc's mouth thinned. "They are not accustomed to being around—"

"Commoners?" Heather interrupted.

"Got it!" Fidelia removed the Glock's trigger lock, then swiveled toward the front door. "Damn, I'm too late. I wanted to do some princess hunting. Mount one of their freaking tiaras over my fireplace."

"Don't let them upset you," Jean-Luc said. "They're only here because of the charity show in two weeks. After that, they'll be gone. Alberto, too. They're all going back to Paris."

He looked so sad about it, Heather couldn't help but wonder why he was here. "Why did you leave Paris?"

"It's a long story."

She bet it was. She also wondered just how close he was to the models from hell. "You've known Simone and Inga for a long time?"

"Yes." He started up the steps, motioning for them to follow. "Come. It's safer inside." He waited by the front door, surveying the grounds with narrowed eyes.

"Do you think Louie's coming here?" Heather escorted her daughter up the steps.

"There's no telling what he'll do next." Jean-Luc held the door open. Fidelia and Bethany went inside, but Heather lingered beside him on the porch.

"Simone and Inga, they're . . . just your models?"

"Yes." His mouth quirked. "Are you concerned, *chérie*?"

"No. I'm fine." She was just a jealous liar, that was all. She entered the elegant foyer that opened into the store's showroom. "Fidelia, put the lock back on your gun. I believe you'll be sharing a room with Bethany and me." She gave Jean-Luc a questioning look.

"Yes. Unfortunately, I have only one guest room upstairs." He shut the front door and locked it, then punched some numbers on a security pad on the wall.

Only one guest room? "Then Simone and Inga aren't living here?"

Jean-Luc frowned. "They are staying here. Alberto and all the guards, too." He motioned to the right. "Would you like a tour?"

"Okay." Heather suspected he was trying to change the subject.

"Look at the big stairs!" Bethany gawked at the grand staircase that began on the right of the showroom and curved gracefully up to a catwalk on the second floor, overlooking the showroom. "Is our room up there?"

"Yes. But first, I want to show you where your mother will be working." Jean-Luc led them to the hallway that began under the curve of the grand staircase.

Heather took Bethany's hand and followed him. There were a lot of people living here. Where did they all sleep?

"I suppose the master bedroom's on the first floor?"

"There are no bedrooms on this floor." Jean-Luc strode down the hallway that dissected the right side of the house. The walls were decorated with black-framed photos of models wearing haute couture by Jean-Luc Echarpe.

He motioned to doors on the right as they passed by. "Women's restroom. Men's restroom. Conference room." There was only one door on the left side of the hall. "This is the design studio." He stopped by the large double doors and pressed some numbers into the keypad.

Heather couldn't see around him. "If I'm working in there, shouldn't I learn the combination?"

He hesitated. "Alberto knows it." He opened the door.

He didn't trust her with the combination? Heather entered the studio, frowning. "Will Alberto be working here, too?"

"*Oui*." Jean-Luc flipped on the lights.

Bethany gasped. "It's so big!"

Fidelia nodded. "*Gigante*."

"Yes, it is." Heather surveyed the huge room. There was no sign of the battle from Friday night. The shattered mannequin had been cleared away.

Jean-Luc pointed at a spiral staircase in the far left corner. "That leads to the catwalk over the showroom. It would be a shortcut to your bedroom upstairs."

"I see. Can we go there now? Bethany's really tired."

He hesitated, then cocked his head, frowning. "It'll be ready soon. Come, you should know where the kitchen is."

Heather followed him back into the hallway and noticed a door at the far end of the hall. "Is that an exit?"

He glanced at the door. "It leads to the cellar. You will have no business there." He strode quickly in the opposite direction, back to the showroom. "We'll be closing the store to the public. It'll be safer that way."

They followed him into the showroom.

Fidelia paused to look at a glass case filled with purses made with Jean-Luc's signature fleur-de-lis fabric. "I could use a bigger purse for all my pistols."

"You may have whichever one you like," Jean-Luc offered as he continued toward the hall on the left.

Heather gave Fidelia a disapproving frown, but the babysitter just grinned back.

"Can I have a purse, too?" Bethany asked.

"No!" Heather grimaced at the thought of a four-year-old carrying an eight-hundred-dollar purse.

As they entered the hallway that bisected the left side of the house, Jean-Luc motioned to the first door. "This is the security office. If you need help, you should go there."

"Got it." Heather noticed the keypad next to the door.

"Storerooms." Jean-Luc gestured to the left. "Alberto's office." He stopped at a door on the right. "This is the kitchen. You may use it as much as you like." He opened the door and stepped aside to let them enter.

It was more than a kitchen. It had a small dining area and a sitting area, complete with a comfy couch, recliners, and a television. It opened onto a utility room with washer and dryer. Heather wandered into the kitchen and admired the pristine appliances, all sparkly new. The cabinets were filled with beautiful glassware and stoneware.

"I love the Tuscan-style dishes," she said. "I was thinking about buying some at the discount store. Where did you get yours?"

His mouth quirked. "Tuscany."

"Oh, right." Her cheeks warmed. The rich lived in another world.

The stainless steel fridge contained nothing but a few crab cakes and cheese puffs, along with three unopened bottles of champagne—leftovers, no doubt, from the party Friday night. The pantry was completely bare.

She shut the pantry door. "What do y'all eat around here?"

Jean-Luc winced. "I forgot about that. I'll have the guards take care of it."

How could you forget about food? Heather noticed her daughter slumped on the couch, about to fall asleep on the yellow bear. "We really need to go to our room."

He tilted his head as if listening to something. "It's ready now."

"Okay." She exchanged a questioning look with Fidelia.

The psychic shook her head slightly. Either she didn't know or she didn't want to talk about it now.

Heather helped her daughter to her feet. "Let's go, sweetie. We're almost there."

As they exited the kitchen, Heather noticed Alberto emerging from a room at the far end of the hall. He stumbled into the hallway, his hand clasped to his neck. In his other arm, he carried two evening gowns.

He looked back at the open door. "I'll fix them just like you wanted."

"See that you do," Simone's voice hissed just before the door slammed shut.

Alberto rushed down the hall. He slowed when he saw them.

Jean-Luc clenched his cane so tight, his knuckles showed white. "Is there a problem?"

Heather glanced at him, surprised by the angry tone of his voice.

Alberto blushed. "They are hard to please."

"Indeed." Jean-Luc glared at him. "A wise man would not make the attempt."

Alberto's gaze lowered. "I know you're right. But they're just so . . . beautiful." He rubbed at his neck.

Heather narrowed her eyes. Was that a bloodstain on his fingers?

"Excuse me." Alberto dashed to the door that led to his personal office and let himself in.

"This way." Jean-Luc gestured for them to follow.

Heather exchanged another look with Fidelia.

He came to a stop. "These are the backstairs."

Sure enough, there was a narrow set of stairs going up to the second floor.

Heather glanced at the end of the hall and the door

Alberto had stumbled through. Another keypad. "Is that the bedroom where the models are staying?"

Jean-Luc glanced at the door, frowning. "It leads to the cellar. You will have no business there." He started up the stairs.

Heather slanted one last look at the forbidden door before following Jean-Luc up the stairs. The ascent was slow since Bethany climbed one step at a time and insisted on carrying the big yellow bear. Heather's mind wandered back to the cellar door. Why was it kept locked? And what about the second door to the cellar, the one at the other end of the hall? Was it locked, too?

What was down there? Monsters? Simone and Inga certainly fit that bill. With a snort, Heather chided herself for having a crazy imagination. It was more likely to be something business-related, like an illegal immigrant sweatshop. She reached the top of the stairs.

"This is my office." Jean-Luc indicated a door with another keypad. "I'll show it to you later."

"All right." She spotted an overhead surveillance camera.

Just then a door down the hall opened, and two men emerged. Or a man and a boy, Heather thought, upon a closer look. She recalled seeing them before with Angus MacKay.

The teenager in a kilt smiled. "Yer room is ready, Mrs. Westfield."

"Thank you. Please call me Heather."

"Verra well. I'm Ian, and this is Phineas."

"What's shakin'?" The black man was wearing the uniform of khaki pants and navy polo shirt.

"We'll be going now." Ian motioned for Phineas to follow. "See ye tomorrow night."

"Good night." She noticed the sword strapped to

Ian's back as he passed by. They clambered down the stairs. How odd that the one who looked fifteen acted like he had seniority. "Isn't he a bit young to be a guard?"

"He's older than he looks." Jean-Luc opened the door that Ian and Phineas had just exited. "This is your room."

Bethany ran inside and squealed.

"What?" Heather rushed inside and halted, stunned.

Fidelia ran inside and bumped into her. "*Ay, caramba*," she whispered, looking around the room.

"My toys!" Bethany dropped the yellow bear on the floor and knelt in front of her dollhouse.

Heather blinked, speechless. Parked next to the dollhouse was Bethany's doll carriage.

She noticed her makeup case on the dresser. "How did you do this? There was a deputy guarding the door."

"My guards are excellent," Jean-Luc said.

They had to be good if they'd managed to sneak all this stuff out of the house.

Fidelia dropped her purse on one of the queen-sized beds and sat. "How did they do it?"

"It is done." He looked worried. "I thought it would make you happy."

"I'm happy!" Bethany announced.

I'm suspicious. Heather looked slowly around the room. The walls were painted a soft green. The two beds were covered with blue damask comforters. A beautiful stained glass lamp rested on a bedside table between the two beds. There was no mirror above the dresser, but a lovely painting by Monet. Against the wall rested the bags of stuff they'd bought at the discount store.

"Heather?" Jean-Luc approached her. "Will this be all right?"

"Yes." She avoided eye contact. "Thank you." He'd obviously tried to make her happy, but the opposite had happened. She didn't know what to think.

"I'll be in my office down the hall for the next hour or so if you need me. Robby will be here soon with your truck."

"Okay." That seemed odd to Heather. Hadn't they used her truck to bring Bethany's toys here?

"I noticed a few boarded-up buildings in town," Jean-Luc continued.

"Yeah, the discount store made them go out of business."

"Robby and I will check them later tonight."

"You mean . . . ?" They thought Louie might be hiding in one of them? "Do you want me to come with you?"

"No," he answered quickly. "You've been through enough tonight. Your daughter, too."

That much was true. Heather didn't think she could handle any more excitement right now. "I'll see you tomorrow?"

"Tomorrow evening, yes. Phil and Pierre will watch over you during the day."

And where will you be? She met his eyes. There was still too much mystery surrounding him.

"Good night, *chérie.*" He took her hand and raised it to his mouth. His lips were soft, sensuous.

Heather's face flooded with heat when delicious memories swept over her. His kiss had been glorious. She'd felt so safe and wonderful in his arms. She wished that feeling could come back, but it was gone. Instead she suffered from a nagging sensation that something was seriously wrong.

"Sleep well." He left the room, closing the door behind him.

"Juan is very romantic," Fidelia observed. "*Muy macho.*"

"*Muy* something," Heather muttered. "Let's get Bethany to bed." *And then we can talk.* The words dangled at the end of the sentence, unsaid.

Thirty minutes later, Bethany was sound asleep in the bed she would share with her mom. Fidelia and Heather took turns washing up.

Heather exited the bathroom and waved a hand toward the dollhouse. "How do you think they managed this?"

"I don't know." Fidelia fluffed the pillows up against the headboard of her bed, then slipped beneath the comforter. "They must have sneaked past the deputy."

Heather rested a hand on one hip. "I don't think Billy and his deputies could be that incompetent."

Fidelia chuckled. "You never know. At least we have the smart ones on our side."

"Smart or just . . . sneaky? There's something very odd going on around here."

Fidelia nodded. "Juan seemed to be listening to someone. He may be psychic."

"I got that impression, too." Heather perched on the end of Fidelia's bed. "Could you hear anything?"

"No, but I'm sensing strange . . . energy. Maybe I'll dream something tonight that'll help."

Heather nodded. She wasn't quite ready to voice her earlier suspicion that Jean-Luc could be immortal. It still seemed too bizarre.

"This is the only bedroom upstairs," Fidelia continued. "And Juan said there are none on the first floor."

"That seemed strange to me, too," Heather conceded.

"Where are all the people in this house sleeping?" Fidelia asked.

Heather winced, remembering the locked cellar doors. "I guess they're in the cellar."

"That's strange," Fidelia muttered. "And what was

that with Alberto? I think those bitches scratched him. Or cut him. There was blood on his fingers."

"I saw that. And Jean-Luc kept telling us to stay away from the cellar. Of course, that could be a good warning with those psycho women living down there."

Fidelia made a clucking noise. "Why were you late to hear Bethany sing? That is not like you."

A blush warmed Heather's cheeks. "I was . . . distracted."

"By Juan? Did he make a pass at you?"

Her blush grew hotter. "I was willing. Far too willing. I . . . I thought I was falling for him."

"And now?"

"I don't know. I'm attracted to him. He's gorgeous and sexy—"

"And rich."

Heather gave her an annoyed look. "That's not what matters to me. Cody had plenty of money, and it sure didn't make me happy."

"Then what do you like about Juan?"

"I think he's an honorable, intelligent, kind man. It was very sweet the way he got that bear for Bethany. And he likes me the way I am. He treats me with respect. He actually listens to me and cares about my feelings."

Fidelia nodded. "He is a good man. I am fairly certain of that."

"*Fairly* certain?"

Fidelia shrugged. "Appearances can be deceiving. I sense something . . . wrong."

Heather snorted. "You don't have to be psychic to know that. There are secrets in this place. Secrets that Jean-Luc wants to hide from me."

"I agree."

"Then how can I trust him?"

Fidelia lounged back against her pillows, frowning. "You must be very careful."

Heather's eyes burned as unwanted tears threatened. She'd so wanted to believe in Jean-Luc. He'd seemed so perfect. But she had no choice. She needed to keep a distance between them. She couldn't let herself fall for Jean-Luc Echarpe.

Chapter 14

Jean-Luc paced in his office. He'd made a stupid mistake. He'd thought the sight of her daughter's toys would cheer her up. It had certainly cheered up Bethany. But Heather—he'd only succeeded in making her suspicious. She was clever. He couldn't underestimate her again. And she was fiercely independent, not as easily impressed by gifts or grand gestures as women he'd known in the past. She didn't seem to need gifts at all. She needed honesty—the one thing he didn't dare give.

Seeing her in proximity to Simone and Inga had confirmed his strong feelings for her. The models were perfection in death, beauty frozen for all time, like statues of goddesses. Heather was life—imperfect and unpredictable. In one evening, she'd melted in his arms, kissing him with passion. And she'd watched him, wary with suspicion. She was volatile, full of emotion. Exciting.

She was also sweet, loyal, and loving. He enjoyed watching her interact with her daughter and Fidelia. They formed such a strong family union, and more and more, he wanted to be part of it.

The thought of losing her made his legs drag with heaviness. He came to a stop by the window overlooking the showroom. His merchandise was there, still on display although the store was closed.

What was it all for? Thirty years ago, he'd enjoyed building a fashion empire, and he'd reveled in his financial success. But somewhere along the line, he'd lost the need to prove himself. It was simply work to fill in the time.

He wanted more, something beyond himself. He wanted Heather to be proud of him. The sort of panic she'd experienced when she feared missing her daughter's show; he wanted her to feel that strongly about his shows. He no longer wanted to create alone. He wanted her to create designs with him. He wanted companionship.

And creating merchandise was no longer enough. He wanted more. What good was a financial empire if he had no child to pass it on to? He wanted children with Heather's hair and eyes, her generous heart and clever mind. All he had to do was keep her safe from Lui and win her heart.

He sighed. Was that too much to ask?

He spotted Robby entering the showroom through the front door. He'd probably left Heather's truck parked in the driveway.

Ian and Phineas walked into the showroom to meet him. Jean-Luc considered teleporting down to join the group. In a second, he was materializing by the base of the stairs.

Robby's hand halted halfway to his sword. "Och, 'tis you. Did yer guests enjoy the surprise?"

"The little girl was delighted, but we may have made Heather too suspicious."

Robby winced. "I was afraid of that. These modern lassies are far too clever."

Ian snorted. "Do ye prefer them stupid?"

Robby shrugged. "I try to avoid the mortal ones altogether." He turned to Jean-Luc. "I was just telling the others here that we need more surveillance cameras. When we planned this building, I thought we'd only be guarding you."

Jean-Luc nodded. Right now, the only cameras were in his office, outside his office, and inside his bedroom. "We need a camera in every room."

"And outside," Robby added. "I know Connor has a stash of spare ones at his security office at Romatech. I'll teleport there to bring them back."

"We also need to buy some food before morning," Jean-Luc suggested. "The bare pantry looked suspicious."

Robby frowned. "Och, I dinna think of that. Pierre's been ordering food in. He was alone here during the day and couldna leave us unguarded."

"I'll go to the store," Ian offered. "What shall I buy—porridge and a leg of lamb?"

"Dude, you are so out of touch with the twenty-first century," Phineas scoffed. "You need Cheetos, Doritos, Oreos, SpaghettiOs—"

"That's food?" Ian asked.

"Damned straight. You know, you old-timers can be really clueless. You'd better let me do the shopping."

"You are a young Vamp?" Jean-Luc asked.

"Hell, yeah. Just over a year. My family's still alive, so I know what people eat."

Jean-Luc arched a brow. "Is your family healthy?"

"Well, my aunt is diabetical, and my little sister's kinda chubby—"

"Healthy food." Jean-Luc handed him the keys to the BMW and several hundred-dollar bills. "Bring back some healthy food."

"Okay, fruits and vegetables and crap. I can do that."

Phineas zipped toward the front door. "Cool! I get to drive the BMW." The door slammed behind him.

"While he's gone, I'll teleport to Romatech and bring back more cameras." Robby paused when they heard the squeal of tires on the driveway.

Jean-Luc winced. "He's new with the company?"

"Dr. Phang?" Ian grinned. "Angus and Emma found him last year. The Russians had transformed him, but he dinna want to bite people. So Angus hired him."

"And what about Phil?" Jean-Luc asked.

"Completely trustworthy," Robby answered. "He's been guarding Roman during the day for over six years."

Ian nodded. "I've known him all that time. He's good."

Jean-Luc recalled the awkward moment when Phineas had claimed Phil smelled different from other mortals. He'd detected something odd, too. "Is there something about Phil I should know?"

Robby's face went blank. Ian seemed suddenly absorbed with the purses on display.

"I'm trusting him with Heather's life. And my own," Jean-Luc added. "I should know."

"'Tis a company matter," Robby muttered. "All I can tell ye is, Phil keeps our secrets, and we keep his. I'll go to Romatech now."

"Hurry back," Jean-Luc told him, aware that Robby was trying to change the subject. "As soon as Phineas returns with the car, I want us to check those empty buildings in town."

"I'll go with you," Ian offered.

"I need you and Phineas to stay here," Jean-Luc replied. "We can't leave the women unguarded."

Ian nodded. "I'll do a perimeter sweep."

He zoomed outside and Robby teleported away, leaving Jean-Luc alone to wonder about Phil. What kind of secret could a mortal have that even vampires were loath to share? He was tempted to call Angus, but the bloody Scotsman would be just as closemouthed as his great-great-grandson Robby. At least Robby and Ian both agreed that Phil was completely trustworthy.

Phil and Pierre would be in the cellar now, sleeping in the dormitory-style bedroom for the guards. As mortals, they were expected to sleep at night, so they could guard during the day. Vamps were totally vulnerable during their death-sleep, so the responsibility of guarding them was huge. Even so, the daytime guards rarely ran into danger. Vampire enemies were also dead during the day, and most of the mortal world was ignorant of their existence.

Alberto was a mortal who knew about vampires. Jean-Luc had confided in his young protégé after Alberto had served faithfully for five years. It was a good arrangement.

Alberto kept their secrets, and in return, he was given opportunities that were rare in the fashion industry. He arranged shows and hobnobbed with powerful, influential people. He was allowed to present his own designs with the advantage of Echarpe distribution and marketing. He'd become Jean-Luc's representative during the day. He was a hardworking perfectionist with only one flaw.

He was obsessed with Simone and Inga. Learning that they were lady Vamps had only increased his desire.

They enjoyed toying with him, but tonight they'd gone too far. Jean-Luc wasn't concerned about Alberto spilling vampire secrets to the media. He and Robby could use mind control to wipe out Alberto's memory if they needed to. But it would be hard to replace Alberto.

Simone and Inga didn't realize it, as vain as they were, but they would be easy to replace.

The memory of Alberto's bloody fingers shot a surge of anger through Jean-Luc. He'd warned Alberto to stay away from Simone and Inga, but obviously the man could not resist the lure of the forbidden. The irony of the situation hit home. Jean-Luc couldn't resist the forbidden, either. It would be so much more convenient if he could fall for a Vamp woman, but no, he wanted Heather.

He teleported back to his office and tried to do some work. Pierre had left an invoice on his desk. The harpsichord he'd ordered had arrived during the day. Good. Jean-Luc didn't consider himself a great musician, but after four hundred years of practice, he was certainly adequate.

Pierre had left a note that he'd instructed the workmen to set up the harpsichord next to the baby grand piano in the music room. Jean-Luc winced at the thought of mortals down in the cellar during the day, but Pierre would have made sure they saw only the main corridor and music room. No mortal would suspect some of the rooms hid vampires in their death-sleep. Still, Jean-Luc was uncomfortable with any mortals knowing about the cellar. He'd have Robby visit these workmen and erase their memories.

And what about Heather? She knew there was a cellar now. How long could he hide his secrets from her? How could he court an honest woman with lies? He'd refused to let her go hunting with Robby and him because he figured the boarded-up buildings were locked. Robby and he could easily teleport inside, but not if Heather was with them.

When they found Lui and killed him, Heather would be free to go on with her life. Would he have to let her go and erase her memory, too?

The thought of spending eternity without her was

difficult to bear. *Merde*, the thought of spending a week without her was painful.

Jean-Luc paced to the sideboard and poured himself a glass of Blissky. The mixture of whisky and synthetic blood burned his throat, but it didn't dull the pain.

He was losing his heart to Heather, and he didn't know how to stop it.

Heather winced as Bethany kicked her again. Between sleeping with a live tornado and her worries about the house and Jean-Luc, Heather had hardly slept a wink.

Fidelia moaned suddenly, jerking Heather more fully awake. She glanced at the bedside table where the clock numbers glowed red in the dark. Five-thirty A.M. The sun would be up soon.

Fidelia moaned again, thrashing her arms and legs. Heather considered waking her, but she really wanted whatever information Fidelia's dream had to offer.

The older woman sat up so suddenly, Heather gasped.

"Fidelia," she whispered. "Are you all right?"

"Eyes, red glowing eyes in the dark. Danger."

That was creepy, but it didn't tell them very much. "Anything else?"

With a sigh, Fidelia rested against the headboard. "I couldn't see much. It was dark. Nighttime. I heard growling. A white flash of long gnashing teeth."

Heather shuddered. The room grew silent except for Bethany's slow and even breathing.

Finally she stood and stretched. She couldn't let a bad dream stop her from living. And since she couldn't sleep, she might as well get to work. The first thing she needed to do was buy some groceries. "Do you want anything from the kitchen?" She snorted. "Some champagne?"

Fidelia chuckled. "I'm fine. I'm going back to sleep. I'll get up when the little one wakes up."

"Okay. Sleep well." Heather stumbled into the bathroom. After a quick shower, she dressed in the new underwear, jeans, and green T-shirt they'd bought the night before. She slipped on her old athletic shoes and exited quietly into the hallway. A window at the end of the hall provided some dim light. The moon was half full, and stars sparkled in a clear sky.

She paused outside Jean-Luc's office. Would he be inside? They'd never discussed the specifics of her job. A red blinking light overhead drew her attention. The surveillance camera was on. Was someone watching her?

She slipped down the backstairs and peeked into the main corridor. Empty. There was a faint sound. Music.

She glanced at the cellar door. After a quick look around, she tiptoed to the door. The sound of music grew louder.

She pressed an ear against the door. Classical music. A piano and something with a tinkling sound. A harpsichord? She curled her fingers around the doorknob and gave it a twist. It turned slightly, then stuck fast. Locked.

"May I help you?" a deep voice spoke behind her.

She whirled to find Robby MacKay standing in the hall. "I . . . good morning. I was looking for the kitchen."

"Over here." He turned to indicate the door on the other side of the staircase.

"Oh, that's right. I'm still learning my way around." She strode toward the kitchen. "I thought I'd make a list of things we need from the grocery store. The pantry's bare, you know."

"'Tis full now. We bought ye some food."

"Oh." She paused outside the kitchen door. "Well, thank you. That was very efficient of you."

He crossed his arms, giving her a thoughtful look. "I found yer handbag in yer truck last night. 'Tis in the security office. I'll bring it to you."

"Great. I might need to run some errands."

He frowned. "If there's anything ye need, tell one of the guards. For yer own safety, ye must stay here."

"Oh." Was she a prisoner? "I see." She let herself into the kitchen, then leaned against the door, taking deep breaths. She wasn't a prisoner, she reminded herself. They were just trying to keep her, Fidelia, and Bethany safe.

And they were keeping their secrets safe, too. *Curiosity killed the cat*, the old saying warned her. But she was no cat. She was woman, hear her roar.

She would uncover all their secrets, one by one.

Chapter 15

Jean-Luc had always loved playing duets. The music swelled back and forth from the piano to the harpsichord. At times he took the lead, and the melody flowed beneath his fingertips. Other times he retreated to the background, pounding the keys to set the rhythm for the other player.

It was a bit like swordplay, he mused. With a good partner, the action swept back and forth—lunge, retreat, thrust, parry. Or like a good night of sex. Taking the lead, then easing back. Setting the rhythm, pounding over and over, sometimes gently, sometimes hard. Using his fingers to make Heather sing.

He smiled to himself. He'd win her over somehow, and it would be glorious. As the closing strain faded away, he kept his fingers on the keys to enjoy the last hint of vibration. *Mon Dieu*, how he wanted her. He'd thought music would help take his mind off her, but it had only made him ache for her.

"Shall we play another, Jean-Luc?" Inga asked from her seat behind the piano.

"Oh yes, please do." Simone had amused herself

by dancing a minuet. "Let's call Robby to come dance with me. It'll be a party, just like old times."

Jean-Luc folded his sheet music. "Actually I have something serious to discuss."

Inga slumped on the piano bench. "You're always serious these days."

"With good reason," Jean-Luc countered. "Lui is back, and he's threatening to kill anyone I care about."

Simone gasped. "That would be us."

Jean-Luc refrained from pointing out that in the two hundred years he'd known Simone and Inga, Lui had never threatened them. He only seemed interested in killing mortals. "You both talked to him Friday night. He was disguised as an old man with white hair and a cane."

"That was Lui?" Inga looked aghast as she pressed a hand to her chest. "He seemed so charming and harmless."

"And rich." Simone flipped her long black hair behind her shoulders. "He offered me twenty thousand dollars for my company."

Inga snorted. "Does he think you're a whore?"

"Actually, I've been considering it." Simone assumed an injured look. "Jean-Luc ignores us terribly."

He'd been hearing that complaint for more than fifty years. "Didn't either of you notice that he wasn't mortal?"

Inga shrugged. "The room was full of smelly mortals."

"And now you've invited some to live under our roof." Simone shuddered. "*Quelle horreur.*"

Jean-Luc pushed back his bench and stood. "They're under my protection. You will treat them with respect. And I have another request. Leave Alberto alone."

Simone waved a hand in dismissal. "He is nothing."

"He's an important employee. You went too far tonight."

Simone scoffed. "It was just a little scratch."

"And I have rules in my household. No biting. If you cannot abide by my rules, you will have to leave."

Simone's eyes flashed. "You would throw us out?"

Inga jumped up from the piano bench. "Come now. We've been friends too long for this silly bickering."

"Indeed." Simone glared at Jean-Luc. "You would not want me for an enemy."

Jean-Luc studied her quietly. "You may leave whenever you wish, Simone."

"Sorry to interrupt," Robby spoke from the open door.

"Robby, you must dance with me," Simone demanded.

"Another time, lass. I need a word with Jean-Luc."

Jean-Luc bowed slightly. "Good night, ladies."

They trudged out the door, pouting.

"Off to bed for yer beauty sleep." Robby stepped aside to let them pass. "Ye're no' getting any younger, ye ken."

Simone gave him a dirty look, but he only chuckled.

Jean-Luc joined him at the door. "You're such a charmer."

"Aye." Robby nodded. "I take pride in it." His smile faded, and his voice lowered. "I found Mrs. Westfield listening to the music at the cellar door."

"Oh." Jean-Luc's heartbeat quickened, just thinking about her. He strode down the hall. "She's up early."

"Aye. And suspicious like we feared. She's in the kitchen now. I returned her handbag to her."

"I see." They had a little time left before sunrise forced them into their daily death-sleep. "I'll try to allay some of her suspicions."

"Good." Robby accompanied him up the stairs. "We made some progress tonight. Six cameras are set up outside."

"Good." But there'd been no progress on finding Lui. Their search of abandoned buildings had yielded nothing. Jean-Luc opened the door to the ground-floor hallway.

"We'll do another check before the changing of the guard." Robby headed to the security office. "See ye tomorrow."

"Good night." Jean-Luc entered the kitchen and stopped in the sitting area. "Heather?"

She peeked out of the utility room. "Jean-Luc! I—I didn't expect to see you." She hurried into the kitchen. "I was just doing some laundry."

She avoided looking at him and shoved her damp, curly hair behind her ears. She fumbled with a pencil and notepad next to her purse on the counter. She seemed nervous, and it irked him that she was no longer comfortable in his presence. "Making a list?" he asked.

"Yes." She waved a hand toward the pantry. "I found it stocked with all sorts of stuff this morning. I really appreciate it, but there are a few things missing. For instance, we have spaghetti, but no tomato sauce."

He had no idea what a spaghetti was, but he'd take her word for it. "Pierre or Phil can get whatever you need."

"I suppose." She tapped the pencil against the countertop. "I guess I'm trapped here until the problem with Louie is resolved."

"It's for the best. I don't want to take any chances with your safety."

She frowned. "I'll need some fat-free milk." She added it to the list. "I have to watch every calorie."

"Heather." He rested his hand on top of hers to stop her fidgeting. "I think you're beautiful the way you are."

She closed her eyes briefly with a pained look. "I

have to know." She gave him a beseeching look. "How did you get Bethany's toys here?"

It was more than a request for information, he realized. She was asking for honesty. She wanted to regain her trust in him. And dammit all, he couldn't tell her the complete truth. That would scare her away faster than anything.

"Robby, Ian, and Phineas worked together," he began. "There was only one deputy, so it wasn't that hard for Phineas to distract him to the back of the house while the others snuck into the front." He didn't mention that part of the sneaking involved teleportation.

She bit her bottom lip. "I suppose that makes sense. How did they bring the stuff here?"

"They had plenty of time to transport it here while we were at the store shopping."

She nodded slowly. "They probably used my truck."

They hadn't, but he didn't disagree. His hand was still covering hers, and she hadn't pulled away. He removed the pencil from her grip. "You're tense. I can tell. It makes your shoulders hunch."

"Of course I'm tense. A homicidal maniac set my house on fire, and he wants to kill me."

"Relax." He circled behind her.

"What are you doing?" She glanced back.

"Trying to ease your tension." He rested his hands on her shoulders, then gently kneaded his fingers into the muscles around her neck. "I want you to know that you and your daughter's safety are more important than anything to me."

"Thank you." With a sigh, she tilted her head forward. "I guess you and Robby didn't find Louie tonight."

"No." He massaged her shoulders. "I would have told you, but I thought you were asleep."

"I couldn't sleep. Poor Bethany. I'm afraid this is taking a toll on her. She was thrashing about in bed."

"I'm so sorry." He led Heather toward the couch. "Come. You look tired."

"I'm exhausted, but I have so much to do. The insurance company to call, and Heather's preschool—"

"They won't be open yet." He shoved a big footstool up to the couch and sat her on it. Then he settled onto the couch behind her, straddling the footstool.

"You must be tired, too." She glanced back at him. "You're still in the same clothes."

"I'll get some rest in a little while." The sun was nearing the horizon. Soon he would feel the pull of death-sleep. But for now, he could enjoy being with Heather. He dug his fingers into her shoulders.

She let out a long moan, then cut it off abruptly. "Sorry, didn't mean to do that out loud."

He smiled. "I like hearing you moan." He massaged circles down her back. "Even more, I like being the cause."

"This feels so good." She sighed. "I don't know what to think of you."

He rubbed the small of her back. "Do you have to think at all?"

"Yes. I've made some bad mistakes in the past. I have to be very careful now, 'cause it's not just my life I could screw up, but Bethany's, too."

He touched her hair, enjoying the feel of the silken strands. "You are my ideal of a good mother."

She twisted to look at him. "That's about the kindest thing I've ever heard."

"Heather." He scooped an arm under her legs to pull her into his lap. "You bring kindness out of me. You make me want to be deserving of you."

She touched his face. "Why wouldn't you be?"

"I'm not perfect."

"No one is." She traced his jaw with her fingers. "You have secrets. About yourself and Louie."

She wanted to know more. He chose his words carefully. "Lui assassinated some important political figures in France. I stopped one of his attempts, and he has plagued me ever since."

"How does a fashion designer stop an assassin?"

"I . . . wasn't a designer then. I worked for the government."

Her eyes lit up. "Like James Bond?"

"Something like that."

"I knew it!" She grinned. "You're just as sexy as James Bond, and you have that aura of danger about you."

He lifted his eyebrows. "You think I'm sexy?"

Her cheeks flushed. "Did I say that?"

"Yes." He brushed her hair back from her brow. "I suppose I shall have to live up to my reputation."

"I suppose." Her gaze lowered to his mouth.

That was an invitation. He brushed his lips against hers. Her arms encircled his neck, pulling him closer. A thrill shot through him. She wanted him. He deepened the kiss, pouring all his desire into the movement of his lips and the swirl of his tongue.

She stroked his tongue with her own and moaned. He slid his hand past her ribs to cup her breast.

"Yes," she breathed against his cheek.

He spread his fingers to cover her breast, then lightly squeezed. "You're so lovely." He nuzzled her ear. Her carotid artery throbbed nearby, sending out pulses of the scent of Type AB blood.

She tilted her head to make it easier for him to kiss her neck, not realizing how intensely erotic that move was to a vampire. His groin began to throb in sync with the coursing of her blood.

"Heather." He feathered kisses along her cheek. *Zut,*

what terrible timing. She needed to be loved properly, and he'd literally be dead in ten minutes.

She ran her hands through his hair. "Kiss me."

How could he resist? He molded his mouth to hers once more and explored her with his tongue. He rubbed his thumb around the tip of her breast and felt the nipple tighten. The swelling in his groin was fast becoming torture. "I want to stay with you. I want to love you, but I have to go."

"Why?" She kissed his cheek. "Where are you going?"

"I have . . . business meetings in San Antonio," he lied. "But I'll be back tonight. In the meantime, I want you to get some rest."

"I'll miss you."

He stroked her hair. "I'll miss you, too." He invaded her mind with one swift plunge and felt her shiver at the cold presence of his mind. *Sleep, my love.*

She exhaled slowly, and her eyes flickered shut. "I'm sleepy," she whispered.

"I know." He laid her gently on the couch. He set pillows beneath her head, then grabbed an afghan from the nearby recliner to cover her up. He kissed her brow. "Sweet dreams, *chérie.*"

Her mouth curled in a smile, then her face went blank.

Jean-Luc turned off the lights, then descended to his lonely bed in the cellar.

Monday passed peacefully, and Heather was grateful for that. She slept till midmorning when Fidelia and Bethany came downstairs and found her on the couch. After a quick breakfast, she began making phone calls concerning her house. She informed the preschool that Bethany would be out for a week. Hopefully, this mess with Louie wouldn't drag on any longer than that. Though she wouldn't mind if her relationship with Jean-Luc continued for weeks or months. Or years. He was such a wonderful combination of sweet and sexy. She couldn't wait to see him again tonight.

She brought some toys downstairs, and once Bethany was happily playing, she asked Pierre to let her into the design studio. She asked for the combination, explaining how she'd be coming and going. Pierre merely smiled and lowered the door stopper to keep the door propped open.

She soon forgot about the mysterious lock combination as she lost herself in work. She decided to remake the white gown from the showroom. She dragged the mannequin into the studio and positioned it next to a worktable. Then she located a dress form that could be adjusted to a larger size and stood it next to the mannequin. Before and after. Size zero and size twelve.

She scoured the shelves along the walls, searching for just the right material. There were so many exceptional fabrics, she soon had the table stacked with ten bolts.

Under the spiral staircase, she found shelves filled with office supplies. She selected a large sketching pad and several Prismacolor pencils. She sketched for a few hours, then went back to the kitchen for lunch.

Phil and Pierre joined them for hot dogs. Pierre made them laugh by insisting they call his lunch *le hot-dog*. Alberto finally made an appearance. He must have stayed up late and slept in. He looked askance at their meal.

Heather noticed how his turtleneck sweater hid the marks on his neck. She exchanged a look with Fidelia.

She grinned. "You'll burn up in that sweater, *muchacho*. It'll be ninety-six degrees today."

"Do you want some lunch?" Heather asked.

He shuddered. "I'll go to town to eat. There's a German bakery on Main Street that's rather good."

"Oh, yeah." Heather knew the one he was talking about, since it was the only German bakery on Main Street. "Finkel's makes the best apple strudel in Texas."

"Vraiment?" Pierre handed Alberto the car keys and a twenty-dollar bill. "You must bring back strudel for all of us, *d'accord*?"

"I'm not an errand boy," Alberto grumbled. "But all right. Ciao." He grabbed the keys and money and left.

"Thank you." Heather smiled at Pierre.

He shrugged. "I am a bit homesick. In Paris, we have the pâtisseries everywhere. The most delicious bread and pastries. I miss them."

"Sounds wonderful." Heather sighed. "I've always wanted to see Paris. I hear the rats are really special."

Pierre sputtered with a horrified look. "Paris is the most beautiful city in the world. I will tell Jean-Luc to bring you. My mother will cook you the best coq au vin you have ever tasted."

"I'm all for that." She went back to work, her spirits lifted. After an hour of sketching, she heard Alberto enter the studio.

"The strudel's in the kitchen." He eyed the fabric on her worktable. "You like colors."

"Yes."

He circled her table, examining her work. "I'm more into black and neutrals. More sophisticated."

"Ah." That must mean she was *less* sophisticated.

He wrinkled his nose at the dress form she'd enlarged to a size twelve. "This is much too big for haute couture."

"I don't really aspire to be that . . . fancy. I want to make something that would look good on someone like me."

His eyes widened. "Why?"

"Why not? I wear clothes, too."

"Well, yes." His gaze drifted painfully over her T-shirt and jeans. "But surely you understand there is a huge difference between mere clothes and fashion."

"I know that. I want to bring fashion to women like me. I want them to enjoy their clothes and take pride in how they look."

He looked like she was speaking an alien tongue. "Take pride in being a size twelve? Does Jean-Luc know what you're doing?"

"Yes. He asked me to do this."

Alberto's brows shot higher. "You must be joking."

She gritted her teeth. "No. I'm very serious. Fashion should be accessible to everyone."

He snorted. "This must be some strange American idea of equality."

"I'll take that as a compliment."

"It is a fantasy. The world of fashion belongs to the beautiful people." Alberto looked her over. "Jean-Luc is humoring you. It is clear what he wants."

Heat flooded her face. "You've not only insulted me, you've insulted Jean-Luc. He has enough business savvy to realize he's missing out on a huge market. A lot of women could never wear some of the bizarre things that come down the runways these days. Jean-Luc has the courage and vision to give women clothes they can actually wear."

Alberto's smile was smug. "I can see he is your hero. I wonder how long that will last. Especially once you know more about him." He sauntered toward the door. "I have work to do in my office. *Real* fashion to create."

Heather tried to get back to work, but found it hard to concentrate. Was Jean-Luc just humoring her because he was attracted to her? She looked over her sketches. They looked good to her, but drawing a good picture didn't guarantee a beautiful gown. And what did Alberto mean with that crack about her and Jean-Luc? Was she supposed to like Jean-Luc less the more she got to know him?

She took a deep breath and let it out slowly. She wouldn't do this to herself. She wouldn't let fear and self-doubt overwhelm her. She was at war with fear.

God knew she had plenty to be afraid of. A new career, a new relationship with Jean-Luc, a psycho killer who wanted her dead. Failure was not an option.

She could do the career. It would be difficult, but nothing worthwhile was ever easy. And the relationship with Jean-Luc was looking better than ever. He'd been so sweet that morning. And sexy. Her heart raced every time she thought about his kisses and the way he'd massaged her back and fondled her breast. Her skin prickled with goose bumps, eager to feel his touch once more.

He'd said he wanted her, and she knew that was the truth. The bulge in his pants had pressed against her rear, and God help her, she had wanted to touch him. She'd wanted to have sex with a man she'd met just a few days ago. Thank goodness she'd fallen asleep when she had.

What was happening to her? *Love*, a small inner voice answered. No, it couldn't be. But then why was he constantly in her thoughts? Why did she keep wishing the time away till she could see him again?

Love.

Unable to concentrate, she left her sketches on the worktable and returned to the kitchen. Fidelia was watching television while Bethany played in the kitchen. The stuffed crocodile was chasing Barbie around the kitchen table while the doll did her best to guard the box of strudel from reptilian attack. Heather helped herself to a piece of strudel, then played with her daughter. Soon they heard Fidelia snoring in the recliner, a sound that always made Bethany giggle.

Heather was making supper when Fidelia jerked awake with a cry. "What is it?" She stepped close to the older woman so Bethany wouldn't hear.

"I had the dream again," Fidelia whispered. "Red eyes, glowing in the dark. Danger."

Heather grimaced. "They still haven't found Louie."

Fidelia rubbed her forehead. "I saw something else. An oil painting. I think I've seen it before."

After supper, Heather took Bethany upstairs for her bath. They came back to the kitchen about eight P.M., so Bethany could have a bedtime snack. Heather wondered if Jean-Luc was back from his business trip.

Fidelia was loading the dishwasher. "I remembered where I saw that painting. I called and talked to the curator, Mrs. Bolton." She handed Heather a piece of paper.

Heather's eyes widened as she read the information. "I've heard of this place. It's a museum now?"

"*Sí*. Mrs. Bolton said she'd keep it open for you till nine o'clock tonight."

"Okay." Heather folded the paper and slipped it into her jeans pocket. What a strange place to take Jean-Luc. She wondered again if he was back. She glanced up at the newly installed surveillance camera with its red, blinking light.

"I know," Fidelia muttered. "I don't like being watched."

Who was watching? Heather wondered. Whoever it was, she hoped they enjoyed the ongoing saga of Barbie versus the crocodile. The kitchen door swung open, and Robby marched in, wearing his usual green and blue plaid kilt.

He smiled. "Good evening. Jean-Luc is in the design studio, and he'd like to see you."

Heather's heart beat faster. She hugged her daughter. "I have to go. Duty calls." Duty and hopeless attraction.

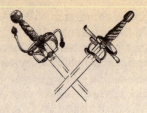

Chapter 16

"Jean-Luc, we need to talk."

He glanced up from one of Heather's sketches to see Alberto coming into the studio. "Is there a problem in Paris?"

"No. The problem is here." Alberto waved at Heather's work. "This—this is a disaster."

Jean-Luc laid the sketch down. "This was *my* decision, Alberto. I do not need to defend it."

He lowered his gaze. "I don't mean to upset you, Jean-Luc, but you taught me yourself that your designs are only for a privileged few."

Jean-Luc's anger was tempered by the desperation on Alberto's face. Clearly the man believed Heather's project was a mistake. "I know this idea is unorthodox, but I want to try it."

"It will make you a laughingstock in the fashion world. None of the Hollywood stars will wear your gowns if they're being worn by the *common* folk."

"You and I both come from common folk."

"Yes, but we rose above that." Alberto gestured at the dress form. "She's making fat lady clothes!"

A small gasp at the door heralded Heather's arrival. Jean-Luc groaned inwardly, knowing she'd heard Alberto's rude remark. He stepped close to his protégé and narrowed his eyes. "You are mistaken, and you will apologize."

Alberto's face flushed. He glanced over his shoulder at Heather. "I am sorry, *signora*."

"Is it true?" Heather walked toward them, her expression worried. "Will my designs damage your reputation?"

She must have heard more than Alberto's insult. Jean-Luc shrugged. "The media is fickle. I never know how they will react. They might laugh at this, or they might call us heroes and visionaries."

She tilted her head, considering. "Does it really matter what they think? I mean, if sales are good, how could it be called a failure?"

Alberto huffed with exasperation. "It is not about money. High fashion is an art."

"I think it's about making people feel good," Heather declared. "And if they're spending their money on something, then that means it's making them happy."

Jean-Luc smiled. Heather's confidence in herself was growing. "We're going to do it, Alberto. Thanks to Heather, fashion will be available to women of all shapes and sizes."

Alberto sputtered while Heather grinned. Jean-Luc wanted to pull her into his arms, but was broadsided with a sudden idea.

"We can use the charity show to gauge how people will react," he suggested. "Heather, can you have a few designs ready by the end of next week?"

"I think so." She nodded. "Sure."

Jean-Luc didn't want to bring in more professional

models, since he didn't want the media to hear about the show or about his presence in Texas. "Do you know some local women who could model your clothes?

Alberto snorted. "The town is full of fat women."

Heather glared at him, then turned to Jean-Luc. "I have some friends who would love to model. And they're not fat." She shot another angry glance at Alberto.

"You can showcase some of your designs, too," Jean-Luc told Alberto. "Simone, Inga, and Sasha will model for you."

"Can we make it a competition?" Alberto asked, his eyes lighting up. "And invite celebrities to judge?"

"No." Jean-Luc gave him a warning look. "No celebrities, no media. You know why."

Alberto sighed.

Heather looked curious. "Why—"

"It'll be a small function just for the local people," Jean-Luc interrupted. "Because the proceeds are only for the local area." He hoped that would make enough sense to keep her from asking more questions.

She smiled. "I think it's wonderful that you're raising money for the school district. Thank you."

He shrugged. "Alberto's handling the matter." It was embarrassing to be considered charitable when he was actually bribing the builder and mayor to keep quiet about his store.

He was beginning to dread the show, for afterward his official exile would begin. The store would close for good. Alberto and the models would return to Paris. People would assume he'd left, too, but he would be hiding in the abandoned building with his two guards for twenty-five long years. How could he live next door to Heather and not be tempted to see her?

"Do you want any of your designs in the show?" Alberto asked.

Jean-Luc shrugged. "It doesn't matter." Nothing seemed to matter when faced with a twenty-five-year-long prison term without hope of seeing Heather. But how could he ask her and her family to share a prison with him? They didn't have the possibility that he had of living for centuries into the future. This was their life now, their only life. They needed to live it. Without him.

"Fine," Alberto continued. "Then Heather and I will each show our designs to the local . . . riffraff, and then we'll see which ones they prefer." He gave her a challenging look, then strode from the room.

She stepped closer to Jean-Luc. "Are you all right?"

"Yes."

She studied him, frowning. "You look like you've lost your best friend."

He was going to, he realized. He was in a no-win situation. In the worst-case scenario, he could lose Heather to Lui's murderous revenge. But he wouldn't let that happen. He'd kill Lui first. Unfortunately, then he would lose Heather because it was the only honorable thing to do. He couldn't ask her to give up twenty-five years of her short life to share his exile.

He would have to send her away. He'd hire her to do her designs in New York or Paris. Then she could have her dream life. And he'd make sure that she and her daughter never wanted for anything. A strong wave of emotion washed over him, and he realized he wasn't planning this simply out of duty or a sense of honor.

He was doing it for love. Somehow, somewhere during the last few days, he'd begun to fall in love.

"I'm all right," he assured her. "I'm just concerned that we haven't found Lui yet."

"I wanted to talk to you about that." She dug a piece of paper from her jeans pocket and handed it to him.

"Fidelia had a dream about an oil painting, and it's located at this museum on the outskirts of town. The curator is keeping it open for us."

"Then we should go." He escorted her toward the door as he glanced at the paper. "Chicken Ranch?"

"Yep. The most famous one in Texas, so they made it into a museum."

He led her down the hall. "They made a museum about chickens?"

She laughed. "It was a house of prostitution."

"Ah. I should have realized."

"Yeah." Heather winced. "I'm just wondering how come Fidelia knows so much about it."

The second they entered the showroom, Jean-Luc noticed Robby installing a camera near the two-story-high ceiling. Unfortunately, he wasn't using a ladder.

He grabbed Heather and turned her away from the levitating Robby. "How . . . was your day?"

"Fine." She smiled slowly. "It started off with a wonderful massage."

He smiled back, then glanced up at Robby. The Scotsman had heard them and was descending to the floor. "I liked your sketches."

Heather's smile widened. "Thank you."

Robby was now on the floor.

"Grab the keys, Robby. And bring our swords. We're going hunting."

"I'm coming, too." Heather dashed toward the kitchen, calling back. "I'll borrow a gun from Fidelia. Don't leave without me!"

Robby frowned, shaking his head. "No' a good idea."

"She's coming," Jean-Luc announced, then went out the front door before Robby could argue.

The front door was bracketed by two outdoor lights that dimly lit the porch. Jean-Luc let his gaze wander over the land that separated his lair from the highway.

He saw no hint of movement. Cedar trees and clumps of palmetto dotted the area enclosed by the long circular driveway. His BMW and Heather's truck were parked nearby. He'd had a gardener plant oak trees along the drive, but they were small now. By the time his exile of twenty-five years was up, they would be large and impressive.

"There you are!" Heather rushed out onto the porch. "I was afraid you'd leave without me."

"I really should, but I've discovered a recent problem where you're concerned."

"What's that?" She hitched her purse onto her shoulder.

"I'm unable to tell you no."

She laughed. "That's not a problem."

"It is if it puts you in danger."

"I can take care of myself. I'm at war with fear, remember?"

"I am impressed by your willingness to confront the villain." He placed a hand on the small of her back and ushered her toward the darker end of the porch. "How do you feel about confronting this attraction between us?"

Her eyes widened. "I . . . suppose we can admit it's there."

"And it's growing stronger. At least for me."

She leaned against a column and gazed toward the highway. "It's happening very fast."

"Do you doubt it's real?"

She glanced at him. "No. It's real. Real enough that I could get hurt."

"I would never hurt you. Not intentionally."

"I know that." She placed a hand on his chest. "I'm . . . very attracted to you, Jean-Luc, but I'm trying not to make any mistakes I'll regret."

"I understand." He planted a hand on either side

of the column, pinning her in. "I know I should resist
you. But whenever you're close, I can only think about
how much I want you."

He kissed her brow. "I keep remembering how good
you feel in my arms and how sweet you taste." He
kissed her cheek. "Remember our first kiss, *chérie*? The
one in the park?"

The corner of her mouth quirked. "What kiss? Did
we kiss?"

"You melted in my arms. You moaned into my
mouth. You tasted me with your tongue."

"Oh. That kiss."

"And you did it again this morning."

"Well, some things you just have to keep doing till
you get it right."

He smiled. "*Chérie*, you have it right." He skimmed
his fingers up her neck. "All I can think about is kissing
you. I can hardly work. My mind has become utterly
useless."

"Poor baby." She tilted her head when he rubbed
his nose against her neck. "We can't have you being
useless."

"I'm sure we'll find something I can do." He touched
his tongue against the pulsing artery in her neck. The
scent of her blood sizzled through him.

"Like trying to seduce me?" She sounded breathless.

He kissed a trail to her ear. "There's no trying. I *am*
seducing you."

He drew her earlobe into his mouth and groaned
when she responded with a shudder. He suckled as he
enveloped her in his arms.

Her hands slipped around his neck. "Yes," she whispered.

He brushed his lips across her cheek. "I want you so."

"I know," she breathed the words against his mouth.
"Why does this feel so right?"

"Because we . . . fit." He molded his mouth against hers and pulled her tight against him. They *did* fit. Her lips were perfect against his. Her breasts moved against his chest in just the right way.

He smoothed his hands down her back. The small of her back arched perfectly against his lower belly, her hips nestled sweetly against his groin, and her belly cushioned his hard erection. She was perfect in every way.

How could he let her go? Maybe she could learn to accept him as a vampire. Maybe he could have the sort of love Roman and Angus had found. Maybe he could even have a family.

A flash of light hit them as a car zoomed up the driveway. He immediately pulled her around the column into the shadow.

"Do you think it's Louie?" she whispered.

"No. He wouldn't be this obvious." Jean-Luc watched the car as it passed Heather's truck and his BMW. It screeched to a halt just past the front door. "It's probably one of your admirers from town."

"I have no admirers," she muttered.

"Then who was that noisy little man I had to dunk in the water?"

"Coach Gunter. He's more of a pest than an admirer." Heather twisted to peek around the column, but Jean-Luc pulled her back into the shadow.

"Careful." He narrowed his eyes as a man exited the car. "Yes. This one is definitely in love with you."

"What?" She scoffed.

"Heather!" the man yelled from the driveway. "I know you're there!"

"Cody?" she whispered with a grimace. "My ex doesn't love me. He hates me."

"He hates that you rejected him," Jean-Luc whispered. "But he still loves you. Believe me, I know the signs."

"You do?" She gave him a dubious look.

"Come on out, Heather!" Cody shouted. "I saw you on the porch, kissing that man."

"Jealousy," Jean-Luc whispered.

"The news is all over town," Cody bellowed. "Everyone knows you're living here. They know you're shacking up with that rich foreigner."

"Shall I skewer him?" Robby asked quietly as he shut the front door.

"No." Jean-Luc stepped from the shadows into the light by the front door. "You are trespassing on private property. I suggest you leave."

"I have a right to be here! You've got my daughter in there. What are you doing to her?"

"Bethany is perfectly fine." Heather moved into the light. "You can pick her up at the appointed time next Friday. Now go home, Cody."

"Why? So you can screw your new boyfriend? I didn't know you were a damned slut, Heather."

"Enough!" Jean-Luc zeroed all his psychic power onto Cody's forehead. The bastard stumbled back a few feet. *Every time you curse Heather, you will become a cockroach.*

Cody crumpled onto the brick pavement.

Heather stepped forward. "What—"

"Leave him be." Jean-Luc touched her arm.

Cody wriggled on the driveway, then rose into a squat. "I am a cockroach," he squeaked.

Heather gasped. "Not again."

Cody crawled toward the BMW, then leaped on top and scrambled across the hood.

Jean-Luc winced at the abuse his car was taking. *You cannot pick up your daughter this weekend.*

Cody lumbered toward his car. "I cannot pick up my daughter this weekend." He dove through the open window of his car and thrashed about.

"Is he drunk?" Heather grimaced when the engine roared to life. "He shouldn't drive like that."

The car shot forward and bounced over a curb where the driveway curved back to the state highway.

You will drive well, Jean-Luc delivered the psychic message, though he wasn't sure Cody could drive at all in his current condition.

The car stopped weaving and zoomed down the driveway in a straight line.

Heather exhaled a long breath. "He's gone crazy. Thank God he doesn't want Bethany this weekend."

"That was different," Robby spoke behind them.

Jean-Luc glanced back to find the Scotsman giving him an amused look. "Are you ready to go?"

"Aye." Robby strode down the steps to the driveway, carrying two swords. "Let me check the car first."

"This is it." Heather studied the Queen Anne house lit by the headlights of Jean-Luc's car as he parked. Between the scraggly azalea bushes in the front flower bed, she spotted a stone cellar.

The two-story wooden frame house was out in the middle of nowhere, but fifty years ago it had drawn customers from all over the state. A large sign by the front steps read *Chicken Ranch, est. 1863*. Heather noted an old Chevy Impala in the parking lot, probably Mrs. Bolton's car.

Heather gathered her purse, containing Fidelia's Glock and a flashlight, and met Jean-Luc on the sidewalk. Robby handed him his foil, and Jean-Luc slid it into a sheath hidden beneath his long black coat. Robby didn't bother to conceal the claymore strapped on his back.

Heather shook her head as they climbed the front steps to the porch. "The curator's not going to let you in with those swords."

"That is the least of my worries." Jean-Luc knocked on the door.

As they waited, Heather admired the elaborate gingerbread work around the covered porch and the wicker furniture. "They've maintained the place well."

Jean-Luc knocked again.

Heather frowned. "She said she would keep it open."

Jean-Luc turned the doorknob, and the door swung open slowly. "She has kept it open." He entered the dimly lit foyer, followed by Robby.

"Hello?" Heather called out as she stepped into the house. No answer. She gazed about, taking in the flocked wallpaper and Oriental rug on the wooden floor. "Maybe she's in the bathroom."

Robby obviously didn't believe in such convenient reasoning, for he drew his claymore. He entered the dark parlor on the right, his sword clenched tight in his fist.

He halted abruptly. "Lord Almighty," he whispered.

"What is it?" Jean-Luc rushed in, then stopped.

Heather couldn't see what they were looking at, so she fumbled along the wall and flipped the light switch. "Good Lord."

The light was aimed at the far wall, where a giant oil painting spread five feet across. Heather swallowed. No wonder Fidelia recognized this painting. Who could forget it? A curvaceous blonde reclined on a velvet chaise, completely nude while she pleasured herself, one hand on a plump breast and the other between her spread legs. Judging from the look on her face, her hands could work miracles.

"Sheesh. That doesn't leave much to the imagination." Heather turned away to look at the rest of the room. Red velvet chaises like the one in the painting lined the walls. She wondered if the prostitutes had reenacted the scene for paying customers.

Robby's head tilted as he studied the painting. "I suppose its purpose is to help a man be prepared."

Jean-Luc stood beside him, his gaze also glued to the painting. "That makes sense from a business point of view. If the men are ready to perform, then they can move the customers through more quickly."

"And make more money," Robby concluded.

"Hello?" Heather waved a hand in front of their faces to get their attention. "We're looking for a homicidal maniac, remember?"

Robby jerked as if coming out of a trance. "I'll take a look around." He returned to the foyer and clambered up the stairs.

Heather glanced at the painting, then frowned at Jean-Luc. "Are you done?"

His mouth twitched. "I feel a bit sorry for her. All the men who came through here, and still, she needs to find pleasure by her own hand."

Heather shrugged. "If you want a job done right, you gotta do it yourself."

He arched a brow. "Has it been that way for you?"

She scoffed. "I wasn't talking about myself."

"Are you sure? Didn't your ex have only three steps?"

Heather felt her cheeks grow warm. "I wonder what happened to Mrs. Bolton." She headed toward a closed door and knocked before cracking it open. "Hello?"

"Allow me." Jean-Luc withdrew his foil, then entered the room first.

Heather smoothed a hand over the wall and found the light switch. A small crystal chandelier hung from the ceiling, circled by a mirror edged in a gold, ornate frame. The mirror reflected the lights, making that part of the ceiling sparkle, but Heather suspected the mirror had other purposes as well, seeing that it was situated over a large bed.

The bed and windows were lined with red satin and lace. Red wallpaper, flocked with black cupids, covered the walls. A large desk with pigeonholes sat in the corner.

"The madam's room, I believe." Jean-Luc looked inside a closet. "Though it looks like she did some entertaining herself."

"Yep." Heather motioned to a pair of handcuffs linked through the bed's wrought-iron headboard. "Looks like she needed to be in charge all the time."

Jean-Luc frowned. "I could never submit to that. I don't like to feel powerless."

Heather snorted. "You would have to trust me not to hurt you." She winced. "I mean whoever was with you." Her face grew hot.

He smiled slowly as he approached. "Are you inviting me to your bed, *chérie*?"

"No. I was speaking theoretically." She crossed her arms. "Though I doubt I would need to chain you to the bed."

"No, you would not." His eyes twinkled. "Would I need to chain you? Theoretically speaking."

She shoved her hair back from her damp forehead. This theory was getting too hot to handle. "I need to feel that I'm in control."

"Ah, now you have given me a challenge." He stepped closer. "To make you lose control."

She swallowed hard. "I think we're getting off course. We need to find Mrs. Bolton." She strode toward another door.

Jean-Luc went through first, and she followed. It appeared to be a less formal parlor, a place for the ladies to relax when off duty. It opened onto the foyer and the next room, which was the kitchen. There they found the door leading into the cellar.

Robby joined them and insisted on going down first. He flipped the light switch. Nothing happened.

"Could be a blown fuse," Jean-Luc said.

Heather retrieved her flashlight from her purse and lit the stairs. Robby went first, followed by Jean-Luc and Heather. At the bottom she shone the flashlight around, illuminating a small storeroom with shelves. The cellar was obviously divided into more than one room.

"Do you smell that?" Robby asked quietly.

"Yes." Jean-Luc grabbed Heather's arm. "I'm taking you back to the car."

"What? Why?" She saw Robby going into the next room. She sniffed the air but could smell nothing but dust.

"Lui's not here," Robby called from the next room. "But I need the torch."

"*Merde.*" Jean-Luc wrapped his left arm around Heather. "Stay with me."

She shivered, and the light wavered as they entered the next room.

"The wall to your left," Robby's voice came out of the darkness. "That's where I smell it."

She pointed her flashlight at the wall and gasped when letters in red appeared. It was a message, but not in English.

"It's French." Jean-Luc took her flashlight and panned across the words. "It says, 'We will meet at the time of my choosing.' Signed with an *L.*"

"Louie," Heather whispered and stepped back. "He was here."

Robby stepped close to the wall and examined the red letters. "'Tis fresh."

With a gasp, Heather realized it wasn't paint on the wall. It was blood. Fresh blood. She stepped back, her skin crawling with gooseflesh. "He left the message for us. He knew we were coming."

"Yes." Jean-Luc continued to study the message.

Bile rose in her throat. Where did all that blood come from? She stepped back and tripped.

"Aagh!" She fell back and landed on something bulky. She screamed again.

Jean-Luc quickly turned the beam of the flashlight on her. And the dead body.

"Oh my God!" She scrambled away.

A woman's body lay on the cellar floor, her throat slit. Jean-Luc and Robby rushed forward.

Heather slapped a hand over her mouth. Jean-Luc grabbed her. Everything went black for a second, and she blinked, nauseated and dizzy.

A breeze wafted over her face, and she realized she was in the parking lot next to Jean-Luc's BMW. She must have fainted for a minute because she couldn't recall getting there.

"Let's get you home," Jean-Luc bundled her into the car.

With shaking hands, she dropped her purse onto the floorboard. Poor Mrs. Bolton. She'd become Louie's first victim in Texas. With a shudder, Heather realized she'd thought the word *first*.

They couldn't let Louie kill again. Especially when she and her daughter were on his list.

Chapter 17

Back at home, Jean-Luc paced the hallway outside the kitchen. Never again. No matter how much Heather pleaded with her pretty green eyes, he was not taking her on another hunt. Not when Lui was leaving dead bodies behind.

Merde. There'd been too much blood on the wall. The smell of it had been so powerful, he hadn't sensed the dead body on the floor.

Heather rushed down the backstairs. Her face was still pale, and her gaze flitted about nervously.

"Are they all right?" he asked.

"Yes. Bethany's asleep, and Fidelia's reading. She could tell something was wrong, but I didn't want to talk about it."

Heather strode into the kitchen, and Jean-Luc followed her. "I don't even want to think about it." She washed her hands in the sink, then wrung them dry with a towel. "It was so awful."

"I shouldn't have let you go." He poured her a glass of water. "Here. Unless you want something stronger."

"This is fine." She gulped down half the glass. "Fidelia was right. Louie was hiding there in the cellar."

"*Oui*. But he's moved on now, and we don't know where."

"Poor Mrs. Bolton." Heather shuddered. "I don't understand. Why would she let a creepy killer stay in her basement? Was he threatening her or tricking her somehow?"

Jean-Luc frowned. He would have to divulge some information. "Lui was probably controlling her. He's adept at manipulating minds."

Heather's eyes widened. "Then Fidelia was right again. He's psychic."

"Yes. He uses people and then discards them." With a gulp, Jean-Luc realized it was time to tell her more. If he wanted their relationship to develop and last, and he did, then he needed to be honest with her. His heart raced. What if she rejected him? He would have to be very careful. He couldn't let her run away and face Lui alone.

She sighed. "I know Robby has already called Billy, but I dread talking to him. I don't want to relive that horrible scene all over again." She turned on the faucet and rinsed her hands once more.

"Heather." He turned the water off. "You can't wash it away."

Her eyes glistened with tears, and her hands shook as she dried them. "I'm trying to be brave, but I keep remembering her body. I just want it all to go away."

The kitchen door cracked open, and Robby peered inside. "The sheriff's outside."

Heather waited on the front steps, drumming her fingers on her thighs. Billy was still in his squad car, taking his time. He thumbed through a notepad. Then he selected a new toothpick from a plastic dispenser.

She groaned, closing her eyes briefly.

"It's all right," Jean-Luc whispered beside her. "The sheriff is claiming control of the situation by making us wait."

She clenched her fists to keep her hands from fidgeting. She could no longer doubt that Louie was a killer. He had no regard for human life whatsoever.

Robby positioned himself on the other side of her.

"We'll no' let any harm come to you, lass."

She was actually very fortunate. She had two macho men who would fight to the death to keep her safe. Not to mention the other guards and Fidelia. She wasn't alone like poor Mrs. Bolton. The memory of her dead body sent another tremor down Heather's spine.

Billy finally set his hat on his head and exited the car. "Good evening, folks." He slammed the car door shut, then circled the squad car to stand in the middle of the driveway. "Now which one of you called about a dead body?"

"That was me, Robby MacKay."

Billy looked him over. "You're a foreigner, too?"

"Aye, from Scotland. Have ye looked at the body yet?"

"I'll ask the questions around here." Billy removed his notepad and pencil from his pocket. "Now, where exactly is this dead body?" He glanced at Jean-Luc. "It's not another squirrel, is it?"

"It's Mrs. Bolton." Heather glared at Billy. "She's the curator at the Chicken Ranch Museum. You'll find her . . . in the cellar." Tears crowded her eyes as the gruesome image filled her mind.

"What were you doing at the Chicken Ranch, Heather?" Billy demanded.

She took a deep breath, willing the tears and the image away. "Fidelia sent us there. She had a vision."

"We've been looking for the man who set fire to

Heather's house," Jean-Luc explained. "Fidelia thought he was hiding at the Chicken Ranch, so—"

"You went there?" Billy interrupted, his nostrils flaring. "You should have called me!"

"There was no way of knowing if Fidelia's vision was correct," Heather said.

"That doesn't matter." Billy stepped toward her, jabbing a finger in the air. "You don't do your own investigation. You call me." He glared at the two men flanking her. "If anything had happened to Heather, I'd hold you two accountable."

"We are protecting her," Jean-Luc said through gritted teeth.

"That's not your job." Billy tossed his toothpick to the ground. "So you're saying the same guy who set Heather's house on fire just killed Mrs. Bolton?"

"Aye," Robby answered.

Billy made some notes on his pad. "Any idea who this guy is?"

"I don't know his name, but he's killed before," Jean-Luc said. "In France."

"Shit. Another foreigner." Billy scowled at him. "How come the French police let this guy get away?"

Jean-Luc sighed. "No one knows who he is. He has threatened Heather, and we have sworn to pro—"

"Whoa!" Billy held up a hand. "Heather, if you're on his hit list, I need to take you immediately into protective custody."

"And where would you put me and Bethany?" Heather asked. "You're not equipped for this sort of thing."

"I'll think of something," Billy said. "There's always the jailhouse."

"No!" Heather grimaced. "I'm not putting Bethany in jail. We're safe here."

Billy's eyes narrowed. "Are you sure about that?

Looks to me like your problems started when you met Mr. Sharp."

"I have five guards, including Robby, and an excellent alarm system," Jean-Luc declared. "I can keep Heather and her family safe."

Billy glowered at him, then turned to Heather. "Is that what you want? You want to trust this foreigner with your life?"

"Yes." Heather felt amazed that she'd answered so easily. Even though there were things she didn't know about Jean-Luc, she really did trust him. She glanced at him and saw the relief on his face.

"I need to talk to you alone." Billy retreated to his squad car and waited for her to join him.

She descended the steps and crossed the driveway. "What is it?"

He glanced back at Robby and Jean-Luc and lowered his voice. "You've only known them a few days. Are you sure you can trust them?"

"Yes."

Billy gave her a dubious look. "I'm not sure you're thinking clearly. Are you here of your own free will? You're not being coerced in any way?"

"No. I truly believe this is the safest place for Bethany and me."

Billy frowned. "Well, that Frog is watching you like a hawk."

Heather glanced back. Jean-Luc was watching them intently. "He cares about me."

"There's something about him I don't trust."

"Billy, you don't trust any foreigners. In fact, you don't like anyone who isn't a native-born Texan."

"Well, yeah, that's true." He turned to a fresh sheet of paper in his notepad. "I'm gonna give you my private cell phone number. You can call anytime night or day, and I'll come running."

"Okay." She accepted the paper.

"I'm serious, Heather. I let you down before. I won't do it again."

Tears returned to her eyes. "Thank you."

"I've gotta go check out this dead body, but I'll come back later with more questions."

She nodded. "I understand."

He laid a hand on her shoulder. "Take it easy."

"Thanks." Heather turned back to the house while Billy circled his squad car. By the time she reached the porch, his car was peeling away.

"Are you all right?" Jean-Luc touched her elbow as he escorted her back into the foyer.

"I'm tired." Heather rubbed her eyes. "But I'm too nervous to sleep, and Billy might come back with more questions."

"Would you like to see my office? We could be alone there to talk."

Talk? He'd end up kissing her again, and as lovely as that sounded, she didn't want to throw herself at him to take her mind off a dead body. "No, not tonight. I—I'd like to be alone for a while. I think I'll get some work done." She headed for the design studio.

"I'll let you in." He walked beside her. "Heather, I don't want you to feel . . . trapped here. I know this is the safest place for you, but if you wish to leave . . ."

She touched his arm. "I'm staying here."

"Good."

She wondered if he'd overheard her conversation with Billy. If so, he had excellent hearing.

He punched the keypad and opened the door for her. "I'll be in my office if you need me. And Robby's in the security office."

"I'll be fine, thank you."

With a sad look, he touched her cheek, then walked away.

Heather meandered to the worktable and looked over her sketches. She took a few deep breaths and tried to push all the wretched memories away. For just a little while, she needed to escape. She needed to create something beautiful.

She selected the design she wanted to make first and the fabric, a royal-blue silk chiffon. Then she went to work making the pattern. After a few hours, she had one she was happy with. She cut out the material.

"Mrs. Westfield?" Robby peeked in the door. "Yer daughter just came down the stairs. Jean-Luc took her into the kitchen. I thought ye'd like to know."

"Yes. Thank you." Heather rushed into the hallway and accompanied Robby across the showroom.

"I saw her pass by the camera outside Jean-Luc's office," Robby explained. "I called him, and he helped her down the stairs and into the kitchen. I hope ye doona mind."

"No, not at all. I'm glad someone was awake to take care of her."

"If ye need me, I'll be in here." Robby let himself into the security office.

"Good night." Heather continued on to the kitchen and eased open the door silently. She heard Bethany's voice.

"I'll be Barbie, and you can be the crocodile."

"Very well," Jean-Luc answered quietly.

"What's he doing?" Bethany asked.

"He's bowing. 'Good day, milady.'"

Bethany giggled. "Crocodiles don't bow."

"They should when they meet a princess."

Bethany laughed some more. "You bow like that when you see me."

"Because you're a princess. This house didn't have a princess till you came."

Heather's heart expanded. What a sweet thing to say.

"I know!" Bethany sounded excited. "Let's pretend I'm the princess, and the crocodile is a frog."

"Ribbit," Jean-Luc croaked.

Bethany burst into giggles. Heather smiled to herself.

"And then the princess kisses the frog." Bethany made a loud smacking noise. "And he turns into a prince. And now, they're in love forever."

There was a pause, and Heather waited to hear what Jean-Luc would say next.

His voice sounded low and tense. "Can the fair maiden love him when he's . . . an ugly creature?"

Heather almost yelled *yes*. But surely Jean-Luc wasn't referring to himself? He wasn't a creature. He was gorgeous and sweet. The most perfect man she'd ever met. There was no point in denying it any longer. She was falling in love with him.

"I think so," Bethany answered seriously. "Princess Fiona fell in love with Shrek, and he's a green ogre."

Heather beamed with pride over her brilliant daughter.

"I haven't heard of this Shrek," Jean-Luc said.

"You don't know Shrek?" Bethany sounded amazed. "I have it at home. You can watch it with me."

"I would like that," Jean-Luc replied.

Heather closed the door with a thud. "Hello?" She walked through the sitting area and spotted them at the kitchen table.

"Mama!" Bethany leaped toward her. "I woke up and you weren't in bed with me."

"I'm sorry." She knelt to hug her daughter. "I was working late."

Jean-Luc stood. "I gave her some milk and cookies. I hope you don't mind."

"No." She smiled at him. "You're a sweetheart."

The corner of his mouth lifted, and his eyes glimmered with emotion. And yet he seemed to be at a loss for words. Heather's heart filled with love and longing.

The door opened behind them, and Robby spoke, "The sheriff is back. He wants to interview us each separately."

"I'll go first." Jean-Luc headed for the door.

"Come, sweetie." Heather ushered her daughter to the door, too. "Let's get you back in bed."

She led Bethany to their bedroom and read a book to her until she fell asleep. Heather glanced at the clock. A little after three A.M. Good Lord, this night was endless. Yawning, she descended the stairs and found Billy waiting for her. After thirty minutes of questioning, he was done, and Robby escorted him from the building.

With a sigh, Heather headed back to the stairs. Finally, she'd get some sleep.

She heard music and stopped to listen. Classical music. She eased toward the cellar door and pressed her ear against it. A piano and harpsichord.

"Can I help you?" Robby sauntered toward her.

"I was just going to bed. Good night." She dashed up the backstairs to her bedroom.

Why were so many people in the cellar, when she and her family were locked out? What was Jean-Luc hiding? A spurt of anger gripped her. She was trusting him with her life and with the lives of Bethany and Fidelia. Why couldn't he trust her?

She knew she was falling in love with him. If they were going to have a successful relationship, there couldn't be secrets between them. And if he wasn't going to divulge his secrets, she would discover them on her own.

Nothing would stop her. Especially not fear.

Chapter 18

Red glowing eyes, danger, the flash of white, gnashing teeth. Mrs. Bolton's dead body sprawled on the floor. Heather jerked awake.

"Mama, are you all right?" Bethany stood by the bed, her eyes wide with worry.

Heather took a deep breath. It was just a bad dream. Fidelia's warning about red glowing eyes had seeped into her own dreams and memories.

"You okay?" Fidelia sat on her bed, tying her shoelaces. She and Bethany were already dressed.

"I'm fine." Heather glanced at the bedside clock. Ten minutes after ten. "I overslept." Not surprising since she'd been up most the night. "Have you had any more dreams?" she asked Fidelia quietly.

The older woman frowned and mouthed the word *fire.*

Fire? Heather raised her eyebrows. She wanted to know more, but didn't want to discuss it in front of Bethany.

The little girl ran to the door. "I'm hungry."

"Let's get some breakfast." Fidelia ushered her out.

"Was it bad?" Heather asked just as Fidelia was closing the door. "The fire?" she whispered.

Fidelia winced. "*Infierno.*" She shut the door.

Hell? Heather shuddered. Was that Louie's plan? To set this house on fire and kill them all? She showered, dressed, and went to the kitchen for a quick breakfast.

Afterward, she asked Pierre to let her into the design studio. "I could let myself in if I knew the combination."

Pierre propped the doors open. "I'll ask Robby. No one can know the combination without his permission."

"I see." She hated the locked doors as much as all the surveillance cameras that were being installed, but it couldn't be helped. She strolled into the room and halted in front of her worktable. For a second, she couldn't believe her eyes. She blinked. No, it was real.

There on the table, her sketches were ripped in two. The royal-blue silk chiffon that she'd cut so carefully the night before was slashed and mutilated. She cried out.

"*Madame?*" Pierre dashed into the room. "Are you all right?"

She pointed at the destruction. "My work."

"What's wrong?" Phil ran into the room.

"My work is destroyed." Heather groaned. "There are so many guards in this house, and so many damned cameras. Why didn't anyone see this?"

"There are no cameras in here," Phil explained. "We're installing them today."

"Who would do something so mean?" Pierre picked up two halves of a sketch.

Phil frowned. "Whoever has the most to gain from it."

Heather sucked in a deep breath. *Alberto.* He didn't

want her designing for Jean-Luc. "I need to talk to Alberto."

"You think he did it?" Pierre asked. "I've known Alberto for years. I don't think he would. But don't worry. We'll investigate the matter thoroughly."

"It won't happen again," Phil assured her.

Heather nodded.

Phil and Pierre left, and she stood there, looking at the destruction. Could Alberto really do something this mean? At least there was plenty of silk chiffon still on the bolt. She would have to cut the dress again. If she started now, she could be sewing by noon.

She smoothed the royal-blue material across the second worktable, then arranged her pattern pieces on top.

"*Buon giorno.*" Alberto strolled into the room. "Pierre said you wanted to see me?"

Heather took a deep breath to remain calm. "What do you know about this?" She motioned to the table behind her.

"Oh my God! What happened?" He rushed over for a closer look.

"I was hoping you would tell me."

He picked up a piece of slashed fabric. "This is terrible!"

She glared at him. "It sure is."

His eyes widened suddenly, and the material slipped from his fingers. "You think I. . . ?" He huffed with indignation. "I have no need to resort to this. Your line of clothing will fail miserably on its own."

Heather hesitated. He seemed genuinely affronted. But if Alberto hadn't done this, then who did? "Oh, of course. It was the models. Simone and . . . Helga."

"Inga." Alberto rubbed at the red scrape on his neck. "They do not control their anger well."

"You can say that again. What is their problem?"

Alberto winced. "Please. Don't tell Jean-Luc. He's already angry at them. He'll fire them for sure."

"They deserve to be fired."

"No! Please. It would destroy them."

Heather snorted. "They're top fashion models. They could work anywhere."

"No, they cannot. Jean-Luc is the only one who would hire them. He—he understands their . . . problem. They have a, uh, disability."

"Right. I recognized that right off the bat."

His eyes widened. "You did?"

"Oh yeah. It's called *psycho bitch*."

"No! They—they cannot go out into the sun at all. Most designers would never tolerate that."

"You mean they're allergic to the sun?"

Alberto shrugged. "You could say that. Imagine—no photo shoots on the beach. No other designer would hire them. They'll be completely ruined if Jean-Luc fires them."

Heather couldn't work up an ounce of sympathy. "They should have thought of that before they went berserk."

"They feel threatened by you. Jean-Luc has never shown so much interest in another woman."

"Really?" She was starting to feel a little magnanimous now. "You mean he hasn't had a long string of girlfriends?"

"No, not at all. He has stayed away from women for years. But that has changed now that he's met you."

"What about the other girls that Louie murdered?"

Alberto winced. "That was a long time ago."

She bet it was. Her immortal theory kept coming back.

Alberto pressed his palms together. "Please don't

tell Jean-Luc about this. I'll talk to them. I'll make sure they never cause you trouble again."

"You can make them behave?" She gave the scrape on his neck a dubious look.

"If they want to model my gowns in the show, they will do as I ask. And I'll help you." He motioned to the table where she was about to recut the first gown. "I'll show you a way to cut the skirt on the bias. It'll flow better when the model's moving down the runway."

"That would be great. Thank you."

"And these sketches—" He picked up two halves. "They won't ever look as good, but you can tape them back together and make copies. In fact, you should always make copies of everything you do. There's an excellent copier in Jean-Luc's office. You should use it."

"I would hate to disturb him."

Alberto laughed. "He's not there during the day."

"Then where is he?"

Alberto visibly gulped. "He's . . . away." He waved a hand vaguely in the air. "On business."

"Where?"

"I'll give you the combination, so you can go to his office," Alberto rushed his words. "Fourteen eighty-five. Don't ask the significance. And it's the same number for the keypad to this room."

"Really?" Was that why they were so reluctant to tell her the combination? How many keypads used the same number?

"Is it a deal?" Alberto asked. "You won't tell Jean-Luc what Simone and Inga did?"

"No, I'll let it pass."

"Please don't tell anyone I told you the combination."

"My lips are sealed." She'd found a new, unlikely ally. Alberto spent the next two hours helping her cut the first gown, and she knew it was an improvement over the one she'd cut the night before.

"Thank you." She gathered up the scraps to throw away. "Would you like to join us for lunch?"

"Sorry, but I can't. I'm meeting Sasha for a late lunch."

"I didn't know she was back in town."

Alberto frowned. "I didn't know she'd left."

"She left Sunday. She went to San Antonio to some fancy spa."

"We made the date last Saturday." He strolled to the door, frowning. "I hope she hasn't forgotten."

"Aren't you worried about making Simone and Inga mad?" Heather winced. She shouldn't have asked. It wasn't her business if Alberto was juggling three women. But when one of them was her old high school buddy and the other two were psycho bitches, it could get messy in a hurry.

"They won't know." Alberto paused by the door. "I have no chance with them, really. I should let it go, but they have some kind of hold on me."

Heather lifted her brows. "A hold? Like a *spell*?" Were the psycho bitches actually psycho witches?

He sighed. "They are . . . different. Nothing good can come from my infatuation."

"That's probably true."

He gave her a worried look. "You should be careful, too. I owe Jean-Luc a great deal. He's a kind and talented man, but . . . you should stay away from him. If you can." Alberto hurried from the room before she could respond or even recover from shock.

Heather spent the afternoon sewing while Pierre and Phil installed two surveillance cameras in the studio. Alberto's strange warning kept echoing in her mind. If he admired Jean-Luc, why would he warn her away? What did he know that she didn't? And what was the significance of fourteen eighty-five? A birth date?

She shuddered. Surely not. Her creative mind was working overtime.

Phil and Pierre joined them in the kitchen for supper. Food supplies were running low, so Pierre offered to run to the store. Since Alberto had taken the BMW for his long date with Sasha, Heather gave Pierre the keys to her truck, along with a shopping list.

Fidelia was clearing the table when she halted suddenly. A plate tumbled from her hand and crashed onto the floor.

"What?" Heather jumped to her feet.

Fidelia shot Phil a panicked look. "Stop him! Now!"

Phil charged down the hallway and out the front door. Heather ran after him and had just reached the doorway when a loud explosion knocked her back. Her heart lunged up her throat. With her ears ringing, she regained her balance and stumbled outside. She halted.

Her truck was engulfed in a huge fire. The flames shot upward. *Pierre.* A wave of nausea doubled her over.

Phil stood in the driveway, his fists clenched. He dropped to his knees, tilted his head back, and roared. It sounded strange through the buzz in her ears. Intense heat from the fire slapped her back, and she stumbled against the doorframe.

"Mama?"

She slammed the door shut and leaned against it. Black dots flickered before her eyes, and she couldn't think of anything to say.

Bethany skipped toward the front door. "Where's everybody going? Can I go?"

Heather swallowed down a wave of bile and shook her head.

Fidelia entered the showroom, hugging her purse to her chest. Her eyes glimmered with unshed tears. "I was too late?"

Heather's own vision blurred with tears. "It was just like you dreamed. *Infierno*."

Chapter 19

Jean-Luc sat behind the desk in his office, staring into space. Every now and then, Robby strode across his line of vision, but he hardly noticed. The voices in the room droned like an annoying swarm of bees. He must be in shock. He never felt like this during battle. It was always afterward when he went numb.

Robby plunked a bottle of Blissky on his desk and suggested he have a wee dram. Jean-Luc regarded the bottle silently. The mixture of synthetic blood and Scotch whisky wouldn't solve anything. It wouldn't bring Pierre back to life. It wouldn't take away the grief or the guilt.

All the men in the room were agitated, their voices loud, their arms waving. He blinked when Robby's fist slammed onto his desk. The bottle of Blissky jumped.

"How could he forget to check the truck?" Robby yelled. "I thought I trained him better than that."

"I'm sure ye did." Ian took a gulp from his glass of Blissky. "Ye shouldna blame yerself."

"I should have checked it myself." Phil collapsed into a chair and pressed the heel of his palms to his temples. "'I can smell explosives. I should have checked the damned truck."

That pricked the fog in Jean-Luc's head. Phil could smell a bomb?

"Pierre should have known better," Robby muttered as he paced across the room. "Bugger!" He pounded his fist on the desk again. The Blissky teetered close to the edge.

Ian grabbed the bottle and refilled his glass. "Where was the BMW?"

"Alberto had it," Phil explained. "He came back about seven o'clock. He had a date with that model, Sasha, but she stood him up. He was upset, so he went shopping in San Antonio."

Jean-Luc leaned back in his chair and closed his eyes. He didn't want to listen to this. He wanted to be with Heather. How was she doing? Did she realize the bomb had been meant for her? Was she battling fear all alone?

As soon as he'd heard the news, he'd tried to see her. He needed to know if she was all right. He needed to see if Bethany was all right. He needed to reassure Heather that they would be protected, that Lui would die for his crime.

Two steps into the kitchen, and he'd been greeted with a Glock pointed at his face. Fidelia had politely asked him to leave. They weren't accepting visitors. He'd only caught a glimpse of Heather, sitting on the couch with her daughter. She'd refused to even look at him.

She blamed him, no doubt. She and her family were in terrible danger because of him. And she was probably angry that he'd shown up three hours after the explosion. In her time of need, he'd been dead to the world. The dreaded feeling of being powerless crept back. It was the worst part of being a vampire, being completely powerless during the day. If Heather needed him then, he would fail her.

He opened his eyes. "How is Heather doing?"

"She kept asking why none of you were there," Phil replied. "I said you were all away on business, but she looked suspicious. She insisted I call the fire department and sheriff. After the fire was put out, the sheriff insisted she go with him, but she refused."

Thank God. Jean-Luc took a deep breath. Hopefully, this meant she still trusted him. Or maybe she was trusting in Fidelia's guns. He stood and moved to the window overlooking the showroom. "I'm sick of people dying because of me."

"Lui does the killing, no' you," Robby grumbled. "I'll call Pierre's mother and—"

"No," Jean-Luc said. "I'll do it." And he would make sure Pierre's family never lacked for anything. "Why are we here? We should be guarding Heather."

"She's fine," Robby said. "Phineas is watching her. And you know if Lui teleports into the building, he'll trigger an alarm. We would be all over him."

Jean-Luc paced across the room. "We need a plan. We need more guards."

"I've asked for more," Robby assured him. "Unfortunately, Angus is using every spare man in the hunt for Casimir."

"I'm alone now during the day." Phil sat forward and braced his elbows on his knees. "Unless you count Fidelia and her guns."

"I can help with that." Ian retrieved a vial from his sporran. "Roman gave me a bunch of these. 'Tis the formula that keeps a Vamp awake during the day."

Robby moved closer to look at the greenish liquid. "I thought Roman banned that stuff."

"I thought so, too," Jean-Luc said. "For every day he used it, he aged an entire year."

"Aye, he did." Ian lifted his chin. "But I volunteered to test it for him."

Jean-Luc frowned. "I appreciate you wanting to look older, but I don't want you experimenting with yourself."

"I doona need a guardian, Jean-Luc." Ian dropped the vial back into his sporran. "I'm four hundred and eighty years old. I can make a bloody decision for myself."

Jean-Luc sighed. He couldn't forbid Ian's use of this drug, but he still didn't like it. "Were there any side effects?"

"Roman's hair turned gray at the temples, that's all," Ian muttered. "I'm doing it. Ye canna stop me."

"All right." Jean-Luc sat on the corner of his desk. "We have to lock the place down completely."

"I agree." Robby resumed his pacing. "We should always keep them together. They'll be easier to guard that way."

Jean-Luc nodded. "We'll cancel the charity show." He knew that would upset Alberto and Heather, but better safe than sorry. "Lui would definitely make a move then."

Robby stopped. "Perhaps we should let him."

Jean-Luc shook his head. "I don't want to use Heather as bait."

"We'll keep her surrounded and safe," Robby insisted. "Do ye prefer the alternative? That we stay locked up here like a flock of frightened sheep?"

"We'll keep looking for him," Jean-Luc said. "Fidelia figured out he was hiding at the Chicken Ranch. Maybe she can find him again."

"She tried that earlier," Phil said. "Before you guys woke up. She was so upset about Pierre, she swore she would find Lui herself and fill him with bullets. I gave her his sword and cane."

"What did she see?" Jean-Luc asked.

"Nothing." Phil shrugged. "She said he was gone. He was too far away for her to reach."

Jean-Luc paced across the floor, digesting this information. Could Lui really be gone? Was killing the museum curator and Pierre enough to satisfy his need for vengeance? But Lui had threatened Heather and him. In fact, Lui had claimed that Casimir would pay him a small fortune to kill Jean-Luc. "He can't be gone. He's not finished."

"I agree." Robby sat, frowning. "He might retreat for a few days, but only to lull us into a false sense of security."

Jean-Luc nodded. "He'll be back. Just like the message he wrote in blood. He'll meet us at a time of his own choosing."

"We should stay here," Phil suggested. "That would force him to come here."

"And we would be ready for him." Ian's eyes narrowed. "I bet he'll come the night of the runway show."

"We don't even know what he looks like," Jean-Luc reminded them. "And he could use mind control on anyone involved with the show or even attending the show. Anyone there could be an assassin."

"Then we'll limit the attendance to just a few," Ian suggested.

Jean-Luc paced across the room. The only way to be rid of Lui was to confront him. He could keep Heather safe. He'd never leave her side. "All right. We'll plan to kill him on the night of the runway show."

Heather lay awake in bed, staring at the ceiling. Her eyes burned with exhaustion, but she didn't want to shut them. Every time she did, her mind flashed the same horrible picture—her truck ablaze with Pierre inside.

She wished she could erase the image from her memory. Or turn back time, so Pierre could still be alive. Or turn it back further, so Mrs. Bolton could be alive. How different everything would be if last Friday, she had done as Jean-Luc had asked and run away. But she had tried to be brave and rescue Jean-Luc. Now she had no choice but to be brave. The bomb had been intended for her.

She had to make sure no one else died. She needed to be brave, cautious, and smart. Why should she rely solely on Jean-Luc and his guards to keep her and Bethany safe? Obviously they were not infallible.

Fidelia had her guns, and she was prepared to use them. Heather needed to be just as tough. She would arm herself with knowledge. That's what professionals did when they were at war. They gathered intelligence.

She sat up in bed. It was time to uncover some of the secrets in this place. After all, it was *her* life on the line. They had no right to keep her in the dark. Fourteen eighty-five. Would those numbers get her into the cellar?

She checked the bedside clock. Three twenty-three A.M. She slipped out of bed and wondered if she should change clothes. No, it would take too long, and the noise might wake Fidelia or Bethany. She'd stay in her blue and yellow Tweety Bird pajamas from the discount store.

She peeked into the hallway. It was empty. Earlier in the evening, Phineas had stayed outside their door, and she'd heard traffic coming and going from Jean-Luc's office. Now everything was quiet.

She noted the camera over the office door. If she went past it to the backstairs, the guards might see her. They'd stop her before she could venture close to the cellar.

She squeezed through the door and tiptoed in the opposite direction. Her bare feet were silent on the thick carpet. The hallway took a sharp turn to the right, where it opened onto the catwalk across the back of the showroom.

Moonlight filtered through the tall back windows, casting long gray shadows across the showroom's marble floor. The mannequins posed, their bare arms gleaming white and stark. There were two cameras high on the walls, but they were aimed at the room below. The catwalk was bracketed on each side with a waist-high wall.

She crouched down so she wouldn't be seen and dashed across the catwalk. It ended by the back door to the design studio. She punched fourteen eighty-five on the keypad and felt a small rush when the door opened. She slipped inside.

The studio was dark except for the slashes of moon-light spilling through the French doors. She carefully descended the spiral staircase. The metal steps were icy cold against her bare feet. She crept across the studio, hugging the dark shadows along the walls and hoping she didn't show up on the cameras.

She cracked open the door and peered into the hall-way. The cellar door was at the end of the hall. And at the other end, close to the showroom, there was a camera.

Damn. There was no way to avoid it. But she'd come too far to give up now. If she ran, she could be at the cellar door in six seconds.

She took a deep breath and charged. With trembling fingers, she punched in fourteen eighty-five. The door opened. Her heart lurched.

She stepped inside, shut the door, and leaned against it. A dim light overhead illuminated a plain stairwell. Bare walls, a cement landing, a metal railing in front of her. The faint sound of music echoed eerily. She breathed deeply to calm her pounding heart.

So far, so good. No bogeyman was here, brandishing his Texan chainsaw. She moved forward to the railing and saw the stairs going down. Each step was lit by a red light. She descended the cement steps to a landing, then turned to go down another short flight of stairs. The concrete was cold and gritty beneath her feet. She reached a plain wooden door. It inched open easily, and the volume of the music increased.

It was the piano and harpsichord again. The melody was slow, beautiful, and terribly sad. They were mourning, she realized. Mourning for Pierre.

She suddenly felt too intrusive. Of course they were mourning for Pierre. They'd known him for years. She'd known him only a few days. She considered going back, but caught a glimpse of the hallway and stopped.

She opened the door further, and her mouth fell open. After the bare stairwell, she'd expected a more spartan environment, but this was . . . opulent. The hallway was wide enough for five people to walk down at once, and the floor was covered with a beautiful hand-carved rug. It felt thick and woolen to her feet. It was a rich ruby-red with golden fleur-de-lis scattered across it in a trellis pattern. Another pattern of gold and ivory roses formed a wide border around the rug.

The hall was illuminated with golden sconces along the walls, each sconce dripping lead crystal teardrops. Even the ceiling was beautiful—ivory with fancy moldings painted gold. The doors were also ivory with gilt woodwork. Interspersed between the doors were bombé chests and ornate armoires. Antiques, Heather guessed, and incredibly expensive.

She padded silently down the hall, past oil paintings that looked like they belonged in a castle. The music grew louder. It emanated from a room where the double doors were ajar, jutting into the hallway.

She eased behind a door and peered through the crack by the doorframe. She saw the piano. It was an old baby grand decorated with gold scrollwork. A woman was playing, her long blond hair loose down her back. Inga.

A woman moved across the room, blocking Heather's view. It was Simone, doing some sort of dance. A minuet? She glided out of the way, and Heather glimpsed the harpsichord. Jean-Luc? She caught her breath and turned away, pressing her back against the wall.

Jean-Luc was the one playing the harpsichord! She stood there, listening to the melancholy music. He was quite good, actually. But why would a modern man play such an old instrument? The more she learned about him, the more the immortal theory made sense.

He was hurting, she realized, as the sad strains tugged at her heart. She should have talked to him earlier. She should have comforted him. She knew him well enough to know he would blame himself. He was an honorable man with a deep sense of responsibility. An old-fashioned guy. And he might have a very good reason for being old-fashioned.

But she'd refused to see him. She'd reached a point where one more emotional stimulus would have sent her over the edge. She had to withdraw and be alone for a while.

The music brought tears to her eyes. He was such an amazing man. How could she not fall in love with him? Fencing champion, fashion designer, musician. One hell of a kisser. Of course, if he was immortal, he'd had centuries to develop his talents.

She tiptoed down the hall, wondering what to do

next. Should she confront him? Maybe. But not with Simone and Inga around.

The music stopped. She turned, suddenly afraid that she'd been spotted. But no, the hallway was still empty. She heard a clicking sound at the other end of the hallway. The door was opening.

She dashed behind a tall armoire and plastered herself against the wall. Footsteps approached, muffled by the thick carpet.

"Robby!" the ladies exclaimed. "You must stay and dance with us."

He was in the music room, Heather realized. Could she make it to the other exit before he came out? He was talking so softly, she couldn't make out his words.

Her attention was snagged by the oil painting right across from her. Definitely an antique. The guy was wearing black leather bucket boots, maroon knee breeches and waistcoat, and a white shirt with a wide lace collar. A short velvet cape was slung nonchalantly over one shoulder. His foil was by his side, the tip planted on the floor, his hand resting lightly on the ornate hilt.

Heather smiled. He looked like one of the Three Musketeers. Or a pirate, except that he was too clean and well dressed. His long black hair curled to his shoulders, and his wide-brimmed hat boasted two plumes—white and maroon. A sharp dresser. Pretty blue eyes.

Her heart froze. Goose bumps tingled down her arms. Good Lord, she knew those eyes. She'd kissed those lips.

It was true. He really was immortal.

"Thank you for the warning," Jean-Luc's voice drifted from the music room. "I'll take care of her."

Her breath caught. Was he talking about *her*? Oh

God, they were leaving the music room. She wasn't ready for this. She needed time to accept this new reality. Immortal men. She opened the nearest door and slipped inside.

The room was dark except for a dim sliver of light to the left. As her eyes adjusted she made out several pieces of furniture—an armoire, a wingback chair and ottoman situated next to a table and lamp. There was no mistaking the largest form in the room. The bed was huge and dark. The headboard stretched halfway to the ceiling.

Great, just what she needed, to be discovered in someone's bedroom. The sliver of light drew her attention. She walked toward it, feeling the smooth coolness of a wooden floor beneath her feet. As she approached the foot of the bed, she stepped onto a thick rug. Hand-carved wool in an Aubusson style.

The dim light emanated from a pair of double doors that had been left partially open. She pushed the doors further open and sucked in a deep breath.

It was the most beautiful bathroom she'd ever seen. Marble floors and countertops gleamed a soft, rosy beige. Ornate gold faucets curved over two scalloped sinks. The shower stall was huge and boasted three shower heads. But the most striking feature was the huge whirlpool bathtub in the middle of the room. It was rectangular in shape, with a marble column at each corner. The columns were topped with a gilded cupola. Marble steps led up to the tub.

She ascended a few steps and peeked under the cupola. It was painted like a summer sky, complete with sun and white, fluffy clouds. As she stared, the sky grew brighter. No, the whole room was brighter. She slowly turned.

Jean-Luc was standing by the door with his hand on the dimmer switch.

She swallowed hard. At least he didn't look angry. "Hi. I know I shouldn't be here, but—"

"Do you like it?" He waved toward the giant bathtub.

"I—yes. It's . . . very nice. I mean, fantastic, really."

"It's great for relieving stress. You can use it whenever you like."

"It's . . . *your* tub?"

He nodded, then glanced over his shoulder. "My bedroom."

"Oh." Of all the bedrooms in the world to stumble into . . .

"Are you all right?" he asked. "I was worried about you."

"I'm fine." He didn't seem too upset about her trespassing. But he did look pale and worried. "I'm really sorry about Pierre."

His gaze lowered to the floor. "So am I."

The poor guy was hurting. She eased down the steps to the marble floor. "It's late. I should be going."

"No." His gaze lifted to her. "We need to talk."

She gulped. Was he going to confess the truth now about being immortal?

"How did you get the combination to the keypad?" he asked.

"Alberto, but he was only trying to help. He didn't expect me to . . . sneak down here."

A corner of Jean-Luc's mouth tilted up, although his smile still looked sad. "He underestimates you."

"I saw the portrait in the hall. The musketeer guy." She wanted to say *you*, but the word stuck in her throat.

"Heather." He stepped toward her, and she moved back. He halted, and a pained look crossed his face. "I would never hurt you."

"I know. But this is all kinda . . . weird."

"I would do anything to protect you and Bethany. You're safe with me." He motioned to his bedroom. "Come and have a seat. We need to talk."

She eased past him into the bedroom. It wasn't quite so dark now, and she could see the bed was covered with a maroon velvet comforter. The wingback chair and ottoman were also maroon. She perched on the ottoman.

He pushed the bathroom doors partially closed, causing the bedroom to grow darker. Then he walked to his bed and sat on the end of it. "There's something I've been wanting to tell you. It may be difficult to believe."

She took a deep breath as if preparing to dive into the deep end. At war with fear, she reminded herself. "It's all right. I already know your secret."

Chapter 20

She knew?

Jean-Luc cleared his throat. "Perhaps I should start at the beginning."

"Fourteen eighty-five?" she whispered. "I—I think that could be the year of your birth."

His breath caught, and it took a moment to force out a reply. "Yes, it is."

Her face paled. "Oh God." She shifted uneasily on the ottoman. "I was right. You're immortal."

"Not exactly. I can be killed."

She nodded. "That's where the swords come in. I saw it on television. I guess Hollywood knows about you?"

He shrugged. "There have been many stories told about us, but not always true."

"The bad guy will try to cut your head off. That's how you die."

He winced. "Decapitation would be effective, but there are a number of ways to kill me." He smiled wryly. "I could make you list if you're keen to know. It might come in handy if I ever forget your birthday."

She smiled briefly, then winced. "So Louie is immortal, too. That's why the names you called him died out centuries ago. I checked it out on the Internet."

"Ah." She'd been suspicious from the start. "You're very clever to figure out so much. I hope you also realize that you can trust me. I'm doing everything in my power to keep you and your daughter safe."

She frowned. "You've done everything but tell me the truth."

"I didn't want to scare you away. You would be too vulnerable on your own, too easy for Lui to kill. I could not allow you to face him alone."

"So you concealed things to protect me."

"Yes. And to protect myself. I could not bear it if something happened to you."

A pained expression crossed her face. "When did the other women die?"

"Yvonne was murdered in 1757 and Claudine in 1832. There's been no one special since then."

"That's a long time."

He shrugged. There'd been numerous short-term affairs and one-night stands, especially before the arrival of synthetic blood. He needed a few pints every night, and a well-pleasured woman tended to be more generous. But this was not something Heather would appreciate. "After Lui murdered Yvonne, I avoided any close relationships. I didn't want another woman to be killed because of me."

"But you . . . fell in love again. With Claudine?"

"Yes. I thought it would be safe. I'd hunted Lui for years, but he'd disappeared. Just when I thought it was safe, he came back."

"Why does he hate you so much?"

"He tried to assassinate Louis XV, and I stopped him. I was one of the king's personal guards at the time."

Her eyes narrowed with a pained look. "You knew King Louis XV?"

"I have known many kings."

She glanced down at her clasped hands. Her fingers looked tense, her knuckles white. "You've seen a lot of people come and go."

"Yes."

She closed her eyes briefly. When she opened them, they glimmered with tears. "I've heard enough. I need to go." She rose quickly and started toward the door.

"Wait." He stood and blocked her path. "There's more."

"No." She shook her head, and the tears welled in her eyes. "There can't be anything more. Not between us. What would be the point? It doesn't matter if I think you're incredibly sweet and gorgeous and intelligent—"

"It matters to me."

"No, it doesn't. Because to you, I'll be gone in the blink of an eye. I'm one of those little *ants* that come and go. I'm surprised you even bother to keep me alive."

"How can you say that?" He grabbed her shoulders. "Do you think I'm totally heartless?"

"No. But why would you care if I live to be thirty or seventy? What's forty years to someone who's over five hundred? My life is just a blip on your radar screen."

Mon Dieu, he wanted to shake her. "You are everything to me! You are the woman I love."

She gasped.

"It's true." He stepped closer. "I love you, Heather."

She shook her head. "I'll grow old and gray."

"And I will still love you. Why would I care if your outer appearance mellows with time? It is *you* who fills my heart, and I have waited five hundred years for you."

She drew in a shaky breath. "You always say the most beautiful things." A tear rolled down her cheek.

"You're the most beautiful man, but I'm afraid this could never work."

He brushed the tear away. "You're at war with fear, remember?" He smoothed his hands across her back, drawing her close. "Trust me, *chérie*."

"I want to." She rested her hands on his chest. "But this is so hard . . ."

"We have this moment." He kissed her brow. "This perfect moment in time." He kissed the tip of her nose. "Let me love you." He hovered over her mouth.

"Jean-Luc." Her hands slipped up to his neck.

He kissed her gently, still aware that she could flee at any moment. He took a slow, leisurely pace, seducing her with softness. Her body responded, molding to his. His groin tightened. He ignored his own urgent need and slipped his hands beneath her T-shirt. He slowly caressed her back.

She shivered, causing her breasts to jiggle slightly against his chest. With a moan, he drew her lower lip into his mouth and sucked. Her fingers delved into his hair.

"Heather." He nuzzled her neck. Her carotid artery throbbed against his cheek. His erection grew harder. "Let me love you."

"I can never resist you," she whispered.

That was good, but he wanted more. He wanted a declaration of love. He felt sure she loved him. Maybe she didn't realize it yet. Or maybe she was afraid to admit it. Either way, he'd make it clear to her. He'd make her scream with pleasure, over and over, until she realized the truth.

He grasped the hem of her T-shirt and eased it up.

"Wait!" She crossed her arms, covering up the little yellow bird on her T-shirt.

His heart plummeted. He released her and stepped back. "Forgive me."

"It's not you." She pointed at the camera in the upper corner of his bedroom. "It's them."

"*Merde.*" He'd forgotten about that. And the damned red light was still blinking. Didn't they realize this was private? He made a cutting motion across his throat. The light went off.

"This is embarrassing," Heather muttered. "What if they turn it back on in five minutes, thinking we're done?"

He arched a brow. "*Five* minutes?"

She huffed. "Okay, so I haven't participated in any marathons." She glared at the camera. "Or any peep shows."

With a smile, he strode to his bedside table and fumbled in his top drawer. He removed a remote control, aimed it at the camera, and pushed the off button. "There. They can't interrupt us."

"Okay." She watched him warily as he approached. "I—I'm still not totally convinced this could work."

"I know, but I can be very persuasive." He took her by the shoulders. "All night long."

She shivered as he nuzzled her neck. "I could use a little persuasion."

"I thought so." He nibbled on her ear. "Where were we?"

"I was about to star in a *Girls Gone Wild* video."

He had no idea what that was, but it sounded interesting. "You wish to go wild, *chérie*?" He grabbed the hem of her T-shirt.

She sucked in a deep breath. "What the hell? You only live once."

That was debatable, but this was not the time. He yanked the shirt over her head and dropped it. The little yellow bird fluttered to the floor.

His first inclination was to admire her breasts for a moment, but he knew that would turn his eyes red, and he didn't want to scare her. Still, he couldn't resist a quick glimpse. Her plump, rosy nipples were turning pebbly and hard. The tightened tips begged to be suckled. He kept his gaze lowered, grasped her around the waist, and tossed her onto the center of his bed.

"Whoa!" She bounced on her rear.

He landed beside her and shoved her back. "Close your eyes."

"What?"

He kept his face turned away as he untied the drawstring on her pajama bottoms. "Close your eyes and relax. Just let yourself feel." He leaned over and touched her belly button with his tongue.

She shuddered.

"Eyes closed?"

"Yes."

He glanced at her face. Her eyes were shut, and her trust in him swelled his heart. "You're so beautiful."

A corner of her mouth tilted up. "Are you looking at my breasts?"

He grinned. "Actually, I was looking at your face." He kissed her cheek. "But your breasts are beautiful, too."

"Thank you."

He rested a hand on her waist. "*Si belle.*" He skimmed his fingers up her rib cage and the valley between her breasts. Her chest rose with a deep breath.

With his fingertips, he circled one breast, then the other. "Your nipples are becoming darker. Tighter. And I haven't even touched them yet." He pressed his mouth against the outside curve of her left breast.

She sighed. He cupped her right breast and massaged gently.

She moaned.

"Do you like it gentle . . . or rough?" He took the hardened tip between his thumb and forefinger and tugged.

She gasped.

"Or perhaps both." He drew the nipple into his mouth and swirled his tongue around the tip.

She splayed her fingers into his hair. "Jean-Luc."

"Hmm?" He kissed her other breast, nibbling and tweaking the nipple. He slipped his hand into her loose pajamas, reaching lower and lower until he encountered her curls. Slowly he massaged the plump mound. Her breathing became faster and more erratic.

He nuzzled her neck. "I want to taste you."

"Oh God," she whispered.

"I want to feel you shudder against my face." He licked her lips, then kissed her. He swept his tongue inside her mouth, then drew back. "It will be like that, but better. Are you ready?"

"Oh yes," she breathed, her eyes squeezed shut.

He grabbed the waistband of her pajama bottoms, yanked them down her legs, and tossed them aside. She covered her face briefly with her hands, then flung her arms wide. Her legs moved slightly, bending at the knee.

He grasped her ankles and planted her feet firmly apart on the bed. Her body jolted, sending a quiver down her legs that he could feel. His erection strained against his trousers, and he prayed for endurance. He needed to make her scream first. He needed her speaking words of love when he fully claimed her.

He clasped her knees and shoved them apart. She gasped.

He stared. *Mon Dieu*, she was beautiful. Dark auburn curls. Rosy flesh along the outer folds. A darker ruby color in the center. She glistened with moisture. Her fragrance called to him. It smelled of sweet desire and rushing blood.

He nestled a cheek against her soft inner thigh. "You're lovely beyond words. So sweet and wet." He skimmed his fingers over her, and her legs trembled.

Her groan sounded urgent and full of need. She clutched at the bedspread and moved her feet to his back.

He moved in closer and touched her with his tongue. One taste and he was lost. He seized her by the hips and swirled his tongue all over her, exploring every bit of her while she squirmed beneath him. He inserted his tongue, but wanted further inside her. He plunged a finger inside, then two, and stroked her while his tongue lapped her clitoris.

She was panting now, her hips rising. He nipped at her, then flicked his tongue, increasing to vampire speed.

She screamed. Her thighs gripped him; her inner muscles clenched his fingers. Her climax rippled through her, over and over, and just when it showed signs of waning, he tugged at her clitoris and wiggled his fingers. She screamed again, and more spasms shot through her.

He smiled. She responded so well, tasted so good. Soon she would confess her love. He unzipped his trousers.

"That was incredible." She pressed a hand to her chest. "You're so good."

"Yes?" Any minute now, she would declare her undying love. Then he would fill her and make her his own.

"You're wonderful and . . . *aack!*" Horror flashed across her face. "Your eyes are red!"

Zut. "It's nothing. I can explain."

"They're glowing!" She scrambled away from him. "That—that's not normal!"

"Heather, relax."

"Fidelia warned me." She hustled off the bed. "Red glowing eyes. Danger."

"I won't hurt you!"

"Fidelia was right about the fire. She dreamed it." Heather grabbed her pajama bottoms and stuffed her legs inside. "And she dreamed about red glowing eyes and gnashing white teeth."

"Dammit, Heather, I'm in complete control." He stood beside the bed. "I won't bite you."

She froze. Her eyes widened. "*Bite* me?"

Merde. She didn't know. He motioned to the bed. "Please have a seat. I can explain."

She retreated a step. "I don't think so." She spotted her T-shirt on the floor and nabbed it. "I thought my theory was right. You admitted you were born in 1485."

"I was."

She pulled the T-shirt over her head. "What are you not telling me?"

"I died in 1513."

She rubbed a hand against her brow. "Okay. That's how the immortal guys discover who they are. They die, then come back."

"I was wounded at the Battle of the Spurs." He sat on the edge of the bed. "My comrades fled, but I refused to retreat. The English surrounded me. I was stabbed many times and left to die."

She pressed a hand to her mouth and looked a bit green. "That's horrible."

"By the time the sun set, I was barely alive. Roman found me and said I could live to fight again. I agreed, and he changed me."

"Into an immortal?"

"No, *chérie*." He took a deep breath to prepare himself for her reaction. "Into a vampire."

Her face paled. He could literally smell the blood draining from her face and hands. He could hear her heart pounding. "That—that can't be true. Vampires aren't real."

"Heather." He stood and moved toward her, but

stopped when she jumped back. "There's no need to fear me."

"I think there is. Don't you—don't vampires feed off people?"

"Not anymore. We drink synthetic blood from bottles."

"Right. Of course. You're not tempted to have your meals fresh?" She raised a hand to stop him coming closer, then pointed at him. "Alberto. He was bitten."

"And I threatened to fire Simone and Inga. They know biting is not allowed in my household."

"How considerate of you." She gave him a dubious look. "How many vampires have I met?"

"Robby, Ian, and Phineas. Simone and Inga. Angus MacKay and Emma."

"Emma?" Heather looked aghast. "I let a vampire watch my baby?"

"We're the best equipped for fighting Lui, since he's a vampire, too."

"And Phil and Pierre?"

"Mortal. We have to rely on mortals to protect us during the day because we're . . . unavailable."

She raised her brows. "Unavailable? You showed up three hours after Pierre's death. That was just rude!"

"I hate being separated from you during the day. I hate that I'm not there to protect you or comfort you. But I can't help it. I'm . . . dead."

She blinked. "You mean really . . . *dead*?"

With a sigh, he sat on the bed. "Completely dead. It's very . . . annoying, but it's only during the day."

"Right." She narrowed her eyes. "I guess you have fangs?"

He touched a pointed tooth. "They're not extended

now. I'm in complete control. You're entirely safe."

She scoffed. "*Safe?* Those things are weapons. Oh sheesh. You had your . . . mouth all over me."

"I knew what I was doing. And you liked it."

She marched up to him and slapped him on the face.

He winced. "Why so angry, *chérie*? I've told you the truth."

"*Now* you tell me." She paced in front of him. "There are certain things you're supposed to say *before* sex. Stuff like, 'By the way, sweetheart, I have herpes.' Or here's a good one—'Guess what? You're about to screw a *dead* man!'"

He stood. "I am *not* dead!"

"Give it a few hours! You will be."

"Does a dead man look like this?" He pushed his trousers down to reveal his bulging cotton briefs. He was no longer fully erect, but he was certainly swollen enough to be noticed. And she did notice. Her eyes widened, then quickly looked away.

"A dead guy who's stiff," she muttered. "Go figure."

"I'm not dead." He stepped toward her. "Did my lips feel dead when I kissed your breasts and sucked your clit?"

She flinched. "Don't—"

"Have you already forgotten how you squirmed and screamed in my arms? You gushed all over me." He licked his lips. "I can still taste you."

She covered her face briefly. "I haven't forgotten. That's why this is so damned hard. I—I thought you were perfect. I thought I was falling in love."

"You are. I know you love me."

"No! I can't . . . handle this right now. It's too much." She ran to the door and wrenched it open.

"Heather." He zipped up his pants and dashed into the

hallway. She was halfway to the cellar door. "Heather, don't leave the building. It's too dangerous outside."

She stopped and glanced back at him with an incredulous look. "It's dangerous *inside*. I'm living with a bunch of freaking vampires!"

"We're good Vamps." He walked toward her. "We would never hurt you. We have sworn to protect you. Please, promise me you won't leave."

She gave him a wry look. "I promise. Believe me, I'm trying very hard not to do anything foolish." She turned and strode to the cellar door.

Jean-Luc sighed with relief. She understood that leaving the house would be foolish. Unfortunately, she was also implying that a relationship with him was foolish.

He would just have to change her mind. Somehow, he'd win her back. He'd show her he could be trusted. He'd prove to her that their love was not foolish.

Chapter 21

Heather dashed up the stairs to the ground floor. *Vampires?* How could that be? But why would Jean-Luc lie about something so awful? *I know you love me.* His words pricked at her. No! She couldn't love a vampire. Vampires were monsters who preyed on the innocent to survive.

She slammed the cellar door behind her and strode down the hallway. Vampires. In Texas. Maybe she should call Immigration. She rushed past the doors to the design studio. Good Lord, her boss was a vampire. And fantastic in bed. She winced and tried to erase that last thought.

I know you love me.

Dammit, she was not going to fall in love with a bloodsucking fiend. A line from an old movie came back to torment her. It required a few sniffles and a thick country accent. *I always fall for the wrong kind of man.*

Yep, that was her. She'd gone from a control-freak husband to a vampire lover. At least a vampire couldn't control her during the day. He was dead. A giggle escaped her mouth. Good Lord, she was losing her mind.

She halted halfway across the showroom when the door to the security office swung open.

Robby exited and gave her a worried look. "Are ye all right, lass?"

Vampire. She stepped back.

He frowned. "Doona be afraid."

Right. He was just a huge, hulking vampire with a sword on his back, a knife in his sock, and fangs in his mouth. She turned and ran up the grand staircase. As she crossed the catwalk, she noticed him standing in the showroom, watching her.

Dammit, she was not going to be afraid. She was at war with fear. She slipped inside her bedroom.

"I have a pistol pointed at your ass," Fidelia's voice whispered in the dark.

"It's me." Heather locked the door. "We need to talk. Keep your gun handy."

"I don't have my guns in bed. I was just bluffing."

"Get them." Heather fumbled across the room to the bathroom. "And come in here. I don't want to wake Bethany."

A minute later, Fidelia waddled into the room, her purse clutched to her chest.

Heather shut the bathroom door and turned on the light. "We're in big danger."

"I thought so." Fidelia dropped her heavy purse on the marble vanity. Her hair shot out in different directions, and her voluminous hot-pink nightshirt boasted the words *Hot Stuff*. "The cards have been warning me."

Heather perched on the edge of the bathtub. An unfortunate memory flashed in her mind. Jean-Luc's bathtub had been incredible. And there was room in there for two. She shook the thought away. "I snuck into the cellar to find out what they were hiding."

"Uh-huh." Fidelia lowered the toilet lid, then sat on it. "Was the sex good?"

Heather's jaw dropped. "Excuse me?"

"I'm psychic." Fidelia pointed at her. "And your shirt's on wrong side out."

Heather glanced down, and heat flooded her face. She quickly changed the subject. "I discovered something important. I was right about Jean-Luc being centuries old. He was born in 1485."

Fidelia nodded her head slowly. "That explains a lot. That's a lot of experience. He must have been good in bed."

Heather scoffed. "That is quite beside the point."

"So he *was* good?"

"Fidelia, his eyes turned red. They were glowing."

Her face paled. "*Santa Maria.*" She crossed herself quickly. "Did you see the white gnashing teeth?"

"No, but he has them. He's a *vampire.* They're all vampires. Except Phil. And poor Pierre. Even Louie is a vampire."

Fidelia's brown eyes widened. "Are you sure? Did Juan-Luc confess?"

"Yes."

She pressed her hands together, close to her mouth, whispered a prayer in Spanish, then crossed herself again. "I have always sensed there were . . . others, but I never—" She stiffened. "Did he bite you?"

"No. I never saw his fangs come out." Heather grimaced at the thought of ugly canines jutting from Jean-Luc's beautiful mouth.

Fidelia leaned forward to examine her neck. "You have no marks."

"He didn't bite me," Heather insisted. "He said he was in complete control."

"Control, yes." Fidelia sat back, frowning. "I have heard they would be very good at mind control. He could bite you and then wipe it from your memory."

"I don't think so. Jean-Luc said he doesn't allow any biting in his house. They all drink blood from bottles."

"Really?" Fidelia's dark brows lifted. "Then none of these vampires attacked you?"

"No."

"Juan-Luc didn't use mind control to force you to do things against your will?"

Heather shook her head, feeling her cheeks grow warm. He'd made her scream, but she'd done that willingly enough. "I don't think he was controlling me. I was sorta out of control. I yelled at him and slapped him."

"Did he yell back?"

"No." Heather shifted her weight on the edge of the tub. "He asked me not to leave the house. He's . . . worried about our safety."

Fidelia took a deep breath. "Let me get this straight. He didn't attack you or bite you or control you at all?"

"No."

"Then why were you yelling and slapping him?"

"Because they're *vampires*. Isn't that reason enough?"

Fidelia shrugged. "As far as I can tell, they've tried very hard to make us comfortable, and they're serious about keeping us safe. They lost one of their own today."

"Pierre was mortal."

"He was their comrade, and they were upset by his death. It could have happened to any of them. Or to us. We're all in danger."

Heather sighed. "So you think we should stay here? Unite with these . . . vampires against the common enemy?"

"Louie's a vampire, no? I say our best protection is more vampires. We should definitely stay here."

Heather nodded. "I agree. But as soon as they kill Louie, we're leaving."

"And what about Juan-Luc? You like him, no?"

"I can't date a man who has survived for centuries by biting women and sucking their blood."

"I bet he gives one hell of a hickey."

"Fidelia! The man is a monster."

She reached for her purse. "You want me to shoot him? I'll kill him tonight."

"*No!*" Heather jumped to her feet.

Fidelia gave her a knowing look. "You failed that test, *chica.*"

Heather gritted her teeth. "It's not what you think."

"That he's very good in bed?"

She sat with a huff. "It has nothing to do with attraction. I simply abhor violence in general."

"You slapped him."

"I was upset. And I feel kinda bad about it now."

Fidelia leaned forward on her elbows. "When did he confess? Before or after the sex?"

"After." Heather rubbed her brow. She was getting a headache.

"Ah. So that is why you slapped him. The bastard. He took his pleasure from you and satisfied his own needs before telling you the truth."

A dull pain throbbed at Heather's temple. "Actually, he never got—I mean, he spent the whole time pleasuring me."

"Oh!" Fidelia's eyes lit up. "That Juan-Luc. He is *muy macho.*"

Heather sighed. She'd had the biggest orgasm ever. Not that she ever intended to think about it again.

"So he never tried to bite you, and he didn't seek

his own pleasure." Fidelia tilted her head, considering. "Then why did he take you to bed?"

Heather swallowed hard. "He said he loves me."

"Ah. *Amor*."

Heather slumped. "He said he'd waited five hundred years for me."

"Mmm. *Romantico*."

"But he's a vampire."

Fidelia shrugged. "Nobody's perfect. My second husband—he had six toes on one foot."

"This is a little more serious than that. Jean-Luc is literally dead half the time."

Fidelia nodded. "For most men, that would be an improvement."

"I'm serious! I have to stay away from him. I want a normal life for me and Bethany. We'll live here for the moment, but I'm going to avoid him at all costs."

"All right," Fidelia agreed. "You must never talk to him, even if he is *muy romantico*. And you must try not to think about how good the sex was. It was really good, wasn't it?"

"You're not helping. Whose side are you on?"

Fidelia patted her knee. "I'm on the side of your heart, *chica*. Your heart will tell you what to do if you listen."

Heather groaned as another jab of pain targeted her temple. This was not the advice she wanted to hear. For when it came to her heart, she feared it was already lost.

After tossing and turning with too many sexy memories replaying in her sore head, Heather gave up on sleep. She took a long hot shower, dressed, and headed down the stairs to the studio by five A.M. As she neared the security office, the door opened.

"Good morning, lass," Robby greeted her.

She mumbled a greeting and hurried past him. If she could just immerse herself in the work she loved, she might be able to forget all the vampires lurking about. They probably all knew by now that their secret was out.

"Hey! Wait up, dudette!"

She glanced back. Great. The one named Phineas was following her. She kept walking.

"Whassup?" He caught up with her.

"Nothing." She stopped in front of the studio doors and punched fourteen eighty-five into the keypad. "I just want to work."

"That's cool. Don't mind me. I'm just hanging out."

"Like a bat?" she muttered as she entered the studio.

"More like your own personal bodyguard." He closed the door behind her. "We want to keep you safe."

"Somehow I'd feel a lot safer without a vampire following me."

Phineas stopped with an injured look. "I ain't gonna hurt you."

Had she actually hurt his feelings? "You've never bitten anyone before?"

He winced. "I ain't perfect, but I've worked real hard to control myself. I know I was a bum before. Hell, I was a real loser when I was alive, but Angus believes in me, and I ain't gonna let him down."

She proceeded to the worktable to organize her supplies. "Are you saying your life is better now that you're dead?"

"I ain't dead. At least not right now. And yeah, my life is better. This is my first real job, and I'm doing real good. I'm sending money home to my family. And I'm learning how to fence and do martial arts. You wanna see?"

Before she could say no, Phineas spun around to face the cluster of mannequins in the center of the room.

"Hai-ya!" He assumed an attack pose. "You're going down, sucker!"

He grabbed a male mannequin by the arm, twisted, and bent over at the waist. Heather assumed the mannequin was supposed to fly over his shoulder and crash on the floor, but unfortunately, the arm simply came off.

Phineas looked surprised for only a second, then he tossed the arm on the floor. "Yeah, I whupped your ass." He pranced back, holding up his dukes. "You won't be messing with me, sucker! I'll turn you into the one-armed man!"

A grin tugged at Heather's mouth, and she turned away. The last thing she wanted was to remember how much she actually liked these guys. She wandered toward the dress form where she'd draped the finished parts of the first gown. There was a note stabbed to the form with a sewing pin. She glanced over the black cursive script to read the signature at the bottom.

Jean-Luc. Her heart lurched. She removed the note.

> *An excellent start on your first gown. The show will take place as planned, a week from this Saturday. Attendance will be restricted. I wish you well with your designs, but my first priority is your safety.*

That was it. Polite and businesslike. She was almost disappointed. He could have written something like, *Sorry I'm a vampire,* or *I'd rather die again than ever bite you.* But no, he didn't even mention his role as a blood-sucking fiend. And he didn't write anything romantic, either.

She crumpled up the note and dropped it in the trash

bin. It was better this way. He was her boss, nothing more. As soon as Louie was dead, she was outta here. She settled down at the sewing machine to finish the skirt.

Phineas perched on the worktable. "Robby thinks you're afraid of him. That's why he sent me to guard you."

"I'm not afraid." Just totally freaked. She stepped on the foot pedal to start the machine.

"It takes time to get used to us. Man, I was totally freaked when I first found out I was a vampire."

Heather stopped sewing. Had he read her mind? More likely, *totally freaked* was just the universal reaction to vampires. "How long have you been . . . like this?"

"Just over a year." Phineas described his transformation at the hands, or teeth, of some evil vampire dudes, and how Angus had saved him.

"The evil ones still feed on people?" Heather asked.

"Yeah. They even kill people. We hate them." Phineas puffed out his chest. "We're the good guys."

"So there are good vampires and bad ones?"

"Yeah. How does Connor say it? *Death doesn't change a man's heart.* So a bad dude's gonna stay bad, you see."

"And a good man stays good?" Like Jean-Luc. She'd always felt he was a good man. A wonderful man. *I know you love me.* His words haunted her.

"Yeah, that's right." Phineas launched into a long story about a really bad dude named Casimir.

Heather returned to her sewing, but found herself drawn into the story and asking questions. Apparently the two factions were called Vamps and Malcontents, and they were on the verge of an all-out war. Angus MacKay had been the Vamp general in the Great Vampire War of 1710.

"Did Jean-Luc fight in the war?" she asked.

"Hell, yeah. He was second in command. Connor told me Jean-Luc never left Roman's side. He took some major cuts to keep Roman safe."

He was a loyal friend, a hero among his own kind. But his world was totally beyond hers. It was a dangerous world, too. Not a good place for her and Bethany. She tried not to think about him. "Who's Connor?"

"Roman's head bodyguard. I'm usually assigned to Roman's house, but Connor insisted on hiding them."

"They're in danger?" Heather recalled meeting Roman briefly. His wife had been very friendly and— Heather stopped sewing with a gasp. "They have a child!"

"Yeah. Roman's like a scientific genius, you know. He makes the synthetic blood we drink. And when Shanna wanted a baby, he figured out a way to make the baby his."

Heather couldn't believe it. "That sweet little boy is the son of a vampire?"

"Yeah. He's a cute little guy, huh?"

"But how could Shanna have a baby? Vampires are dead, sorta." This was too confusing.

"Shanna's mortal." Phineas grinned. "Like you."

Heather gulped. A mortal married to a vampire? And giving birth to his son. How could Shanna do that? But she seemed so happy. And the baby boy was beautiful.

"Mama!" Bethany skipped into the room, followed by Fidelia with her purse and Ian.

Heather glanced at the clock. It was after six. She hugged her daughter. "You're up early."

"I'm hungry," Bethany announced.

"Come have breakfast with us." Fidelia stepped closer and whispered, "They want us to stay together all day."

"But I have to work," Heather protested.

"Doona worry," Ian said. "We'll bring some furniture in here and make sure ye're all comfy."

Soon Heather and her family were sitting around the kitchen table eating cereal while Phineas stood guard. Ian plucked the recliner off the floor and left, carrying it over his head as if it weighed no more than five pounds.

"Hmm, *muy macho*." Fidelia leaned to the side to watch his exit.

Heather swallowed her cereal with a gulp. Apparently vampires were very strong. She recalled how easily Jean-Luc had picked her up and tossed her on the bed. Other memories rushed back. Good Lord, he was so hot. But off limits. She shoved the memories away.

"It's a little warm in here, no?" Fidelia gave her a sly grin.

Heather groaned inwardly. It could be really annoying to have a friend who was psychic.

Robby came in, and without a word, he hefted the entire love seat onto one shoulder and sauntered from the room.

"Ooh." Fidelia waggled her dark brows. "Roberto. I wonder if he wears anything under that skirt."

"It's a kilt." Heather motioned with her head toward her daughter. "Let's keep breakfast G-rated, okay?"

"Fine, I'll just imagine it." Fidelia scowled at her cereal. "At my age, that's all I have left."

Phineas grinned. "You're a baby compared to some of the old-timers around here."

"*Gracias, muchacho*." Fidelia gave him a grateful look. "I like all you men around here. You're *muy macho*." She gave Heather a pointed look. "Don't you think so?"

She glowered back. "Don't push it."

Ian and Robby returned for the television and TV stand.

"Thank you!" Fidelia called after them. "Now I won't miss my soaps. These men are very sensitive to our needs, don't you think?"

Heather made a face at her.

Phineas's laugh turned into a yawn. "The sun's coming. I can feel it. I'll have to leave soon."

Meaning he would be dead soon. Jean-Luc would be dead, too. Heather shuddered at the thought. Where was he? Was he climbing into that big bed of his so he could lie there all day dead as a doornail?

Phineas stood. "Hey, bro! Whassup?"

"Hey." Phil walked toward them. "Good morning."

Heather greeted him with a smile. At last, another normal human being.

Phil eyed the empty sitting area. "What happened?"

"We moved everything to the studio so Heather could work," Ian explained as he entered the kitchen. He inclined his head toward Heather. "Ye're all set up for the day."

"Thank you." Heather gathered up bowls and took them to the sink.

"Phineas, ye can go downstairs," Ian told him. "Robby's already headed that way."

"Sure. So long." Phineas waved at Heather. "See ya tomorrow night."

"Sleep well." She winced. What was the appropriate thing to say? *Die well?*

"What about you, bro?" Phineas asked Ian.

"I took the drug," Ian responded, his voice low. "I'm staying up."

Phineas grimaced. "Man, that's wack."

Phil looked the young Scotsman over carefully. "Do you feel all right?"

Ian shrugged. "I was a wee dizzy at first, but I feel fine now."

Phineas shook his head. "I've dealt with drugs before. They're no good, man."

"I'll be fine," Ian insisted. "Now go on downstairs."

"Okay." Phineas looked at Heather. "Keep an eye on him." He strode from the room.

Heather approached the two remaining guards. "What's going on?"

"Nothing." Ian crossed his arms, frowning.

"He's taken an experimental drug that will allow him to stay awake during the day," Phil explained.

"Is it dangerous?" Heather asked.

"Nay," Ian answered. "I feel fine, and we need more than one guard during the day."

Heather bit her bottom lip. These vampires were going to great lengths to protect her and her family. It was becoming increasingly hard to think of them as monsters.

As they all walked back to the design studio, she noticed the darkness. Shutters had been drawn over all the windows. The lights were on, but it was still gloomy without sunlight.

"They did a lot of stuff while we were eating breakfast," she whispered to Phil.

"They can move very fast," he replied.

Super fast and super strong. *And super sexy.* She mentally slapped herself for that last thought. "Why does it have to be so dark?"

"Sunlight would burn Ian," Phil whispered. "It'll kill him if he's exposed to too much."

Heather grimaced. The young Scotsman was putting himself in too much danger. "I don't see why we need two guards in the daytime. Louie's a vampire, right?"

Phil nodded.

"Then he would only attack at night," Heather concluded. "Unless he's taking the same drug Ian is."

"I'm sure he isn't. But he's an expert at controlling the minds of mortals. He used mortals to assassinate the French kings. He could brainwash anyone to come here and kill us, even during the day."

Heather gulped. "So anyone who comes to the door could be an assassin? Like . . . the mailman?"

"Correct."

The doorbell rang.

Chapter 22

Heather moved close to her daughter. Ian unsheathed his sword, and Fidelia removed a pistol from her purse.

Phil peered through the blinds on the window beside the front door. "It's the UPS man." He punched a button on an intercom speaker. "Leave the packages on the porch."

"This could be legitimate." Ian rested the sword blade against his shoulder. "Jean-Luc was ordering things online Sunday night."

"What's going on, Mama?" Bethany whispered as she took hold of Heather's hand.

"It's . . . a surprise." A pleasant one, Heather hoped.

Phil continued to spy through the window. "We've got four boxes. He's leaving now. Stay back. The sun's up."

Ian moved out of the way. Phil opened the door, and a slash of sunlight shot across the showroom floor. Above the shiny marble, golden dust motes danced in sunlit air.

Heather glanced at Ian to see if he was all right. His eyes glistened with moisture.

She walked toward him. "Are you in pain?"

He shook his head. "It's been a verra long time since I've seen sunlight. I never thought I'd see it again. 'Tis so . . . beautiful."

Heather turned away. It was hard to stay prejudiced against these vampires. The slash of light disappeared as Phil exited and shut the door. She moved to the window where Phil had peeked out earlier.

"You shouldna stand so close," Ian warned her.

Did he think the packages would explode like her truck? She peeked out the window to make sure Phil was all right. "Oh my gosh, he's *sniffing* the boxes."

"Phil can smell a bomb," Ian said. "Please move back."

"Phil can smell—" Her question was interrupted when the door opened and Phil pushed a box inside.

"This one's safe." He shut the door.

"Who's it for?" Bethany ran forward to look at it.

"Bring it here." Ian sheathed his sword, then drew the smaller blade from his knee sock. "I'll open it for you."

Bethany pushed the box to Ian just as Phil shoved a second box inside. "This is fun!" She pushed the second box to Ian. "Open it!"

Ian had already sliced the packaging tape on the first box. He dug through some Styrofoam peanuts and pulled out a beautiful doll wearing an elaborate dress.

Bethany squealed and held out her arms. "It's for me!"

"Good Lord," Heather whispered, moving closer.

Ian removed several plastic bags, each one containing another lovely outfit for the doll. "Och, ye can tell a fashion designer picked these out. Verra fancy."

"I love her!" Bethany spun around, holding the doll.

Heather turned to Fidelia. "We can't keep this stuff."

Fidelia snorted. "Try taking that away from your daughter."

Heather winced. "He's being sneaky and manipulative."

"I'd say he's clever and generous," Fidelia muttered. "But then, what the hell do I know?"

Ian emptied the first box and found a few picture books. Heather sighed. Jean-Luc would make an excellent father if he wasn't a monster. With a jolt, she remembered that Roman was a father. What if Jean-Luc used the same procedure? Could he actually become a father?

"All done." Phil shoved the last two boxes inside, then shut and locked the front door.

Meanwhile, Ian had the second box open. It contained an antique set of hand-painted tarot cards.

Fidelia clasped them to her chest. She looked at Heather. "You're *loco* if you let him go."

Heather frowned at her. "I can't be bought."

Ian opened the third box and pulled out something made of a rich black taffeta. He handed it to Heather.

It was a black cocktail dress, and just her size. Jean-Luc was probably trying to replace the one he'd torn last Friday. She admired the classic styling and superb craftsmanship. It had probably cost a small fortune.

"Can't be bought?" Fidelia asked wryly.

"No." Heather laid the dress back into the box. "I'll be returning this."

Ian dug into the fourth box, then quickly closed it. With a blush staining his youthful face, he pushed the box toward Heather. "It's for you."

"What did you get, Mama?" Bethany danced over, waving her doll in the air.

Heather pulled out something red and lacy. A bra. She stuffed it back in. "It's nothing. Just clothes."

"Oh." Bethany turned away, disappointed.

"Let me see." Fidelia inched closer.

Heather fumbled under the peanuts and pulled out another item. Black lacy underwear. She stuffed it back in.

Fidelia chuckled. "That Juan-Luc. He's a naughty one."

Heather shook her head. He'd ordered this stuff Sunday night? Had he planned on seducing her all along? She pulled out a midnight-blue silk nightgown, edged with lace. Yep, apparently, he had.

"Mmm, *muy romantico*," Fidelia whispered.

Heather closed the box, feeling the heat of a blush. Even Ian and Phil looked embarrassed. They were studying a shadow on the wall.

"I'm not keeping this stuff." She stacked her two boxes neatly. "I refuse to be in his debt."

Fidelia shook her head. "I don't care what you say. I'm not giving back my new cards."

They all proceeded to the design studio. Curtains had been drawn across the French doors along the back wall. The furniture from the kitchen had been arranged in a front corner, away from Heather's sewing machine. She could sew all day without interfering with Fidelia's ability to watch television.

The morning passed without further incident. Lunch was a little creepy when Ian sauntered into the kitchen, sipping something red from a glass.

Alberto joined them a bit later. "Do you have any idea where Sasha is? She never showed up for our lunch date."

Heather shrugged. "She's at some spa in San Antonio."

"I called there, and she checked out."

"Oh." Heather took a bite of her turkey sandwich while she considered. "Her mom lives nearby. Sasha might be visiting her." Or she might be avoiding Alberto.

He frowned at his sandwich. "I suppose."

"I'm sure she'll be back in time for the charity show," Heather said. "There's no way she'd miss that."

Alberto nodded. "That reminds me. We need to set up a runway in the showroom. Do you know any local carpenters?"

Phil shook his head. "We don't want strange workmen coming in."

"I've got an idea." Heather carried her plate to the sink. "The high school where I teach put on a musical last year, and they built a runway into the orchestra pit. I could check to see if they still have it."

"Good." Alberto looked relieved. "See if they can bring it here. I'll work on the invitation list."

"No more than twenty guests," Ian warned him.

Alberto scoffed. "That's ridiculous!"

Ian arched an eyebrow. "Ye can say that after what happened to Pierre?"

"But once I invite the school board members, and the mayor and city council, that will be almost twenty guests," Alberto protested.

"The show will be small," Ian repeated. "Jean-Luc's orders. Safety first."

Alberto left the room, grumbling.

The rest of them returned to the studio where Heather worked while Fidelia and Bethany tried all the outfits on the new doll. It was almost six o'clock when Ian stumbled and caught the edge of a worktable to steady himself.

"Something wrong?" Phil walked toward him.

"I feel . . . strange."

Heather stopped sewing to watch.

Ian doubled over with a long moan.

She rushed over to him. "Are you all right?"

"Nay." He stumbled forward, then collapsed to his knees. He breathed heavily, and sweat glistened on his brow. "I feel verra—" With a groan, he covered his face.

Heather knelt beside him. "Is there anything we can do?"

He cried out, then fell on the floor.

Heather looked at Phil. "We've got to do something."

With a grimace, he shook his head. "We can't take him anywhere. The sun would fry him. And there's no way to explain this to a doctor."

Ian let out a long moan.

"But he's suffering," she whispered.

"Mama, what's wrong with Ian?" Bethany started toward them, but Fidelia pulled her back.

"Don't worry, sweetie," Heather responded. "He's just a little . . . sick. Something he ate."

Ian cried out again and suddenly stretched out stiff. His hands gripped his face, the knuckles white.

"What can we do?" Heather leaned over him. "Where does it hurt?"

"Everywhere," he breathed. "My face. It feels like it's ripping in two."

Heather touched his shoulder. "You can't take that drug anymore."

"I have to."

"No, you don't. Phil can watch over us during the day. I won't have you suffering because of us."

"'Tis not just for you," Ian groaned. "'Tis for me."

"What do you mean?"

Phil squatted beside them. "He'll age a year for each day he takes the drug."

Heather couldn't imagine why anyone would want to age.

"I'm four hundred and eighty years old," Ian muttered. "I'm a full grown man trapped in the body of a fifteen-year-old. I canna go on like this."

"But this is hurting you," Heather protested.

"I doona care." Ian cried out again and rolled into a fetal position. "I—I need to look older. I want to find true love . . . like you and Jean-Luc."

She started to deny that she felt anything like love for Jean-Luc, but she noticed that Ian's body had gone still. His hands fell away from his face. "He—he's not breathing."

Phil pressed fingers against Ian's neck. "His heart has stopped."

"Oh my God." Heather fell back onto her rear. "This can't be happening." She scrambled to her feet. "He can't be . . ." *Dead?* Weren't vampires already dead? "What—what's going to happen to him?"

"I'm not sure." Phil ran a hand through his thick brown hair. "I can think of two possibilities. It could be that the drug has worn off, and Ian has simply gone into his daily death-sleep. That would be good since he's no longer feeling any pain."

"And the second possibility?"

Phil frowned. "The drug might have killed him."

"No!" Tears sprang to her eyes. "He can't die. All he wanted was an older face and a chance at true love." Dammit, these vampires were way too human.

"I don't think he's dead. At least, not permanently." Phil studied the inert body. "In my experience, a truly dead vampire will turn to dust."

"When will we know for sure?" Heather wiped her eyes.

"When the sun sets. If he's all right, his heart will start beating again." Phil pointed at his face. "Does he look different to you?"

"No." Heather examined him more closely. "Actually, yes. I think his jaw is a little bigger. And he has more of a five o'clock shadow."

Phil nodded. "Growing pains. That's what he was feeling. A year's worth of growing pains. I think he might be a little taller, too."

Heather frowned at the dead body. "Didn't the inventor of this drug know this would happen?"

Phil shook his head. "Roman never felt any pain. Of course, he was already about thirty years old. Since he was full grown, it wasn't such a shock to his body."

"Roman took the drug himself?"

"Yes. After his son was born, he took it for a week to help out with the baby. But then his hair started turning gray, and they realized what was happening."

Heather rose to her feet. "I don't think Ian should take it again. Surely there are female vampires who would understand his problem and accept him as he is?"

Phil stood. "I don't know. But I think this is *his* decision."

Heather disagreed and decided to talk to Jean-Luc about it. Right after she returned the clothes he'd bought. Shoot, so much for her plan to avoid him completely.

She looked down at Ian's body. "We can't just leave him lying here on the cold hard floor."

Phil's blue eyes twinkled with humor. "He's not feeling anything, believe me."

"It just looks so uncomfy." Heather searched the shelves and located two bolts of soft flannel. She slid one under Ian's head for a pillow and unrolled the other to make him a blanket.

They took a break for supper. She called the insurance company to check on her house, then she called the drama coach from Guadalupe High. Liz Schumann was delighted to offer her runway and to model one of Heather's gowns in the show. Liz promised to have her new boyfriend deliver the runway over the weekend, and Heather promised to give him a few tickets to the event.

After supper, they returned to the design studio and the dead body on the floor. Heather finished the first gown and looked at the clock. Seven-thirty. The sun would set soon. She said a silent prayer for Ian that he would wake up. Then she shook her head in dismay. It was happening. She could no longer view these vampires as monsters.

And she was getting drawn into their world.

Jean-Luc woke with the usual electrifying jolt that shot through his body and jump-started his heart. He rushed through his shower and breakfast, for he needed to know as quickly as possible that nothing bad had happened during the day. Was Heather all right? How had Ian fared his first day on the stay-awake drug?

He dressed in gray slacks and a maroon polo shirt—normal clothes. He only hoped Heather wouldn't look at him like she had last night, with that look of horror and disgust in her eyes. He had to win her back somehow.

He checked the kitchen, but they weren't there. As he exited, he saw Fidelia leading Bethany toward the stairs.

"Oh, Juan-Luc!" She grinned. "Thank you for the lovely presents." She cradled the box of tarot cards against her chest.

"I love my new doll." Bethany held it up so he could see. "Her name is Princess Katherine."

"I like that." So the items he'd ordered on Sunday night had arrived. "Do you know where your mother is?"

Bethany pointed down the hall.

"They're all in the studio." Fidelia lowered her voice. "Waiting for Ian to wake up."

Jean-Luc stiffened. "He's not . . . awake?"

Bethany giggled. "He sleeps too much."

Fidelia winced. "Come on, little one. Let's get you in the tub." She hustled Bethany up the stairs.

Jean-Luc zoomed to the studio and stopped.

Heather was kneeling on the floor beside Ian, with Robby, Phineas, and Phil surrounding them. She glanced up at Jean-Luc. His heart lurched in his chest. Her eyes no longer showed disgust, but they were glistening with pain. Her generous nature was taking Ian's dilemma to heart.

"I need to talk to you." She rose to her feet and moved away, obviously so they could have some privacy. She didn't know yet that it was unnecessary, for Vamps had super hearing. "How could you let him do something so dangerous?"

"I objected," Jean-Luc answered quietly. "But in the end, I couldn't force him to abstain. It was *his* decision."

"But he may have killed himself just so he can have a chance at true love." Heather wiped her eyes. "It's sad."

"An honorable man will sacrifice all for true love."

She glanced at him, her eyes widening.

"When Roman took the drug, he was late to wake, too." Jean-Luc turned to watch Ian. "I believe he will wake."

A silence fell between them as they waited.

Robby turned to Phineas. "Go see if Fidelia and the wee lass are all right. We'll let ye know what happens here."

"All right." Phineas trudged out of the room.

"And ye're off the clock, lad," Robby murmured to Phil. "Ye doona need to stay."

"Yeah, I do." Phil folded his arms across his chest.

Heather drew a deep breath. "We got the boxes of stuff you ordered."

Jean-Luc faced her. "Did you like the dress?"

"It's lovely." She avoided looking at him. "But I can't keep it."

"Why not?" Was she punishing him?

"I don't want to be . . . beholden to you. You've already given me a great job and a safe place to stay."

"You saved my life, Heather. I am beholden to you."

"Oh, I'm sure you could have handled Louie on your own." She waved a hand in dismissal. "You're the European fencing champion, remember?"

"But I didn't have a sword, remember?"

Scowling, she turned to face him. "I'm quite sure you could have defeated him without my help. You're . . . *muy macho*, as Fidelia would put it."

"*Merci*. Though you needn't look so annoyed by it."

She crossed her arms. "I still can't keep the dress or the other . . . stuff."

He stepped closer. "You mean the bras?"

"There was more than one?"

"Three bras, three panties." He raked his gaze over her body. "I was very careful to get the right size."

Her cheeks flushed pink. "They're going back."

"No, they're not." When she opened her mouth to protest, he continued, "Because of me, you and your family are in danger. Because of me, your house was ruined. Most likely everything in your house has sustained smoke damage and will need to be replaced. I have cost you a fortune. The few things I purchased don't begin to repay you. It is I who is in debt to you."

She gave a sigh of defeat. "All right. Thank you."

"How are you feeling?" He didn't like to think he'd caused the dark smudges under her eyes.

"I'm very tired. I couldn't sleep last night."

"I apologize for the way you learned the truth. I should have told you earlier."

She slid her hands into her jeans pockets and regarded the floor. "Why didn't you?"

He closed his eyes briefly, wondering how to explain. "I was . . . beguiled by the way you looked at me and talked to me. As if I was normal. It was like being human again, with a home and family and a beautiful woman who actually found me attractive. I—I never had that when I was mortal."

"You never had women throwing themselves at you? That's hard to believe."

"I never had a home and family." He stepped closer to her. "It's taken me a long time to realize that's what I want more than anything."

She looked away, but he caught the glimmer of tears in her eyes.

"Will you allow me the honor of courting you?"

She gave a short nervous laugh. "You sound so old-fashioned."

"Perhaps." He smiled wryly. "But I'm also very determined."

"I—I don't belong in your world."

"You can belong anywhere you want."

She rubbed her brow. "That's the problem. I don't want to belong there. But I don't want to hurt you. I—"

Ian jolted, and his chest heaved with a big breath.

"He's alive!" Robby exclaimed with a grin.

"Yes!" Phil punched the air with a fist.

Jean-Luc grinned. "Thank God."

"Oh, yes, yes!" Heather bounced up and down. "Yes!" She flung her arms around Jean-Luc's neck.

His heart swelled as he enveloped her in his arms. "Yes."

With a gasp, she pulled back. "Oh, I didn't mean—sorry. I was just so happy, I forgot . . ."

"That I was a monster?" he finished her sentence.

Her cheeks stained pink. "I don't think—"

"What happened?" Ian sat up.

"Ye've been sleeping on the job." Robby crossed his arms, frowning. "I should dock yer pay."

Ian glanced around with a confused look. "I'm . . . late?"

Robby laughed and extended a hand to help him up. "Ye had us worried, lad. How are ye feeling?"

Ian grabbed Robby's hand and slowly eased to his feet. "I'm all right, I think."

"You're at least an inch taller," Phil announced.

"I am?" Ian grinned. "It worked! I'm a year older. And I'm bloody well starving."

"Go downstairs and have yer breakfast," Robby ordered.

"I wish you wouldn't take the drug again," Heather said. "You were in so much pain."

"I'm sorry ye had to see it," Ian told her. "But I willna stop." He and Phil strode from the room.

"I'll leave ye two alone." Robby bowed and left the room.

"I should be going, too." Heather started for the door.

"What about your work?" Jean-Luc asked.

"Oh." She turned. "I finished the first gown." She motioned toward the dress form.

He walked toward it. "You decided not to do sleeves after all."

"No." She moved closer. "They were interfering with the fit of the bodice. So I thought I'd make a matching stole that can be draped like a scarf or worn like a shawl."

He nodded. "Good idea."

"I've been wondering—" She bit her bottom lip. "Who does the handwork on your designs?"

"Different women from France and Belgium, depending on what I need done. There's a woman in Brussels who makes the best lace, and another one in Brittany who does the most beautiful embroidery."

"Oh."

Had she suspected him of running a sweatshop somewhere? "I consider them artists and pay them very well. I could take you to see them, if you'd like to see their work."

"I—I don't think so." She backed away. "I should be going. I'm really tired."

He nodded. "You put in a long day."

"Yes. Good night." She practically ran from the room.

Jean-Luc sighed. She'd refused to let him court her. She still seemed a little afraid, but at least she no longer looked disgusted. He was making progress, but it was very slow.

He walked down the hall to Alberto's office and discussed the charity event. Then he teleported to his office to catch up on business. There were more than a hundred e-mails and a dozen reports from Paris to respond to. He was also coven master of Western Europe, so there were a few disputes to settle. He took a small break after midnight, downing another glass of synthetic blood from the stash he kept in his office.

It was after two in the morning when the alarm went off. Jean-Luc grabbed his sword, zoomed to Heather's bedroom, and flung open the door. They were in bed asleep. The alarm hadn't wakened them, for it was set at a frequency only vampires and dogs could hear. The alarm meant one thing—a vampire had teleported into the building.

He strode to the bathroom and checked inside. It was empty.

"What's wrong?" Heather asked sleepily.

"Nothing," he whispered. "Just making sure you're all right. Go back to sleep."

He spotted Robby in the hallway, so he zoomed into the hall and shut the door partway. "What happened?"

"It was Simone," Robby explained. "She claims she was bored, so she went out."

"Where did she go?"

"She wouldna say," Robby replied. "She teleported out with no one noticing, but when she came back, she triggered the alarm."

Jean-Luc recalled how Simone had boasted that she might have an affair with Lui. "She could be compromised."

"I know. Shall I send her away?"

"No. We want Lui to make his move so we can catch him."

"Fine. I'll keep an eye on her." Robby zipped down the stairs.

Heather peered through the half-opened door. "What's going on?"

"Everything's fine," Jean-Luc assured her.

She stepped into the hallway. "I heard you talking. You think Simone could be under Louie's control?"

"It's possible. He usually uses mortals, but he could manage to control a vampire, especially if she has a grudge."

"Like Simone." Heather frowned. "This mind control—you never used it on me, did you?"

He stiffened. "No, that would be dishonorable."

"I didn't mean to insult you."

His gaze wandered over her wonderfully mussed hair and rumpled pajamas. "If you were under my control, you would be downstairs right now in my bed."

"Oh."

"And you would be naked. And I would be—"

"All right! I get the picture."

He smiled slowly. "Was it good for you?"

She gave him an annoyed look.

"You look beautiful."

She snorted. "I don't have any makeup on."

"You're a natural beauty."

"It'll be short-lived. I'll get old and wrinkly."

"Time doesn't scare me." He stepped closer. "Let me court you."

She gave him an odd look, as if wariness and desire were battling inside her. "I'll think about it." She eased into the bedroom and shut the door.

Yes, he was slowly making progress.

Chapter 23

Heather was looking for something to hate about Jean-Luc. His vampire status no longer seemed a good enough reason to reject him. All the Vamps in the house were drinking their meals from bottles. All the male Vamps were well-mannered and considerate. Simone and Inga appeared selfish and vain, but Heather strongly suspected they'd been that way before acquiring fangs.

Fidelia confirmed the theory that death didn't change a person's character. She'd seen proof of that through her experience with helping lost spirits. So Heather could no longer avoid the truth. Jean-Luc was just as gorgeous, intelligent, and honorable as he'd been as a mortal.

His sense of honor carried over into the way he conducted business. There were no sweatshops, no employees being abused in the pursuit of wealth. Phil confided in her that Jean-Luc was taking care of Pierre's family. He was a good man. If he had been mortal, Heather knew she wouldn't hesitate to pursue a relationship with him. She wouldn't be constantly denying her feelings for him. So the real question was, could she accept him and love him as he was?

Thursday was a peaceful day until suppertime, when Ian suffered another attack. Fidelia immediately whisked Bethany off to the kitchen, so the little girl wouldn't have to witness Ian's torment. Heather hated seeing him suffer and begged him to take some painkillers, but he stoically refused. After a half hour of twitching and sweating, he finally fell into a peaceful death-sleep.

Heather finished the stole for the first gown and proceeded to the pattern-making stage for the second outfit. As time went by, she found herself looking forward to seeing Jean-Luc again.

He showed up about eight-thirty, as handsome as ever. Her breath caught, just looking at him. *I know you love me.* God help her, was he right? What else could explain how she was drawn to him even when she knew the truth about him?

He looked over her work while they waited for Ian to wake up. Ian woke and stumbled to his feet to see if he'd grown. Heather handed Robby a measuring tape.

"Congratulations, ye're now six feet tall," Robby announced. "And ye need to shave."

Ian grinned, rubbing the whiskers on his jaw.

"We should have some Blissky to celebrate," Phineas suggested.

Ian laughed. "Ye're always looking for a reason to have some Blissky."

"I have a bottle in the security office," Robby said. "Let's go."

The three male Vamps sauntered off, leaving Heather alone with Jean-Luc.

"What's Blissky?" she asked.

"A mixture of synthetic blood and Scottish whisky,"

Jean-Luc explained. "Roman has made our meals much more interesting with his Vampire Fusion Cuisine."

Heather made a face. "Are you kidding me?"

"No. We now have Chocolood, blood with chocolate, a favorite among the lady Vamps, and Bubbly Blood, blood with champagne for those special vampire occasions."

Heather laughed. "What would that be? Moving into a new, improved coffin?"

The corner of his mouth tilted up. "Now you're mocking me. You know exactly where I sleep, and it's not a coffin."

Her face warmed with the memory of his bed.

"Would you like to see what I've been working on? It's in my office."

She hesitated, not knowing if she was ready to be alone with him behind closed doors.

His smile faded. "I would never harm you, *chérie*. I would do anything to protect you from harm."

Anything but stop her from falling in love with him. And that might cause her great pain sometime in the future. She sighed. Love never came with a guarantee. It was always a leap of faith. She just wasn't sure she wanted to take that leap.

Was she letting fear rule her life again? Sometimes caution was the wise choice. Then again, too much caution could be really boring and . . . sad. What if she spent the rest of her life regretting her cautious wisdom?

She took a deep breath. "I can stop by for a few minutes."

"Good." He walked slowly toward the door, waiting for her to accompany him. He made no attempt to touch her, and she was grateful for that. He seemed to understand that she needed time. And she needed answers.

"Why did you come to Texas?" she asked as they started down the hallway.

"I needed to disappear. The media was questioning why I never grew older."

"So you're in hiding?"

He nodded. "For twenty-five years. Then I can return to Paris, posing as my son."

She wanted to ask if he ever considered having a real son, but she lost her nerve. "So you're going to be in Schnitzelberg for a while." How could she go back to her normal life, knowing that a vampire who loved her lived right down the highway?

"I can still go places. I just have to be careful. I can't afford to be spotted by the media."

"How on earth do you travel?" She paused as they entered the showroom. "Don't tell me—you're stashed in a coffin in the cargo bay of a 747."

He winced. "That would be awful. Travel is actually very easy for us. We just teleport."

"*Teleport?* Nobody teleports, except in sci-fi shows."

"Vampires teleport."

She gazed around the showroom, speechless. She turned back to Jean-Luc, and he vanished.

She gasped. "Jean-Luc?"

"Yes."

She jumped and spun around. He was behind her. "Oh. That was too sneaky."

"It comes in very handy. That's how my guards were able to bring your daughter's toys here."

She narrowed her eyes. "You could teleport into my bedroom whenever you like, even with the door locked?"

"Yes. But don't forget—I'm an honorable man."

She winced with a sudden thought. "Then Louie could teleport here. He could go straight to my bedroom—"

"Heather," he interrupted her, touching her shoulder. "An alarm goes off the second anyone teleports into the building. It went off last night when Simone returned."

"Oh. So that's why you barged into my bedroom."

"Yes."

He really was protecting her. "I appreciate how hard all of you are working to keep us safe."

He smiled. "When this is all over, I think we should go on a date."

"You mean dinner and a movie?" She scoffed. "I'm not volunteering to be dinner."

He chuckled. "No, but I could take you somewhere out of the public eye, like Angus's castle in Scotland or Roman's villa in Tuscany."

What a rascal. He was dangling a carrot that she found hard to resist. She'd always longed to travel.

"I have Vamp friends all over the world who would welcome us," Jean-Luc continued. "We just have to be sure that I'm not recognized. Or that the sun hasn't risen."

"You mean you would take me with you when you *teleport*?"

"Yes. It's quite simple, really."

She snorted. "That's easy for you to say. You're talking about turning me into some kind of . . . vapor, then hoping I materialize with my head on straight."

"It's perfectly safe."

"It doesn't sound safe."

He tilted his head, considering her. "I'll show you how it works now, then you won't have to worry about it."

She stepped back. "I'm okay with worrying. I'm really quite good at worrying."

"We'll just go to my office." He pointed to the second-floor window that overlooked the showroom.

"And then later, when I take you on a longer trip, you won't be afraid."

Good Lord, he was so enticing. "I might agree to a date sometime in the future. But that doesn't mean I've agreed to that courtship idea of yours."

"Fine. We'll do a practice run now." He moved closer.

Her heart lurched. Oh God, she'd agreed to teleport.

He placed his hands lightly around her waist. "There are a few things you must do for it to work."

"Like what?"

"Put your arms around my neck and hold tight."

She slowly moved her hands up to his neck. "What now?"

He wrapped his arms around her. "Now you kiss me."

She scoffed. "They never did that on *Star Trek*."

"Their loss."

"What if you're teleporting alone or with a guy?"

He winced. "All right. I lied." He gave her a rueful smile. "But you can't blame me for trying."

She swatted his shoulder.

He chuckled. "You do have to hold me tight, though."

The room began to waver, and Heather grabbed his neck for dear life.

"Trust me." His soft words whispered in her ear just before everything went black.

She felt a floating sensation, then a solid floor beneath her feet. She opened her eyes. She was in a large office. "That was spooky."

"You'll get used to it."

She stepped back, and he released her. She wandered around the office, noting the two leather wingback chairs, the desk, computer, and file cabinets. She stopped by a worktable that was strewn with beautiful fabric in shades of green and blue. A pile of peacock feathers begged to be touched. She stroked the soft fronds.

"I knew you would have to touch," he spoke quietly behind her. "You like texture."

Her skin prickled with goose bumps. "How did you know?"

"I've been watching you." He moved close beside her. "You like the smoothness of silk against your bare skin. You like to touch chenille and velvet." He picked up a peacock feather. "This reminded me of you. It holds all the different shades of green and turquoise that I see in your eyes. They change slightly when you're smiling or frowning or . . . climaxing."

She shot him an annoyed look. "Your eyes change, too."

He smiled and handed her a stack of sketches. "What do you think?"

She looked them over. He was so talented. He managed to draw on centuries of fashion experience and create something both classic and new. "They're beautiful."

"So is my inspiration." He stroked the edge of the feather down the side of her face and down her neck.

She dropped the sketches and paced toward the window. She gazed down at the mannequins, stark white in the dark showroom. "I need to know more about you."

"What do you wish to know?"

She leaned her forehead against the cool glass. "Everything. You know everything about me."

He sighed. "There's not much to tell. I was born a poor peasant, the son of Jean who cleaned out the stable. I don't recall a family name."

She turned to face him. "What about Echarpe?"

"I acquired that name after I was transformed. Some

Vamps gave it to me as a jest. After women . . . encountered me, they would wear a scarf to hide the marks."
He shrugged. "*Echarpe* means 'scarf.'"

She winced. "A sad joke."

"Much of my life has been a sad joke. I have . . .
fought to be where I am today."

She could relate to that. "Is it true what you said the
other night—that your mother died when you were
young?"

Frowning, he sat in one of the wingback chairs. "Both
my parents died. I was orphaned by the age of six. The
baron allowed me to sleep in the stable and take over
my father's duties."

Heather huffed. "Well, that was kind of him."

"It was better than being homeless."

She walked toward him, stopping at the desk. "Go
on."

"The baron was a seasoned warrior, and he had several wards living at the chateau with his son. He was
training them all for knighthood. I would hide behind
barrels to watch. Then I practiced at night in the stable
with a staff."

She nodded. "I bet you were good."

"The baron's son was a bully, and he would beat
the other boys to a pulp. The baron did nothing, for
he was proud of his son. One day, when I was about
ten years old, the son had one of the wards down on
the ground, and he was pummeling him with a club. I
grabbed my staff and shoved him away. We engaged
in battle."

Heather winced. As a history teacher, she understood the severe consequences if a peasant attacked
one of his superiors.

"The servants were yelling at me to stop and run
away," Jean-Luc continued. "The other wards ran to
alert the baron. And I continued to fight. I fought like

a madman. All my years of frustration and misery erupted with so much anger."

"I can believe that." She'd been so angry at herself for her years of being a doormat. "What did the baron do?"

"He ordered us to stop. I realized then what I had done. I thought I was going to die." Jean-Luc rubbed his brow, frowning. "That was the first time I felt the full extent of being powerless. My fate was entirely in the hands of another man."

"How terrible." Heather moved to the chair next to him.

"To everyone's surprise, the baron walked up to his son and backhanded him across the face so hard, the boy fell to the ground with a cut lip. The baron called it punishment for failing to kill an inferior in battle. Then he said if I wanted to fight, I could. I was astonished, but it seemed much better than mucking out the stables for the rest of my life, so I agreed."

"You trained with the other boys?"

"Yes. The next few years were difficult. I had to be on guard constantly, for the baron's son was always trying to ambush me and beat the hell out of me."

"What a creep."

Jean-Luc smiled. "He was. The king at that time, Louis XII, was trying to take over Italy. He demanded his nobles send him their best knights. The baron was linked to the powerful de Guise family who wanted the king to fail, so the baron was told to send his worst. And so I was quickly knighted. Another sad joke."

Heather winced. "You couldn't have been the worst."

"I had no real battle experience. And no family, so I was expendable. I was given a poor excuse for a horse, and some pathetic old weapons."

"Oh my gosh, they sent you to die."

"Exactly. I remember the baron laughing, saying that his decision to train me had paid off. I was sent instead of his son to die in a war that was doomed to fail." Jean-Luc closed his eyes briefly. "I swore that day that I would never be powerless again. I would never be a pawn again."

Heather touched his arm. "I'm so sorry."

He took her hand in his. "My first battle was in 1500. I survived."

"You were only fifteen."

He nodded. "I continued to do well. I was noticed and given a better horse and equipment. I was working my way up the ranks until 1513 and the Battle of the Spurs."

"That's when you . . ."

"Died. The English invaded France at Guinegate, and my comrades fled in battle. I was so angry that I stood my ground and slashed the first Englishman who approached me. A stupid mistake, for soon I was surrounded and stabbed many times. They left me to die."

Heather shuddered, and he tightened his grip on her hand.

"That night, Roman found me. I didn't want to die."

"Of course not. You were so young."

"Yes, but it was more than that. I wanted to be in charge of my own destiny. I was sick of being powerless. I wanted power, even power over death."

Heather swallowed hard. "I guess you got it."

He smiled wryly. "I can still die. And the final joke to my short life as a mortal—the following morning, my body was gone, so the Battle of the Spurs has gone down in the history books as a bloodless battle. I was the one forgotten casualty."

"I'm sorry."

He squeezed her hand. "Only a few know my story. I hate to even remember how pathetic I was."

"I felt pathetic, too, that I let everyone boss me around. But you know, we're not pathetic at all. We're conquerors. We have both struggled to change our lives for the better." She winced inwardly. She'd just admitted his life as a vampire was an improvement.

"I won't lie to you, *chérie*. The vampire world is just as violent as the mortal one. The Malcontents are growing an army, and another war could break out. That would be a disaster for us all. Such a war could not escape notice. The media would be all over it."

She took a deep breath. "Your secret would be out."

He nodded. "Exactly."

And there would be people determined to hunt down all vampires and kill them. "That would be a disaster." She withdrew her hand and leaned back in her chair. The vampire world was a dangerous one. How could she drag her daughter into it?

He stood and wandered to the window overlooking the showroom. "I need to warn you about the runway show a week from Saturday. I thought about canceling it, since it gives Lui an opportunity to attack you. But we decided to go ahead with it."

She gulped. "So I'm going to be a sitting duck?"

He turned to face her. "I will be by your side the entire evening. We will be well prepared. It is better this way. Better to draw him here where we can control the situation. And better for it to happen at night when all the Vamps are awake and able to protect you."

She nodded slowly. "Better to get it over with, too." She didn't want to live with the threat of Louie any longer than necessary. "But we have to keep my daughter and Fidelia safe. I won't let you put them in danger."

"Agreed." He paced over to his worktable. "Now you

know what I fear the most. I hate being powerless. Being a vampire has given me many powers, super strength and speed, and so on, but it also has one terrible weakness. I am totally powerless during the day."

She rose to her feet. "You have your guards to keep you safe."

He shook his head and picked up a swatch of green silk. "It is not my safety that worries me. Every morning at sunrise, when I slip into my death-sleep, I am gripped with a terrible fear that something will happen to you while I lie there powerless to help you." He crushed the fabric in his fist. "I could not bear it."

"It'll be all right." She rushed to the table. "I have Phil and Ian, and Fidelia with her guns. And I'm not totally helpless myself." She touched his arm. "We all have fears that plague us."

"And are you still afraid of me? Of what I am?" He dropped the fabric on the table. "How can I convince you that it changes nothing? I will still love you no matter what. I will always love you."

Tears stung her eyes, and she turned away. "It's not that I don't—I think you're a wonderful man."

He picked up a peacock feather and dragged the soft fronds up her bare arm. "I'm trying so hard not to touch you."

Her arm tingled. Her heart ached with a need to comfort him. He so needed to be loved. He deserved all the love that a good life should have, the love he'd never had.

With a small cry, she wrapped her arms around his waist and hugged him tight. "You're a good man, Jean-Luc. A beautiful man."

"Heather." He held her lightly as if trying to retain control. "I want you so." His hand skimmed up and down her back, inciting delicious little tingles.

She needed to back away, but he was so solid. So

easy to lean on. She felt his chin rub against her hair. His lips brushed against her brow. The familiar tug of desire spread through her.

His arms tightened. "Let me court you." He nuzzled her neck, then whispered in her ear, "Let me love you."

She glanced at his face, and her breath stuck in her throat. The light blue irises in his eyes were changing. "Your eyes are turning red."

He smoothed her hair back from her brow. "It's a problem I keep having whenever I'm around you."

"Why? Do I make you hungry?"

"You make me ache with desire. My eyes are merely a reflection of the passion burning inside me."

"You mean they turn red when you're . . . turned on?"

"Yes." He smiled slowly. "You could help me alleviate the problem. But I'm afraid it would continue to arise, over and over again."

Oh God, would that be such a bad way to spend the rest of her life? A seed of panic rose in her stomach. She wasn't ready to commit to such a different life for her and her daughter. "I—I need to go." She stepped back.

He released her. "As you wish, *chérie*."

She left and slipped inside her dark bedroom. Good Lord, what should she do? She had no doubt that Phineas was correct, and being a vampire didn't change a person's character. Jean-Luc was just as noble and honorable as he'd been when alive. Maybe even more so. His additional years of existence had given him a wisdom and maturity that Heather found very appealing. And of course, he was very sexy. He was wonderful with Bethany, kind and generous to Fidelia. He was perfect in every way but one. He was a vampire.

But being a vampire hadn't changed Jean-Luc, and

it wasn't changing how she felt about him. Now that she was over the initial shock, she realized she was still attracted to him, still in love with him. And that scared her more than his pointed teeth ever had. For she was seriously considering a relationship with him.

Part of her told her that was crazy. She'd known Jean-Luc a week now. How could she make a decision that would affect her entire life? And Bethany's, too. How could she explain to her daughter that Mommy's new boyfriend was dead during the day? How could she burden a young child with such secrets? But the alternative, keeping the truth from her daughter, would make Heather feel dishonest and guilty.

Overall, it was a difficult situation. She would age, and Jean-Luc wouldn't. She would be dragging her daughter into a bizarre world. On the other hand, she might be giving her daughter a wonderful and loving stepfather.

But he would be dead during the day. Heather's mind flipped back and forth between the pros and cons. It was enough to give her a major headache. She fumbled across the room in the dark to the bathroom, then she closed the door and turned on the light.

She looked at herself in the mirror. Fidelia had told her to follow her heart. Her heart longed for Jean-Luc, but her head urged caution. If Jean-Luc became part of her family and it didn't work out, she wouldn't be the only one with a broken heart. Bethany would suffer, too.

Heather sighed. She was at war with fear, but in this particular battle, fear was winning. The safest course of action was retreat. She should pull back before her love for Jean-Luc overwhelmed her.

Heather worked hard Friday, trying not to think about Jean-Luc. That night, he asked if she'd like to talk in his office, and she declined. The sad look in his eyes pierced her heart, and she hurried to her bedroom. Fidelia asked what was wrong, but she could only shake her head with a lump in her throat.

During lunch on Saturday, she discovered another super power that vampires possessed. Great hearing. In the kitchen, Ian heard a car coming up the driveway. Heather accompanied the two guards to the foyer of the showroom.

Phil peered outside the window. "It's a pickup truck, pulling a flat trailer."

Heather peeked out the window to see who was exiting the truck. "Oh no, it's Coach Gunter."

"Is he a threat?" Ian asked.

"Only to every woman on earth," Heather muttered. She noted the big black boxes in the back of the truck and piled on the flat trailer. "He's brought the runway." And that had to mean he was Liz Schumann's new boyfriend. Good Lord, Liz had to be out of her mind.

Coach strode to the front door, ignored the doorbell, and pounded on the door with his fist.

Heather winced. "You'll have to let him in. I'll fetch Alberto." She rushed down the hall to Alberto's office. Even from there, she could here Coach's booming voice as he entered the foyer.

"The runway's here," she told Alberto. "And I promised Liz three tickets to the show."

Alberto reluctantly handed over three tickets. "I barely have enough for the school board and big shots in town."

Heather winced. "I guess with only twenty guests, we won't be raising much money."

Alberto snorted. "These local people don't have any money. Jean-Luc's giving the donation. Twenty thousand."

"Dollars?" Heather gulped. "That's awfully generous."

"He has his reasons." Alberto waved a dismissive hand. "Not that he isn't generous. Jean-Luc gives a lot to charity. But in this case, he's paying for silence. When the store closes after the show, Jean-Luc wants this place to be forgotten. I believe your job will be over."

She remembered that he'd hired her for only two weeks. "You mean no one will come here at all?"

"Hopefully not. If they do, there'll be a guard here to turn them away. I'll be returning to Paris with the models, and Jean-Luc will go into hiding."

It sounded so lonely. Heather recalled the first card Fidelia had turned over for Jean-Luc. The Hermit. He would be so lonesome. But she could change that if she agreed to let him court her.

"Well, I should take a look at this runway." Alberto strolled from the office.

Heather took her time returning to the foyer. Phil and Coach had set several runway sections in the showroom, and Alberto was examining them.

"Hey, Heather!" Coach yelled as he headed outside for another section of runway. He pointed at Ian, who stood in the shadows looking embarrassed. "That kid's no help at all. You should fire his lazy ass."

Heather gave Ian a sympathetic look. She knew he had to stay out of the sunlight, but apparently Coach was giving him hell. After twenty more minutes, the runway was completely unloaded.

She gave Coach his tickets.

"You know I'm dating Liz Schumann now." He paused by the front door.

Heather nodded. "I figured that."

"Yep." He flexed his biceps. "She's one lucky little lady. You don't know what you're missing."

"I'm devastated. Please tell Liz to drop by on Friday so I can make sure her gown fits." Heather had already arranged for two other teacher friends to model.

"How fancy is this shindig?" Coach asked. "Do I have to dress up?"

Her gaze drifted over his tank top and gym shorts. "You might consider wearing pants. And leaving your whistle at home."

"Oh, really fancy, huh?" He marched out the door. "See ya next Saturday."

Heather went back to the design studio to work on her second outfit. Alberto left to hand-deliver the rest of the tickets.

About six P.M., Ian collapsed again. Heather was relieved her daughter was having supper in the kitchen and didn't see it. Still, Ian was starting to look older, and she was at a loss how to explain that to her daughter.

She was walking to the kitchen with Phil when the doorbell rang.

Phil peeked out the window. "It's the sheriff."

Heather opened the door and let him in.

"I wanted to make sure you were all right." Billy looked her over while he stuck a toothpick in his mouth.

She shut the door. "We're fine. Any news?"

"Nope. I can't find this Louie guy." Billy strode into the showroom and looked around. "We got some fingerprints from the museum, but they're not in any system. And we don't know his real name, so we're at a dead end."

"I see." Heather followed him into the showroom.

"Did you find anything useful from Heather's truck?" Phil asked.

"Nope." Billy wandered around the runway sections. "So you're getting ready for the show Saturday?"

"Yes," Heather replied. "Since I'm going to be at the show, Jean-Luc thinks Louie will come."

Billy wheeled around to face her. "He's using you as bait?"

Heather shrugged. "He's bait, too. Louie wants to kill us both."

Billy chewed on his toothpick, frowning. "I'll need to be there, along with my two deputies."

"We'll be glad to have your help," Heather assured him. Ian had told her that if the mortals saw anything they shouldn't, the Vamps would erase their memories.

Billy strolled back to the front door. "Cody's acting weird again. He was at Schmitty's Bar last night. Got drunk and started raising a stink about you. Then, all of a sudden, he says he's a cockroach and scrambles all over the pool tables, messing up everybody's games."

Heather sighed. One more problem to deal with.

"I had to lock him up for the night." Billy opened the door and paused on the front porch. "He was fine this morning, but I'm telling you, the guy's psycho."

"I understand. Thanks for stopping by." She closed the door and locked it.

It was a strange world when the vampires appeared more normal than the mortals.

Chapter 24

That night, Heather learned about another super power the vampires possessed. She stood in the showroom, amazed, while Robby and Ian hung material from the catwalk to make a curtain that partitioned off the back of the showroom. The models would use the back section as their dressing room during the runway show.

What amazed Heather was the two Scotsmen didn't need a ladder. They simply levitated in the air.

"I guess you can do that, too." She slanted a glance at Jean-Luc, who stood beside her.

"Yes." He leaned toward her. "In my arms, we could rise to new heights together."

She wasn't sure he was referring to levitation. "I'm fine being a lowly mortal."

"There's nothing lowly about you. And I've had some trouble lately with certain parts levitating on their own."

She snorted. "What other powers do you have?"

"Superior vision and hearing. An advanced awareness of my surroundings. For instance, did you know Fidelia is hiding behind the scarf display case?"

"No. Why on earth would she do that?"

Jean-Luc's mouth twitched. "You can't guess?"

Heather lifted her gaze. Above the display case, Robby was hovering in the air, wearing his blue and green plaid kilt. "Good Lord. This is embarrassing." Thankfully, Bethany was in the kitchen, eating cookies, while Phineas stood guard.

Ian dashed into the showroom, carrying more bolts of fabric to use as curtains. He moved so fast, his body was a blur.

"You're super fast and strong," Heather observed.

"We have great endurance." Jean-Luc smiled. "We can last all night long."

She scoffed. He had a one-track mind tonight. In that respect, Vamp men had not advanced one iota from their mortal beginnings. "Your eyes put you at a disadvantage."

"How's that? Don't you like knowing when you turn me on?"

"Yes, but if I ever see you look at another woman, and your eyes turn red, you'll be in big trouble."

He winced. "I never thought about it that way. Fortunately, I plan to be faithful."

How could he remain faithful when she was old and gray? Heather sighed. "What other powers do you have?"

"Telepathy. We don't do it that often, because it's not private. Any Vamp could pick up a message being broadcast. That's the problem with vampire sex."

"What?"

"Vampire sex. Any Vamp can join in and play along."

Heather grimaced. "That's disgusting."

He arched an eyebrow. "You might like it."

"I am not into group sex."

"Good, because I refuse to share you."

Time to change the subject. "What other powers do you have?"

"Mind control. We can manipulate and erase thoughts."

She nodded. "You think Louie might use mind control on someone involved with the show. Even Simone."

"It's possible, but don't worry. I won't leave your side."

She wondered whom Louie would choose. Would his victim act strangely, making it obvious? "Oh my gosh, what if he's messing with Cody?"

Jean-Luc blinked. "Excuse me?"

"Cody's been acting weird ever since Louie arrived on the scene. Maybe Louie's using him to get to me."

Jean-Luc shook his head. "No, he's not."

"How can you be so sure? Cody went berserk again last night."

"He must have cursed you."

"Billy said he was ranting about me, but—how would you know?"

Jean-Luc sighed. "He is being manipulated. By me."

Heather gasped. "Why would you do that?"

"He was cursing you. He deserved it."

"He's been running around like a cockroach."

"Exactly." Jean-Luc nodded. "It suits him perfectly."

"That's not your decision to make."

"I was protecting you."

"No." Anger sizzled inside her. "You were scaring the hell out of me. I've been worried for days. I had to call my lawyer to see about changing visitation rights."

"I'll pay your bill."

"That's not the point! You had no right to interfere in my personal life."

"I thought I *was* part of your personal life." He

crossed his arms, frowning. "The next time I see your ex, I'll erase the command. He'll go back to being his usual repugnant self."

"Thank you. I can't believe I've been worrying over this, and it was just a joke to you."

"I was not laughing, Heather. I wanted to kill the bastard for the way he was treating you. A hundred years ago, I would have."

Her chest constricted, making it hard to breathe. She felt . . . closed in. Suffocated. She wasn't ready for this.

"Are you all right?" He touched her shoulder. "You're heart is pounding."

She stepped back. "I have fought too hard for my freedom just to throw it away now." She turned and stalked to the kitchen to be with her daughter.

He was losing her, and he didn't know what to do about it. Vampires weren't accustomed to rejection. In the old days, if Jean-Luc wanted a pint, he could always resort to mind control. That way, the lady in question never said no.

But it wasn't blood he wanted from Heather. He wanted her love, and that was proving much harder to obtain. His sense of honor precluded using mind control on something this important. He wanted her love to be true.

His old methods of seduction hadn't quite worked on Heather. She had her own career, her own home, her own family. She valued her independence, and she didn't really need him.

Merde. The more she pulled away, the more he ached for her. In the days that followed, he was tempted several times to whisk her down to his bedroom and make love to her till she couldn't see straight. He also considered using vampire sex to seduce her while she slept, but he rejected that idea, too. She'd not reacted well to his manipulating her ex's mind. She would not appreciate his playing games with her head.

So he was left with a totally lame course of action—being a nice guy. He'd always considered himself somewhat nice, so it was surprising how much he had to work at it. He had to constantly remind himself not to tease her with his usual lewd sense of humor. He had to force himself, over and over, not to touch her.

She immersed herself in work, and every evening, he reviewed her daily accomplishments in a businesslike manner. He made polite suggestions while he mentally pictured her clothes falling off. He gave her sincere encouragement while he imagined her screaming his name in the throes of a massive climax.

As the week wore on, he even pictured her beautiful body growing ripe with his child inside her. Dammit to hell, he wanted to start a life with her. He wanted to be her husband. This being-nice crap was for the birds.

By Friday, Heather was ready to scream, and she didn't know why. Jean-Luc was being very polite. He didn't even try to touch her. Unfortunately, he also stopped teasing her and making jokes. He no longer looked at her like he was ready to devour her. Had his love for her already gone cold? If that was the case, then she was right to withdraw.

She had felt angry about his turning her ex into a cockroach, but when she'd gone to Fidelia to complain about it, they'd both ended up rolling with laughter.

Heather sighed. She missed the old Jean-Luc. In the last few days, all the fun had gone out of him. Even Fidelia noticed the difference.

"Poor Juan-Luc," she moaned. "He has lost his mojo. You must help him get it back."

"How?" Heather was hesitant to ask.

"Go down to his bedroom and take off your clothes while you do the tango."

"I don't know how to tango. Will the Cotton Eye Joe work?" Heather pictured herself stripping while doing a country-western line dance.

"I'm trying to help you, *chica*. If you don't tell him you love him, you could lose him. Do you want to lose him?"

No. The answer sprang to her mind. No, she couldn't bear to lose him. "I miss him. I miss the fun conversations we used to have. I miss the way he was always trying to steal a kiss or touch me. I miss the way he made me feel." She'd felt loved by him. Oh God, she missed his love.

She kept herself occupied by working long hours. By Friday morning, she finished the last of the three outfits. That afternoon, her three teacher friends came by for their fittings. Everything was set for the show on Saturday. Her two weeks of employment would be over. Jean-Luc had said she could stay until her house was ready. Was he reluctant to see her go? She didn't know how she could leave him and go back to her old life like nothing had happened.

Ian collapsed as usual about six P.M. They always made sure Bethany was in the kitchen when it happened. Heather had told her Ian was a special person who was aging very fast. Bethany seemed to accept that, although she announced she wanted to age fast, too.

A little after seven P.M., Sasha showed up. After fussing at her, Alberto fitted her for the outfit she was supposed to wear.

"Heather, your designs are fabulous!" Sasha hugged her. "I'm so happy for you."

"Thank you." Heather was surprised. "You do know that my designs are for a size twelve?"

"Oh, I know. And I may be wearing them someday." Sasha whirled in a circle, grinning. "Guess what? I'm going to retire! And start eating again!"

"Wow. Congratulations. When did you decide this?"

"When I fell in love." Sasha clasped her hands together over her heart. "I met him in San Antonio. He's so handsome. And rich. And he's crazy about me!"

"Great! When do we get to meet this guy?"

"Soon. Henry is so fabulous. You'll just love him. I do. Can you believe it?" Sasha practically danced to the front door. "I'll see you tomorrow!"

Later that evening, after the Vamps awoke, Simone and Inga put on their gowns and tried out the runway. They pronounced it ugly, but adequate.

Meanwhile, Jean-Luc paced around the showroom, making sure everything was in order. The mannequins and display cases had been moved to storage. The black runway was flanked on each side by two rows of white folding chairs. The lengths of silk hanging from the catwalk glimmered in shades of black, gray, and white. The whole room looked very elegant.

Jean-Luc stopped beside Heather. "Your outfits are ready?"

"Yes. And my models were fitted this afternoon."

"Good." He paced toward the silk curtains and back. "You did well to have three outfits ready in such a short time."

"Thank you."

He paced toward the front door, then turned and came back. He glowered at her. "I'm about to explode."

She blinked. "Excuse me?"

"I can't take it anymore."

Was he rejecting her? Heather's heart began to pound. "I realize you only hired me for two weeks, and my time is up."

"I'm not talking about employment. I'm talking about us." He paced away, but returned after a few steps. "I've gone almost a week without touching you. I don't know how to . . . act. I want to grab you and kiss you, but I don't dare frighten you away. And I'm tired of waiting for Lui to make his move. You're trapped here until I can get rid of him."

"I think we're all suffering from cabin fever. I'm nervous about tomorrow, too, but I'll be glad when it's over."

"When it's over, you'll be free to go." He dragged a hand through the dark curls on his head. "Will you accept full-time employment?"

She blinked. "You're offering me a job?"

"Yes. I want to manufacture some of your designs. You can work out of New York or Paris. I'll help you relocate."

Heather's heart lurched. Designing clothes in New York or Paris? It was all she'd ever dreamed of. "But where would you be?"

He sat heavily in a foldout chair. "I'll be here in hiding."

She sat beside him. Her dream job didn't sound so wonderful if it didn't include him. "Could I work here?"

"I suppose the daytime guard could let you in." He gave her a wary look. "You can always go home before I wake."

She bit her lip. "Is that you want?"

"No! I know exactly what I—" He leaned back in the chair. "But I shouldn't tell you. It'll scare you away."

"Tell me. If Louie was gone, what would you do?"

"I would take you and your family to New York. We would stay at Roman's townhouse. You would see the tourist places during the day, and then at night . . ."

"Yes?"

"We'd go to the Diamond District to pick out a ring."
Her mouth dropped open.

"And then I would ask you to marry me."
Her mouth snapped shut, and she gulped.

"I would be a good father to Bethany, and I would love to have more children with you. Two, I think."

Did he have their colleges picked out? He certainly did know exactly what he wanted. She struggled to breathe.

He tilted his head, watching her. "What do you think?"

"I think you found your mojo," she whispered.

"Is that an answer?" He looked confused.

"No." Heather clenched her hands together.

"I'd better leave you alone. I've said too much already. *Merde*. I've probably scared you away." He strode from the room.

Heather's heart pounded in her ears. Good Lord, he wanted to marry her. Marriage to a vampire. And children.

Was he scaring her away? Didn't she have enough to be scared about? Tomorrow was Saturday, the day of the runway show. And the night they expected Louie to try to kill her.

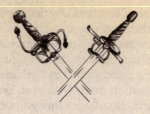

Chapter 25

"Thank you for coming." Jean-Luc shook hands with Gregori, who had just teleported into his office.

"No problem, bro." Gregori peered through the window at the showroom below. "So you want me to emcee your show?"

"If you don't mind." Jean-Luc thought Gregori was the best choice since he'd once hosted a reality show on the Digital Vampire Network. "I need to be at Heather's side."

Gregori nodded. "She's the chick Lui wants to kill?"

"Yes." Jean-Luc glanced at the silk curtain. She was behind there with her models. Phineas was standing guard, but Jean-Luc was anxious to take over that duty.

"This will be fun." Gregori adjusted the tie to his tuxedo. "Lots of hot babes. Is Simone here?"

"She's with Inga. They put on each other's makeup. I have a digital camera and monitor set up in the cellar so they can see themselves." Jean-Luc retrieved a piece of paper from his desk. "This is everything you need to know."

Gregori glanced over the script. "Okay. Let's do it."

Robby strode into the office. He nodded at the vice president from Romatech Industries. "Gregori."

"Hey, bro." Gregori shook his hand.

"Everything's ready to go," Robby announced. "One of Heather's models was a bit nervous and had too much to drink. Heather has her drinking some coffee."

Jean-Luc frowned. "If she's drunk, her mental facilities will be weak."

"Ye're thinking she would be easy for Lui to control," Robby said.

"*Oui.*" Jean-Luc picked up his cane with the hidden sword inside.

"I'll keep an eye on her. Simone, too," Robby added.

"Unfortunately, everyone in the building is a suspect." Jean-Luc strode to the office door, carrying his cane. "Let's go."

The three male Vamps zoomed down the backstairs and into the kitchen. Phil and Fidelia were having a late-night snack with Bethany.

"You can go to my office now." Jean-Luc hunched down beside Bethany. "You can watch your *maman* through the window." The little girl nodded, her mouth full of cookies.

He passed by Phil and whispered, "Keep them safe."

"Yes, sir." Phil nodded. He'd been instructed earlier to shield Bethany's view if things turned ugly.

Jean-Luc strode to the showroom with Robby and Gregori.

Robby pointed at the catwalk. "I'll be up there during the show. Phineas and Ian will be down here. The sheriff's already here with two deputies."

Jean-Luc noted Billy leaning against a wall with a toothpick in his mouth. His deputies were standing on the opposite side of the room.

"I'll check the guests as they come in," Robby continued, "and make sure they're all mortal."

Simone and Inga strode into the room, ignoring the deputies who turned to gape at them.

"Hey, Simone." Gregori walked toward her, smiling.

She stopped. "Gregori." She lifted her hand and allowed him to escort her and Inga to the backstage area.

Gregori lifted the curtains to let them pass. "I'll be back here," he told Jean-Luc.

"Tell Heather I want to see her." Jean-Luc waited.

Heather peeked out. Her eyes widened. "You're looking good."

"Thank you." He'd worn his best tux. "We're ready to start."

"Okay." She glanced back. "Good luck, ladies."

Jean-Luc smiled when he saw she was wearing the black cocktail dress he'd purchased for her. "You look lovely."

"Thank you." She smoothed down the skirt. "I know a guy with great taste."

"That's right." Jean-Luc escorted her to the front row of chairs. "I heard one of your models is a little drunk."

She winced. "Liz. I would have never believed that a drama coach would suffer so much from stage fright. But they're all dressed and ready to go." She was talking fast and her gaze was flitting about. She was nervous, Jean-Luc realized, and with good reason.

"Come." He sat in a chair at the end of the row and motioned for her to sit beside him. He took her hands in his. They were icy cold, and he rubbed them. "I will protect you, Heather. I promise."

She took a deep breath. "I've been waiting for this for two weeks, and now I just want it over with."

"You'll do fine. Your outfits are beautiful."

"Well, that seems really unimportant compared to someone trying to kill me."

"No one will hurt you. I won't let them." He glanced at the front door. Robby was checking everyone and examining purses as they came in.

"Oh no," Heather moaned. "Coach Gunter has arrived."

The short coach didn't wait in line, but burst into the showroom. "Hey Heather!" His booming voice rang out. "I brought some moral support for Liz." He blew his whistle, and two cheerleaders from Guadalupe High skipped into the showroom, waving pom-poms and squealing.

"Oh no." Heather scooted down in her chair.

Jean-Luc chuckled. "I've never seen this before at a fashion show."

"Only in Texas," Heather muttered.

Coach and the cheerleaders sat in the front row across from Jean-Luc and Heather.

More people arrived, and soon all the seats were filled. Robby shut the door, then walked down the hall. A few seconds later, he strolled onto the catwalk. Obviously he'd used vampire speed once he was out of sight.

Gregori stepped onto the platform next to the runway. "Good evening, and welcome to Schnitzelberg's first fashion show."

The small crowd cheered. Pom-poms waved.

Gregori grinned. "This is a charity event. For each person in attendance, Jean-Luc Echarpe is donating one thousand dollars to the Schnitzelberg Independent School District."

More cheers.

Jean-Luc scanned the room. Every visitor was mortal. None of them had approached him to talk or thank him, so it looked like his identity was still a secret.

"We'll start with two designs by Alberto Alberghini," Gregori continued. "May I introduce our world-famous models—Simone and Inga!"

The crowd clapped politely. Jean-Luc suspected they'd never heard of his famous models.

Music started. Alberto was controlling that from backstage. At the front door, Ian dimmed the sconces on the walls, so the runway would look brighter.

Simone stepped onto the runway. There was an appreciative gasp among the crowd.

"Simone is wearing a black silk evening gown that shimmers with thousands of bugle beads," Gregori read from his notes. "The draped back gives it just the right dramatic touch. A stunning design."

Simone marched down the runway and struck a pose. Jean-Luc watched her carefully. She glared at him, but then she always modeled with an angry expression. She was halfway back when Inga began her walk.

"Inga is wearing an ivory cocktail dress of shantung silk," Gregori announced. "Note the slanted neckline which leaves one shoulder bare and how this is echoed in the asymmetrical hem. An elegant creation by Alberto Alberghini."

The crowd clapped politely.

"Did Alberto write this script?" Heather whispered.

Jean-Luc nodded. "I edited it." He knew Simone and Inga would be busily changing into their next outfits. Alberto had set up a screen so the mortal models wouldn't see them using vampire speed to change clothes.

"And now," Gregori continued, "we have three designs by Schnitzelberg's very own designer, a promising new talent in the fashion world, Heather Lynn Westfield."

The crowd cheered. Coach Gunter circled a fist in the air and hooted. The cheerleaders shook their pom-poms.

Heather ducked her head. "I can't believe this."

"The town loves you," Jean-Luc whispered. "I can see why."

She looked at him, her eyes sparkling with emotion. "Thank you for believing in me."

He took her hand. "It doesn't have to end tonight."

"All right!" Gregori grinned. "Our first model is Miss Gray, an English teacher from Guadalupe High."

Miss Gray stepped hesitantly onto the runway, wearing Heather's first gown.

The cheerleaders leaped to their feet, their pom-poms in the air. "Go, Miss Gray!" Shake, shake, shake. "Go, Miss Gray!"

Alberto started the music up again. Miss Gray smiled and apparently realized she was among friends. She walked down the runway, her smile growing.

"Miss Gray is wearing an evening gown of royal-blue silk chiffon," Gregori read from his notes. "Notice the expert flow of the skirt and the versatility provided by the matching stole."

The second teacher started down the runway.

"Go, Ms. Lawson!" Shake, shake, shake. "Go, Ms. Lawson!"

"Ms. Lawson is wearing a black cocktail dress, topped with a bolero-style vest," Gregori announced. "The red soutache trim on the bolero is repeated on the hem of the skirt. A creation both elegant and bold."

Heather clung to Jean-Luc's hand.

"You're doing great," he whispered.

"If someone wants to attack me, I wish they'd just do it," she whispered back. "The suspense is killing me."

The third teacher stepped onto the runway.

Coach jumped up and hooted. "Way to go, Liz!"

"Go, Miss Schumann!" Shake, shake, shake.

Liz started down the runway, wobbling a bit in her maroon stiletto heels.

"Miss Schumann is wearing a maroon jacket dress," Gregori said. "The fitted dress is topped with an elegant jacket, featuring a pleated portrait collar, three-quarter-length sleeves, and a faux gem button."

She posed at the end of the runway while Coach whipped out a camera.

Jean-Luc ducked, not wanting his picture taken. *Zut*, Robby must have been too busy checking purses. He'd missed this camera.

A light flashed, apparently blinding Miss Schumann, for the woman stumbled back, then squealed as she teetered on the edge of the runway and fell off.

"I got you, Liz!" Coach rushed toward her and helped her up. "She's okay!" He raised his arms like she'd scored a touchdown.

The crowd cheered. Heather started toward her friend, but Jean-Luc stopped her.

"You need to stay with me." He exchanged a look with Robby. It looked like the three mortal models were safe. But Lui could have still taken over someone's mind in the audience. And Simone still had one walk left.

The crowd gave Liz another round of applause as Coach Gunter escorted her back to the curtained-off area.

Gregori cleared his throat. "And now, we have three more designs by Alberto Alberghini. First up, Schnitzelberg's own world-famous model, Sasha Saladine."

Sasha started down the runway, and the crowd cheered.

"Sasha is wearing a three-piece outfit, all in beige

silk," Gregori continued. "The tightly fitted pants and top make a stunning contrast to the loose and flowing full-length coat."

Jean-Luc noticed Sasha had her hands in the coat pockets. That was normal for a model, but . . .

Sasha pulled out a gun, aimed at Heather, and pulled the trigger.

Jean-Luc leaped in front and felt a sharp sting in his right arm. As thin as Sasha was, the recoil from the pistol sent her flying off the runway. Phineas jumped on her. The deputies and sheriff were running toward her.

"Are you all right?" Jean-Luc looked at Heather. She was shaking, her eyes wide. He pulled her close.

He glanced at the catwalk. Robby was gone. Ian was gone, too. No doubt they'd teleported outside to look for Lui, in case the bastard was lurking about.

The crowd pushed toward the door, screaming.

The sheriff jumped onto the runway. "Calm down! The danger is over."

Coach blew his whistle, and the crowd quieted. "All right, let's go." He steered the crowd out the door. "Form a double line. Move it! Move it!"

Billy jumped down to where Phineas had Sasha pinned on the floor. He helped her up, and she looked around, dazed.

"What happened?" She looked at the sheriff. "Oh hi, Billy. I remember you from high school."

With a frown, he pulled her hands behind her back and cuffed her. "Sasha Saladine, you're under arrest for attempted murder. You have the right to remain silent."

"What?" Sasha turned pale. "I wouldn't hurt anyone."

Billy used a handkerchief to pick up her gun. "You just tried to shoot Heather with this."

Sasha gasped. "I don't know how to shoot. I would never hurt Heather."

"Yeah, right." Billy led her toward the front door. "You probably blew up her truck, too."

Sasha gasped. "No! I don't know what you're talking about. Billy, please." She gave him a beseeching look. "Don't you remember me?"

He looked sadly at her. "Yeah, I do."

Heather pulled away from Jean-Luc. "Billy, she's telling the truth. She's not responsible."

He gave her an incredulous look. "She shot at you. Everyone saw it." He led Sasha out the front door. "You have the right to an attorney . . ."

Heather turned to Jean-Luc. "We can't let her pay for Louie's crime."

"I'll take care of it," Jean-Luc assured her. "For now, it's more important that we find Lui." He removed the sword from his cane, wincing when his arm objected.

Heather gasped. "Oh my God!"

"What are you doing?" Gregori strode toward him.

"I want you and Phineas to guard Heather while I hunt for Lui."

Gregori shook his head, frowning. "Dude, you're not in any shape to fight. Let Robby and Ian do it."

"But it's my responsibility." Jean-Luc tightened his grip on his sword. For some reason, his hand was tingling and unresponsive. "I have to kill that bastard once and for all."

Heather touched his left arm. "Jean-Luc. Darling, you're bleeding. You've been shot."

Two hours later, Jean-Luc relaxed in his giant bathtub. The hot water swirled around, producing white foam, while the jets pummeled his back with pulsating water. He sat in the corner, his injured right arm propped along the side to keep the bandage dry. His left arm rested along the other edge, close to the bottle of Blissky.

Jean-Luc had been surprised by the gunshot wound. He'd been so determined to protect Heather and kill Lui that his mind had ignored the pain. Gregori and Heather had escorted him down to his bedroom, while Alberto dealt with the aftermath of the disastrous show.

Gregori knew a Vamp doctor from Houston who had helped deliver Shanna's baby. He called Dr. Lee, and the Vamp teleported straight to Jean-Luc's bedroom with his medical kit. Once Heather was assured that Jean-Luc would live, she ran upstairs to see her daughter.

The bullet had to come out. Gregori handed Jean-Luc a bottle of Blissky to help with the pain. Dr. Lee removed the bullet, bandaged him up, left a bill, then teleported back to Houston.

Gregori wandered off to see Simone and Inga. Ian and Robby were still hunting for Lui, while Phineas and Phil guarded Heather and her family. Jean-Luc knew Lui had to be close by. He'd been controlling Sasha, and she'd been in the area for the last two days. He had to be close. The bastard would want to be close to relish the damage he'd caused.

Jean-Luc took another sip of Blissky. Here he was, once again helpless. He couldn't fight tonight. He was useless. The pain had become a dull throb, but anger and frustration were steadily growing.

Lui had to be found. This had to end. Jean-Luc couldn't force Heather to stay here forever like a prisoner. But if he let her go, Lui would kill her. *Mon Dieu*, she had every reason to hate him. She'd lost her newfound freedom because of him. He was crazy to even hope for her love.

He heard his bedroom door open and shut. "Robby, is that you? Please tell me Lui is dead."

Soft footsteps approached. Jean-Luc turned to look, his gaze blurred by pain. He blinked. He had to be dreaming. She was wearing the blue nightgown he'd bought for her. Yes, he had to be dreaming. It was a good dream.

Heather slowly walked toward him. "Jean-Luc."

He blinked. "You're real."

She smiled slowly. "Oh yes."

Chapter 26

Heather's eyes adjusted to the dim light of Jean-Luc's bathroom. "Are you all right?"

"I'm devastated. My best tuxedo was ruined."

She figured his sarcasm was pain-induced. "At first I thought vampires might not feel any pain, but Gregori assured me that you do."

Jean-Luc leaned his head back on the marble edge of the tub and closed his eyes. "I have all kinds of feelings. Anger that Lui has escaped me once again, frustration that you're forced to accept my protection whether you like it or not."

"I'm not complaining. You took a bullet for me."

He waved a hand as if that was nothing. "Then there are all my positive feelings. Devotion to you, respect for you, desire for you, and the joy I feel in your company." He opened his eyes and looked at her. "Everything positive in my life revolves around you."

She moved to a corner of the raised tub and wrapped an arm around the slender column. The marble was cool against her cheek. "You have a lot to be proud of,

Jean-Luc. You're very clever and talented. You've come a long way in life, and you've built a highly successful business."

He rested his head back again. "I worked hard, so I could be the one in charge, so I wouldn't be powerless to the whims of other men." He sighed. "But Lui keeps coming back, and I'm powerless to stop him. Worthless."

Her heart squeezed in her chest. "Don't you dare say that. You risked your life to save me." She moved up the stairs and sat on the edge of the tub.

"I feel worthless right now. If Lui showed up tonight, I wouldn't be able to fight." Jean-Luc smiled slightly. "Don't worry. I would still protect you."

"I believe you." She knew he'd die if he had to. She touched the soft black curls on his head.

"I have an emergency plan. I'd teleport you and Bethany to Romatech Industries. There's a safe room there, completely encased in silver. No vampire can teleport in or out. You would be safe there."

"I see." She stroked his hair, and he closed his eyes. "Silver's bad for vampires?"

"Mmm." The lines of pain in his face slowly smoothed.

She kept stroking his hair. Now she understood why the silver belts had hurt Louie so much. "Gregori told me you would heal completely during your death-sleep. You won't even have a scar to commemorate your bravery."

A corner of his mouth tilted up. "It was more like desperation. I couldn't bear to lose you."

"I think you were very brave. I wanted to thank you."

He opened his eyes and regarded her sadly. "We've rescued each other now, so we're even. As soon as I kill Lui, you will be free to go."

She took a deep breath. "I'm not going anywhere."

He stared at her blankly. "You're accepting the job?"

She straightened so she was standing on the bottom step of the stairs leading up to the tub. Her heart began to race. "I'm accepting you."

His eyebrows rose. He sat up.

She slipped the straps of her nightgown off her shoulders, and then peeled the bodice down to reveal her breasts. His eyes darkened.

She had to wiggle a little to get the nightgown over her hips. His eyes began to glow. The nightgown fell in a puddle around her feet.

Her heart was pounding now, echoing in her ears. The fear and uncertainty she'd felt the last two weeks had all melted away, leaving her with a sense of elation. Her mind was made up. She was following her heart. And she was declaring victory over fear. "Remember what you said? You were right about me."

His eyes glimmered bright red. "What did I say?"

"You said I loved you." She ascended the steps, and a glorious feeling of power washed over her. "And I do." She eased into the hot water.

"You do?" He moved over to give her room.

She settled beside him. "Yes, I do. I was thinking about you all week, trying to get up the courage to follow my heart."

"So you've defeated that fear?"

"Yes. There was a scripture that helped me. The one that says there's a purpose for everything under heaven. I realized you were here for a noble purpose. You protect the innocent from bad vampires." She touched his face. "How could I not love you?"

He gave her a wry look. "You're trying to make me noble?"

"You are noble, you silly goose. Deal with it."

He chuckled. "I love you, too." He glanced at his

bandaged arm. "But I may have trouble proving it."

"You don't have to do anything." She nestled against his left side and rubbed a thigh against his leg. "I'm here to seduce you."

"Really?"

"Uh-huh." She planted kisses along his shoulder and up his neck. "I hope you don't mind. I know how you hate feeling powerless."

His mouth quirked. "Strangely enough, I'm all right with this."

"Good." She skimmed a hand down his chest, reached his stomach, and bumped into the tip of his swollen manhood. "Oh. You're not completely out of action."

"No." He hissed in a breath when she wrapped her hand around him and squeezed.

She stroked the shaft, enjoying the way it grew thicker and harder. The tip remained velvety soft. She kissed his chest. "I never could resist you. From the first time I met you, I wanted you."

"Heather, I love you so much." With his left arm, he pulled her half on top of him. He kissed her on the mouth. A hungry, demanding kiss.

She tasted a hint of whisky on his tongue. She explored his mouth and skimmed her tongue across the edge of his teeth. The sharp points on his canine teeth didn't faze her. She knew who he was, and she loved him.

She straddled him, and they continued to kiss. His left hand stroked her back. She nestled against his erection, rubbing herself against the length. Her breasts moved against his chest.

"Come up higher." He wrapped his left arm around her waist and lifted her up so her breasts were even with his mouth. He drew a hard nipple into his mouth and suckled.

She moaned and arched into him. Tingles spread all over her body, and a deep need flared inside her. Good Lord, Fidelia had been right. A man who had sucked blood for centuries knew how to use his mouth.

Somewhere in the daze of sensual pleasure, Heather realized he'd taken charge. "Hey." She gasped as he tugged on her nipple. "I'm supposed to be seducing you."

"You were wildly successful. Consider me seduced." With one arm, he lifted her out of the water and sat her on a corner of the tub.

Wow, super strength came in handy. Goose bumps prickled her body as cool air caressed her skin and her back came in contact with a cool marble column.

"Hold on." He eased her hips to the edge of the tub.

"Like this?" She raised her arms overhead and grasped the column. She gasped when he buried his head between her legs.

Oh God, that mouth of his. That tongue. She pressed her fingers against the marble. Her heels dug into his back.

He stroked and nibbled till she was panting and writhing with tension. Just when she was ready to explode, he pulled back.

"You're beautiful," he whispered. Then he twirled his tongue around her, and she shattered.

Her body was still shuddering when he pulled her back into the hot, bubbly water. The swirling currents pulsed against her sensitized skin and sent another wave of tremors through her body.

"Oh God." She fell limp against him. "I should seduce you more often."

"Every night, *chérie*. Hold on."

Everything went black for a second, then Heather felt herself falling back onto his bedspread. He must have teleported them straight to bed.

He zoomed back to the bathroom. She sat up to see him zipping back to her with a towel.

"Here." He dried her back, then pushed her gently onto the bed so he could dry the front of her body.

"Wait!" She pointed at the camera.

He zoomed to the bedside table and grabbed the remote. "Don't worry. The guys are out looking for Lui. No one's seen you." He turned off the surveillance camera, then jumped on the bed.

He leaned over to kiss her breasts, then winced. "Wait a minute." He moved to the other side of her so he could prop himself up on his left arm.

"I have a better idea." She shoved him flat on his back. "You're the injured hero. So just lie there and take it like a man."

His mouth twitched. "You're cute when you're bossy."

"Cute? You think this is cute?" She cupped his balls and lightly squeezed.

He moaned. "I take it back. You're an incredibly erotic seductress."

"That's more like it." She sat beside him and ran her fingers over his body. This was the first time she was getting a good look at him naked. He was lean and muscular. A few scars marked his pale skin. She traced them, realizing they had to be centuries old, dating back to his days as a mortal. Curly black hair shaded his upper chest. She traced the thin line of black hair down his torso to the thicker patch surrounding his erection.

She stroked the shaft and it twitched. "It's alive!"

He gave her a wry look. "I need inside you."

"All in good time." She leaned over and kissed the soft tip.

He winced. "I really need inside you."

"We have all night." She dragged her tongue up the shaft, then took him in her mouth.

He groaned. "Take me inside you. Now."

She swirled her tongue around the tip, then released him. "Hmm, yummy."

"Dammit, woman!" His eyes blazed red. "Ride me."

She blinked in surprise. "Oh. You're so cute when you're bossy."

"I'm not bossy. I'm dying." He pulled her on top.

She straddled him, then tried to position him in the right place. "I'm not very experienced in this—aagh!" She gasped when he shoved himself into her and pulled her down at the same time. "Okay, that'll work."

She settled down on him, letting him fill her completely. "You feel so good."

"So do you," he breathed. He caressed her breasts. "Love me."

"I do." She rocked on him slowly, then leaned forward to kiss him.

He pulled down on her hips, urging her to go faster. She did, feeling the tension coiling tighter and tighter. He reached between her legs to rub her clitoris, and she went frantic. Somewhere, in the back of her mind, she realized she'd never behaved so wildly before. It was liberating. It was glorious.

He tweaked her as she came down hard on him. Convulsions shook her, and her body went limp. She fell beside him. He rolled with her, then grasped her bottom as he drove into her. He groaned, grinding his hips against her as his climax shuddered through him.

Slowly their breathing returned to normal, and they lay on their sides, gazing into each other's faces.

"Wow," Heather breathed.

"Indeed." The red in his eyes slowly faded.

She touched the curls on his head. "I love you." She felt tears crowding her eyes. "I love you so much."

"Will you marry me?"

Before she could answer, he sat up and continued, "I promise to get rid of Lui. You won't have to live a life of entrapment. We'll be able to travel and enjoy life. And we can—"

She put a finger on his mouth. "The answer is yes."

He grinned and kissed her finger, then kissed the palm of her hand.

She shivered. "Let's get under the covers."

He pulled back the bedspread, and they snuggled between the sheets. He winced when she accidentally bumped against his injured arm.

"Oh, I'm so sorry." She kissed the shoulder.

"I'll be out of pain in a few more hours."

"When the sun comes up?"

"Yes. Heather, will you leave before I go into my death-sleep?"

"It doesn't scare me, Jean-Luc. I've seen Ian that way every afternoon."

"I know. But I want our first night together to be perfect for you. I don't want your last memory of it to be my dead body."

"All right." Maybe with time, he wouldn't feel embarrassed about it. She kissed his cheek. "I love you just the way you are."

Heather woke around noon in her bedroom upstairs. She stretched, smiling as memories of lovemaking replayed in her mind. After an hour of rest, Jean-Luc had suggested they find another position that didn't put any weight on his injured arm.

They had rolled around, laughing, till she ended up sitting in his lap, facing him as they kissed and fondled each other. They rolled around some more. Eventually she found herself on all fours while he stood beside the bed and entered her from behind. He reached around to stroke her with his fingers while he drove into her, and the combination sent her over the edge.

Exhausted, she fell asleep in his arms. He'd nudged her awake with kisses about five-thirty A.M., and she put on her nightgown to sneak upstairs. She took a long hot bath to ease sore muscles. Then she put on her pajamas and climbed into bed next to Bethany.

She vaguely recalled Bethany trying to wake her up sometime later. She'd mumbled something, and Fidelia had chuckled.

"Your mama's worn out, little one. And about time, too. Let her sleep."

Now Heather rested in bed, half asleep, thinking about Jean-Luc. She'd agreed to marry him! Her fears that it wouldn't work out had been cast aside.

She dressed and went downstairs to the kitchen. Ian and Phil had moved the furniture back. She greeted them and gave Bethany a hug.

Fidelia hefted herself out of the recliner and waddled into the kitchen. "Come have some breakfast."

Heather followed her.

Fidelia grinned as she took a box of cereal from the pantry. "So how was it?"

Heather snorted. "It was very private."

"That good, huh?" Fidelia poured the cereal into a bowl while Heather fetched the milk.

"I had a bad dream last night." Fidelia lowered her voice. "The red glowing eyes and gnashing white teeth."

"We already know what that means." Heather poured milk into the bowl.

"I'm not so sure." Fidelia frowned. "I'm getting a real sense of danger. And then there was this stone building. Ruins. An old church, I think."

"Interesting."

Fidelia sighed. "Ian told me they still haven't found Louie. They'll go hunting again tonight."

And Jean-Luc would be fit and ready to fight tonight. Heather's breath caught when she realized he'd be risking his life again. She stared at the bowl of cereal, her appetite suddenly gone.

"There's a car coming up the driveway," Ian announced.

Heather followed Ian and Phil to the front door.

Phil peered out the window. "A woman driver. She looks like one of the models from last night."

"It's Miss Gray!" Alberto called as he strode down the hallway, pulling a suitcase behind him. "She's here for me. I'm off to Paris, and Linda's giving me a ride to the airport."

Heather peeked out the window. Linda Gray was one of her friends from Guadalupe High. "I didn't realize she knew you."

"She didn't until last night." Alberto entered the foyer. "When Sasha started shooting last night, I flung myself over Miss Gray to protect her." He grinned. "She thinks I'm a hero."

"Well, I guess you are." Heather offered her hand. "Have a good trip."

Alberto shook her hand. "I might be back to visit soon, if things work out with Miss Gray."

Phil opened the door while Ian moved away from the sunlight.

"Good luck to you all." Alberto rolled his suitcase out the door. "Ciao."

Heather went back to the kitchen to enjoy a day off with her daughter. Around suppertime, Ian collapsed on the kitchen floor.

Bethany giggled. "He takes naps like a baby."

"Yes." Heather smiled. But he no longer looked like a baby. Ian had aged twelve years over the last twelve days.

"If I take a nap, will I get older, too?" Bethany asked.

"Sweetie, you get older every day, just much slower than Ian."

"But I want to grow up faster," Bethany protested.

"I know, but I don't want to lose you any faster than I have to." Heather stood. "Let's see what we can find for supper."

After their meal, the doorbell rang, followed by pounding on the door. Heather and Phil went to see who was there. Cody was outside, pacing on the front porch.

She sighed. Too bad Jean-Luc wasn't awake. He needed to undo the cockroach spell. Maybe she could get Cody to come back after sunset. But for now, he should be safe to talk to. He was under Jean-Luc's control. And Bethany was in the kitchen with Fidelia, so if Cody started acting strangely, his daughter wouldn't see it.

Heather opened the door.

Cody whirled around to face her. "I didn't get to see Bethany this weekend."

"You said you weren't able to see her."

"I know I did." Cody scratched his head. "But I don't know why. Something's wrong with me."

Heather stepped onto the porch. "It'll be all right, Cody. You can see Bethany next weekend."

"Is she all right? I heard there was some trouble here last night."

"She's fine. We didn't let her see anything bad."

"Okay." Cody descended the steps, headed for his car, then turned. "I bet that witch is doing this to me."

"What witch?"

"That gypsy psychic lady you let take care of our daughter. She's a bad influence."

Heather sighed. Just when she thought Cody was going to behave, he ruined it with something stupid. "Fidelia's a wonderful, loving person, and she'd do anything to protect Bethany."

"Right! Like put some kind of spell on me." Cody paced in front of his car. "I'm gonna sue, that's what. I'll have her arrested."

"On what charge? She hasn't done anything." Heather noticed Billy's squad car coming up the driveway. Phil stepped out onto the porch.

Cody grinned. "Great timing. I'll have Billy drag that witch off to jail."

"Fidelia hasn't done a thing to you." Heather descended the porch steps.

The squad car rolled to a stop, and Billy climbed out.

"You're just in time, Sheriff." Cody walked up to him. "I want you to arrest that gypsy woman. She's put a spell on me."

"That's ridiculous," Heather snapped. "Fidelia's not a gypsy, and she doesn't do spells."

"Then why did she force me not to see Bethany this weekend?"

"Cody, come back next weekend. You can take Bethany then."

"You can't tell me what to do!" Cody yelled. "Billy, I want you to arrest Heather. She's in violation of the divorce decree."

She scoffed. "Billy, will you please make him leave?"

Billy had been calmly watching the argument. He walked to the back of his car and motioned to Cody to follow him.

"A father has rights, too, you know." Cody stopped next to Billy and turned to give Heather a dirty look.

In one quick movement, Billy removed his pistol and clonked Cody on the head with the handle. Cody crumpled to the pavement.

Heather gasped and ran down the steps. "What are you doing? I just wanted you to talk to him."

Billy stuffed his gun back in the holster. Then he opened the back door of his squad car and shoved Cody inside.

"Billy?" Heather stepped closer.

Phil ran to her and grabbed her arm. "Come back inside. Something's not right."

Billy whipped out his gun and shot Phil in the leg.

Heather screamed. Phil tumbled onto the driveway. Blood oozed from his wounded calf.

"What the hell?" Fidelia looked out the front door, then pulled a gun from her purse.

"Mama!" Bethany cried.

Fidelia pushed her back, dropped her purse, and frantically worked at unlocking the trigger lock on her pistol.

"Get inside!" Phil hissed as he lay on the driveway.

Heather started, then hesitated. How could she leave Phil behind?

"Get in the car." Billy motioned with his gun toward the open door of his squad door.

She noticed the glassy look to his eyes.

Billy aimed his pistol at Phil's head. "Get in the car."

Phil gritted his teeth. "Don't do it."

Billy cocked his pistol.

"Wait! I'll do it." Heather climbed into the car.

"Drop the gun, sucker!" Fidelia yelled, aiming her Glock at Billy.

He yanked Phil up and used him as a shield. He moved to the back of the car, dragging Phil with him.

He opened the trunk and shoved Phil inside. The minute he slammed the trunk shut, Fidelia fired her pistol.

She missed. She shot again. Heather ducked down. Fidelia's aim was bad.

Billy jumped in the front seat and sped away.

Heather sat up and pounded her fists against the screen separating her from the sheriff. "Billy, wake up! You're under Louie's control."

He kept driving.

Heather looked out the rear window. Fidelia was in the middle of the driveway. Bethany ran after the car, crying, and Fidelia pulled her back.

A chill swept over Heather. Was this the last time she'd see her daughter? No, she couldn't bear that. Jean-Luc would come to the rescue. The sun was on the horizon. He would wake soon.

Unfortunately, so would Louie.

Chapter 27

Heather estimated that Billy had driven about ten minutes when he pulled onto an old dirt road. The car bounced over dried ruts, and she tried to keep Cody from falling off the seat. She winced at the thought of poor wounded Phil, getting jostled in the car trunk.

She tried several times to talk to Billy, even asking him about Sasha, but he was totally unresponsive.

Cody groaned. "What's going on?" He rubbed the back of his head and scowled at Heather. "Did you hit me?"

"No. Billy did."

Cody looked around the squad car with a confused expression. "We're going to jail?"

"I wish." Jail was in town where there were people.

The car rolled to a stop in what looked like an old courtyard overgrown with weeds. An old stone wall encircled the yard. Sections had fallen over and crumbled.

"This looks familiar." Heather shielded her eyes against the harsh glare of the setting sun. There, in the distance, was an old stone chapel. She caught her breath. This must be the place Fidelia had dreamed about.

Billy exited, then opened her door and pointed his gun at her. "Out!"

She climbed out very slowly. Her chances of survival would greatly increase if she made it past sundown. As soon as the sun set, Jean-Luc and his Vamp buddies would come charging to the rescue.

Cody clambered out of the car. "What the hell are you doing, Billy?"

The sheriff motioned toward the chapel. "Walk."

"You'll be hearing from my lawyer," Cody growled.

Billy lifted his pistol even with Cody's face.

"Okay! I'm walking!" Cody stalked through the weeds.

"Slow down," Heather whispered. She glanced back at Billy. His face was still expressionless.

She remembered this place now. As a young girl, she'd come here with her family for a picnic. They'd left early because her mother had been afraid the old building would collapse on them.

You're at war with fear, she reminded herself. She needed to stay calm and look for windows of opportunity.

"Lots of good memories here, huh, Billy?" Cody looked back at the sheriff. "Remember that time we brought two cheerleaders here?"

Billy didn't answer.

"This was our favorite place to go parking during high school," Cody explained to Heather. "Didn't Billy bring you here?"

"No." So Billy must have cheated on her during high school. That wasn't surprising since he'd gone out with her only so he could be around Sasha. "Billy, where's Sasha? What have you done with her?"

"Sasha!" Cody snorted. "Boy, she was here, making

out, every Saturday night. We never did get a turn with her, did we, Billy?"

"What are you doing?" Heather whispered.

"I'm trying to remind him that we're old friends," Cody hissed.

"He stopped being your friend when you married me," Heather reminded her ex.

"Yeah." Cody sneered at her. "It's all your fault."

They arrived at the double wooden doors of the chapel. Heather glanced at the sun. It was just peeking over the horizon, shooting its last golden rays through the gaps in the tree line. The sky was pink in the west, but already dark in the east where a full moon was rising.

"Inside," Billy ordered.

Cody pushed at the right half of the double door, and it swung open with a loud creak. Heather and Cody stepped inside. She moved out of Billy's way as he entered and slammed the door shut.

The air inside was cool and musty. The ceiling soared high overhead. A section behind the altar had collapsed, leaving a gap in the roof. The top half of the rising moon crept into the gap, illuminating the altar below.

The altar was nothing more than a long wooden table, scarred with years of abuse. Visitors had carved their names into it. Teenage lovers had chiseled hearts with their initials. Three pillar candles were clustered in one corner.

Along the walls, windowpanes had been smashed out. The long arched windows now served as gateways for the birds that fluttered in to make nests in the high rafters.

Close to the entrance, in the nave of the chapel, an old staircase led up to a lopsided wooden choir loft. Beneath the choir loft, the chapel was dark. Heather detected movement in the shadow beneath the stairs.

Sasha stepped into the dim light. "Welcome." Her eyes were glassy and unfocused, her skin deathly pale, and she seemed thinner than ever. A surge of anger gripped Heather. Louie was feeding from Sasha. He wasn't just controlling her, he was killing her!

"Sasha!" Heather walked toward her. "You have to fight this. He's going to kill you."

She blinked. "He loves me."

"No! Wake up!" Heather reached for her, planning to give her a good shake.

"Back off." Billy pointed his pistol at her.

Heather stepped back. "He's controlling both of you."

"What the hell?" Cody turned to Heather. "Who's controlling them?"

"Louie," Heather replied.

"Henry." Sasha sighed with pleasure.

"Henry?" Heather asked.

"Henry," Billy repeated like a robot.

"Who's Henry?" Cody asked.

"He's Louie," Heather explained.

"Sheesh!" Cody shook his head. "You're all crazy."

"Henry came to rescue me from the jailhouse last night," Sasha whispered. "He rescued Billy, too."

"Who the hell is Henry?" Cody demanded.

"He's an assassin," Heather whispered.

"Get over by the wall," Billy ordered them.

Heather inched over slowly.

"Why does this Henry want to kill us?" Cody cried. "I don't owe him any money."

Billy tossed some rope to Cody. "Tie her up."

"Why? So you can kill us?" Cody screamed. "Why should I do anything you say?"

Billy fired his pistol. The bullet hit a flagstone by Cody's feet, splintering the rock into a cloud of gravel.

"Fine!" Cody marched over to Heather.

"Sit!" Billy pointed his gun at her.

She eased down with her back to the rough stone wall. Her heart thundered, echoing in her ears.

Cody squatted in front of her and tied up her ankles. "What the hell does this Henry got against us?"

"He wants to kill me."

"Dammit, I should have known this was your fault." Cody looped more rope around her wrists, then straightened. "You stupid bitch, you're going to get *me* killed, damn you!" He stiffened suddenly and fell on the floor.

His body twitched, then he flipped over onto all fours. "I am a cockroach!" He scurried into the shadows near the stairs.

"Stop him!" Sasha cried.

Billy fired his pistol.

"No!" Heather cried, straining at the ropes.

"I am a cockroach!" Cody squeaked from the shadows.

Billy shot again. There was a scurrying sound on the staircase.

He was climbing up to the old choir loft. Heather winced. It couldn't be safe up there. Of course, it wasn't any safer down here.

She could barely make out Cody's dark figure as he scrambled across the choir loft. Billy took aim and fired. Cody jumped and ran in the opposite direction. Billy shot again.

Heather watched, horrified. It was like shooting a duck at the firing range of an amusement park.

Just then, a tremendous howl filled the air. Billy stopped shooting to listen.

Heather caught her breath. She'd never heard a dog or coyote howl so loud. The sound was deafening. And it had to come from a very large creature.

"What was that?" Sasha whispered.

"I don't know," Billy replied. "But it sounds close."

Heather jumped when she heard a loud noise in the courtyard. It sounded like metal being ripped apart.

The chapel grew darker. The sun must have set. The only light was from the stars and full moon that gleamed through the hole in the roof.

Billy and Sasha stiffened and turned to face the altar.

"The master awakes," Sasha whispered. She hurried to the altar and picked up a box of matches off the table. She lit the three candles.

Billy set his pistol on the table. A few feet behind the table, he leaned over and hooked his fingers through a large metal ring in the floor. He pulled, and a wooden door screeched open.

A figure in black levitated through the opening in the floor. He kept floating up toward the hole in the ceiling. Moonlight surrounded him like a silver nimbus. Heather couldn't see his face, but she felt him looking at her.

She jumped when Billy slammed the cellar door shut.

The vampire Louie lowered to the floor. His hair was no longer white, but black like his trench coat. He looked about thirty-five years old, Heather estimated, but she knew he was probably well over five hundred.

Billy and Sasha bowed. "Master."

"You brought me Jean-Luc's latest whore," Louie said quietly. "Very good." He glanced at the choir loft. "And you brought me another mortal."

Cody scurried into the shadows.

"He will amuse me before he dies." Louie turned to look at Heather.

She swallowed hard. She'd never seen such cold, black eyes. In that terrible moment, she realized there was nothing human left in him. He'd simply become a creature that preyed on humanity.

He stepped toward her. "Allow me to introduce myself. I am Henri Lenoir." His lips curled in a humorless smile. "You won't live long enough to tell Jean-Luc. It'll be our little secret."

She bent her knees to conceal her hands in her lap. Cody hadn't tied them very well, so it might be possible to work them free. For now, it might be best to keep Louie talking. That would give Jean-Luc and his friends more time to find her. And it would give her more time to get her hands free. "Why do you hate Jean-Luc so much?"

Louie removed his black leather gloves and stuffed them into the pocket of his trench coat. His hands were pale, the fingernails long and painted black. "Casimir has offered me a small fortune to kill Jean-Luc. And I will have his position as Coven Master of Western Europe once Casimir takes over. The reward is great for such a small task. But I want to make Jean-Luc suffer first. That is where you come in. I'll be killing you for free."

"What if I paid you not to kill me?"

A corner of his mouth twisted. "You are an amusing one, but I doubt you could afford me." His black eyes raked over her. "Besides, I enjoy killing women."

Her stomach twinged.

"I plan to kill you slowly." He moved closer. "You don't seem very afraid."

Was that what he wanted? To see her cry and beg? Sure she was terrified, but she wouldn't give him the pleasure of seeing it. She lifted her chin and glared at him.

"I shall, of course, rape you while I feed on you. It's more insulting to Jean-Luc that way."

Her stomach roiled, and she swallowed hard at the

bile rising in her throat. Rape was a lot more insulting to her, but Louie obviously didn't care. She was simply a way to hurt Jean-Luc. She had no other value. Nothing to bargain with.

"I am ravenous now." Louie strolled back to the altar. "I must take the edge off my appetite. I would hate to accidentally kill you too quickly."

A heavy feeling of doom invaded her. She wouldn't be able to reason her way out of this. She tugged at the ropes.

"Come, my dear." Louie lifted a hand toward Sasha. She ran to him. "Yes, Master."

He led her to the altar and pushed her sleeve up her arm. Heather winced at the sight of puncture wounds.

Sasha reclined on the table, her head close to the candles. Louie leaned over to lick the inside of her wrist.

Heather turned her head away, not wanting to watch. But when she heard a hissing sound, she took a quick peek. She gasped. His fangs were extended, long and sharp. He drove them into Sasha's wrist.

Heather shuddered. She couldn't let him near her. She strained at her ropes, wincing as they chafed and burned her skin. It was now or never. Louie was busy eating, and Billy was just standing there like a zombie.

A loud howling sound permeated the room.

Louie raised his head to listen. Blood dripped from his fangs onto Sasha's pale skin.

Another howl began, long and plaintive. It echoed around the stone walls. Birds, frightened from their nests in the rafters, took flight out the windows.

"We have company." Louie retrieved the pistol from the table and handed it to Billy. "Prepare yourself."

"Yes, Master."

Louie returned to Sasha, lifted her arm, and bit her.

Heather slipped one hand free. Yes! She loosened the

ropes on the other hand. She might just manage to escape.

Just then, a large black blur shot through an open window. It landed on the stone floor just a few feet away from Heather. She froze, unable to breathe.

It was a huge, dark wolf with long and shaggy fur. A growl vibrated in its throat.

Billy stepped back, his face pale.

Louie straightened. His fangs retracted, and he released Sasha's arm. It fell limp onto the table. Sasha appeared unconscious.

The wolf turned its massive head to look at Heather. It bared its teeth and growled.

She gasped. Red glowing eyes. White gnashing teeth. Oh God, this was Fidelia's dream of danger.

She could be killed slowly by a vampire, or mauled to death quickly by a huge wolf. Either way, it looked like her time was up.

Chapter 28

Jean-Luc jolted awake, coughing as something foreign slid down his throat. Someone was grasping his chin, forcing his mouth open. He shoved the hand away.

"It worked!" a woman's voice shouted.

He tried to sit up, but a wave of dizziness knocked him back. Strong hands caught him. His vision was blurred with a greenish tint. A foul taste tainted his tongue. *Mon Dieu*, poison. He struggled to get out of bed, but his body wouldn't respond.

"'Tis all right, Jean-Luc." The strong hand moved to his shoulder. "It takes a wee moment to adjust."

He recognized Ian's voice, though the Scotsman's face was still a greenish blur. "What have you done?"

"I gave ye some of the stay-awake drug." Ian showed him the vial of green liquid. "The sun hasna set."

It was still daytime? Jean-Luc's vision cleared, and he noticed Fidelia hovering in the doorway of his bedroom. She was holding Bethany, whose face was streaked with tears. His heart plummeted. His worst fear—something had gone wrong while he'd rested powerless in his death-sleep.

"What happened?" This time his body obeyed his command to move. He slid to the edge of the bed, and realized he was still naked. "Turn the little one away."

Fidelia hugged Bethany, burying the little girl's face in her blouse, and Jean-Luc zoomed into his walk-in closet.

"Tell me what happened," he called out as he ripped the bandage off his right arm. The gunshot wound was gone. With vampire speed, he pulled on some pants and a shirt.

"I woke Ian up," Fidelia confessed. "I knew he had the drug in his purse—"

"Sporran," Ian grumbled.

"And I poured some down his throat," Fidelia continued. "I figured it couldn't hurt, you know. He was already dead. When he woke up, we came here to wake you."

"Where's Heather?" Jean-Luc stuffed his feet into socks and a pair of black boots. His chest constricted when he realized they weren't answering. He ran from the closet. "Where's Heather?"

Bethany started crying.

Fidelia's face crumpled. "Billy took her away. I think he's under Louie's control."

Jean-Luc's heart wrenched. *God, no.* His worst fear. But at least it was still daytime. Lui would still be dead, so Heather was safe for the moment. He grabbed his belt with the leather scabbard and buckled it around his hips. "How long ago?"

"About ten minutes." Fidelia shook her head. "I didn't know what to do. I wanted to follow them in your car, but I didn't have the keys, and I couldn't leave

Bethany here alone, and Ian was dead on the floor—"

"You did right." Jean-Luc selected his best foil and slid it into the scabbard. "Where's Phil?"

"Billy shot him and stuffed him into the trunk of his car."

"All right." Jean-Luc joined Fidelia in the hallway. "Ian, if you have more of that drug, go wake up Robby and Phineas."

"Aye." Ian zoomed past them to the guardroom.

"You have to save her," Fidelia whispered.

"I will." He rested a hand on her shoulder. "You did the right thing."

Fidelia hung her head. "I messed up. I shot at Billy, but I missed."

"I want my mama," Bethany wailed.

"I'll bring her home, *chérie*. She'll be all right." He wished he could believe that.

Bethany wrapped her arms around his neck. When he realized she wasn't going to let go, he settled her on his right hip, opposite his scabbard.

"Come." He strode down the hall to the cellar kitchen. "You say Billy took her about ten minutes ago?"

"Yes." Fidelia followed.

"How long till sunset?" He turned into the kitchen. It was small, consisting of a fridge, a microwave, a small dishwasher, and a cabinet of glasses.

"I don't know." Fidelia paused in the doorway. "About five minutes, I guess."

"So Billy has given himself fifteen minutes to take her to Lui." Jean-Luc retrieved four bottles of synthetic blood from the fridge. "Lui's hideout could be fairly close." He set Bethany on the counter, so he could unscrew the tops off the bottles.

"I suppose." Fidelia grabbed one of the bottles to help him.

He set all four bottles in the microwave and turned it on. "Did you see which way Billy went?"

"I did!" Bethany raised her hand. "He went down the driveway."

"That's good." Jean-Luc smoothed back her strawberry-blond curls.

"They turned onto the highway, headed south," Fidelia said. "Last night I dreamed about an old stone church. I think that's where he's taking her."

"Where was it?" Jean-Luc removed a bottle from the microwave and guzzled down the warm blood.

"In the countryside." She leaned against the doorjamb, frowning. "It would be south of here." She straightened suddenly. "There's an old Spanish mission down the highway. It's only about ten minutes away."

Robby, Ian, and Phineas gathered around the doorway. They were all dressed and fully armed.

"We have a location." Jean-Luc handed them each a bottle. "A Spanish mission, ten miles south."

"Good." Robby turned to Phineas. "Ye'll stay here with the ladies."

"Oh, come on, man." Phineas grimaced. "I want some real action."

"And ye may get it if Lui comes back here for more victims," Robby muttered. "Ye could get more action here than ye can handle."

"I can do it." Phineas nodded. "Just let me at that sucker. He'll be sorry he ever messed with me."

"Phineas." Robby gave him a stern look. "If he comes here, the first thing ye do is send out a psychic message to us. We can teleport here in a second."

"Gotcha." Phineas upended his bottle of blood and gulped it down. He wiped his mouth with the back of his hand. "I'll protect the women with my life."

"And I have my guns," Fidelia added. "We'll be fine."

"Let's go." Jean-Luc set his empty bottle in the sink and gathered Bethany back into his arms.

They strode down the hall and up the stairs to the ground floor.

"Let's take the car." Jean-Luc stopped next to the security office.

"We could run there just as fast," Ian protested.

"Jean-Luc's right." Robby opened the door and grabbed the keys off the hook. "We need to conserve our energy."

"Can you check the sun for us?" Jean-Luc asked Fidelia.

"Sure." Fidelia ran to the window next to the front door.

"'Tis still up," Ian murmured. "I can feel it."

Fidelia peered through the blinds. "There's only a sliver left on the horizon."

"Good." Jean-Luc handed Bethany over to Phineas. "He'll take care of you till I bring your mother back."

Bethany nodded.

Jean-Luc stepped back and drew his sword. He warmed up with some thrusts and lunges. His heart pounded, but not from exercise. He couldn't allow himself to think about how frightened Heather might be. Just the thought brought bile to his throat. At least Lui was a sick enough bastard that he'd take his time with her. The stay-awake drug had given them a few precious extra minutes to prepare, and those minutes might make all the difference.

Robby emerged from the security office with an extra sword in his right hand. "We'll need to check the car for explosives. I'll look under the carriage. Ian, look under the bonnet."

"Aye." Ian tightened the straps that held the sheath and claymore on his back.

"Is it true," Robby asked, "that the sheriff tossed Phil into the trunk of his car?"

"Yes." Fidelia continued to peer out the window. "I doubt Phil can help you very much. He was shot in the leg."

Robby exchanged a look with Ian. "'Tis a full moon tonight."

Ian nodded. "Good. 'Twill give us another advantage."

"What advantage?" Jean-Luc sheathed his sword.

"The sun's down!" Fidelia threw open the door. "Go!"

"The keys!" Jean-Luc caught them, and zoomed out the door with Robby and Ian. He climbed behind the driver seat, and the second they told him it was safe, he started the engine. They jumped in, and he floored the accelerator. He turned south on the highway, then gained more speed.

After a few minutes, Robby held up a hand. "Pull over!"

"Why?" Jean-Luc veered onto the shoulder and stomped on the brakes.

"Listen," Robby whispered.

Jean-Luc heard a strange howling sound, coming from the south. "What is that?"

"Focus on it and teleport there now," Robby ordered. He and Ian wavered, then disappeared.

Jean-Luc ripped the keys from the ignition and concentrated on the sound. Everything went black.

This was no ordinary wolf. Heather had never seen one close up before, but she knew they didn't have red glowing eyes. This one had to be bigger than normal, too.

Billy lifted his pistol and took aim.

"Wait." Louie raised his hand. "We can always kill it later. I want to see if it will chew on her first."

Heather gulped. Those jaws looked incredibly strong. And the teeth—very sharp. The wolf moved toward her. She pressed back against the wall.

It was limping, favoring a back leg. The fur was matted with something dark and shiny. As the wolf limped forward, it left a bloody paw print on the stone floor.

Heather glanced at its eyes. The glow had faded, and the red was turning pale blue. It stopped in front of her and tilted its head like it was studying her. Maybe it was. The eyes looked intelligent. And somehow familiar.

It inched closer, its muzzle over her drawn-up knees.

"No," she breathed, lifting a hand to ward it off.

It leaned forward and licked her palm.

With a gasp, she closed her hand. Her mind raced. The wounded leg. The screeching sound of metal being ripped. The sniffing for bombs. The familiar eyes.

"Phil?" she whispered.

The wolf whimpered.

"Oh my God." She closed her eyes briefly against the sting of hot tears. She wasn't alone. Phil was here to protect her.

Louie sighed. "What a disappointing beast. Billy, kill it."

Billy lifted his pistol.

Phil spun around, growling. And charged.

Billy pulled the trigger, but nothing happened. He backed up, frantically pulling the trigger over and over.

Phil knocked him down and snapped his jaws on Billy's arm.

Heather grimaced. She didn't want Billy to die.

A loud howl reverberated through the room. Phil had pinned Billy to the floor and appeared to be enjoying his victory. He threw his massive head back and howled again.

"Damned creature." Louie circled the altar, unbut-

toning his long black coat. "I'll take care of it myself."
He whisked off his coat and tossed it on the table. It
landed on Sasha.

Just then, two forms wavered before Heather's eyes
and became solid. She cried with relief. Robby already
had a sword in his hand. Ian drew his claymore.

A third form appeared.

"Jean-Luc!" Heather cried.

He glanced at her. "Thank God." He drew his foil
and spotted Louie by the altar. He strode toward him.
"Let's finish this now."

Louie sneered. "Agreed." He vanished.

"No!" Jean-Luc shouted.

Louie suddenly appeared next to Heather. His left
hand gripped her arm. Good Lord, he meant to teleport away with her!

A dagger spun through the air and sliced Louie's
arm before falling on the ground. He cried out and released her.

Heather grabbed the dagger, then scooted away. It
must have come from Robby or Ian. She sawed at the
ropes binding her ankles.

A warm nose nuzzled her shoulder, and she jumped.
"Oh, it's you." Phil sat beside her. Her personal guard
was back. "Good boy."

"A sword, Robby!" Jean-Luc yelled. He dropped
his foil and kicked it toward Heather, then caught the
sword Robby tossed him.

Heather scrambled to get the foil, then froze when
she saw Jean-Luc circling Louie. Oh God, this was it.
The final showdown. Louie had a huge broadsword.
No wonder Jean-Luc had discarded his foil.

Louie attacked, making a swipe that whistled past
Jean-Luc's stomach.

"You missed." Jean-Luc jumped and levitated to the
ceiling.

Louie levitated to meet him. Jean-Luc crashed his sword against Louie's with so much force, it caused Louie to flip over backward in the air. He banged against a rafter and fell to the floor.

Jean-Luc landed on his feet next to Louie's sprawled body. He raised his sword for the killing blow, but Louie rolled suddenly and sliced upward.

Jean-Luc jumped back. His shirt was sliced, and a thin red line crossed his pale skin. The tip of Louie's sword had left its mark.

Louie leaped to his feet, smiling. "You're pitiful. I grow tired of toying with you."

Jean-Luc attacked. The swords clashed again and again. Heather glanced at Robby and Ian. Surely they wouldn't let Louie win. Ian was hovering nearby, his claymore drawn and ready.

Robby had drawn the sword from his back. He strode over to Billy and placed a hand on Billy's brow.

Heather's gaze flitted back and forth. Her ears rang with the constant clanging of swords crashing together. Both Jean-Luc and Louie were breathing heavily now.

Billy stiffened and pulled away from Robby. He looked around and cradled his wounded arm to his chest. His eyes met Heather's. "What have I done? I'm so sorry."

"Heather, move!" Jean-Luc yelled at her.

Move where? Then she realized what he was doing. Jean-Luc was driving Louie toward her and Phil. She scrambled away, and Robby grabbed her.

Jean-Luc continued to force Louie to retreat. Phil sat still and quiet. When Louie was a few feet in front of Phil, the wolf let out a tremendous howl.

Louie jumped and glanced behind him. In that second, Jean-Luc stabbed him through the heart. Louie turned completely gray, then disintegrated into a pile of dust on the floor.

Jean-Luc stepped back, lowering his sword. He closed his eyes and let the sword clatter onto the floor. "It's done," he whispered. He turned to Heather. "We're free."

With a cry, she ran to him and threw her arms around his neck. He held her tight.

"It's over," Heather whispered. "It's over."

He kissed her brow. "You're free now. You can have your old life back, if you want."

She cradled his face with her hands. "I want my new life with you."

"We can do that, too." He squeezed her tight. "It was my worst fear. I woke up to find you were in danger."

"It's all right," she whispered. "You killed him. Louie will never torture you again."

Robby walked over to retrieve his sword. "Well done, Jean-Luc."

He glanced around the chapel. "Is everyone all right?"

Sasha moaned. She struggled to sit up, but fell back onto the table.

"Sasha!" Billy ran toward her. "Thank God you're all right."

"Billy." She stretched out a hand to him. "I never meant to hurt anyone. Please believe me."

"I believe you." Billy took her hand. "He controlled me, too. It was terrible. I was fighting it, but there was nothing I could do." He kissed her hand.

"He remembers everything," Robby whispered. "I broke the hold Lui had on him, but I dinna erase his memory."

Jean-Luc nodded. "That's probably for the best. It would be difficult to explain all this."

"Sasha's lost too much blood," Heather whispered.

"We'll have Dr. Lee make another house call," Jean-Luc said. "He can give her a blood transfusion."

"She won't become a vampire?" Heather asked.

"Nay," Robby replied. "She'll be fine. Her blood wasna completely drained. I just hope Dr. Lee can remove the bullet from Phil."

Jean-Luc looked at the werewolf. "Why didn't you tell me about him?"

Robby shrugged. "'Tis a company secret."

"How many are there like him?" Heather asked.

Robby's mouth quirked. "If I told ye, it wouldna be a secret."

"He bit Billy," Heather said.

Robby's smile faded.

"Bugger," Ian whispered. He gave Billy a worried look.

"Oh no," Heather breathed. "It's contagious?"

Robby nodded. "Aye."

Heather winced. Poor Billy. She glanced at the altar. Billy was sitting on the table, holding Sasha in his arms. Well, he'd finally gotten the girl he wanted. Hopefully, Sasha wouldn't mind a boyfriend who went furry every now and then.

"I'll explain it to him later," Robby said. "Ian, go ahead and teleport them to the house. And call Dr. Lee."

"Verra well." Ian strode toward the wounded couple, and soon they all vanished.

Heather stepped back to look at Jean-Luc's wound. "You need to see Dr. Lee, too."

He shrugged. "It's just a scratch."

She snorted. "That scratch nearly gave me a heart attack. You have got to stop getting injured every night."

He grinned. "You're cute when you're bossy." He pulled her closer and whispered in her ear, "We'll have to find some new positions that won't strain my injury."

She laughed.

Robby strolled over to the table and blew out the candles. "I'll teleport back with Phil, and we'll be done." He glanced up at the choir loft. "Is there something up there? I thought I heard something."

"Probably a tiny Texan mouse." Jean-Luc nuzzled Heather's neck.

"I am a cockroach!"

Heather gasped. "Cody! I forgot he was there."

Jean-Luc frowned. "I'm tempted to leave him there."

"No," Heather protested. "He actually came in handy. Billy ran out of bullets, shooting at him. In a weird way, he saved Phil's life."

"All right. I'll remove the command." Jean-Luc walked over to the choir loft and levitated. "Cockroach."

"Yes, Master!"

Jean-Luc hovered in the air for a few minutes. Then he sank to the floor. "It's done."

"What the hell?" Cody yelled. "How did I get here?"

Jean-Luc gathered Heather in his arms. "There will be a little girl very happy to see you."

Heather's eyes filled with tears. "Thank you."

Cody clambered down the stairs. "What the hell is going on?"

"I believe ye'll find the sheriff's car outside," Robby said. "I suggest ye take it back to town."

Cody noticed the giant wolf and backed toward the door. "You guys are crazy!" He ran from the chapel.

Robby chuckled. "Come on, Phil. Let me take ye home." He halted in midstep. "Och, ye wee beastie."

Heather grimaced. Phil had raised a leg and was dousing the pile of dust that had been Louie. "Oh, ick." How could she ever look Phil in the face again?

Phil finished, then sat on his haunches. He gave them a wolfish grin, his long tongue lolling out.

With a laugh, Robby wrapped an arm around the furry beast. The two vanished.

"Our turn." Jean-Luc smoothed a hand up Heather's back. "You remember how to do this? You hold me tight."

"I remember." She wrapped her arms around his neck.

His mouth twitched. "And then you kiss me."

"Absolutely." She pressed her mouth against his and let the world fade away.

Epilogue

Three weeks later . . .

On the drive home from the wedding, Heather realized that she now led a dual life. Living in two worlds had meant they needed two wedding receptions.

Both mortals and Vamps had attended the small wedding at Heather's church. While the Vamps had discreetly left, Heather's mortal friends had gathered in the church's fellowship hall for wedding cake and punch.

Jean-Luc had happily shoved a piece of wedding cake into Heather's mouth, but she'd purposely missed his mouth, smearing it on his cheek. Everyone had laughed, never realizing that Jean-Luc had not eaten any cake at all. Then Heather tossed the bouquet over her shoulder.

"He scores!" Coach Gunter caught the bouquet and lifted both arms up, signifying a touchdown.

Heather and Jean-Luc made an early exit to the limousine parked out front. Her friends thought they were rushing off to catch a plane, but their next stop was the Vamp reception at the studio.

Heather understood why the Vamps wanted to party in private. How else could they drink Bubbly Blood and perform old dances like the minuet? She was actually looking forward to the dances. Jean-Luc had spent the last few weeks teaching her the steps when he wasn't busy making love to her or overseeing the production of her wedding dress.

She smoothed out the ivory silk, trying not to crush the skirt in the back of the limo. "It's the most beautiful wedding gown ever."

"For the most beautiful bride ever." Jean-Luc kissed her cheek, then nuzzled her ear. "I plan to ravish you thoroughly tonight."

"Shh." Heather didn't want her daughter to overhear.

Bethany was busily opening and shutting all the cabinets in the limo. She looked adorable in the blue flower girl dress Heather had made for her.

Fidelia, the matron of honor, had scooted down the seat to the window behind the chauffeur. She knocked on the glass. "*Hola*, Roberto!"

The limo sped up.

Heather chuckled. Poor Robby.

They pulled to a stop in front of Jean-Luc's studio—their home, Heather corrected herself. Robby opened the door so they could get out. Fidelia fussed behind her, making sure the long train of her skirt was perfect.

"Ready?" Jean-Luc took her hand.

"Yes." She climbed the steps with Jean-Luc as Robby opened the door.

The showroom was bright with light gleaming off the polished marble. The room had been cleared for the reception. A few round tables lined the walls, topped with white tablecloths and bouquets of flowers. There was a small buffet of real food, punch, and champagne for the few mortals in attendance, plus another table covered with champagne flutes and Bubbly Blood chilling in ice buckets.

The center of the room was left empty for dancing. A band called the High Voltage Vamps had teleported in from New York and were set up beneath the catwalk. Cascades of voile and flowers hung from the catwalk, leaving the air scented with roses and gardenias.

It wasn't a surprise to Heather since she'd helped with all the plans and decorations, but she still felt a thrill upon seeing it. It was perfect.

Vamps lined up to meet her. Her worries that they might not approve of her melted away. Angus and Emma MacKay were first in line, and both gave her a big hug. They invited her and Jean-Luc to use their castle in Scotland whenever they liked. Next in line was a handsome Italian Vamp named Giacomo. He kissed her cheeks and invited them to visit his palazzo in Venice. A few more of Jean-Luc's coven members from Western Europe had made the trip.

"I see that Simone and Inga didn't make it," Heather whispered to Jean-Luc. The two models had teleported back to Paris after the runway show.

He grinned. "What a shame."

"Did you ever find out where Simone was sneaking off to at night?"

Jean-Luc nodded, still smiling. "You won't believe it. She was fishing."

"For men?"

He laughed. "For fish. In the river. Apparently she likes to fish, but doesn't want to admit it."

"Weird." Heather figured Simone liked stabbing the worms with the hook. She was suddenly grabbed for a big hug.

"I'm so thrilled for you!" Shanna Draganesti squeezed

her, then stepped back. "I've never seen Jean-Luc so happy. You're good for him."

Heather felt her eyes tearing. She'd never felt so happy, either. "Where's your little boy?"

"I left him with your daughter and Fidelia." Shanna pointed at their table. "He was hungry, and Fidelia was sweet enough to fix him a plate of food. She's a hoot."

Heather smiled. "Yes, she is."

"Oh dear." Shanna shook her head. "There he goes again."

Heather's mouth dropped open. Constantine was floating up to the ceiling. Bethany squealed with delight.

"He's just showing off," Shanna muttered. "He loves the attention."

Heather pressed a hand to her chest. "But he—he's a mortal."

"With a Vamp daddy." Shanna smiled at her husband.

Heather turned to Jean-Luc. "Did you know about this?"

He was watching Constantine with a stunned expression. "No. I'd heard that our DNA was a bit different, but I didn't realize . . ."

"Oh dear." Shanna gave them a worried look. "I hope this won't stop you from having your own children. Constantine is a very loving and sweet child."

"I'm sure he is." Heather watched him descend to his chair. He was giggling along with Bethany. "Does he do anything else?"

"His main talent appears related to healing," Roman explained. "Everyone who comes in contact with him feels better afterward."

"Oh." Well, that wasn't bad at all. Heather watched the little boy stuff some crackers in his mouth.

"Constantine is so special that we decided to have another one." Shanna grinned. "We're expecting!"

"Oh my!" Heather hugged her. "That's wonderful!"

"Congratulations, *mon ami*." Jean-Luc slapped Roman on the shoulder.

Roman smiled. He looked handsome in the Echarpe tuxedo Jean-Luc had given him as a present for being best man.

"I'm very proud of you, Jean-Luc. You've come a long way." Roman slanted a wry look at Heather. "Did he tell you that I taught him how to read and write?"

"No." Heather curled her hands around Jean-Luc's arm and leaned against his shoulder.

"And I taught Roman how to fight," Jean-Luc said. "He was a slow student."

Roman snorted. "I was reluctant to kill. My mission has always been to save lives."

"Isn't he wonderful?" Shanna hugged him. "I have more news. I've decided to change over eventually, probably about ten years from now. I want the children to be old enough to handle it."

"Excuse me?" Heather wasn't sure what she meant.

"Shanna has agreed to become a vampire," Roman said quietly.

Heather's heart lurched. She released Jean-Luc's arm. "Oh. Con-congratulations." Good Lord, the woman wanted to be a vampire!

Roman and Shanna moved on to see how their son was doing. The rest of the reception line flowed by in a daze.

"Are you all right?" Jean-Luc whispered. "Do you need to sit down? You look pale."

"I—I think I'll sit down."

Jean-Luc led her to the table reserved for them, then he dashed away at vampire speed and returned with a plate of food and a cup of punch.

"I wasn't sure what you liked." He set the food in front of her.

"This is great, thank you." She popped a grape in her mouth.

He sat beside her. "You were shocked by Shanna's announcement."

"Yes. It never occurred to me that we have another . . . option. I can understand her wanting to be with her husband forever, but she'll have to give up her days with her children."

"I know." Jean-Luc took her hand in his. "I would never ask you to do it."

"But you hope that I would."

He lifted her hand to his mouth and kissed her knuckles. "Let's take it one day at a time. Or rather, one night at a time."

She smiled. "I would like to have children with you. Even if they do end up floating around the nursery."

He squeezed her hand. "Good. I want more little girls who look like their *maman*."

She ruffled the black curls on his head. "I want a little boy who looks like his father."

He leaned over to kiss her. A flash of light caught their attention.

"Gotcha!" Gregori was holding a digital camera and grinning.

The music started with a waltz.

"The first dance." Jean-Luc stood and held out a hand. "I'd like to dance with my wife."

Heather stood and let him escort her to the dance floor. Everyone clapped. Heather just hoped she wouldn't trip and fall on her face in front of everyone.

The music slowed.

"No waltz?" Heather asked.

"We can do one later." Jean-Luc slipped his arms around her waist. "For now, I just want to hold you close."

"Sounds good." She wrapped her arms around his neck.

They swayed gently in time with the music.

Jean-Luc kissed her brow, then rested his cheek against her temple. "I love you. I will always love you."

With a sigh, she closed her eyes. "I love you, too."

His grip tightened. "From now on, we battle our fears together."

"Yes."

"Are you afraid of heights, *chérie*?"

"A little. Why?"

"Open your eyes," he whispered.

She did. "Good Lord."

"Look! Mama's flying!" Bethany stood, pointing up in the air.

Heather tightened her hold around his neck. They were floating up to the ceiling, gently rotating. The long train of her skirt swirled in the air.

"Jean-Luc," she breathed. "You naughty man."

He chuckled. "Stay with me, *chérie*. I will take you places you've never dreamed of."

Next month, don't miss these exciting new love stories only from Avon Books

How to Propose to a Prince by Kathryn Caskie
An Avon Romantic Treasure

Elizabeth Royle has dreamt she's going to marry a prince and now all she has to do is find him. The one thing Lizzie never counted on was that her prince might not actually be royalty. Lizzie knows there's something about Lord Whitevale and prince or no, she won't stop until they are where they belong—together forever.

Making Over Mr. Right by Judi McCoy
An Avon Contemporary Romance

Zoë, the Muse of Beauty, has been banished from Mount Olympus and she's not going to let anyone stand in the way of her return, certainly not a reluctant businessman with a poor sense of style. But once she meets handsome Theodore Maragos, Zoë starts to wonder what's so bad about a life on Earth?

The Return of the Rogue by Donna Fletcher
An Avon Romance

Cavan Sinclare returns home after being held captive by barbarians only to find himself married to a woman he once rejected. Frustrated with the fear he sees on his new bride's face, Cavan must find a way to gentle the harshness his difficult life has left him with. Will he and his new wife ever learn to trust . . . and to love?

The Kiss by Sophia Nash
An Avon Romance

Georgiana Wilde has been in love with Quinn Fortesque for as long as she can remember. Unfortunately, he seems to harbor no feelings for her other than friendship. When Quinn is offered a second chance at enduring love, will he be ready to open his heart to the lady standing behind the veil of friendship . . . a true bride for all seasons?

DISCOVER ROMANCE at its
SIZZLING HOT BEST FROM AVON BOOKS

Be Still My Vampire Heart
by Kerrelyn Sparks
978-0-06-111844-9/$5.99 US/$7.99 Can

One Night With a Goddess
by Judi McCoy
978-0-06-077460-8/$5.99 US/$7.99 Can

At the Edge
by Cait London
978-0-06-114050-1/$5.99 US/$7.99 Can

When She Was Bad
by Cindy Kirk
978-0-06-084790-6/$5.99 US/$7.99 Can

The Forever Summer
by Suzanne Macpherson
978-0-06-116126-1/$5.99 US/$7.99 Can.

Dead Girls Are Easy
by Terri Garey
978-0-06-113615-3/$5.99 US/$7.99 Can

Witch in the House
by Jenna McKnight
978-0-06-084369-4/$5.99 US/$7.99 Can

Not the Marrying Kind
by Hailey North
978-06-058247-0/$5.99 US/$7.99 Can

Satisfaction
by Marianne Stillings
978-0-06-085066-1/$5.99 US/$7.99 Can

Hello, Doggy!
by Elaine Fox
978-0-06-117569-5/$5.99 US/$7.99 Can

CRO 1007

Visit www.AuthorTracker.com for exclusive
information on your favorite HarperCollins authors.

Available wherever books are sold
or please call 1-800-331-3761 to order.